THE HANDBOOK OF FIXED INCOME OPTIONS

Strategies, Pricing and Applications

Revised Edition

FRANK J. FABOZZI
Editor

IRWIN
Professional Publishing®
Chicago • London • Singapore

© Frank J. Fabozzi, 1996

Times Mirror
Higher Education Group

Library of Congress Cataloging-in-Publication Data

The handbook of fixed income options: strategies, pricing, and
    applications / Frank J. Fabozzi [editor]. — Rev. ed.
        p. cm.
    Includes bibliographical references and index.
    ISBN 0–7863–1023–5
    1. Options (Finance). 2. Fixed-income securities. I. Fabozzi,
Frank J.
HG6024.A3H36   1996
332.63'228—dc20   96–3753

Printed in the United States of America
1 2 3 4 5 6 7 8 9 BS 0 3 2 1 0 9 8 7 6

This book is dedicated to the memory of
Fischer Black

PREFACE

When properly utilized, options offer market participants a vehicle for controlling market risk. Stock index options offer equity managers the opportunity to control the market risk associated with holding a diversified portfolio of common stocks. Options on fixed-income instruments and options on futures on a fixed-income instrument allow borrowers and lenders to control interest rate risk. There are other contracts with option-like features that can be used to control interest rate risk. Interest rate agreements (caps, floors, and collars) are nothing more than a package of interest rate options. Compound (or split fee) options are options on options. In the interest rate swap market, options on interest rate swaps (called *swaptions*) are available.

There are also options that are embedded in fixed-income securities. Examples include callable bonds, putable bonds, and mortgage-backed securities. To understand the risk/return characteristics of these securities and to control the market risk associated with a portfolio that includes these securities, it is necessary to understand the investment characteristics of options.

The Handbook of Fixed Income Options provides detailed information about the investment characteristics of fixed-income options and other option-like vehicles, how they are priced, how they can be employed in investment management and the analysis of securities with embedded options.

— *Frank J. Fabozzi*

LIST OF CONTRIBUTORS

Scott Amero Managing Director, BlackRock Financial Management

Keith Anderson Managing Director, BlackRock Financial Management

Mark J.P. Anson, PhD Vice President, Salomon Brothers Inc.

David Audley, PhD Director of Investment Systems and Technology, Tiger Management Corporation

David F. Babbel, PhD Associate Professor, Wharton School, University of Pennsylvania

William A. Barr Vice President, Fuji Securities Inc.

Anand K. Bhattacharya Managing Director, Manager, Taxable Fixed-Income Research, Prudential Securities

Peter Bouyoucos Vice President, Morgan Stanley

Jane Sachar Brauer, PhD Vice President, Merrill Lynch

Richard Chin First Vice President, Co-Director of Equity Products and Strategies Group, Prudential Securities Incorporated

Lawrence J. Dyer Kidder Peabody & Co.

Frank J. Fabozzi, PhD, CFA Adjunct Professor of Finance, School of Management, Yale University

William J. Gartland, CFA Vice President, Bloomberg Financial Market

Gary L. Gastineau Senior Vice President, New Product Development, American Stock Exchange

Laurie S. Goodman, PhD Managing Director, Mortgage Strategy Group, PaineWebber

Lawrence E. Grannan Director, Senior Foreign Exchange Advisor, Bank of Montreal

Victor J. Haghani Partner, Long-Term Capital Management

Jeff Ho Vice President, Mortgage Strategy Group, PaineWebber

David P. Jacob Managing Director, Normura Securities International, Inc.

Frank J. Jones, PhD Chief Investment Officer, Guardian Life

Beth A. Krumholz

Nicholas C. Letica Director, Bear Stearns & Co.

Linda Lowell First Vice President, Mortgage Strategy Group, PaineWebber

Scott McDermott Vice President, Goldman, Sachs & Co.

Steven L. Nutt Vice President, Chemical Futures & Options, Inc.

Yiannos A. Pierides Assistant Professor of Finance, Department of Public and Business Administration, University of Cyprus, Nicosia, Cyprus

Shrikant Ramamurthy Vice President, Fixed-Income Research and Product Management, Prudential Securities Incorporated

Ehud I. Ronn, PhD Associate Professor of Finance, University of Texas at Austin

Robert D. Selvaggio, PhD Director, Fixed Income & Mortgage Research Group, The Chase Manhattan Bank, N.A.

Robert M. Stavis Managing Director, Salomon Brothers Inc

Robert Strickler Vice President, Citicorp

Klaus Bjerre Toft, PhD Assistant Professor of Finance, University of Texas at Austin

BRIEF CONTENTS

PART 1

FUNDAMENTALS OF OPTIONS AND RELATED PRODUCTS

1   Overview of Fixed-Income Options   3
William J. Gartland, Nicholas C. Letica, and Frank J. Fabozzi

2   Fixed-Income Option Contracts   37
Lawrence E. Grannan and Steven L. Nutt

3   Exotic (Nonstandard) Options on Fixed-Income Instruments   49
Gary L. Gastineau

4   A Survey of Spread Options for Fixed-Income Investors   75
Scott McDermott

5   Options on Mortgage-Backed Securities   127
William A. Barr

6   Interest-Rate Caps, Floors, and Compound Options   143
Anand K. Bhattacharya

PART 2

OPTION PRICING

7   An Overview of Fixed-Income Option Models   167
Lawrence J. Dyer and David P. Jacob

8   The Binomial Model for Valuing Options and Bonds with Embedded Options   201
Frank J. Fabozzi

9   Valuing Embedded Options in Interest Rate Caps, Floors, and Collars   225
Mark J.P. Anson

10   A Model for the Valuation of Callable Bonds   245
Ehud I. Ronn

11   Valuing Options on Treasury Bond Futures Contracts   261
Ehud I. Ronn and Klaus Bjerre Toft

ix

12   An Intuitive Approach to Fixed-Income Option Valuation   283
David Audley, Richard Chin, and Shrikant Ramamurthy

13   Valuation of Credit Risk Derivatives   297
Yiannos A. Pierides

14   An Options Approach to Valuing and Hedging
Mortgage Servicing Rights   311
Robert D. Selvaggio

15   Choosing the "Correct" Volatility for the
Valuation of Embedded Options   319
David Audley and Richard Chin

16   Measuring, Interpreting, and Applying
Volatility within the Fixed-Income Market   331
Keith Anderson and Scott Amero

PART 3

APPLICATIONS

17   Hedging with Options and Option Products   345
Jane Sachar Brauer and Laurie S. Goodman

18   Scenario Analysis and the Use of Options in
Total Return Portfolio Management   369
Keith Anderson and Scott Amero

19   Covered Call Writing Strategies   401
Frank J. Jones and Beth A. Krumholz

20   Capping the Interest Rate Risk in Insurance Products   437
David Babbel, Peter Bouyoucos, and Robert Strickler

21   Putable Swaps: Tools for Managing Callable Assets   465
Robert M. Stavis and Victor J. Haghani

22   Using Options to Enhance the Total Return
of a Mortgage Portfolio   483
Laurie S. Goodman, Linda Lowell, and Jeff Ho

INDEX   499

CONTENTS

PART 1

FUNDAMENTALS OF OPTIONS AND RELATED PRODUCTS

Chapter 1

Overview of Fixed-Income Options   3
William J. Gartland, Nicholas C. Letica, and Frank J. Fabozzi

How Options Work   4
The Option Price   9
Options Strategies   24
Classic Option Strategies   26
Volatility   33
Summary   35

Chapter 2

Fixed-Income Option Contracts   37
Lawrence E. Grannan and Steven L. Nutt

Options on U.S. Treasury Bond Futures   39
Options on 10-Year U.S. Treasury Note Futures   40
Options on 2- and 5-Year U.S. Treasury Note Futures   41
Options on Eurodollar Deposit Futures   42
Options on Nondollar Interest Rate Futures   46
Over-the-Counter Interest Rate Options   46

Chapter 3

Exotic (Nonstandard) Options on Fixed-Income Instruments   49
Gary L. Gastineau

Barrier Options   50
No Regrets Options   56
Deferred Premium and Deferred Strike Options   63

Chapter 4

A Survey of Spread Options for Fixed-Income Investors   75
   Scott McDermott

Introduction   75
SYCURVE Options   77
The SYCURVE Option's Equivalent Portfolio   80
SYCURVE-DUOP Options   88
MOTTO Options   90
ISO Options   97
CROSS Options   103
SPREAD-LOCK Options   108
Summary of Spread Options for Fixed-Income Investors   112
Appendix 4–A: An Analytic Formula for Valuing European
SYCURVE Put and Call Options   114

Chapter 5

Options on Mortgage-Backed Securities   127
   William A. Barr

Introduction   127
Market Conventions: OTC Options on Mortgage-Backed Securities   128
Differences among Treasury Options, OTC and Exchange-Traded
Options, and OTC Mortgage Options   129
Institutional Differences between Exchange-Traded Treasury Options and OTC
Mortgage Options   129
The Impact of Prepayments on Mortgage Option Pricing   131
Hedging the Option Embedded in the Mortgage Pipeline   133
Split Fee Options   137
Mortgage Options to Enhance Portfolio Returns   140
Summary   141

Chapter 6

Interest-Rate Caps, Floors, and Compound Options   143
   Anand K. Bhattacharya

Features of Interest-Rate Caps and Floors   144
Pricing of Caps and Floors   144
Interest-Rate Caps   145
Participating Caps   148
Interest-Rate Floors   151

Interest-Rate Collars   153
Interest-Rate Corridors   154
Cap/Floor Parity   156
Termination of Caps and Floors   158
Compound Options   158
Summary   163

PART 2

OPTION PRICING

Chapter 7

An Overview of Fixed-Income Option Models   167
Lawrence J. Dyer and David P. Jacob

The Basics of Option Pricing   169
Comparison of Major Models   177
Which Model Should Be Used?   193
Summary   199

Chapter 8

The Binomial Model for Valuing Options and Bonds with Embedded Options   201
Frank J. Fabozzi

Valuing Option-Free Bonds: A Review   202
The Binomial Interest Rate Tree   204
Constructing the Binomial Interest Rate Tree   210
Valuing an Option-Free Bond with the Binomial Tree   215
Using the Binomial Tree to Value an Option   216
Valuing a Bond with an Embedded Option   220
Summary   223

Chapter 9

Valuing Embedded Options in Interest Rate Caps, Floors, and Collars   225
Mark J.P. Anson

Introduction   225
Interest Rate Caps   226
Pricing Embedded Options in Interest Rate Caps, Floors, and Collars   228

A Modified Option Pricing Approach to Pricing Embedded Options in Caps   237
Summary   240
Appendix 9–A: Extending the Binomial Formula to Continuous Time   241

Chapter 10

A Model for the Valuation of Callable Bonds   245
Ehud I. Ronn

Introduction   245
Criteria for Selection of Interest Rate Models for the Valuation of
Callable Bonds   246
The Model's Inputs   248
Valuation of Callable Bonds   250
Richness/Cheapness Analysis: The Calibration of Interest Rate Volatility   253
Summary   256
Appendix 10-A: Matching the Term Structure in a No-Arbitrage
Recombining Interest Rate Lattice: A Numerical Example   258

Chapter 11

Valuing Options on Treasury Bond Futures Contracts   261
Ehud I. Ronn and Klaus Bjerre Toft

Introduction   261
Options on Treasury Bond Futures Contracts   263
Valuation   272
Summary   281

Chapter 12

An Intuitive Approach to Fixed-Income Option Valuation   283
David Audley, Richard Chin, and Shrikant Ramamurthy

Computations versus Intuition/Historical Data   284
Sector Yield Curve   284
Sector Curve and Embedded Options   285
Sector Price and Sector OAS   285
Estimation of Option Value   287
Callable Bond Example   288
Method 1: Sector Price of the Callable Bond   289
Method 2: Refunding Costs versus Costs of Noncallable Bond   291
Effect of Interest Rate Models on Option Value   292
Putable Bond Example   293

Estimating the OAS to the Treasury Curve   294
Mean Reversion Revisited   295
Summary   296

Chapter 13

Valuation of Credit Risk Derivatives   297
Yiannos A. Pierides

The Black and Cox Model of Coupon Corporate Bond Pricing   298
An American Put Option on the Cum-Coupon Bond Price (*G*)   299
Another Credit Risk Derivative: An American Call on the Bond's Spread   304
Summary   309

Chapter 14

An Options Approach to Valuing and Hedging Mortgage Servicing Rights   311
Robert D. Selvaggio

What Is Mortgage Servicing?   311
How Are Mortgage Servicing Rights Valued?   312
Hedging Mortgage Servicing Rights: An Option Replication Approach   314
Conclusions and Suggestions for Defending a Hedge Policy   318

Chapter 15

Choosing the "Correct" Volatility for the Valuation of Embedded Options   319
David Audley and Richard Chin

What Is Volatility?   320
One-Factor Interest Rate Models and Short-Rate Volatility   320
Effective Maturity and Effective Yield Volatility   321
Volatility Benchmarks   322
Implied Volatility   326
Summary   328

Chapter 16

Measuring, Interpreting, and Applying Volatility within the Fixed-Income Market   331
Keith Anderson and Scott Amero

Historical versus Implied Volatility   331
Calculating Historical Volatility   332

Price versus Yield Volatility   334
Developing a Volatility Forecast   336
The Importance of Scheduled Market Information   337
Patterns of Implied Volatility   337
Implications of a Volatility Forecast   338
Volatility and Expected Return   338

PART 3

APPLICATIONS

Chapter 17

Hedging with Options and Option Products   345
Jane Sachar Brauer and Laurie S. Goodman

Using Options in Asset Management   346
Liability Management   359
Asset/Liability Management   364
Summary   367

Chapter 18

**Scenario Analysis and the Use of Options in Total
Return Portfolio Management   369**
Keith Anderson and Scott Amero

Scenario Analysis   370
Options   380
Option Strategies to Structure Portfolio Return Patterns   382
Summary   396

Chapter 19

Covered Call Writing Strategies   401
Frank J. Jones and Beth A. Krumholz

Call Writing   401
Writing Treasury Bond Futures Calls against Treasury Bonds   412
Managing the Covered Write   418
Conceptual Observations   428
Summary   429
Appendix 19–A: Rate of Return on a Covered Write on a Treasury Bond   432

Chapter 20

Capping the Interest Rate Risk in Insurance Products   437
David Babbel, Peter Bouyoucos, and Robert Strickler

Keeping Risk under a Cap   437
Description of Interest Rate Caps   440
Considerations in Valuing Caps   445
Adding Caps to a Bond Portfolio   451
Example: Interest-Sensitive Life Insurance   452
Summary   463

Chapter 21

Putable Swaps: Tools for Managing Callable Assets   465
Robert M. Stavis and Victor J. Haghani

Risk and Return from Noncallable Corporate Bonds   466
Asset-Based Interest Rate Swaps with Noncallable Bonds   467
The Problems of Callable Assets   468
Using a Putable Swap to Manage a Callable Asset   471
Determinants of Value of a Put on an Interest Rate Swap   476
Summary   479

Chapter 22

Using Options to Enhance the Total Return of a Mortgage Portfolio   483
Laurie Goodman, Linda Lowell, and Jeff Ho

OTC Treasury and Mortgage Option Markets   484
Covered Call Writing   486
Writing Options to Monetize Positive Convexity   488
Using Options to Augment Up- and Down-in-Coupon Mortgage Trades   492
Using Options to Bet on the Directionality of Mortgage/Treasury Spreads   496
Summary   498

Index   499

P A R T

1

FUNDAMENTALS OF OPTIONS AND RELATED PRODUCTS

1

⑥ OVERVIEW OF FIXED-INCOME OPTIONS

William J. Gartland, CFA
Vice President
Bloomberg Financial Market

Nicholas C. Letica
Director
Bear Stearns & Co.

Frank J. Fabozzi, Ph.D, CFA
Adjunct Professor of Finance
School of Management
Yale University

As the sophistication and diversity of investors have grown, the need for derivative instruments such as options has increased accordingly. Knowledge of option strategies, once the province of a few speculators, is now necessary for everyone who wishes to maintain a competitive edge in an increasingly technical market. Moreover, the new options technology has been applied with increasing success to securities with optionlike characteristics such as callable bonds and mortgage-backed securities.

In this chapter we will review how options work, their risk/return profiles, the basic principles of option pricing, and some common trading and portfolio strategies. More detailed discussions of option pricing and hedging strategies are provided in later chapters. The next chapter describes option contracts: exchange-traded options on physical securities, exchange-traded options on futures, and over-the-counter options.

Throughout most of the discussion, we will focus on options on physicals. The principles, however, are equally applicable to options on futures or futures options.

HOW OPTIONS WORK

An *option* is the right, but not the obligation, to buy or to sell a security at a fixed price. The right to buy is called a *call,* and the right to sell is called a *put;* a call makes money if prices rise, and a put makes money if prices fall.

If the owner of an option used the option to buy or sell the underlying security, we say that the option has been exercised. Because the holder is never required to exercise an option, the holder can never lose more than the purchase price of the option; an option is a limited-liability instrument.

An option on a given security can be specified by giving its strike price and its expiration date. The *strike price* is the price on the optional purchase; for example, a call with a strike price of par is the right to buy that security at par. The *expiration date* is the last date on which the option can be exercised; after that it is worthless, even if it had value on the expiration date. If an option is allowed to expire, it is said to be *terminated.* On or before the expiration date, the option holder may decide to sell the option for its market value. This is called a *pair-off.*

Some options can be exercised at any time until expiration; they are called *American* options. On the other hand, some options can be exercised only at expiration and are called *European* options. Because it is always possible to delay the exercise of an American option until expiration, an American option is always worth at least as much as its European counterpart. While exchange-traded options are either American- or European-type options, in the over-the-counter market the exercise can be tailored to the objectives of a dealer's clients. For example, some options can be exercised before the expiration date, but only on designated dates. Such options are called *Atlantic* options or *Bermuda* options.

The easiest way to analyze a position in a security and options on that security is with a *profit/loss graph.* A profit/loss graph shows the change in a position's value between the *analysis date* ("now") and a horizon date for a range of security prices at the horizon.

Suppose a call option with a strike price of par (100) is bought today for 1 point. At expiration, if the security is priced below par, the option will be allowed to expire worthless; the position has lost 1 point. If the security is above par at expiration, the option will be exercised; the position has made 1 point for every point that the security is above par, less the initial 1-point cost of the option. Exhibit 1–1 shows the resulting profit/loss graph.

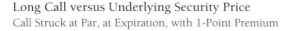

E X H I B I T   1–1

Long Call versus Underlying Security Price
Call Struck at Par, at Expiration, with 1-Point Premium

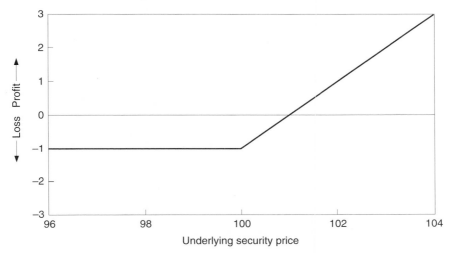

Note that if the price of the underlying security increases by 1 point, the option buyer breaks even. This happens because the value of the option at expiration is equal to the initial purchase price. A price of 101 is the break-even price for the call: The call purchase will make money if the price of the underlying exceeds 101 at expiration.

A put is the reverse of a call. Look at Exhibit 1–2, which is the profit/loss graph of a put option struck at par bought for 1 point. At expiration, the put is worth nothing if the security's price is more than the strike price and is worth 1 point for every point that the security is priced below the strike price. The break-even price for this trade is 99, so the put purchase makes money if the underlying is priced below 99 at expiration.

Put/Call Parity

A put and a call struck at the money split up the profit/loss diagram of the underlying security into two parts. Consider the position created by buying a call and selling a put such that the strike price of the two options is equal to the price of the underlying. If the price of the security goes up, the call will be exercised; if the price of the security goes down, the put will be exercised. In either case, at expiration the underlying is delivered

E X H I B I T   1–2

Long Put versus Underlying Security Price
Put Struck at Par, at Expiration, with 1-Point Premium

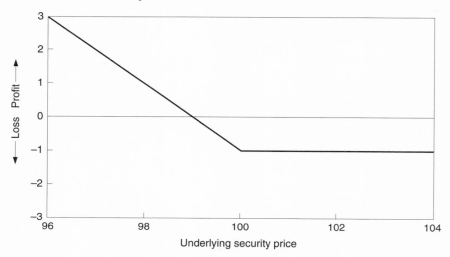

at the strike price. So in terms of profit and loss, owning the call and selling the put is the same as owning the underlying.

Exhibit 1–3 divides the profit/loss graph of the underlying security into graphs for a long call and a short put, respectively. The following three facts can be deducted:

Long security = Long call + Short put	(see Exhibit 1–3)
Long call = Long security + Long put	(see Exhibit 1–4)
Long put = Short security + Long call	(see Exhibit 1–5)

This relationship is called *put/call parity*; it is one of the foundations of the options markets. Using these facts, a call can be created from a put by buying the underlying, or a put can be made from a call by selling the underlying. This ability to convert between puts and calls at will is essential to the management of an options position.

Differences Between Options and Futures/Forward Contracts

An option is one basic type of derivative instrument. A derivative instrument is one whose value is derived from the underlying security, com-

E X H I B I T   1–3

Long Security = Long Call + Short Put

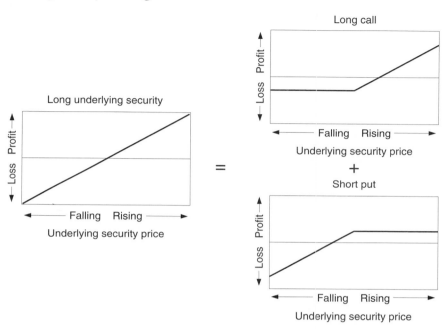

modity, or interest rate. We have seen how the value of an option is derived from the value of the underlying security.

Two other basic types of derivative instruments are a futures contract and a forward contract. Both a futures contract and a forward contract require a party to the agreement to either buy or sell something at a designated future date at a predetermined price. Futures contracts are standardized agreements regarding the delivery date (or month) and quality of the deliverable security, and are traded on organized exchanges. A forward contract differs in that it is usually nonstandardized (that is, the terms of each contract are negotiated individually between buyer and seller), no clearinghouse is involved, and secondary markets are often nonexistent or extremely thin. Unlike a futures contract, which is an exchange-traded product, a forward contract is an over-the-counter instrument.

Notice that unlike the parties to a futures or forward contract, the buyer of an option contract has the right, but not the obligation, to transact. The option writer does have the obligation to perform. In the case of a futures or forward contract, both buyer and seller are obligated to

Long Call = Long Security + Long Put

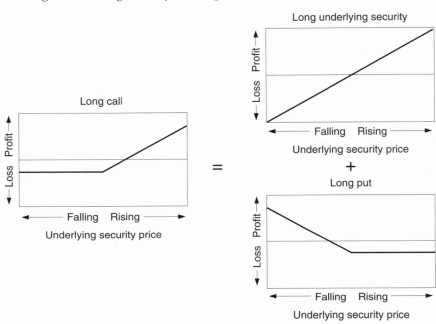

perform. Of course, a futures or forward buyer does not pay the seller to accept the obligation, whereas an option buyer pays the seller an option price.

Consequently, the risk/reward characteristics of the options and futures/forward contracts also differ. In the case of a futures/forward contract, the buyer of the contract realizes a dollar-for-dollar gain when the price of the contract increases and suffers a dollar-for-dollar loss when the price drops. The opposite occurs for the seller of a futures/forward contract. Options do not provide this symmetric risk/reward relationship. The most the buyer of an option can lose is the option price. However, while the buyer of an option retains all the potential benefits, the gain is always reduced by the amount of the option price. The maximum profit the writer may realize is the option price; this is offset against substantial downside risk. This difference is extremely important because investors can use futures/forward contracts to protect against symmetric risk and options to protect against asymmetric risk.

E X H I B I T   1–5

Long Put = Short Security + Long Call

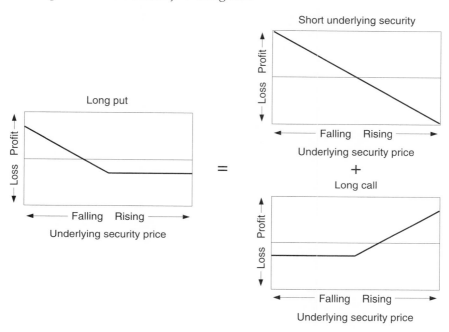

THE OPTION PRICE

The option price reflects the option's *intrinsic value* and any additional amount over its intrinsic value. The premium over intrinsic value is often referred to as the *time value.*

Determination of the theoretical or fair value of an option is complicated. For this reason, Part 3 of this book is devoted to this important topic. Here we focus only on the two basic components of an option and the factors that affect the price of an option.

Intrinsic Value

The intrinsic value of an option is the option's economic value if it is exercised immediately. If no positive economic value would result from exercising the option immediately, the intrinsic value is zero.

For a call option, the intrinsic value is positive if the current security price is greater than the strike price. The intrinsic value is then the difference between the two prices. If the strike price of a call option is greater than or equal to the current security price, the intrinsic value is zero. For example, if the strike price for a call option is $100 and the current security price is $105, the intrinsic value is $5. That is, an option buyer exercising the option and simultaneously selling the underlying security would realize $105 from the sale of the security, which would be covered by acquiring the security from the option writer for $100, thereby netting a $5 gain.

When an option has intrinsic value, it is said to be *in the money*. When the strike price of a call option exceeds the current security price, the call option is said to be *out of the money;* it has no intrinsic value. An option whose strike price is equal to the current security price is said to be *at the money*. Both at-the-money and out-of-the-money options have an intrinsic value of zero because they are not profitable to exercise. Our call option with a strike price of $100 would be (1) in the money when the current security price is greater than $100, (2) out of the money when the current security price is less than $100, and (3) at the money when the current security price is equal to $100.

For a put option, the intrinsic value is equal to the amount by which the current security price is below the strike price. For example, if the strike price of a put option is $100 and the current security price is $92, the intrinsic value is $8. The buyer of the put option who exercises the put option and simultaneously sells the underlying security will net $8 by exercising, since the security will be sold to the writer for $100 and purchased in the market for $92. The intrinsic value is zero if the strike price is less than or equal to the current market price.

For our put option with a strike price of $100, the option would be (1) in the money when the security price is less than $100, (2) out of the money when the security price exceeds $100, and (3) at the money when the security price is equal to $100.

Exhibit 1–6 summarizes these relations.

Time Value

The time value of an option is the amount by which the option's price exceeds its intrinsic value. The option buyer hopes that at some time prior to expiration, changes in the market price of the underlying security will increase the value of the rights conveyed by the option. For this prospect, the option buyer is willing to pay a premium above the intrinsic value. For example, if the price of a call option with a strike price of $100 is $9 when the current security price is $105, the time value of this option is $4 ($9

E X H I B I T   1–6

Intrinsic Values of Options

	Call Option	**Put Option**
If Security Price > Strike Price		
Intrinsic value	Security Price – Strike Price	Zero
Jargon	In the money	Out of the money
If Security Price < Strike Price		
Intrinsic value	Zero	Strike Price – Security Price
Jargon	Out of the money	In the money
If Security Price = Strike Price		
Intrinsic value	Zero	Zero
Jargon	At the money	At the money

minus its intrinsic value of $5). Had the current security price been $90 instead of $105, the time value of this option would be the entire $9 because the option has no intrinsic value. Other factors equal, the time value of an option will increase with the amount of time remaining to expiration, since the opportunity for a favorable change in the price is greater.

There are two ways an option buyer may realize the value of a position taken in the option: (1) exercise the option and (2) sell the call option. In the first example above, since the exercise of an option will yield a gain of only $5 and will cause the immediate loss of any time value ($4 in our first example), it is preferable to sell the call. In general, if an option buyer wishes to realize the value of a position, selling will be more economically beneficial than exercising. However, under some circumstances it is preferable to exercise prior to the expiration date, depending on whether the total proceeds at the expiration date would be greater by holding the option or by exercising it and reinvesting any cash proceeds received until the expiration date.

Relationship between Put and Call Prices

A relationship exists between the price of a call option and the price of a put option on the same underlying instrument with the same strike prices and the same expiration dates. To see this relationship, commonly referred to as the *put/call parity relationship,* let's use an example.

Consider a put option and a call option on the same underlying security with one month to expiration and a strike price of $100. The price of the underlying security is $100. Suppose the call price and put price are $3 and $2, respectively. Consider this strategy:

1. Buy the security at a price of $100.
2. Sell a call at a price of $3.
3. Buy a put option at a price of $2.

This strategy involves

1. Long the security.
2. Short the call option.
3. Long the put option.

Exhibit 1–7 shows the profit-and-loss profile at the expiration date for this strategy for selected security prices. For the long security position there is no profit, because at a price above $100, the security will be called from the investor at a price of $100, and at a price below $100, the security will be put by the investor at a price of $100. No matter what the security's price is at the expiration date, this strategy will produce a profit of $1 without anybody making any net investment. Ignoring (1) the cost of financing the long position in the security and the long put position and (2) the return from investing the proceeds from the sale of the call, this situation cannot exist in an efficient market. By implementing the strategy to capture the $1 profit, the actions of market participants will have one or more of the following consequences, which tend to eliminate the $1 profit: (1) The price of the security will increase, (2) the call option price will drop, and/or (3) the put option price will rise.

Assuming the security's price does not change, the call price and the put price will tend toward equality. This is true only when we ignore the time value of money (financing cost, opportunity cost, cash payments, and reinvestment income). Also, our illustration does not consider the possibility of early exercise of the option. Thus, we have been considering a put/call parity relationship that is applicable only to European options.

It can be shown that the put-call parity relationship for an option on a bond is

Put price = Call price + Present value of strike price + Present
          value of coupon payments – Price of underlying bond

E X H I B I T   1–7

Profit/Loss Profile for a Strategy Involving a Long Position in a Security, a Short Call Option Position, and a Long Put Option Position

Assumptions: Price of security = 100

Call option price = $3

Put option price = $2

Strike price = $100

Time to expiration = 1 month

Price of Security at Expiration Date	Profit from Security*	Price Received for Call	Price Paid for Put	Overall Profit
$150	0	3	−2	1
130	0	3	−2	1
120	0	3	−2	1
110	0	3	−2	1
100	0	3	−2	1
90	0	3	−2	1
80	0	3	−2	1
70	0	3	−2	1
60	0	3	−2	1

* There is no profit, because at a price above $100, the security will be called from the investor at a price of $100, and at a price below $100, the security will be put by the investor at a price of $100.

This relationship is actually the put/call parity relationship for European options; it is approximately true for American options. If this relationship does not hold, arbitrage opportunities exist. That is, portfolios consisting of long and short positions in the security and related options that provide an extra return with (practical) certainty will exist.

Factors That Influence the Option Price

Five factors influence the option price:

1. The price of the underlying security.
2. The strike price of the option.
3. The time to expiration of the option.
4. The volatility of the underlying security over the life of the option.
5. The cost of financing the underlying security.

Exhibit 1–8 summarizes the factors that affect the value of an option and the degree to which increasing each factor affects that value.

Price of the Underlying Security

The option price will change as the price of the underlying security changes. For a call option, as the price of the underlying security increases (holding all other factors constant), the option price increases because the intrinsic value increases. The opposite holds for a put option: As the price of the underlying security increases, the price of a put option decreases.

Strike Price

The strike price is fixed for the life of the option.[1] All other factors equal, the lower the strike price, the higher the price of a call option. For example, if the security price is trading at $110, the intrinsic value for a call option with a strike price of $100 will be $10, while the intrinsic value for a call option with a strike price of $105 will be only $5. For put options, the higher the strike price, the higher the option price.

Time to Expiration of the Option

An option is a "wasting asset." That is, after the expiration date passes, the option has no value. Holding all other factors equal, the longer the time to expiration of the option, the greater the option price. This occurs because as the time to expiration decreases, less time remains for the underlying security's price to rise (for a call buyer) or to fall (for a put buyer)—that is, to compensate the option buyer for any time value paid—and therefore the probability of a favorable price movement decreases.

EXHIBIT 1–8

The Effect of an Increase of a Factor on Option Values

	Call	Put
Underlying price	Increase	Decrease
Strike price	Decrease	Increase
Carry	Decrease	Increase
Time to expiration	Increase	Increase
Volatility	Increase	Increase

---

[1] Chapter 3 discusses exotic options. For such options, the strike price may not be fixed.

Consequently, for American options, as the time remaining until expiration decreases, the option price approaches its intrinsic value.

Exhibit 1–9 graphs the value of an option as time to expiration increases. Exhibit 1–10 compares the value of an option at expiration with the values of options with one and three months to expiration. At the strike price, there is a sharp corner in the graph that becomes more pronounced as the time to expiration decreases. This sharp corner makes an at-the-money option increasingly difficult to hedge as expiration approaches.

If the option is out of the money, it has some time value because there is a chance that the option will expire in the money; as it get further out of the money, this is less likely to occur, and the time value decreases.

If the option is in the money, its time value is due to the fact that it is better to hold the option than the corresponding position in the underlying security because if the security trades out of the money, the potential loss on the option is limited to the value of the option; as the option gets further in the money, this possibility becomes more far-fetched, and the time value decreases.

E X H I B I T   1–9

Call Option Value versus Time until Expiration
Three Calls: At the Money, 1 Point In the Money, 1 Point Out of the Money

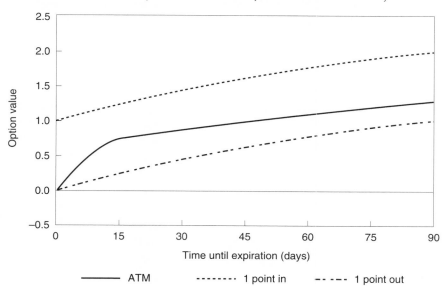

EXHIBIT 1–10

Call Option Value versus Underlying Security Price
Call Struck at Par with 1 and 3 Months to Expiration

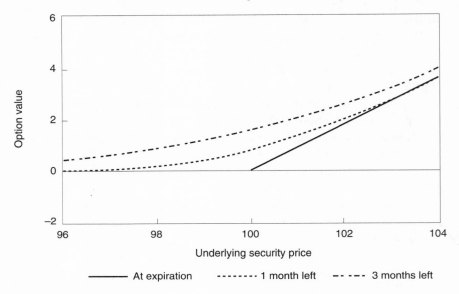

Either way, the time value depends on the probability that the security will trade through the strike price. In turn, this probability depends on how far from the strike price the security is trading and how much the security price is expected to vary until expiration.

Expected Volatility

Volatility measures the variability of the price or the yield of a security. It measures only the magnitude of the moves, not the direction. Standard option pricing models make no assumptions about the future direction of prices, but only about the distribution of those prices. Volatility is the ideal parameter for option pricing, since it measure how wide this distribution will be. We discuss volatility in more detail at the end of this chapter.

The higher the volatility of a security, the higher the prices of options on that security. If a security had no volatility, for example, that security would always have the same price at the time of purchase of an option as at its expiration, so all options would be priced at their intrinsic value. Increasing the volatility of a security increases the time value of options on that security as the chance of the security price moving through the strike price increases. Increases in the value of an at-the-money option are approximately proportional to increases in the volatility of the underlying. Exhibit 1–11 shows how the price of an option behaves as the volatility of the underlying security increases.

Cost of Financing the Underlying

Carry is the difference between the value of the coupon payments on a security and the cost of financing that security's purchase price. With the usual upward-sloping yield curve, most securities have a positive carry.

The effect of the carry can be seen by comparing the price of an at-the-money call with the price of an at-the-money put where the underlying security has a positive carry. The writer of the call anticipates the chance of being required to deliver the securities and thus buys the underlying as a hedge; the put writer loses the carry, so the call should cost less than the put. When the yield curve inverts and short-term rates are higher than long-term rates, carry becomes negative and calls cost more than puts.

E X H I B I T   1–11

Call Option Value versus Percent Price Volatility

Three Calls: At the Money, 1 Point in the Money, 1 Point Out of the Money;
3 Months from Expiration

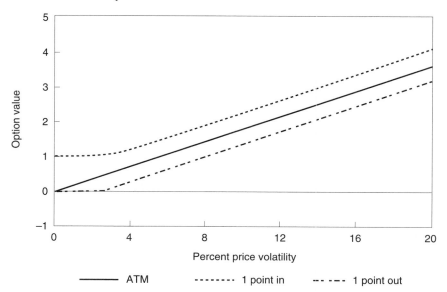

By put/call parity, selling an at-the-money call and buying an at-the-money put is equivalent to shorting the underlying security. The cash taken out of the option trade, accounting for transaction costs, compensates the option holder for the carry on the position in the underlying until expiration. This trade is called a *conversion,* and it is frequently used to obtain the effect of a purchase or sale of securities when buying or selling the underlying is impossible for accounting reasons.

Exhibit 1–12 compares the cost of an at-the-money call and put for a range of financing rates. The two graphs intersect where the call and the put have the same value: This happens when the cost of financing the underlying is equal to the coupon yield on the security; thus, the carry is zero and there is no advantage to holding the underlying over shorting it.

Delta, Gamma, and Theta: Hedging an Option Position

More precise quantitative ways to describe the behavior of an option are needed to manage an option position. Option traders have created the concepts of delta, gamma, and theta for this purpose. Delta measures the

E X H I B I T   1–12

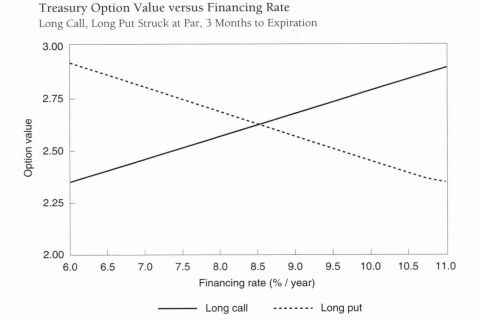

Treasury Option Value versus Financing Rate
Long Call, Long Put Struck at Par, 3 Months to Expiration

price sensitivity of an option, gamma the convexity of the option, and theta the change in the value of the option over time.

Delta

For a given option, the *delta* is the ratio of changes in the value of the option to changes in the value of the underlying security for small changes in the underlying. A typical at-the-money call option would have a delta of 0.5; this means that for a 1-cent increase in the price of the underlying, the value of the call would increase by 0.5 cents. On the other hand, an at-the-money put would have a delta of –0.5; puts have negative deltas because they decrease in value as the price of the underlying increases.

The standard method of hedging an option position is called *delta hedging,* which, not surprisingly, makes heavy use of the delta. The idea behind delta hedging is that for small price moves, the price of an option changes in proportion to the change in the price of the underlying security, so the underlying security can be used to hedge the option. For example, 1 million calls with a delta of 0.25 would, for small price movements, track a position of 250,000 of the underlying bonds; thus, a position consisting of 1 million of these long calls and 250,000 of the security sold short would be delta hedged. The total delta of a position shows by how much that position is long or short. In the example above, the total delta is

$$0.25 \times 1,000,000 - 1 \times 250,000 = 0$$

Thus, the position is neither long nor short.

Intuitively, the delta of an option is the number of bonds that are expected to be delivered into the option. For example, an at-the-money call has a delta of 0.5, which means that one bond is expected to be delivered for every two calls that are held. In other words, an at-the-money call is equally as likely to be exercised as not. An option that is deeply out of the money will have a delta that is close to zero because there is almost no chance that the option will ever be exercised. An option that is deeply in the money will almost certainly be exercised. This means that a deeply-in-the-money put has a delta of –1 because it is almost certain that the holder of the option will exercise the put and deliver one bond to the put writer.

Put/call parity tells us that a position in the underlying security may be duplicated by buying a call and selling a put with the same strike price and expiration date. Thus, the delta of the call less the delta of the put should be the delta of the underlying security. The delta of the underlying is 1, so we get the following equation:

$$\text{delta}(call) - \text{delta}(put) = 1$$

where the call and the put are options on the same security with the same strike price and expiration date. This says that once the call is bought and the put is sold, the bond is certain to be delivered; if the call is out of the money, the put is in the money. Moreover, as the chance of having the underlying security delivered into the call becomes smaller, the chance of having to accept delivery as the put is exercised becomes larger. Exhibit 1–13 compares the deltas for a long and a short put.

Gamma
Making the position delta neutral does not solve all hedging problems, however. This is demonstrated in Exhibit 1–14. Each of the three positions shown is delta neutral, but position 1 is clearly preferable to position 2, which in turn is better than position 3. The difference among these three positions is *convexity*. A position such as position 1, with a profit/loss graph that curves upward, has a positive convexity, whereas position 3 has a graph that curves downward and thus has negative convexity.

Gamma measures convexity for options; it is the change in the delta for small changes in the price of the underlying security. If a position has

E X H I B I T   1–13

Option Delta versus Underlying Security Price
Long Call, Long Put Struck at Par, 3 Months to Expiration

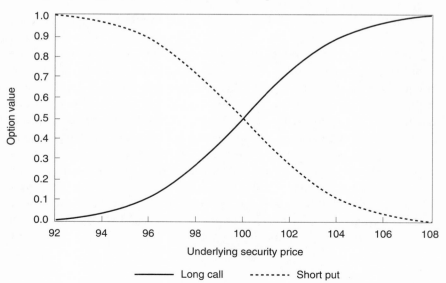

E X H I B I T   1–14

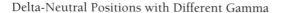

Delta-Neutral Positions with Different Gamma

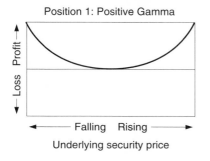

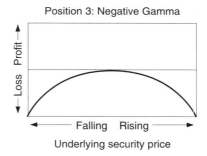

a positive gamma, then, as the market goes up, the delta of the position increases and as it declines, the delta increases. Such a position becomes longer as the market trades up and shorter as the market trades down. A position like this is called *long convexity* or *long volatility.* These terms come from the fact that if the market moves in either direction, this position will outperform a position with the same delta and a lower gamma. Exhibit 1–15 shows this phenomenon.

A long option always has a positive gamma. The delta of a call increases from 0 to 1 as the security trades up, and the delta of a put also increases, moving from –1 to 0. Because the profit/loss graph of options curves upward, option traders often speak of buying or selling volatility as a synonym for buying or selling options.

A position with a zero gamma is called *flat convexity* or *flat gamma.* Here a change in the underlying security price does not change the delta of the position. Such a position trades like a position in the underlying with no options bought or sold. If the position has in addition a delta of zero, its value is not affected by small changes in the price of the underlying secu-

E X H I B I T   1–15

Profit/Loss Diagram with Convexity
Long Security with Flat and Long Convexity

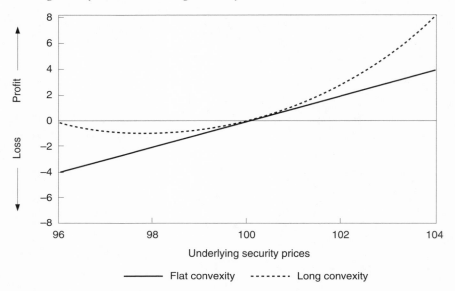

Flat convexity   -------- Long convexity

rity in either direction. Position 2 in Exhibit 1–14 is a profit/loss graph for a position with no delta or gamma.

A position with negative gamma is called *short volatility* or *short convexity*. The profit/loss curve slopes downward in either direction from the current price on the underlying; thus, the position gets longer as the market trades down and shorter as the market trades up. Either way, this position loses money if significant price movements occur. Position 3 demonstrates this behavior.

A position that is long volatility is clearly preferable to an otherwise identical position that is short volatility. The holder of the short-volatility position must be compensated for this. To create a position that is long volatility, it is necessary to purchase options and spend money; moreover, if the market does not move, the values of the options will decrease as their time to expiration decreases, so the position loses money in a flat market.

Conversely, creating a position that is short volatility involves selling options and taking in cash. As time passes, the value of these options sold decreases because their time value falls, so the position makes money in a flat market. Large losses could be sustained in a volatile market, however.

Exhibit 1–16 shows the effects of different volatility exposures.

Theta

To describe the time behavior of options, there is one last measure called *theta*. The theta of an option is the overnight change in value of the option if all other parameters (prices, volatilities) stay constant. This means that a long option has a negative theta, because as expiration approaches, the time value of the option will erode to zero. For example, a 90-day at-the-money call that costs 2 points might have a theta of –0.45 ticks per day.

Option Pricing Models

Theoretical boundary conditions for the price of an option can be derived using arbitrage arguments. For example, it can be shown that the minimum price for an American call option is its intrinsic value; that is,

Call option price ≥ Max [0, (Price of security – Strike price)]

This expression says that the call option price will be greater than or equal to the difference between the price of the underlying security and the strike price (intrinsic value), or zero, whichever is higher.

The boundary conditions can be "tightened" by using arbitrage arguments coupled with certain assumptions about the distribution of the securi-

E X H I B I T   1–16

Comparison of Different Volatility Positions (All Positions Are Delta Neutral)

	Short Volatility	Flat Volatility	Long Volatility
Convexity	Position has negative convexity: gamma < 0	Position has no convexity: gamma = 0	Position has positive convexity: gamma > 0
Options purchased	More sold than bought	As many sold as bought	More bought than sold
Time value	Position earns value as time passes: theta > 0	Position stays flat as time passes: theta = 0	Position loses value as time passes: theta < 0
Market moves	Position loses money if the market moves in either direction	Position is invariant with respect to market moves	Position makes money if the market moves in either direction

ty's price. The extreme case is an option pricing model that uses a set of assumptions to derive a single theoretical price rather than a range.

Several models have been developed to determine the theoretical value of an option. The most popular model was developed by Fischer Black and Myron Scholes in 1973 for valuing European call options.[2] Several modifications to their model have followed since then. Another pricing model that overcomes some of the drawbacks of the Black-Scholes option pricing model is the binomial option pricing model.

The basic idea behind the arbitrage argument in deriving these option pricing models is that if the payoff from owning a call option can be replicated by (1) purchasing the security underlying the call option and (2) borrowing funds, the price of the option will be (at most) the cost of creating the replicating strategy.

Chapter 7 provides an overview of the various option pricing models and their underlying principles and demonstrates the limitations of employing the Black-Scholes option pricing model. Other option pricing models are explained in Part 3.

OPTIONS STRATEGIES

Investors have many different goals, including reducing risk, increasing rates of return, or capturing gains under expected market moves. Often these objectives are simply to rearrange the profit/loss graph position in accordance with the investor's expectations or desires. By increasing the minimum value of this graph, for example, the investor reduces risk.

Options provide a precise tool with which to accomplish this rearrangement. Because it is impossible to replicate the performance of an option position using just the underlying, options allow a much broader range of strategies to be used. The following characteristics of options provide an explanation.

Directionality

Both a put and a call are directional instruments. A put, for example, performs only in a decreasing market. This property makes options ideal for reducing directional risk on a position. Take, for example, a position that suffers large losses in a downward market and makes a consistent profit

---

[2] Fischer Black and Myron Scholes, "The Pricing of Corporate Liabilities," *Journal of Political Economy,* May–June 1973, pp. 637–59.

if prices rise. By purchasing a put option, the investor gives up some of these profits in exchange for dramatically increased performance if the market declines.

Convexity

Buying and selling options makes it possible to adjust the convexity of a position in almost any fashion. Because OTC options can be purchased for any strike price and expiration, convexity can be bought or sold at any point on the profit/loss graph. For example, an investor holding mortgage-backed securities priced just over par might anticipate that prepayments on this security would start to increase dramatically if the market traded up, attenuating possible price gains. In other words, the investor believes that the position is short convexity above the market. To adjust the profit/loss graph, calls could be purchased with strike prices at or above the market. This trade sells some of the spread over Treasuries in exchange for increased performance in a rising market.

Fee Income

An investor who wishes to increase the performance of a position in a stable market can sell convexity by writing options and taking in fees. This increases the current yield of the position, at the cost of increasing volatility risk in some area of the profit/loss graph. A typical example of this approach is the venerable covered call strategy, where the manager of a portfolio sells calls on a portion of the portfolio, forgoing some profits in a rising market in exchange for a greater return in a stable or decreasing market.

Leveraged Speculation

Investors with a higher risk/reward profile wish to increase their upside potential and are willing to accept a greater downside risk. In this case, options can be used as a highly leveraged position to capture windfall profits under a very specific market move. A strongly bullish investor might purchase 1-point out-of-the-money calls with 30 days to expiration for ½ point. If the market traded up 2 points by expiration, the option would then be worth 1 point and the investor would have doubled the initial investment; a corresponding position in the underlying would have appreciated in value by only about 2 percent. Of course, if the market did not trade up by at least 1 point, the calls would expire worthless.

CLASSIC OPTION STRATEGIES

This section gives a brief explanation of some of the simplest pure option strategies.

Straddle

The purest convexity trade is called a *straddle,* composed of one call and one put with the same strike price. Exhibit 1–17 shows the profit/loss graph of a straddle struck at the money at expiration and with three months to expiration.

    This position is delta neutral, as it implies no market bias. If the market stays flat, the position loses money as the options' time value disappears by expiration. If the market moves in either direction, however, either the put or call will end up in the money, and the position will make money. This strategy is most useful for buying convexity at a specific strike price. Investors who are bearish on volatility and anticipate a flat market could sell straddles and make money from time value.

E X H I B I T   1–17

Profit/Loss Diagram for a Long Straddle
Struck at Par, at Expiration, and 3 Months Out

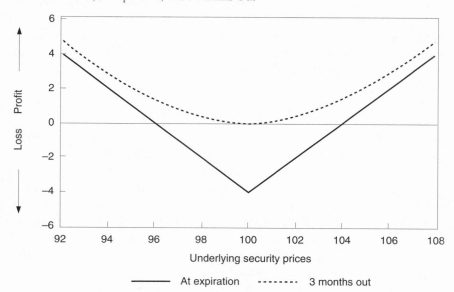

Strangle

A *strangle* is the more heavily leveraged cousin of the straddle. An at-the-money strangle is composed of an out-of-the-money call and an out-of-the-money put. The options are struck so that they are both equally out of the money and the current price of the security is halfway between the two strikes. The profit/loss graph is shown in Exhibit 1–18.

Just like a straddle, a strangle is a pure volatility trade. If the market stays flat, the position loses time value, whereas if the market moves dramatically in either direction, the position makes money from either the call or the put. Because the options in this position are both out of the money, the market has to move significantly before either option moves into the money. The options are much cheaper, however, so it is possible to buy many more options for the same money. This is the ideal position for the investor who is heavily bullish on volatility and wants windfall profits in a rapidly moving market.

Writing strangles is a very risky business. Most of the time the market will not move enough to put either option much into the money, and the

EXHIBIT   1–18

Profit/Loss Diagram for a Long Straddle
Struck at Par, at Expiration, and 3 Months Out

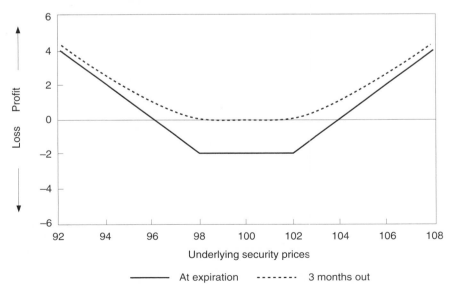

writer of the strangle will make the fee income. Occasionally, however, the market will plummet or spike, and the writer of the strangle will suffer catastrophic losses. This accounts for the picturesque name of this trade.

Spread Trades

Spread trades involve buying one option and funding all or part of this purchase by selling another. A bull spread can be created by owning the underlying security, buying a put struck below the current price, and selling a call above the current price. Because both options are out of the money, it is possible to arrange the strikes so that the cost of the put is equal to the fee for the call. If the security price falls below the put strike or rises above the call strike, the appropriate option will be exercised and the security will be sold. Otherwise, any profit or loss will just be that of the underlying security. In other words, this position is analogous to owning the underlying security except that the final value of the position at expiration is forced to be between the two strikes. Exhibit 1–19 shows the profit/loss graph for this position at expiration and with three months left of time value.

E X H I B I T   1–19

Profit/Loss Diagram for a Bull Spread
Struck at Par, at Expiration, and 3 Months Out

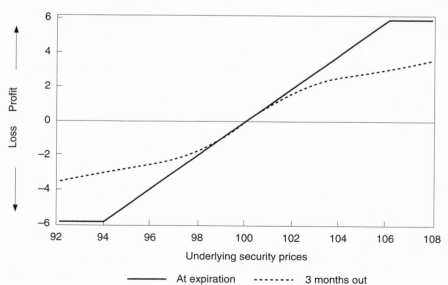

The other spread trade is a *bear spread;* it is the reverse of a bull spread. It can be created by selling a bull spread. Using put/call parity, it can also be set up by holding the underlying security, buying an in-the-money put, and selling an in-the-money call. A bear spread is equivalent to a short position in the underlying, where the position must be closed out at a price between the two strike prices. Exhibit 1–20 shows the profit/loss graph for a bear spread.

PRACTICAL PORTFOLIO STRATEGIES

The strategies discussed in the previous section are the basic techniques used by speculators to trade options. The usual fixed-income investor has a lower risk/reward profile than the speculator and specific objectives that must be accomplished—a floor on rate of return or an increase in current yield, for example. Such investors need a class of strategies different from that needed by speculators; even though the same strategies are often used, the risk is carefully controlled.

E X H I B I T   1–20

Profit/Loss Diagram for a Bear Spread
Struck at Par, at Expiration, and 3 Months Out

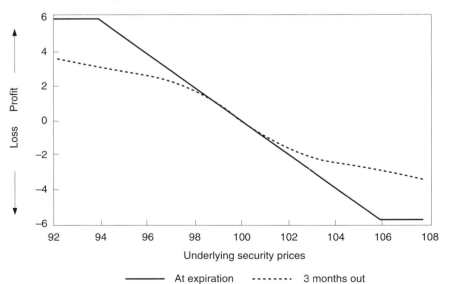

Protective Put Buying: Portfolio Insurance

The protective put buying strategy is the most obvious and one of the most commonly used option strategies. An investor with a portfolio of securities who fears a decreasing market buys puts on some or all of the portfolio; if the market rate falls, the puts are exercised, and the securities are sold at the strike price. Alternatively, the investor may keep the under-lying security and pair off the in-the-money puts, receiving cash in com-pensation for the decreased value of the security. Either way, the investor has limited losses on the portfolio in exchange for selling off return in a stable or rising market.

As the strike price of the put increases, so does its cost and the resul-tant impact on the stable market rate of return. Often out-of-the-money options are used: the floor on returns is lower because the strike price is lower, but the lower cost of the options means that less return is given up if the market is flat or rises. By put/call parity, such a position is equiva-lent to holding a call option struck at or in the money.

Another popular strategy is to buy at-the-money options on a por-tion of the portfolio. This reduces but does not eliminate downside risk. Exhibit 1–21 shows the profit/loss graphs at expiration for positions with

E X H I B I T   1–21

Hedged Underlying Security with Puts
Long Puts Struck at Par, at Expiration

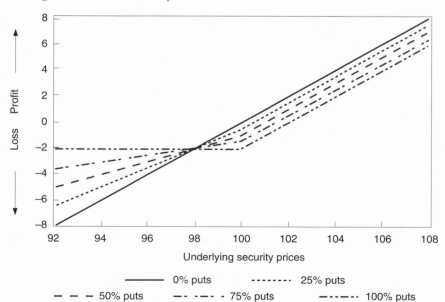

different percentages of the portfolio hedged with an at-the-money put. Note that all the graphs intersect at a single point. This is the point where the initial cost of the option is equal to the value of the option at expiration, which is the break-even price for this trade.

It is not possible to buy options on many classes of securities that may well be held in a portfolio. Perfect insurance for such securities is unattainable, but cross-market hedging will often permit a reduction in downside risk to acceptable levels. This is discussed further in Chapter 17.

Covered Calls

Writing covered calls is a strategy that sells volatility in return for fees. An investor who holds a portfolio sells calls on some or all of the portfolio in return for fees. If the market stays the same or falls, the investor pockets the option fees. If the market increases until the calls are in the money, the investor is called out by the option holder. In other words, possible gains on the portfolio are sold for fee income.

Often the investor wishes to preserve some upside potential. Just as in the portfolio insurance example, there are two different ways to do this. The calls can be struck out of the money, that is, above the current market price. This strategy allows gains up to the strike price to be captured. If the bonds in the portfolio are currently trading below the original purchase price, a popular strategy is to sell calls struck at this purchase price. This provides fee income and increased current yield but prevents the possibility that the bonds will be called at a price below the original purchase price and the portfolio will book a capital loss.

Otherwise, calls can be sold on a portion of the portfolio. This allows unlimited price gains to be captured on the remainder. Exhibit 1–22 shows the profit/loss graph for a covered call program where different portions of the portfolio have calls sold against them.

Buy-Writes and Writing Puts

Buy-writes and writing puts are two very closely related strategies for selling volatility that most investors think of as being entirely different. To execute a buy-write, a bond is purchased, and simultaneously a call is written on this bond to the same dealer for the fee income. If the security is trading above the strike price at expiration, the security is called, and the investor is left with just the option fee. If the price of the security has fallen, the investor is left holding the security, but the total cost of the

E X H I B I T   1–22

Covered Call Writing Program
Short Calls Struck at Par, at Expiration

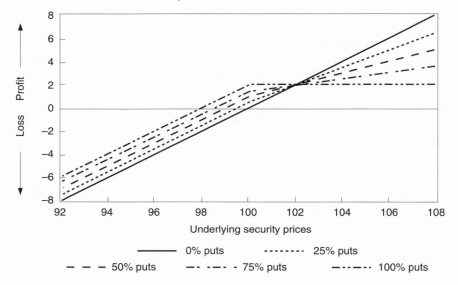

Underlying security prices

——— 0% puts   ········ 25% puts
— — — 50% puts   —· ·—· · 75% puts   —·—··· 100% puts

security is reduced by the fee from the call. By put/call parity, this trade is identical to writing a put struck at the money. In both cases, the investor is delivered the security only if the price of the security is lower than the price of the original sale.

In the mortgage-backed securities (MBS) market, a buy-write is composed of forward purchases and short calls on forward delivery contracts. If the call is exercised, it offsets the forward sale; the buyer never takes delivery of the security and keeps the fee income. Otherwise, the buyer will receive the security on the forward settlement date for the original forward sale price, although the total price is decreased by the value of the option fee.

Put writing is a more general strategy that applies to all fixed-income options markets. The investor writes a put for the fee income and receives the underlying instrument at expiration if the security trades below the strike price. This can be a very effective strategy if carefully structured. An investor may believe that a security offers real value if bought at a certain price below the market. The investor could then write puts struck at the price. If the security falls below the strike, it is delivered at a price that is more agreeable than the current price. Otherwise, the investor simply pockets the fee income.

VOLATILITY[3]

Volatility plays a key role in the valuation of options and in option strategies. In this section, we focus on methods for estimating volatility. Statistically, volatility is a measure of the dispersion or spread of observations around the mean of the set of observations. If volatility seems strangely like a standard deviation, you remember your statistics. When people speak of volatility, they are really talking about a standard deviation.

For fixed-income securities, volatility is expressed in yield or price units, either on a percentage or an absolute basis. Price volatilities can be computed for any security. Yield volatilities should be computed only for those securities with a consistent method for computing yield. Given the complexity of calculating a yield on a MBS and the variation of results, the predominant volatility measure in the MBS market is price volatility. The government bond market, where yields are easily calculated, favors yield volatility.

There are two types of volatility: empirical volatility and implied volatility. Each is described next.

Empirical Volatility

Empirical volatility is the actual, historical market volatility of a specific security. These numbers are typically calculated for various time periods (10 days, 30 days, 360 days) and are usually annualized.[4] Calculating an empirical volatility is nothing more than calculating the standard deviation of a time series. Thus, an absolute volatility is the annualized standard deviation of daily price or yield changes, assuming a normal distribution.

Percentage volatility is the annualized standard deviation of the daily change in the log of prices or yields, assuming a lognormal distribution of prices or yields. Similar to the daily absolute yield changes, the logs of the daily yield changes have a slight bias toward lower yields. The intuitive approach to calculating a percentage volatility is to find the standard deviation of daily *returns,* assuming a normal distribution. This approach is

---

[3] The discussion in this section draws from Nicholas C. Letica, William J. Curtin, Andrew Lawrence, and John Drastal, "Behavior of Volatility and Trading Characteristics of Fixed Income Options," *The Handbook of Fixed Income Securities,* 3rd ed., ed. Frank J. Fabozzi (Homewood, IL: Business One Irwin, 1991), Chapter 35.

[4] When annualizing a volatility, certain assumptions are inherent to the calculation. To convert from daily to yearly volatility, for example, the daily volatility is multiplied by the square root of the number of business days in the year, approximately 250.

equivalent to the lognormal assumption as long as the distribution can be characterized as being equally normal and lognormal and the changes in prices are taken on a small interval, such as daily.

As previously mentioned, empirical volatility can be measured over various time periods. The most common interval on which the standard deviation is taken is 30 days; other common intervals are 10 days and 360 days. The choice of interval determines how quickly and to what degree an empirical volatility responds to deviations. As the time period shortens, volatility increasingly reflects current conditions but is more unstable as each sample asserts greater influence in the deviation. Conversely, as the interval increases, a greater lag and a smoothing are introduced into the calculation.

The interval used to calculate an empirical volatility should be chosen to match the length of the option contract. This provides the investor with an indication of how volatile the underlying security has been recently and how this relates to the volatility employed to price the option.

With no industry standard for volatility units, converting between the price and yield expression of absolute or percentage volatility is a useful skill. The path to follow to convert from one unit to the next is shown in Exhibit 1–23. The modified duration of a security provides the link between price and yield volatilities. Modified duration is defined as the percentage change in price divided by the absolute change in yield.

Implied Volatility

Implied volatility is merely the market's expectation of future volatility over a specified time period. An option's price is a function of the volatility employed, so where an option's price is known the implied volatility can be derived. Although it sounds straightforward, calculating an implied volatility is far more complicated than calculating an empirical volatility because expectations cannot be observed directly. An option pricing model along with a mathematical method to infer the volatility must be employed. The result of this calculation is a percentage price volatility that can be converted to the various types of volatility measures discussed previously (see Exhibit 1–23).

Owning to the existence and liquidity of fixed-income options, proxies for implied volatilities can be derived from Treasuries. The bond futures market on the Chicago Board of Trade (CBT) is one of the most liquid markets for fixed-income options and provides the information necessary to calculate an implied volatility. The resultant implied volatility provides a good indication of the market's expected volatility for the

E X H I B I T   1–23

Converting Volatility Measures

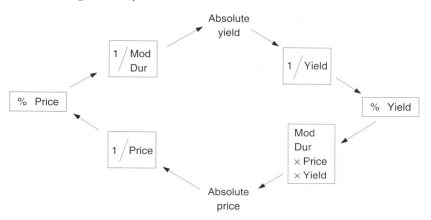

Treasuries with maturities similar to that of the particular bond futures contract in question. The implied volatility on the 20-year bond futures contract, for example, is a useful proxy for the market's expected volatility on long-term Treasury securities.

Exhibit 1–24 shows implied percentage prices and absolute yield volatilities for calls and puts on the bond futures contract of March 1990 over a range of strike prices. Exhibit 1–25 provides a specific example of how an implied percentage price volatility can be converted into an implied absolute yield volatility (from Exhibit 1–24). In particular, the absolute yield volatility for calls on the March 1990 bond contract with a strike price of 92 is derived from this option contract's percentage price volatility.

SUMMARY

Options are no longer merely toys for speculators and dealers. Any investor with specific goals can use option strategies to tailor the performance of a portfolio. Because it is impossible to obtain the effects of options by using only the underlying securities, a whole new universe of strategic possibilities is opened up. In particular, investors with contingent liabilities cannot create an adequate hedge without the use of options.

Increased liquidity in the options markets and a better understanding of the properties of options make option strategies more accessible to the average investor and allow these strategies to be used for a wider range of securities. In particular, the over-the-counter options markets allow the purchase and sale of options with any desired strike price and expiration date.

EXHIBIT   1–24

Implied Volatilities for Options on Bond Futures
(Based on Closing Prices for January 18, 1990)

		March 1990 Contract Closing @ 95%₂ *(Modified Duration = 8.61)*		
		*Strike Price**		
	92	**94**	**96**	**98**
Closing call option price	3:21	1:45	0:38	0:12
Closing put option price	0:07	0:27	1:21	2:59
Percentage Price Volatilities				
Implied call volatility	9.28	9.34	8.90	9.82
Implied put volatility	9.71	8.94	8.78	9.76
Absolute Yield Volatilities				
Implied call volatility	108	109	103	114
Implied put volatility	113	104	102	113

* Option prices are quoted in points and 64ths (i.e., 3:21 = 300 + ²¹⁄₆₄).

EXHIBIT   1–25

Sample Calculation for Converting from Percentage Price Volatility to
Absolute Yield Volatility for Bond Futures Calls Struck at 92

$$\text{Modified duration} \quad = \frac{\% \text{ Change in price}}{100 \text{ bp change in yield}}$$

$$\text{Absolute yield volatility} = \text{Percentage price volatility} \times \frac{1}{\text{Modified duration}} \times 100$$

$$\text{Absolute yield volatility} = 9.28 \times \frac{1}{861} \times 100 = 107.8 \text{ basis points}$$

2

FIXED-INCOME OPTION CONTRACTS

Lawrence E. Grannan
Director
Senior Foreign Exchange Advisor
Bank of Montreal

Steven L. Nutt
Vice President
Chemical Futures & Options, Inc.

Futures exchanges have experienced unprecedented growth in trading volume and open interest over the past two decades. This has resulted largely from the introduction of a plethora of new products and the innovations associated with financial engineering and derivatives. Futures contracts based on debt instruments, currencies, interest rates, and indices, as well as put and call options based on many of these contracts, have all made their debut. Each new addition has made the hedging and trading possibilities inherent in futures and option contracts available to an increasing number of end users. The use of these financial instruments has transcended the relatively specialized world of commodity trading. Today options and futures are utilized by derivative dealers, commercial banks, major corporations, pension fund managers, and money managers. In each case, end users have benefited from the introduction of products designed to meet their particular needs and offering all the advantages of the centralized marketplace.

Most exchanges are organized as not-for-profit associations, governed by a board elected by the membership. Committees of exchange members, elected by the members or appointed by the board, assist in the management of the exchange. A professional and an administrative staff round out the organization of most exchanges, implementing the decisions and policies of the board and the committees. In most countries, the exchanges are self-regulatory bodies (futures exchanges are also subject to government regulation in most jurisdictions) that set standards for exchange membership, develop a body of rules and regulations for members and their firms to ensure fair dealing, determine contract specifications and margin requirements, and resolve disputes between members. Most trading is done by open-outcry, and prices are reported to quotation vendors and news services. Hence, market participants are assured that their trades will take place in a competitive environment and that all trades will be public knowledge. These safeguards serve to protect members and nonmembers alike. By making price data available to the public, the exchanges play an important role in the price discovery process. This economic function provides vital information to decision makers everywhere, whether or not they actually trade futures or options. In addition, many exchanges now offer their most widely traded products on electronic trading systems. In many cases, these computer-based systems allow for virtual 24-hour market access.

The standardized terms of futures and option contracts enhance their fungibility, which in turn increases their liquidity. Market participants are able to offset trades prior to delivery, as the clearing corporation interposes itself in all trades, acting as the buyer to all sellers and the seller to all buyers. This greatly streamlines the recordkeeping for futures and option positions and frees buyers and sellers from the need to negotiate directly with each other. The clearing corporation, as third-party guarantor to all trades, ensures performance of the contract and protects the financial integrity of the marketplace.

The exchanges also require clearing members to post performance margin deposits against their respective futures positions. Member firms, in turn, collect performance margins from their clients in accordance with exchange rules. These deposits do not represent equity in the futures contract, but instead represent a performance bond or good-faith deposit. Buyers of options pay for the premium in full and consequently need not post a margin deposit. However, sellers of options are generally required to maintain a margin deposit plus the amount of the short premium, marked to market. This margin deposit can be as high as the futures margin. Specific requirements vary from exchange to exchange and from contract to contract.

Spread positions in either futures or options may have margin requirements that differ from the sum of the individual contracts' requirements. In the case of futures contracts, intramarket spreads frequently have reduced margin levels, as have some intermarket spreads. Remember, however, that these requirements are always subject to change. In some instances, option spreads can also have margin requirements that are less than the sum of the outright margins and purchase prices of the individual spread components. As with futures, these requirements are subject to change at any time.

With this background in mind, a survey of some of the more successful exchange-traded option contracts follows. It is important to note that the futures and option markets are dynamic and contract specifications are frequently updated to better serve the needs of market participants. Be certain to contact the exchanges or member firms to determine current contract specifications.

OPTIONS ON U.S. TREASURY BOND FUTURES

Options on the Chicago Board of Trade's (CBT) U.S. Treasury bond futures began trading in 1982 and have become one of the most liquid of all the interest rate option contracts. It is not surprising that this particular contract is so successful given that the underlying instrument is the "long bond," which was initiated in 1977 and is now one of the most actively traded futures contracts in the world. The growth in the CBT contract's volume and open interest has paralleled the increased issuance of debt by the U.S. government since the early 1980s. The option contract is an American-style option. The option's exercise can occur on any business day prior to the option's expiration and results in a long or short position in the underlying futures contract.

The futures are settled by delivery of a cash Treasury bond with at least 15 years until its maturity or call date. They normally track the eligible cash bond that has the narrowest spread, or basis, to the futures. This cash bond is known as the *cheapest-to-deliver.* The cheapest-to-deliver will normally be a high-coupon bond (generally greater than 8 percent) when Treasury bond yields are below the 8 percent futures "coupon" level and will usually be a low-coupon issue when the Treasury bond yield exceeds 8 percent. It is important to remember that the futures do not pay a coupon as do the cash fixed-income instruments they represent. The CBT contract is listed as having a nominal value of $100,000. It is quoted in $\frac{1}{32}$ increments equal to $31.25, and one full point equals $1,000. Like all of the exchange-traded interest rate futures contracts, it trades on a quarterly basis of March, June, September, and December.

The options on the bond futures trade in $\frac{1}{64}$ increments that are worth $15.625. In addition to having the same March quarterly cycle as the futures, options are listed for the first two serial months. Trading terminates in the month prior to futures delivery for options in the March quarterly cycle, and similarly (in the month preceding the option's name) for serial options. When the options are exercised, a long call position results in a long futures position at the call's strike price and a long put position results in a short futures position. A short call position results in a short futures position upon exercise. The short put, when exercised, leaves the option writer with a long futures position.

In addition, the CBT has introduced Flexible Treasury Options on the bonds, as well as the rest of the Treasury complex. Essentially, these products allow the counterparties to customize (within limits) the strike price, expiration date, and exercise style (American or European) of the options while retaining the benefits of an exchange-listed product. These options represent an attempt by the exchange to offer its members and their customers a product that provides some of the flexibility of similar over-the-counter contracts.

The liquidity of the options on Treasury bond futures is due to several factors. The "locals," as independent exchange floor traders are called, and institutional trading firms will arbitrage the options against futures or make markets in option arbitrage trades such as conversions, reversals, or "boxes." This results in relatively tight bid-offer spreads across most strike prices. While traders on the floor may lock in arbitrage profits from such trades, the majority of speculative trades on these options will usually try to capitalize on three factors: market direction, time remaining until the option's expiration, and the outlook on volatility. At the CBT, most of the liquidity will be in the nearby option contract until the last few weeks before its expiration.

Dealers in U.S. Treasury securities have been among the most active users of the bond options to hedge their inventories of long-term debt as well as their positions during the regular cycle of auctions. Portfolio managers not only alter the durations of their fixed-income holdings with options but may also try to enhance the returns of these instruments by writing call options against their portfolios. Just as with the futures, the issuers of long-term corporate debt, who do not plan to bring their issues to market for several weeks or months, can construct an anticipatory hedge with options. These issuers can buy puts on the bond futures to lay off the risk of having to sell their bonds with a larger coupon if interest rates rise in the interim.

OPTIONS ON 10-YEAR U.S. TREASURY NOTE FUTURES

In virtually every respect, the specifications for the options on the underlying futures contract resemble those of the bond futures. Both futures contracts have a nominal value of $100,000. However, short positions would deliver, and long positions could eventually receive, a U.S. Treasury note of at least 6½ years but not more than 10 years until its maturity.

Since trading in 10-year T-note futures and options began, portfolio managers and traders have used these instruments to lay off their risk or enhance yields in that sector of the yield curve. Investors in dollar-denominated medium-term corporate debt or mortgage-backed issues employ the note options with less yield curve risk than they might face if they used bond options. Statistical regressions have frequently demonstrated relatively good correlations between the T-note futures and credit instruments such as investment-grade dollar Eurobonds, U.S. corporate debt, and federally insured mortgage-backed issues. The liquidity of these options and their familiarity to many financial risk managers have made them adaptable to numerous types of hedges. A medium-term fixed-income instrument's duration can be increased by the purchase of a call or decreased by the purchase of a put. Therefore, the options can be a valuable tool in immunization strategies. Derivative products risk managers may use the note options to manage a portion of their swap book.

Since the CBT is the arena for the options on both T-notes and T-bonds, traders will often take positions in one option's maturity against another's to capitalize on a shift in the yield curve. The note-over-bond trade, or NOB, in futures can be duplicated using calls and puts in the bond and note options to take advantage of an anticipated flattening or steepening of the yield curve.

OPTIONS ON 2- AND 5-YEAR
U.S. TREASURY NOTE FUTURES

Following on the heels of the successful futures and options contracts on the bonds and 10-year notes, the CBT introduced futures and options on 5-year and 2-year Treasury notes. These contracts are modeled on the bond and note futures and options. The 5-year futures have a nominal value of $100,000 and call for the delivery of a U.S. Treasury note with an original maturity of not more than five years, three months, and a remaining maturity of not more than five years, three months and not less than four years, three months. The 2-year futures have a nominal value of $200,000 and call for the delivery of a U.S. Treasury note with an original maturity of not more than five years, three months, and a remaining maturity of not greater than two years and not less than one year, nine months. The tick size for the 5-year futures is ⅟₆₄, while the tick size for the 2-year futures is ⅟₁₂₈.

Most participants in the bond and 10-year note futures and options markets employ these instruments in conjunction with their trading and investment activities in the underlying cash market. However, the 2- and 5-year futures and options markets evolved to serve the needs of derivatives book risk managers and, secondarily, participants in the underlying cash market. The 5-year note futures and options have been particularly useful in the management of medium-term swap books. In addition, the 5-year futures have benefited from the migration of corporate debt financing to that sector of the yield curve. The 2-year note futures and options have fared less well, since they compete directly with the very liquid 2-year Eurodollar futures strip.

OPTIONS ON EURODOLLAR DEPOSIT FUTURES

On the short end of the yield curve, trading is concentrated in options on three-month Eurodollar futures contracts. These contracts are traded on the International Monetary Market (IMM) division of the Chicago Mercantile Exchange (CME). Eurodollars are U.S. dollars on deposit in banks outside the United States. The Eurodollar deposit futures contract began trading in 1981 and is now the dominant short-term interest rate futures contract in terms of volume and open interest. The explosive growth of Eurodollar futures trading has been fueled by the tremendous growth in the short-term forward rate agreement and interest rate swap markets. Not surprisingly, options on Eurodollar futures, traded on the IMM, have also enjoyed great popularity among a range of end users.

The Eurodollar futures contract represents the London Interbank Offered Rate (LIBOR) for a three-month Eurodollar deposit of $1 million and is traded on the customary March, June, September, and December expiration cycle. To facilitate trading, the IMM uses a simple price quotation index that allows "prices" to be quoted rather than interest rates. The "price" of a Eurodollar futures contract (the IMM index) is equal to 100 minus the add-on interest rate. For example, a price of 93.75 corresponds to an add-on rate of 6.25 percent ($100 - 93.75 = 6.25$), expressed as an annual figure. Hence, when rates increase, the short has a profit while the long has a loss. Since Eurodollar futures are quoted in hundredths of an index point (0.01), the dollar value of one tick (the minimum fluctuation) is equal to $25.

Eurodollar futures are a cash-settled futures contract. On the last trading day, the exchange conducts a survey of the cash market, at a randomly selected time during the last 90 minutes of trading and at the termination of trading of the expiring futures contract, to determine an average LIBOR for three-month deposits to top-tier banks. This rate is then used to determine the settlement price at which the expiring contracts are marked to market for the last time. This process ensures that the futures price will reflect values in the cash market upon settlement. Trading in Eurodollar futures ceases at 3:30 P.M. London time on the second London bank business day preceding the third Wednesday of the contract month. If the third Wednesday of the month is a bank holiday in Chicago or New York, the last trading day is one day later than usual.

Options on Eurodollar futures are also quoted in hundredths of an index point, the minimum premium fluctuation being $25. In general, strike prices are 0.25 index points apart for IMM index levels above 91.00 and 0.50 index points for index levels below 91.00. Options are listed for the six nearest Eurodollar futures contracts in the regular March quarterly cycle. In addition, two serial expirations are listed. An interesting innovation on the part of the CME was the introduction of mid-curve options on Eurodollar futures. Mid-curve options represent short-dated options on deferred Eurodollar futures contracts. These contracts offer the benefits of a high gamma option on futures at various points along the Eurodollar strip. Derivatives book risk managers find these contracts useful in managing their positions. Volatility and directional traders also find these contracts useful because the deferred futures are usually more volatile than the first contract expiration in the strip. With the exception of the mid-curve options, futures and options expire on the same day. Eurodollar options are of the American type.

It might be useful to see an example of how call and put premiums are quoted. Exhibit 2–1 contains quotations for the CME Eurodollar futures and options on futures from *The Wall Street Journal* for Friday, May 12, 1995. The upper table indicates the settlement prices for the Eurodollar futures contracts. In this example, the June 1995 Eurodollars contract settled at 93.88. Included in the exhibit are the day's opening price of the contract, its high price on the day, and the day's low price. The "yield" 6.12 percent is simply the settlement level of the Eurodollar index, 93.88, subtracted from 100. Since the June 1995 was the nearby futures contract, the open interest is the largest for this maturity. Open interest is the amount of futures contracts that have not yet been offset by opposite long or short transactions. The volume figures indicate the number of contracts sold (or bought) on that day.

The lower table in Exhibit 2–1 shows the settlement prices of the call and put premiums for the options on Eurodollar futures. These premiums

EXHIBIT   2–1

Prices for Eurodollar Futures and Options for May 12, 1995

Est vol 4,500; vol Thur 6,105; open int 19,850, – 7,386.
The index: Close 92-25; Yield 6.21.

EURODOLLAR (CME) - $1 million; pts of 100%

	Open	High	Low	Settle		Chg Settle	Yield Chg	Open Interest
June	93.90	93.90	93.82	93.88	–	.02	6.12	+ .02	406,872
Sept	93.97	93.98	93.82	93.96		....	6.04	....	371,392
Dec	93.91	93.94	93.72	93.89		....	6.11	....	315,416
Mr96	93.91	93.96	93.72	93.92	+	.02	6.28	– .02	260,700
June	93.77	93.80	93.56	93.76		....	6.24	....	186,373
Sept	93.66	93.68	93.45	93.63	–	.02	6.37	+ .02	161,850
Dec	93.37	93.49	93.27	93.44	–	.03	6.56	+ .03	129,934
Mr97	93.34	93.45	93.23	93.40	–	.03	6.60	+ .03	100,902
June	93.27	93.37	93.24	93.34	–	.03	6.66	+ .03	88,744
Sept	93.22	93.31	93.20	93.29	–	.03	6.71	+ .03	70,135
Dec	93.18	93.23	93.12	93.21	–	.03	6.79	+ .03	60,934
Mr98	93.17	93.22	93.11	93.20	–	.03	6.80	+ .03	56,889
June	93.13	93.16	93.08	93.14	–	.03	6.86	+ .03	53,097
Sept	93.09	93.12	93.04	93.10	–	.03	6.90	+ .03	41,890
Dec	93.01	93.04	92.96	93.02	–	.03	6.98	+ .03	35,016
Mr99	93.00	93.03	92.95	93.01	–	.03	6.99	+ .03	29,511
June	92.94	92.98	92.91	92.95	–	.03	7.05	+ .03	23,348
Sept	92.88	92.92	92.85	92.89	–	.03	7.11	+ .03	15,303
Dec	92.79	92.83	92.76	92.80	–	.03	7.20	+ .03	12,546
Mr00	92.79	92.83	92.76	92.80	–	.03	7.20	+ .03	10,553
June	92.73	92.77	92.70	92.73	–	.03	7.27	+ .03	7,848
Sept	92.67	92.71	92.64	92.67	–	.03	7.33	+ .03	7,855
Dec	92.56	92.62	92.55	92.58	–	.03	7.42	+ .03	7,089
Mr01	92.57	92.60	92.54	92.57	–	.03	7.43	+ .03	5,776
June	92.49	92.52	92.46	92.49	–	.03	7.51	+ .03	6,704
Sept	92.39	92.44	92.38	92.41	–	.03	7.59	+ .03	8,129
Dec	92.30	92.35	92.29	92.32	–	.03	7.68	+ .03	7,749
Mr02	92.29	92.34	92.29	92.32	–	.02	7.68	.02	4,611
June	92.27	92.28	92.27	92.26	–	.01	7.74	+ .01	3,534
Sept	92.17	92.21	92.16	92.19	–	.01	7.81	+ .01	2,519
Dec	92.08	92.12	92.07	92.10	–	.01	7.90	+ .01	1,890
Mr03	92.11	92.12	92.10	92.10	–	.01	7.90	+ .01	2,049
June	92.03	92.06	92.03	92.06	–	.01	7.94	+ .01	5,147
Sept	91.97	91.99	91.97	91.99	–	.01	8.01	+ .01	3,232
Dec	91.88	91.90	91.88	91.90	–	.01	8.10	+ .01	3,893
Mr04	91.87	91.89	91.87	91.89	–	.01	8.11	+ .01	4,037
June	91.83	91.83	91.83	91.83	–	.01	8.17	+ .01	3,312
Sept	91.77	91.77	91.77	91.77	–	.01	8.23	+ .01	3,358
Dec	....	....	....	91.67	–	.01	8.33	+ .01	2,475
Mr05	91.66	91.67	91.66	91.68	–	.01	8.32	+ .01	2,740

Est vol 875,473; vol Thur 836,501; open int 2,524,847, –11,108.

EURODOLLAR (CME)
$ million; pts. of 100%

Strike Price	Calls—Settle			Puts—Settle		
	May	Jun	Sep	May	Jun	Sep
9350	0.38	0.39	0.55	0.00	0.01	0.09
9375	0.13	0.16	0.37	0.00	0.03	0.16
9400	0.00	0.02	0.23	0.12	0.14	0.27
9425	0.00	0.00	0.13	....	0.37	0.42
9450	....	0.00	0.07	....	0.62	0.60
9475	....	0.00	0.04	....	0.87	0.82

Est. vol. 193,397;
Thur vol. 84,750 calls; 67,475 puts
Op. Int. Thur 954,122 calls; 1,343,206 puts

2 YR. MID-CURVE EURODOLLAR (CME)
$1,000,000 contract units; pts. of 100%

Strike Price	Calls—Settle			Puts—Settle		
	Jun			Jun		
9275	0.63	....	....	0.04	....	....
9300	0.42	....	....	0.08	....	....
9325	0.27	....	....	....	....	....
9350	0.13	....	....	....	....	....
9400	....	....	....	....	....	....

Est vol 0   Thur 25 calls 0 puts
Op int Thur   7,860 calls 6,835 puts

consist of intrinsic value and time value (extrinsic value). Intrinsic value is the amount by which the Eurodollar futures price is above the strike price of a call or beneath the strike price of a put. Time value is the amount by which the price of a put or a call exceeds its intrinsic value. Holding everything else constant, the greater the amount of time until expiration, the greater will be an option premium's time value. The relationship between an option's strike price and its underlying futures price determines whether that option is in, at, or out of the money. If an option's strike price equals the underlying futures price, that option is at the money. If an option premium has no intrinsic value, such as when a call (put) strike is above (below) the underlying futures price, that option is out of the money. If the call (put) strike is below (above) the underlying futures price, that option has intrinsic value and is in the money. For example, if the underlying futures were at 94.00, the 94.00 strike calls and puts would be referred to as being at the money. The 94.25 strike call would be out of the money, and the 93.75 strike call would be in the money.

Looking at the lower table from *The Wall Street Journal*, which shows settlement prices for calls and puts, illustrates how much these respective calls or puts were in, at, or out of the money. With the June 1995 futures at 93.88, the 93.75 call, priced at 16 ticks, has intrinsic value of 13 ticks and time value of 3 ticks. With a price of 39 ticks, the 93.50 strike call has 38 ticks of intrinsic value and 1 tick of time value. Hence, the 93.50 strike call is 38 ticks in the money. If the holder of this American-style call exercised it, he or she would be long a Eurodollar futures contract at 93.50. The seller of this call would be left with a short futures position at 93.50, resulting in an immediate loss of 38 ticks on the futures position. At a value of $25 per tick, the seller's loss would be $950, and this would then be marked to market on a daily basis.

Premiums for puts work on the same principle as the calls. The 93.75 strike put is out of the money and its 3-tick premium is composed entirely of time value. The 94.00 put, which has a premium of 14 ticks, is in the money by 12 ticks. Consequently, the remaining 2 ticks of premium in this option's price represent time value. A trader who was long the 93.75 put might have little incentive to exercise this option with its current price at 3 ticks and the underlying futures at the 93.88 level. Instead, the trader could sell the option on the IMM and realize its time value.

The Eurodollar futures and options market has grown dramatically in the past decade. Fueled by the interest rate volatility of the 1980s, financial institutions and corporations turned to the over-the-counter interest rate derivatives market to meet their hedging needs. Derivatives dealers, in turn, saw in the Eurodollar futures and options market an ideal, standard-ized hedging vehicle. Hence, the exchange has become a wholesale risk market. Later, as end user expertise evolved, many risk managers chose to access the exchange-traded market directly. These cash market partici-pants use Eurodollar futures and options to hedge their day-to-day activi-ties in the debt market. Borrowers can lock in rates on loans that have yet to be taken down, as well as to create caps with options. Lenders can pro-tect their capital from adverse moves in interest rates and use options to create floors. Writers of over-the-counter options can use the IMM con-tracts to hedge their risk as well. In addition, institutional traders can uti-lize both options and futures in taking risk positions in the market, thus adding to the level of liquidity.

Increasing internationalization of futures and options markets led the IMM to seek a link with the Singapore International Monetary Exchange, Ltd. (SIMEX). Under this arrangement, Eurodollar futures traded on SIMEX can be used to offset positions initiated on the IMM, and vice versa. However, while options on Eurodollar futures are traded on the SIMEX, these options are not part of the Mutual Offset System.

OPTIONS ON NONDOLLAR INTEREST RATE FUTURES

The success of the Chicago futures exchanges has been duplicated in a number of overseas financial centers over the past decade. Many of these relatively new exchanges have been loosely modeled on the Chicago exchanges. As has been the case in Chicago, most of the growth in vol-ume on the overseas exchanges over the past decade has come from trad-ing financial futures and options. Option market participants now trade a panoply of financial instruments on exchanges from Paris to Sydney. These contracts allow hedgers and speculators to apply the same tech-niques used in the dollar fixed-income markets to most of the principal nondollar markets.

OVER-THE-COUNTER INTEREST RATE OPTIONS

Although many traders concentrate on exchange-traded options, the market in over-the-counter (OTC) interest rate options fills an important need for risk managers. For over a decade, options have been written and traded on various capital, money market, and derivative instruments, such as interest rate caps and floors. Many market participants are familiar with interest rate caps, which banks have offered to commercial borrowers to lay off risks of rising interest rates. They may be less familiar with options offered on other instruments in the over-the-counter market.

Options on mortgage-related instruments make up a large portion of the OTC interest rate option market. Since there are currently no exchange-traded options on such issues, these options fill an important niche for end users such as mutual funds or other investment portfolios. Another large sector in the OTC interest rate options market are those based on U.S. Treasury issues. Although the CBT offers actively traded options on Treasury futures, the popularity of these OTC options persists due to their being custom tailored to customers' needs by option writers. While these options may have a fairly wide bid-offer spread, there are definite advantages to using them for some hedgers. First, a buyer who purchases puts on a specific issue he or she holds as a hedge can avoid the basis risk encountered with exchange-traded options on futures. Further, the buyer can negotiate an OTC option maturity from a few days to several years. However, exchange-traded Flex Options offer customized expiration dates, as well. Holders of large portfolios may write OTC calls against their cash positions for the purpose of yield enhancement just as they might employ exchange-traded calls. In some cases there are limits on the maturity of options, depending on who is writing them.

In contrast to the highly liquid options on U.S. Treasury futures traded by the open-outcry method, the over-the-counter market consists of a relatively small network of individual dealers. Whereas it is usually simple to cover an exchange-traded option position before its expiration, it might be rather difficult in the OTC market. Additional concerns exist in the OTC markets about the creditworthiness of the institution with which a trader is dealing, since there is no clearing corporation to stand as the intermediary between the two parties to a trade. However, regardless of the concerns regarding the use of OTC options, their features of customization and the dearth of exchange-traded alternatives should lead to a continued expansion of these markets.

⑥ EXOTIC (NONSTANDARD) OPTIONS ON FIXED-INCOME INSTRUMENTS

Gary L. Gastineau
Senior Vice President
New Product Development
American Stock Exchange

Exotic options get a lot of attention. A casual reading of an option course outline or glance at an option seminar agenda may suggest that exotic options dominate the option markets. In fact, most option transaction volume is concentrated in standard or "plain vanilla" option contracts.

No reliable industry figures are available, but there is general agreement that exotic or nonstandard options account for little more than 10 percent of currency options and only a small percentage of fixed-income or equity options. Even if you never intend to buy or sell one of these more complex instruments, understanding them is still important. Exotic options can be very useful, and understanding nonstandard options can also improve your knowledge of traditional options and underlying markets.

Since only options used in fixed-income markets are covered in this book, we will not describe average rate or price options (used primarily in currency markets) or cliquet and quanto options (used in equity markets). The specialty options we will look at have significant fixed-income applications. We will also spend very little time distinguishing between options on the price of an instrument and options on an interest rate. Most of the options described here can be struck at a bond price or at an interest rate, and most features can be incorporated into caps and floors as well as into bond options and longer-term rate options.

BARRIER OPTIONS

Barrier options are specialty options whose payout patterns and survival to the nominal expiration date depend not only on the final price or rate of the underlying instrument but also on whether or not the underlying sells at or through a barrier (*in-strike* or *out-strike*) during the life of the option. By far the most common barrier options in fixed-income markets are *in* options and *out* options. We will also look briefly at roll-up put and roll-down call options.

In Options

An *in option* is similar to a standard option, but an in option has a start price or in-strike as well as a start or trade date. If the market price of the *underlying* drops through the in-strike of a *down-and-in call* or rises through the in-strike of an *up-and-in put*, the payoff of these instruments will be identical to the payoff of standard options with otherwise similar terms. However, if the in-strike is not breached, the in option expires worthless even if the equivalent standard option would have been deep in the money at expiration. The in-strike is also referred to as the *in-price* or *knock-in price*.

Because of the possibility that an in option will be valueless at its expiration date even if a standard option would have been deep in the money, an in option will sell for a lower premium than a comparable standard option. An in option is more difficult to evaluate than a standard option because its payoff is path dependent. Path dependency means that an option's value depends not only on the underlying instrument's value at expiration or exercise but also on the price path the underlying takes in getting there.

Exhibit 3–1 illustrates the payout of a down-and-in call under two possible conditions. In the top graph, the in-strike is breached, and the option pays off like a standard call. In the bottom graph, the in-strike is not breached during the life of the call, and the option expires valueless on its expiration date.

Exhibit 3–2 compares the premium values on down-and-in calls and standard calls at a variety of underlying prices, ranging from below the in-strike (for the standard call) to substantially above the in-strike for both options. The closer the underlying is to the in-strike at the time of valuation, the greater the possibility of activation and the greater the expected value of the in option relative to the standard option.

The fact that the in option is worth a larger fraction of the standard option as the market price of the underlying moves closer to the in-strike

E X H I B I T 3–1

Payout of a Down-and-In-Call: Activated versus Nonactivated

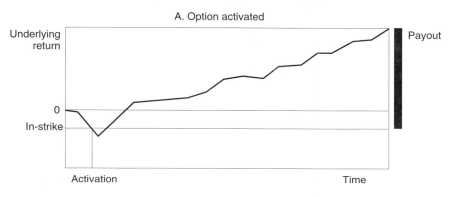

A. Option activated

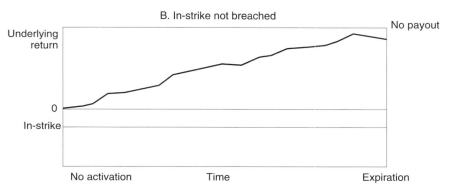

B. In-strike not breached

may not be precisely reflected in the in option's market price. The most common reason for a deviation from the predicted price relationship is that the issuer of an in option may face unusual risks in taking a position in the underlying or in another option as a hedge against liability on the in option. At other times, possible activation of the in option may create no problem for an issuer. If in options are available at attractive prices and an investor has a high degree of confidence that the in-strike will be breached and the underlying will subsequently change direction and move significantly into the money, an in option can be a bargain.

The examples illustrated assume that the in-strike becomes the strike of the standard option created by the breach of the in-strike. In some applications, the strike of the option may be unrelated to the in-strike.

Whether they are asset or liability managers, buyers of in options tend to be either hesitant, price-sensitive buyers or buyers who hope to

EXHIBIT 3–2

Valuation of a Down-and-In Call

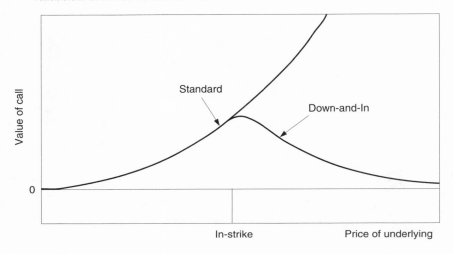

buy participation in a market reversal for a minimum option premium. Price-sensitive option buyers may focus more on the size of the premium relative to the possible payoff than on the probability of breaching the in-strike. If the in option premium is low enough relative to a standard option premium and the buyer correctly anticipates a price movement that activates the in option and then reverses to provide a large payoff, the risk/reward ratio can be very favorable.

The viewpoint of the investor who uses an in option to implement market reversal expectations may be complex. This investor might believe that the farther the market moves in one direction, the stronger its reversal will be. A standard option struck at or out of the money does not express the investor's expectations accurately, and it costs too much relative to the payoff he or she expects. The in option provides a potentially larger pay-off with the same ultimate move, provided the ultimate move is preceded by a breach of the in-strike.

An in option can be a stand-alone position or a sophisticated port-folio risk management device that acts as a hedge for an existing long or short position in the underlying. For investors expecting a movement in one direction followed by a strong reversal, down-and-in calls and up-and-in puts can be attractive substitutes for standard options.

Out Options

Out options are similar to standard options except that the out option has an expiration price or *out-strike* as well as an expiration date. If the market price of the underlying does not drop through the out-strike of a *down-and-out call* or rise through the out-strike of an *up-and-out put*, the payoff of these instruments will be identical to the payoff of standard options with otherwise similar terms. However, if the out-strike is breached, the out options expire immediately. The out-strike is often referred to as the *out-price* or the *knock-out price*.

Because of the possibility that the option will be valueless before its nominal expiration date, an out option will sell for a lower premium than a comparable standard option. An out option, like an in option, is more difficult to evaluate than a standard option because its payoff is path dependent.

Exhibit 3–3 illustrates the payout of a down-and-out call under two possible conditions. In the top graph, the out-strike has been breached, and the option expires valueless at its expiration price rather than on its expiration date. In the lower graph, the out-strike is not breached during the life of the call, and the option pays off like a standard call option.

Exhibit 3–4 compares the premiums on down-and-out calls and standard calls at a variety of underlying prices—ranging from below the out-strike (for the standard call) to substantially in the money for both options. The closer the underlying is to the out-strike at the time of valuation, the greater the possibility of early termination and the lower the expected value of the option, both absolutely and relative to the standard option.

The fact that the put option is worth a smaller fraction of the standard option as the market price of the underlying moves to the out-strike may not be precisely reflected in the out option's market price. The most common reason for a deviation from the predicted price relationship is that the issuer of an out option may face unusual risks in holding a position in the underlying or in another option as a hedge against liability on the out option. At other times, early termination of the out option at the out-strike may fit an issuer's needs unusually well. If out options are available at attractive prices and an investor has a high degree of confidence that the out-strike will not be breached during the term of the option, an out option can be a bargain.

Whether they are asset or liability managers, buyers of out options tend to be either highly confident buyers or, buyers who hope to participate in a high-volatility environment or event for a minimum option pre-

EXHIBIT   3–3

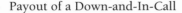

Payout of a Down-and-In-Call

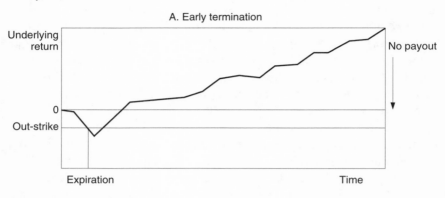

A. Early termination

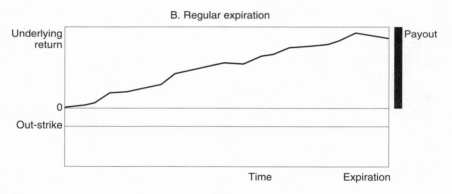

B. Regular expiration

mium. Highly confident buyers see the chance of breaching the out-strike as being quite small. If their view is correct and the out option premium is significantly lower than a standard option premium, they are buying a "bargain-priced" option.

The viewpoint of investors expecting a volatility event or a period of extreme uncertainty is more complex. Typically, such investors will have a strong—but not unequivocal—view of the direction of movement in the underlying. In the event these investors' expectations are incorrect—something that may be nagging at the backs of their minds—they believe they could be very wrong and that any remaining value in a standard call would be small if the underlying hit the out-strike. In the minds of investors with this kind of market view, down-and-out calls and up-and-out puts are potential substitutes for standard options.

E X H I B I T   3–4

Estimated Values of Down-and-Out and Comparable Standard Calls

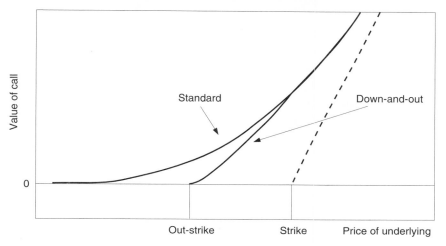

An out option can be a sophisticated portfolio risk management device as a hedge for an existing long or short position in the underlying. For example, an up-and-out put can provide low-cost insurance for a fixed-income position if an investor feels confident that a movement through the out-strike means the insurance feature of the option is unlikely to be needed in the subsequent market environment.

Roll-Up Put and Roll-Down Call Options

Roll-up put and *roll-down call options* are specialized options with provisions that automatically exchange the initial option position for an early exercise or barrier option in the event of an adverse price move prior to expiration. In the case of a roll-down call, the initial option position is exchanged (typically without payment of an additional premium) for a down-and-out call with a lower strike than the original call. The exchange occurs when the underlying drops to a *trigger price* or *rate*. The down-and-out call behaves like a standard call with a lower strike than the original call as long as the out-strike is not breached by further decline in the underlying.

Roll-up puts operate in the opposite direction: The initial put position is exchanged for an up-and-out put when the underlying breaches a roll-up strike. The up-and-out put behaves like a standard put option with a higher strike, unless and until the underlying breaches an even higher out-strike, which causes the option contract to expire.

Exhibit 3–5 compares roll-up and standard put option payouts under three price scenarios that illustrate the significant differences between these specialized options and standard options. Although the illustration features a roll-up put, the principles apply equally—in reverse—to roll-down calls.

In Exhibit 3–5A, the underlying does not rise by enough to trigger the roll-up, and the payout is the same as the payout on a standard put option with otherwise similar terms. Exhibits 3–5B and 3–5C illustrate two circumstances where a roll-up put and, by analogy, a roll-down call behave differently than their standard option counterparts. When a rise in the underlying triggers the roll-up strike, the option becomes an up-and-out put with a strike equal to the roll-up strike and an out-strike typically higher by approximately the difference between the initial strike and the roll-up strike (Pricing varies in response to a buyer's requirements, and call and put prices behave slightly differently.) In Exhibit 3–5B, the out-strike is not breached, and the roll-up strike remains the effective strike. Since the option expires *in the money*, the put with the higher strike (i.e., the rolled-up put) has a higher payout than the standard put. Exhibit 3–5C shows the consequences of a breach of the out-strike (i.e., early expiration of the rolled-up put). In this case, too, the standard put option finishes in the money, but the breach of the out-strike leads to early termination of the rolled-up put, which has no value at expiration—in contrast to the standard put's positive payout.

Roll-up puts and roll-down calls appeal primarily to investors who believe they may be early in implementing a bullish or bearish position in a specific market. Roll-up puts and roll-down calls give an investor the opportunity for a favorable reset of the strike, but provide an obvious penalty—in the form of early expiration—if the out-strike is breached by the underlying. Roll-up puts and roll-down calls may sell in line with standard options because the out-of-the-money options that are exchanged for out options may have approximately the same value as the out options.

NO REGRETS OPTIONS

No regrets options are less common in fixed-income markets than barrier options and have little in common with them except for the protection they offer an investor or issuer from wishing something had been done

E X H I B I T   3–5

Comparison of Roll-Up and Standard Put Option Payouts
under Three Price Scenarios

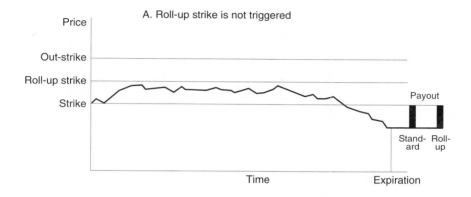

A. Roll-up strike is not triggered

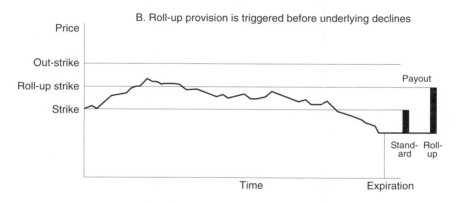

B. Roll-up provision is triggered before underlying declines

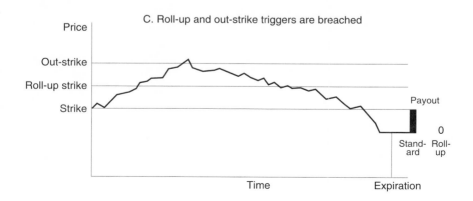

C. Roll-up and out-strike triggers are breached

differently. These options often provide this comfort in exchange for a higher premium than a standard option. In this section, we will examine reset, lookback, alternative, and outperformance options.

Reset and Lookback Options

A *reset option* is a put or call option whose strike may be reset—to a lower strike in the case of a call or a higher strike in the case of a put—if the option is out of the money on the reset date or during the reset period. There may be a limit to the magnitude of the strike adjustment, and the reset may be triggered by a specific price on the underlying, set on a specific reset date, or set during a limited reset period. Reset options come in many variations and are called by many names, including *anti-crash warrants*, *election warrants*, *partial lookback options*, *step-down warrants*, and *strike reset options*.

The reset call option illustrated in Exhibit 3–6 lets the holder reset the strike to the lowest market price the underlying reaches during the reset or partial lookback period. If the underlying instrument sells below the initial strike during the reset period, the value of a reset option that is in the money at expiration will be greater than that of a standard option with a strike equal to the underlying market price at the time of option purchase. Once the reset or partial lookback period is over, the reset option is equivalent to a standard call option with a strike fixed at the lower level determined during the reset period.

The bar graph at the right side of Exhibit 3–6 illustrates that the payoff of a reset option will always be at least as great as the payoff of a standard option with otherwise similar terms. Correspondingly, the reset option will command a higher initial premium than a comparable standard option. The valuation modification consists of an adjustment for the fact that the strike can be reset to a more favorable level during some part of the life of the option.

An investor would have to pay a substantially increased premium for a full *lookback option*. (A full lookback option would extend the reset period to the full term of the option and payoff on a strike set at the lowest underlying price reached during the life of the call in Exhibit 3–6 or the highest underlying price reached during the life of a full lookback put.)

The fixed-date resettable strike call option illustrated in Exhibit 3–7 lets the holder reset the strike to the market price of the underlying on the reset date. If on that day the underlying instrument sells below the initial strike (i.e., the original call option is out of the money), the strike of the

EXHIBIT 3–6

The Reset Effect of a Partial Lookback Call Option

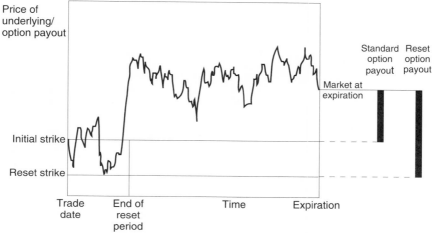

fixed-date resettable call option is set at the money at no additional cost to the holder. Thus, the value of this type of reset option, if in the money at expiration, will be greater than that of a standard option with a strike equal to the underlying market price at the time of option purchase. As in the first example, once the reset period is over, the option is equivalent to a standard call option with a strike fixed at the lower of the original strike or the reset strike.

The bar graph at the right side of Exhibit 3–7 illustrates that the payoff of the fixed-date resettable strike option will always be at least as great as the payoff of a standard option with otherwise similar terms. Correspondingly, this reset option will command a higher initial premium than a comparable standard option, although compared to the *partial lookback* option (illustrated in Exhibit 3–6), an investor would pay a lower premium for the downside protection provided by this European-style reset feature. The valuation modification consists of an adjustment for the fact that the strike can be reset to a more favorable level.

Interest in limited-period reset options stems primarily from the opportunity to pay an additional premium for the right to a more attractive strike set during a reset period or on a reset date. Buyers of reset options ordinarily anticipate that a near-term development will cause a setback in their longer-term expectations, but that the impact will be only temporary.

EXHIBIT   3–7

The Reset Effect of a Fixed-Date Resettable Strike Call Option

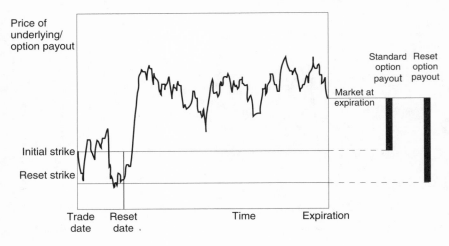

Election- or other event-oriented instruments are probably the most common variety of reset options. Other applications include options whose lives span possible currency realignments, central bank interest rate policy shifts, or any other natural or policy-dictated phenomenon, which can bring on a period of substantial short-term volatility or a significant, temporary adverse price change.

To many investors, an important attraction of reset options is that they do not require an active decision by the holder to time the reset. If an investor wants the ability to modify a position in response to events and the passage of time, it is possible to create roughly similar payoff patterns with separate put and call contracts, *switchback options,* or other option structures. However, the alternative strategies require preset strike adjustment levels or a decision by the option holder during the life of the contract. Active monitoring and involvement by investors may hold less attraction than the automatic feature of a reset option.

Alternative and Outperformance Options

An *alternative option,* (sometimes called an *either-or option* or *best-of-two option*) pays the *independent* performance of the most profitable of two distinct call options on the settlement date. Any payoff is equal to the positive percentage change from the strike on the best performing of the two assets times a prespecified *notional* or *face amount.* The alternative option contract consists of two separate call options with separate strikes on different underlying assets. The strikes are usually at the money, and the face values of the underlyings are usually equal at the outset of the contract. When the alternative option expires, the option holder receives the payout (if any) of the more valuable of the two component options. There is no payout on the other option even if it is in the money at expiration.

As Exhibit 3–8 illustrates, the payout of the alternative option is equal to the better payout of the two call option components that make up the contract. The payout is based not on the relative performance of the two underlying instruments or indexes (as in the case of the outperformance option described below) but on the performance of the better of the two instruments. Comparing the payout of the alternative option with the payout of an outperformance option with similar terms is useful in understanding the important differences between these two structures. The alternative option can have an attractive payout when the outperformance option is valueless, and vice versa. The premium on an alternative option is always greater than the premium on an option on *either* of the two component options separately, and it is always less than the total cost of *separate* options on the components.

A variant of the alternative option is a put version sometimes called the *worst-of-two option,* with a payout based on the worse performing of two underlyings.

Alternative options are used by asset managers who want exposure to the better performing of two asset classes in one market (stocks or bonds) or the better performing of two markets (U.S. bonds or Japanese bonds). In some respects, the applications of alternative options parallel the applications of outperformance options. The major difference is that

E X H I B I T   3–8

The Payout Pattern of an Alternative Option

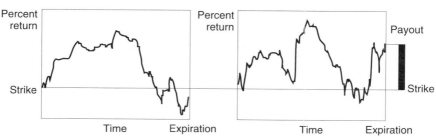

the alternative option will be more attractive to an investor who believes that *both* instruments or indexes will appreciate and when the objective in the transaction is to benefit from the one that does better. In contrast, the outperformance option will appeal more to an investor who believes that one of the two instruments will have a positive return and the other will have a significant negative return. The buyer of the outperformance option also has to pick the better performing of the two underlying assets. The buyer of an alternative option does not have to designate the better performer in advance.

An *outperformance option* is a special-purpose call option that allows an investor to capitalize on anticipated differences in the relative performance of two underlying instruments or indexes. The outperformance option's payoff at maturity is the performance of one instrument minus the performance of a second instrument (both expressed as percentages) times a fixed notional or face amount. The underlying instruments whose performances are compared may be any combination of stocks, bonds, currencies, commodities, or indexes based on any of these instruments. Two popular outperformance pairs are the *bond over stock (BOS) option*, which pays off on the superior performance of a bond or bond index relative to a stock or stock index, and its complement, the *stock over bond (SOB) option* which pays off if a stock or stock index outperforms a bond or bond index. Cross-border yield or index outperformance options are also popular.

As Exhibit 3–9 illustrates, the value of the outperformance option at maturity is proportional to any *positive* spread between the index or instrument that the investor expects to be the better performer and the index or instrument that she or he expects to be the poorer performer. As the payout bar indicates, the value of the payout can be greater than the absolute performance of the better-performing index or instrument if the worse performer declines. If the index or instrument expected to be the poorer performer turns in the better performance, the option has no payout even if the absolute performance of both is positive. As noted, a comparison and contrast with the alternative option is useful in understanding the subtleties of these very different specialty options. The key to the attractiveness of the outperformance option relative to alternative and conventional options is the investor's ability to select not only indexes and investments that perform well but also those that perform poorly.

Outperformance options are used principally by asset managers who find the structure an attractive way to take advantage of an expected change in the spread or the return differential between two instruments or

The Payout Pattern of an Outperformance Option

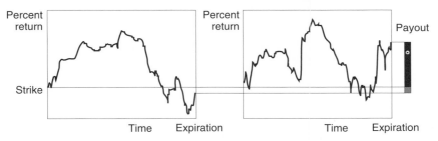

indexes. A particularly popular form of outperformance option in recent years has been the yield spread option, which pays off based on differences between yields on fixed-income securities in two different countries or at two different points on one country's yield curve. This structure often combines interest rate and currency effects.

DEFERRED PREMIUM AND DEFERRED STRIKE OPTIONS

The common characteristic of *installment options, contingent premium options,* and *compound options* is the fact that the option buyer does not pay the entire premium at the time of purchase. The deferred strike option is a very different instrument than the deferred premium option. We include it here because its buyers are also anxious to reduce their premium outlays.

Installment Options

An installment option has two characteristics that differentiate it from a standard option. First, the option premium is paid periodically—usually monthly or quarterly—over the life of the option. Second, the holder has the right to stop making payments, thereby terminating the option on the date of the first missed payment. The significance of this feature is that if the option is not worth the present value of the remaining payments, the holder does not have to continue to make payments. In return for the right to terminate payments, the premium charged for an installment option, if all payments are made, is greater than the premium for a standard option.

Exhibit 3–10 compares installment and standard put options under two price scenarios. (Similar comparisons using installment call options

E X H I B I T   3–10

Comparison of the Profit/Loss of Installment and Standard Put Options
under Two Price Scenarios

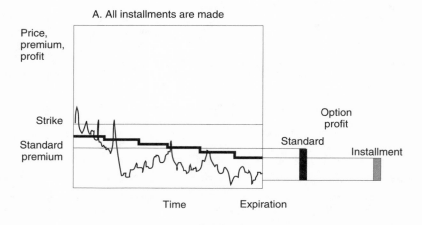

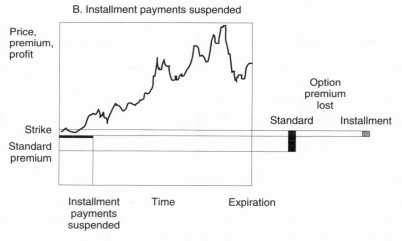

would illustrate the same points.) In the top graph, the price of the underlying falls, the underlying is comfortably below the strike on each installment date, and all installment premium payments are made. The put is in
the money at expiration, so both the standard and the installment put
options have value. Because the holder of the installment option has made

greater total premium payments, the profit on the position is smaller by the amount of the additional premium.

The lower diagram in Exhibit 3–10 illustrates a price advance and early termination of the installment payments. When an installment payment is missed, the option expires. Only one installment payment was made in the lower diagram, so the total premium paid (and lost) was much less than the premium on the standard option. The underlying is above the strike at expiration, and the standard option, which was "alive" prior to expiration, expires worthless. The loss on the standard option is the entire premium, whereas the loss on the installment option is only one of six possible installments—although this one installment is more than one-sixth of the standard option premium.

The bottom line of this exercise is that the gains from the profitable installment option are less than the gains from a comparable standard option, but so are the losses, at least under the assumptions illustrated. Furthermore, the holder of the installment option has periodic opportunities to review the desirability of making additional installment payments, based on whether owning the option is still attractive on each installment date.

A variant of the *European-style* installment option illustrated here is an *American-style* option contract which permits the investor to exercise an in-the-money installment option at any time during its life, canceling the remainder of the contract and ending the obligation to make additional installment payments.

An installment option will appeal to an investor who is willing to pay a little extra for the opportunity to terminate payments and reduce losses if the investment position is not working out. Installment options may have particular appeal in markets where most or all option contracts are traded over the counter (OTC) rather than on exchanges. An over-the-counter option premium can be difficult to recover, even in part, if the option is out of the money when an investor's viewpoint on the market price of the underlying changes. While most OTC option market makers quote two-sided markets in their products, their bid-ask spreads may expand at times. In this context, an installment option can be a partial remedy to concerns over OTC option marketability. If an installment option is selling below the value of making an installment to keep it alive, the investor need not be concerned about losing the value of a fully paid-for standard option. He or she can simply walk away from the installment option on any installment payment date. Unless the option is an American-style contract, however, it usually makes sense to continue payments on installment options that have a net present value on a payment date.

Contingent Premium Options

A *contingent premium option* differs from a standard option in that the option buyer pays a premium only if the option is in the money at expiration. As with any standard option, the buyer and seller agree on the strike price or strike rate, the expiration date, and the option premium. While the option payoff will be identical to the payoff of a comparable standard option contract, the premium on a contingent premium option is substantially higher than a standard option premium. The premium is higher because the option seller collects the premium only when the option is in the money at expiration. The upfront premium the option buyer pays for a standard option belongs to the option seller if the option expires with the underlying price or rate out of the money. In contrast, the contingent premium option costs the buyer nothing (and pays the seller nothing) if the underlying is out of the money at expiration. If the underlying is even slightly in the money, however, the contingent premium must be paid. This premium can dwarf the value of the option payout unless the option is substantially in the money. Contingent *caps* and *floors* have an added twist, because they consist of *strips* of individual *caplets* and *floorlets,* each covering a specific period. The contingent option premium is collected only for periods in which the cap or floor has value at the reset date.

Exhibit 3–11 compares the premium and payoff pattern and illustrates the profit/loss characteristics of a contingent premium call option. Exhibit 3–12

EXHIBIT 3–11

The Premium, Payoff, and Profit/Loss of a Contingent Premium Option

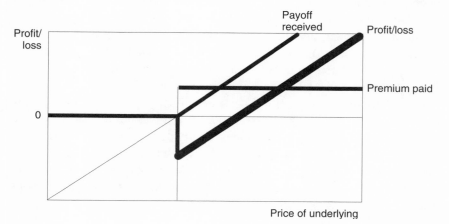

E X H I B I T   3–12

Comparison of a Standard and Contingent Premium Call Option
Buyer's Profit and Loss

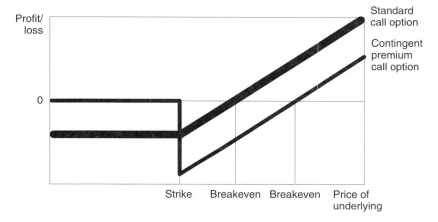

compares the profit/loss lines of hypothetical standard and contingent premium call option buyers at expiration. The option buyer will prefer the contingent premium option if the underlying is out of the money at expiration. If the underlying is in the money, the standard option will give the buyer a better result.

Contingent premium options are priced as a function of the value of the comparable standard option adjusted for the probability that the seller will receive the premium and for the discount appropriate for the delay in the premium payment. Contingent option and swaption premiums are quoted in currency units, percentages, or basis points, whatever units are used for the standard option. Contingent caps and floors can be quoted as a level premium payable at each reset date if the caplet or floorlet is in the money or as a variable premium that reflects the value and probability of exercise of individual caplets or floorlets.

Compound Options

A *compound option* is literally an option to buy or sell another option. The concept of an option on an option is sufficiently elusive that compound options are used less frequently than their inherent usefulness and flexibility justify. Compound options are particularly attractive if an investor or a liability manager believes a strong possibility exists that the underlying will move in the "wrong" direction in the near term or if there is a need for specific contingent protection.

Although we illustrate this product structure primarily with a long call on a long call, any combination of a long or short put or call on a long or short put or call position is theoretically possible. Once the basic call on call structure is understood, the other possibilities will be easier to understand.

In the case of a compound call option (i.e., a call on a call), the buyer of the first leg of the compound option has the right to buy a standard call option at a premium called the strike premium. The strike premium is the premium or price the buyer of the compound call pays for the second leg of the compound option. The higher the strike premium, the less valuable the option to buy the second option will be. Conversely, if the strike premium is very low, the premium on the first option leg will be greater. Exhibit 3–13 illustrates a simple example. This graph compares the premium of a *standard* 12-month call option struck at 100 with the cost of a compound option that gives its holder a 6-month call option to buy a 6-month call option struck at 100. In this illustration, the strike premium is the premium of a 6-month at-the-money 100 strike option. The premium on the initial 6-month call on a call (1) is less than the premium on the standard 12-month option. However,

E X H I B I T   3–13

Premium Comparison of a Call on a Call versus a Standard Call
(Strike Premium Fixed at Value of 100 Strike 6-Month Call)

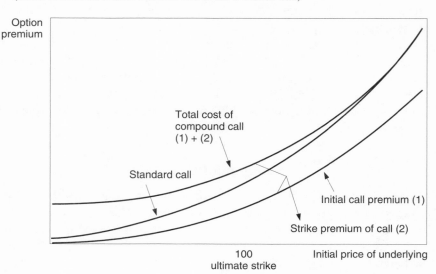

if the initial option is exercised, the buyer of the compound option will pay a greater total premium.

Exhibit 3–14 provides another view of the relationship between the separate and combined cost of the two legs of a compound option and a standard option. Clearly, the higher the strike premium, the lower the premium on the first leg of the compound option; conversely, the lower the strike premium, the higher the premium on the first leg. As the sum of the premiums on the two legs illustrates, a compound option in which both premiums are paid will cost more than a standard option with an initial term equal to the sum of the terms of the two legs of the compound option. The advantage of the compound structure stems from the fact that the loss on the first leg of a compound option can be less than the loss in premium on a standard option held for only part of its life. This feature is illustrated in Exhibit 3–15.

Based on the assumption that all options are struck at the money at issuance, Exhibit 3–15 compares the gain or loss on the first leg of a compound option at its expiration in six months with the gain or loss on a 12-month standard option held for the same period and sold with six months of life remaining. If the underlying is near or above the ultimate strike (on the standard call and on the second leg of the compound call), the 12-month standard call will show a smaller loss than the first leg of the com-

E X H I B I T   3–14

Cost Relationships of Compound and Standard Options

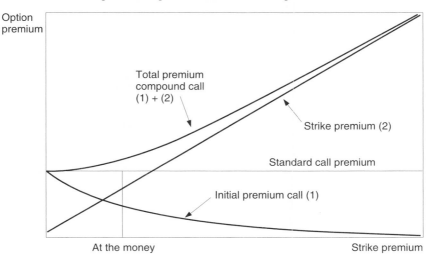

EXHIBIT   3–15

Gain or Loss on the First Leg of a Compound Option versus Holding
a Standard Option for Half of Its Life

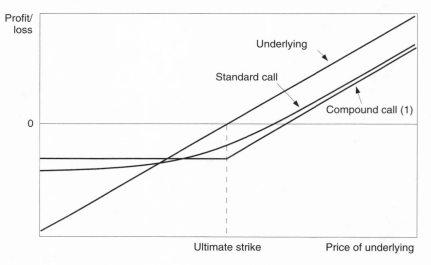

pound call. If the underlying moves down sharply during the life of the
first leg, or if the expected volatility of the underlying declines, the compound option will be a better bargain.

A compound interest rate option can be useful to investors in mortgage-backed securities. An option to buy or sell an option on a specific
interest rate-sensitive instrument can provide appropriate risk management features at a low initial premium. For example, an investor with a
position in mortgage-backed securities that have substantial prepayment
risk may face an uncertain inflow of cash that she or he needs to reinvest.
Remaining fully invested at attractive yields may be extremely important
in the achievement of overall investment objectives.

A call on a call on a noncallable long-term bond could provide the
opportunity to invest in a bond with a relatively favorable yield if rates decline.
Prepayment of mortgage-backed securities in a declining-rate environment
gives the investor a larger than anticipated cash inflow, and the compound
option provides a combination of interest rate risk management and reinvestment risk management. The compound option structure has a lower initial cost
than a standard option on a long-term bond, and the standard option has features that will not be needed if rates do not fall and the investor's mortgage-
backed securities do not prepay at an accelerated rate.

Mortgage bankers may buy calls on puts (caputs) to hedge their "pipeline risk" in case their anticipated loan commitments do not close. Exhibit 3–16 compares the cost of a standard put 10 percent out of the money with a call on a shorter-term put with otherwise similar terms.

Deferred Strike Options

A *deferred strike option* allows an investor or a corporate risk manager to lock in the level of volatility used to calculate the premium of an option at a time when the market's volatility expectations are low. All the terms of the option contract except the strike and (sometimes) the start date are set, and a premium is paid by the buyer and received by the seller. The level of the strike is ultimately set at a specific relationship to *spot* (for example, at spot, 5 percent over spot, etc.) during a period, usually beginning on the trade date and ending on a date agreed upon at the time of the trade. Once the strike is set under the terms of the contract, the deferred strike option becomes a standard option until exercise or expiration. Exhibit 3–17 illustrates option premium savings that might result from an advance purchase of volatility with a deferred strike option.

The implied volatilities illustrated in Exhibit 3–17 are based on close-to-the-money options maturing after the spot month. To the extent that historical volatilities and implied volatilities in exchange-listed options play a major role in the determination of premiums for options in

E X H I B I T   3–16

Comparison of a Call on a Put with a Standard Put

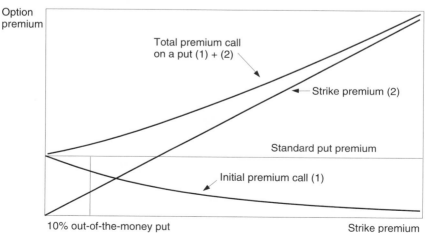

10% out-of-the-money put   Strike premium

E X H I B I T   3–17

Comparing the Effective Costs of Deferred Strike and Standard Options

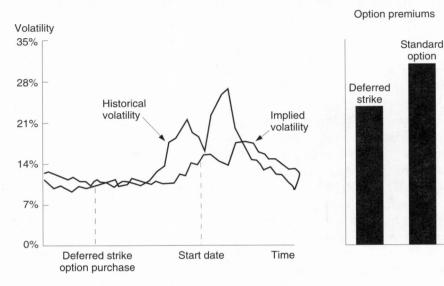

all markets, opportunities often exist to acquire volatility commitments when implied volatilities have declined relative to a long-term average levels. To the extent that an investor or liability manager can purchase a deferred strike option when volatility is cheap and set the option strike later—when volatility may be more expensive—the superior pricing associated with the timely volatility acquisition may more than compensate for the modest additional cost of the deferred strike structure.

Volatility estimation is not the only element of the deferred strike option that provides an opportunity for superior performance. To the extent that the investor or liability manager has any market-timing skill, the ability to set the deferred strike at a relative market low in the case of a call or a relative high in the case of a put may provide an additional opportunity for outperformance. While an option buyer could buy a standard option at market volatility levels on the start date, high volatility near that date might make the price of the standard option less attractive.

Investors are most likely to use deferred strike options when the bargain volatility element and, to a lesser extent, the market-timing element can be combined with another investment objective. For example, an investor in fixed-income markets may anticipate a need to extend duration with the purchase of long-term bonds, perhaps in response to the liquidation of a CMO tranche held by a pension fund. The investor may want to exercise market-timing skills in the reestablishment of a long-duration position, perhaps taking advantage of a volatility decline associated with a period of stable interest rates to buy a deferred strike option. Ideally, the strike would be set when rates changed to permit a more favorable strike, and volatility increased.

4

🌀 A SURVEY OF SPREAD OPTIONS FOR FIXED- INCOME INVESTORS

Scott McDermott
Vice President
Goldman, Sachs & Co.

INTRODUCTION

In the late 1980s, Goldman, Sachs & Co. began trading a new family of fixed-income derivative products that are options on the spreads between different fixed-income asset classes. These new products include SYCURVE[SM] options, which are put and call options on the slope of a yield curve; MOTTO[SM] options, which are put and call options on the spread between mortgage and Treasury securities; ISO[SM] options, which are put and call options on the spread between foreign fixed-income securities and other foreign fixed-income securities or U.S. Treasury securities; CROSS[SM] options, which are put and call options on fixed-income securities in which the option's strike price is established in a currency other than the currency in which the underlying securities are denominated; and finally, SPREAD-LOCK options, which are put and call options on interest rate swap spreads.[1]

These new fixed-income derivative products were introduced in response to a growing client need for hedges against different types of spread exposure. For reasons that we will examine below, it is difficult to hedge against spread exposure using only over-the-counter (or listed) put or call options on individual fixed-income securities. In fact, there is no way

---

[1] SYCURVE, MOTTO, ISO and CROSS are service marks of Goldman, Sachs & Co.

to replicate an option on a spread merely by purchasing and holding combinations of options on individual securities. As a result, the growth of the market for over-the-counter options on spreads has been quite rapid. This chapter presents a summary statement of the spread options market, surveying the available products and giving examples of their use.

For spread options, there are two ways in which the in-the-money value of the option is realized on exercise: (1) through a change in ownership of the securities underlying the option contract or (2) through a cash payment equal to the in-the-money value. By their nature, spread options can have two or more underlying securities, which makes settlement through a change in ownership particularly complex. For convenience, some investors prefer to settle the intrinsic value of spread options with a cash payment (cash settlement) and without a change in ownership of the underlying securities. The cash payment usually takes place on the business day following the expiration or exercise date of the spread option.

Other investors, however, prefer options that involve a physical exchange of securities, and for these investors we have developed the DUOP^{SM} structure.[2] Any spread option can be structured as a DUOP. For example, SYCURVE-DUOP options are put and call options on the slope of the yield curve that—if the options expire in the money or are exercised—involve the purchase of Treasury securities in one maturity sector and the simultaneous sale of Treasury securities in another maturity sector at a strike price spread. In our experience, the majority of MOTTO and CROSS options have DUOP structures, while a majority of SYCURVE, ISO, and SPREAD-LOCK options are cash-settled. This chapter contains examples of both cash-settled options and spread options with the DUOP structure.

Before we describe each of the spread options individually, it is important to emphasize that over-the-counter spread options carry special risks. The value of any spread option, for example, will be determined by the changing relationship (the spread) between prices or yields of the securities underlying the spread option's contract, and not necessarily by changes in prices or yields of any individual security. Accordingly, there is no theoretical limit on the amount of the spread and on the liability of the party that is short the spread option. In certain instances, a performance assurance deposit may be required. Over-the-counter spread options are individual agreements between a buyer and a seller, and each counterparty must evaluate the credit risks involved. In

---

[2] DUOP is a service mark of Goldman, Sachs & Co.

general, these agreements cannot be transferred or assigned without the consent of both counterparties, so over-the-counter spread options may lack liquidity. These special risks are inherent in the over-the-counter spread options market; they are in addition to the risks—exchange rate risk, for example—normally found in the market for the spread option's underlying securities.

SYCURVE OPTIONS

Movements in the shapes of yield curves around the world, and uncertainty as to their future course, have left many market participants looking for efficient ways either to take positions with respect to the future shape of a yield curve or to reduce the risk to their existing portfolios associated with yield curve movements. SYCURVE (slope-of-the-yield-curve) options meet this need, offering the opportunity to "buy" (call options) or "sell" (put options) the yield curve. In our terminology, buying the yield curve means buying the shorter-maturity instrument and simultaneously selling a duration-matched amount of the longer-maturity instrument. Selling the yield curve is the reverse strategy. Thus, SYCURVE call options increase in value as the yield curve steepens (or becomes less inverted), while SYCURVE put options increase in value as the yield curve flattens (or becomes more inverted).

Goldman, Sachs & Co. first introduced SYCURVE options in mid-1989.[3] We have found that the most commonly traded SYCURVE options are on the U.S. Treasury yield curve and, more specifically, on either the 2- to 10-year yield spread or the 2- to 30-year yield spread (see Exhibit 4–1). Accordingly, the examples that follow are drawn from the U.S. Treasury market. However, SYCURVE options can also be structured on most foreign yield curves, and investor interest in SYCURVE options on the Japanese and Canadian yield curves is especially strong.

Definition of Terms

Before we give specific examples of the uses of SYCURVE options, let us first consider the terms of the SYCURVE option contract. As with most over-the-counter options, the strike spread level, expiration date, and underlying securities can be tailored to meet an individual client's needs. In what follows, we review the most common structures.

---

[3] See *SYCURVE[SM] Options: Puts and Calls on the Slope of the Yield Curve,* Goldman, Sachs & Co., November 1989.

E X H I B I T   4–1

The U. S. Treasury Yield Curve
(For Settlement August 16, 1991)

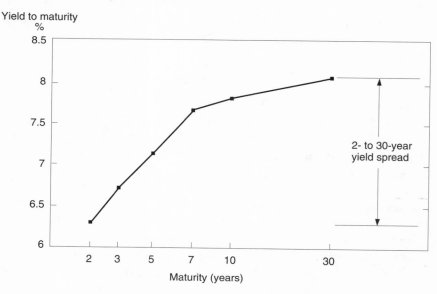

SYCURVE options may be either European, which can be exercised only on the expiration date, at any hour before the close of trading, or American, which can be exercised at any time prior to (or on) the expiration date. Because American options give the owner of the option more flexibility, the option premium for an American option is usually larger than the premium for a European option. Typically, clients prefer European options, and all of the examples that follow will assume European exercise.

The strike price of a SYCURVE option is quoted as a yield spread, in basis points, between two underlying fixed-income securities that are specified at the trade date. SYCURVE options are cash-settled, based on bid-side yields for both underlying instruments. The spread that determines the SYCURVE option's payoff will be the yield spread between the two specific securities.[4] Typically, for example, a SYCURVE call option on the yield spread between the 30-year Treasury bond and 2-year

---

[4] SYCURVE-DUOP options would settle by a physical exchange of the underlying securities at the exercise date or expiration date of an in-the-money option. The payoff of SYCURVE-DUOP options is based on a price spread between two underlying fixed-income securities that are specified on the trade date. We describe SYCURVE-DUOP structures beginning on page 88 of this chapter.

Treasury note is based on the on-the-run 2-year note issue and the on-the-run 30-year bond issue that are outstanding at the trade date, even though new 2-year notes or 30-year bonds may be issued prior to the option's expiration date.

The SYCURVE option's payoff at expiration depends only on the yield spread between the two underlying securities, not on whether general yield levels have increased or decreased during the term of the option. As the payoff is not affected by changes in market rates, the duration and convexity of SYCURVE put and call options are approximately zero.[5]

For example, assume that an investor has purchased a SYCURVE put option based on the yield spread between the 30-year Treasury bond and 2-year Treasury note, with a strike spread of 150 bp, one month until expiration, and European exercise. Assuming a trade date of August 15, 1991, the underlying securities would be the 6⅞s of July 31, 1993, and the 8⅛s of August 15, 2021, and the option would expire on September 15, 1991. We would say that the investor is long a SYCURVE 2/30 put at 150 bp.[6]

The SYCURVE option will expire in the money if the yield spread between the 8⅛s of August 2021 and the 6⅞s of July 1993 is less than 150 bp on the expiration date. Otherwise, the option will expire worthless. SYCURVE options that are in the money will be exercised automatically on expiration.

If the option expires in the money or an in-the-money option is exercised, the holder of a SYCURVE option with a notional principal amount of $1 million is entitled to receive a payoff equal to the difference in basis points between the strike yield spread and the actual yield spread at expiration, multiplied by $10,000. (We use a convention of $10,000 per basis point per $1 million notional principal amount of SYCURVE option contracts.) The notional principal amount of a SYCURVE option is always specified at the trade date. Assuming our investor is long a SYCURVE 2/30 put at 150 bp with a notional principal amount of $1 million, and assuming the yield spread at expiration is 130 bp, the SYCURVE option's payoff at expiration would be

---

[5] A parallel shift in the forward yield curve (the expected yield curve at the option expiration date) will not affect SYCURVE option values. But a parallel shift in today's yield curve does not necessarily imply a parallel shift in the forward yield curve. Especially if today's yield curve is steeply upward sloping or inverted, parallel changes in today's yield curve may imply small changes in the slope of the forward yield curve. So, strictly speaking, and prior to the expiration date, SYCURVE put and call options do retain a small exposure to yield levels.

[6] We present this example, and all other examples in this chapter, for illustrative purposes only. Examples are not meant to reflect actual market conditions.

Strike yield spread of SYCURVE 2/30 put option	150 bp
Less: Yield spread at the expiration date	– 130 bp
In-the-money amount	20 bp
Multiply by: Payoff per $1 million SYCURVE contract	× $10,000 per bp
Dollar payoff per $1MM SYCURVE contract	$200,000
Notional principal amount of SYCURVE 2/30 put at 150 bp	$1 [million]
Multiply by: Dollar payoff per $1 million SYCURVE contract	× 200,000
Net option payoff at the expiration date	$200,000

We calculate the premium on a SYCURVE option in a similar fashion. A SYCURVE option premium is quoted in units of basis points, with a dollar cost equal to $10,000 per $1 million notional principal amount per basis point of quoted premium. For example, if the premium on the SYCURVE 2/30 put option was quoted as 12 bp, the dollar cost for the investor to buy $1 million notional principal amount of the option would be $120,000.

We have intentionally chosen to quote the SYCURVE option premium in the same units as the strike yield spread so that the break-even yield spread at expiration is easy to calculate. For the investor who paid a 12 bp premium for a SYCURVE put at 150 bp, the break-even yield spread is

Strike yield spread of SYCURVE 2/30 put option	150 bp
Less: Quoted option premium	– 12 bp
Break-even yield spread at the expiration date	138 bp

The SYCURVE Option's Equivalent Portfolio

Suppose we formed the following model portfolio of 30-year U.S. Treasury bonds and 2-year Treasury notes: long $8.9 million face amount of the 8⅛s of August 15, 2021, and short $54.8 million of the 6⅞s of July 31, 1993. This portfolio has a dollar duration of zero, meaning that it is insensitive to parallel movements in the yield curve.[7] However, the port-

---

[7] Dollar duration is defined as the change in dollar value of a security per unit face amount of that security per unit change in the security's yield. For the 6⅞s of July 31, 1993, we assume a dollar duration of $182.60 per $1 million face amount per basis point. For the 8⅛s of August 15, 2021, we assume a dollar duration of $1,123.78 per $1 million face amount per basis point. In the illustration, the portfolio dollar duration and dollar sensitivity of the portfolio to changes in yield curve slope have been rounded to the nearest $100 per basis point.

folio is very sensitive to the yield spread between the 30-year bonds held long and the 2-year notes held short. When the 2- to 30-year yield spread narrows, the portfolio gains $10,000 per basis point decrease in the yield spread. For comparison, our investor's $1 million notional principal amount SYCURVE 2/30 put option also gains $10,000 per basis point decrease, assuming the put option expires in the money.

In fact, we could use our model portfolio to reproduce synthetically the returns from a SYCURVE 2/30 put option. At the expiration date, we would want to own our model portfolio if the SYCURVE 2/30 put option expired in the money. Otherwise, we would not want to own our model portfolio at all. Prior to the expiration date, we would want to own only a fraction of our model portfolio, with the fraction roughly corresponding to the probability that the SYCURVE 2/30 put option will finish in the money. In practice, we would want to own a fraction of the model portfolio equal to the hedge ratio (the delta) of the SYCURVE 2/30 put option.[8] For example, if the SYCURVE 2/30 put option had a delta equal to 0.5, we would want to hold only half of our model portfolio: long $4.45 million face amount of the 8⅛s of August 2021 and short $27.4 million face amount of the 6⅞s of July 1993. By continuously adjusting the amount of our model portfolio that we own, we could synthetically reproduce the returns from the SYCURVE 2/30 put struck at 150 bp.

In practice, most investors would find such dynamic hedging extremely tedious, expensive, and difficult to reproduce. These investors use over-the-counter SYCURVE options as a simple and convenient substitute.

Pricing SYCURVE Options

To value a SYCURVE option, we first determine the forward yield spread (the expected yield spread at the expiration date) between the two securities underlying the SYCURVE option. Then, using an estimate, perhaps the historical level, of the volatility of the yield spread, we estimate the probability that the SYCURVE option will finish in the money. This gives us the expected in-the-money portion of the option, the amount of the equivalent portfolio we need to own (the hedge ratio), and therefore the option value.[9]

---

[8] Strictly speaking, an option's delta is defined as the change in dollar value of the option per unit change in dollar value of the underlying security, and is not necessarily equal to the probability that the option will finish in the money. We present an analytic formula for the delta of European SYCURVE put and call options in the appendix to this chapter.

[9] In the appendix to this chapter, we derive an analytic formula for the value of European SYCURVE put and call options.

Notice that the SYCURVE option's price is based on the forward yield spread between the option's underlying securities. The forward date is the option's expiration date. The forward yield spread will usually differ from the yield spread at the trade date (termed the *spot yield spread*) and can differ by a large amount in a steeply sloping yield curve environment. A steeply sloping yield curve, such as that occurring in the U.S. Treasury market throughout much of 1991, reflects expectations of both a rapid rise in yield levels and a narrowing of yield spreads between long- and short-maturity securities (i.e., a yield curve flattening).[10]

Therefore, in a steeply sloping yield curve environment, SYCURVE put options with a strike yield spread equal to the spot yield spread tend to be deeply in the money on a forward basis and hence command a high premium. Conversely, SYCURVE call options with a strike yield spread equal to the spot yield spread in a steeply sloping yield curve environment tend to be out of the money on a forward basis and hence carry a much lower premium.

Investors who believe that the yield curve will remain steep for a long period (longer than implied by forward rates) will be natural sellers of SYCURVE put options and buyers of SYCURVE call options. Investors who believe that the yield curve is likely to flatten very soon (sooner than implied by forward rates) will be natural sellers of SYCURVE call options and buyers of SYCURVE put options.

The implied forward yield is usually determined by a combination of the security's yield on the trade date, the security's repo rate between the trade date and the forward date, and the volatility of those rates. Note that repo rates are important, since they help to determine forward yields. Therefore, SYCURVE option values prior to the expiration date are sensitive to the level of repo rates (all else held constant), while the option's payoff depends only on yield spreads at the expiration date.

An Application of SYCURVE Options

SYCURVE options can be used by portfolio managers whose performance is measured against the performance of a bond market benchmark index. Suppose a portfolio manager is measured against an index of 10-

---

[10] Technically speaking, in a steeply sloping yield curve environment, implied forward yields are above spot yields at all maturities. Also, the difference between implied forward yields of short-maturity securities and their spot yields is much larger than the difference between implied forward yields of long-maturity securities and their spot yields. In sum, when the yield curve is steep, implied forward yield spreads between long- and short-maturity securities are narrower than spot yield spreads.

year maturity Treasury notes, with a duration of approximately seven years. The manager anticipates a yield curve flattening and, accordingly, has positioned the portfolio to be long 30-year Treasury bonds and short Treasury note futures contracts to achieve the target 7-year duration.

The manager estimates that the portfolio will outperform the index by $1.1 million if the 10- to 30-year yield spread narrows by 10 bp over the next three months but will underperform the index by $1.1 million if the yield spread widens by 10 bp over that period. Suppose the spot 10- to 30-year yield spread is 25 bp.

In the discussion that follows, we will give three examples of how this investor could use SYCURVE options in his or her portfolio. These examples are not meant to be trading recommendations; rather, they serve to show how investors can use SYCURVE options to either increase or reduce their exposure to changes in yield spreads.

Very Bullish Strategy

Suppose a manager anticipates a yield curve flattening and believes that, at worst, the 10- to 30-year yield spread could widen by no more than 3 to 5 bp in the next three months. In that case, the manager might be willing to increase his or her exposure to yield spreads still further, and could sell $11 million notional principal amount of SYCURVE 10/30 calls at a strike of 20 bp. Exhibit 4–2 illustrates this "very bullish" slope-of-the-yield-curve strategy.

Let's assume that SYCURVE 10/30 call options are priced at 7.9 bp so that $11 million notional principal amount SYCURVE 10/30 call options would be valued at $869,000 (the premium the manager receives). If these options expire 10 bp in the money, their payoff will be $1.1 million. We chose the notional principal amount of $11 million in this example so that the manager's portfolio and the SYCURVE 10/30 call options would have equal dollar sensitivity to changes in yield curve slope. Under these circumstances, if the 10- to 30-year yield spread is 27.9 bp after three months and the SYCURVE options expire 7.9 bp in the money, the portfolio manager breaks even on the option position. If the yield spread is between 20 and 27.9 bp, the manager profits on the SYCURVE call option position, because the option finishes in the money by less than the option premium received.

If the portfolio manager's view is correct, and the yield spread is less than 20 bp after three months, the manager will profit both because (1) the portfolio will outperform the benchmark index and (2) the SYCURVE call option will expire worthless and the entire option premium may be

EXHIBIT   4–2

Very Bullish Slope-of-the-Yield-Curve Strategy

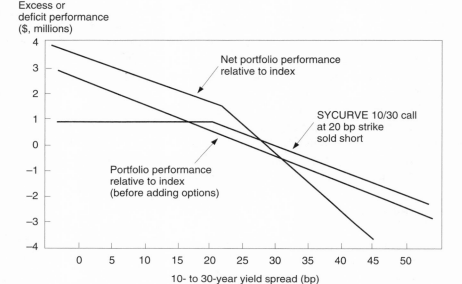

retained. By selling the SYCURVE 10/30 call option, the manager increases his or her performance in a yield curve flattening. However, if the 10- to 30-year yield spread is wider than 27.9 bp after three months, the manager risks dramatically underperforming the benchmark index.

Bullish Strategy

Alternatively, suppose the manager anticipates a yield curve flattening but is not willing to risk dramatically underperforming the benchmark index. In that case, the manager could follow a "bullish" slope-of-the-yield-curve strategy (Exhibit 4–3) and sell $11 million notional principal amount of SYCURVE 10/30 puts at a strike of 20 bp, effectively guaranteeing that the portfolio will modestly outperform the benchmark index over a wide range of yield spreads. Suppose these options are also priced at 7.9 bp ($869,000). Again, notice that we chose the notional principal amount of $11 million so that the manager's portfolio and the SYCURVE 10/30 put options would have equal dollar sensitivity to changes in yield curve slope.

E X H I B I T   4–3

Bullish Slope-of-the-Yield-Curve Strategy

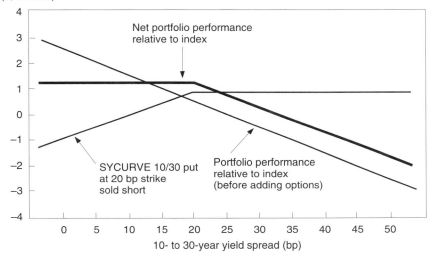

Under these circumstances, if the 10- to 30-year yield spread is less than 32.9 bp after three months, the manager's portfolio will have outperformed the benchmark index. If the yield spread is less than or equal to 20 bp after three months, the manager will have outperformed the benchmark index by a constant dollar amount equal to the sum of the SYCURVE put option's premium plus $550,000. If the 10- to 30-year yield spread is wider than 32.9 bp after three months, the manager's portfolio will have underperformed the benchmark index, but by less than what would have occurred had the manager not sold the SYCURVE put options.

Conservative Strategy

Finally, in a "conservative" slope-of-the-yield-curve strategy (Exhibit 4–4), a manager could buy $11 million notional principal amount of SYCURVE 10/30 call options at 20 bp to eliminate the risk of dramatically underperforming the benchmark index in the event that yield spreads widen. In this case, the portfolio's performance would equal that

E X H I B I T   4–4

Conservative Slope-of-the-Yield-Curve Strategy

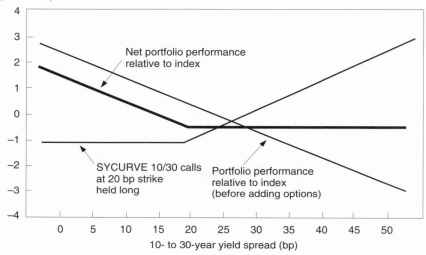

of the benchmark index if the 10- to 30-year yield spread fell to 17.1 bp after three months. If the yield spread narrowed to less than 17.1 bp, the manager would outperform the benchmark index. If the 10- to 30-year yield spread were between 17.1 bp and 20 bp, the manager would modestly underperform the benchmark index (by $319,000 at worst). If the 10- to 30-year yield spread were greater than 20 bp, the manager would underperform the benchmark index by a constant $319,000.

Compare this to the manager's original position, where his or her underperformance versus the index would be greater than $319,000 if the 10- to 30-year yield spread were to widen substantially. In this example, the manager has used SYCURVE 10/30 call options to limit losses in the event that his or her views turned out to be incorrect.

Portfolio managers are not the only users of SYCURVE options. Financial institutions, for example, can also face yield curve risk even when their assets are duration-matched to their liabilities. These institutions could use SYCURVE options to maintain the integrity of their balance sheets by protecting against losses caused by changes in the slope of the yield curve.

Does a SYCURVE Option Equal a Portfolio of Options on Individual Securities?

Before the development of the SYCURVE option, an investor seeking an option on the yield spread between the 30-year Treasury bond and 2-year Treasury note might have bought the following portfolio of over-the-counter options expiring on September 15, 1991: long call options on $8.9 million face amount of the 8⅛s of August 15, 2021, with a strike price of 100, and long put options on $54.8 million face amount of the 6⅞s of July 31, 1993, with a strike price of 100¹⁴⁄₃₂. We have chosen the strike prices so that the 2- to 30-year yield spread is approximately 150 bp if both options are at the money on the expiration date. If both options expire in the money, the net payoff at expiration is equal to approximately $10,000 per basis point decrease in the yield spread. Therefore, the investor has bought a portfolio that has optionlike payoffs—with losses limited to the premiums paid to purchase the options therein—and is sensitive to changes in the slope of the yield curve. Nevertheless, this portfolio is not the same as a SYCURVE option, as we shall show below.

Even though the portfolio of options appears to provide the same $10,000 payoff per basis point decrease in the 2- to 30-year yield spread as does the $1 million notional principal amount SYCURVE 2/30 put option, the two are not identical substitutes for each other. For one thing, the owner of the portfolio of options has more flexibility than the owner of a SYCURVE 2/30 put option. The owner of the portfolio, for example, can choose to exercise one of the options while letting the other option expire worthless. This added flexibility means the portfolio of options is more valuable than the SYCURVE 2/30 put option, and that is reflected in the option premiums paid. Typically, such a portfolio of options would be three to four times more expensive than a SYCURVE 2/30 put option.

To see why the portfolio of options is not equivalent to a SYCURVE 2/30 put option, consider the dollar duration of each. By construction, the SYCURVE option's payoff is insensitive to the overall level of Treasury yields (only yield spreads matter), and its dollar duration is zero. The portfolio of options is insensitive to the overall level of Treasury yields only when both the put and call option expire in the money. If either of the two options in the portfolio were to expire out of the money while the remaining option expired in the money, the payoff of the portfolio would depend only on the overall level of rates (in particular, it would depend on the yield of the underlying security of the in-the-money option) and not on the yield spread. The dollar duration of the portfolio of options is therefore not zero.

For example, assume that neither the SYCURVE option nor any option in the portfolio of individual put and call options is in the money, and consider what would happen after a very large market move. For convenience, assume that the very large market move occurred just before the options' expiration date. Assume that the market move did not change the slope of the yield curve but did change the overall level of rates dramatically. In this case, the SYCURVE option's payoff would be unchanged, and it would expire worthless, since we have assumed that it was out of the money before the market move and that the market move did not affect yield spreads. With the portfolio of options, however, assuming the market move is very large, it is certain that either the call option or the put option, but not both, would be deep in the money at expiration.

The only time a portfolio of options on individual securities will behave like a SYCURVE option over a wide range of market conditions is when all of the options in the portfolio must be exercised together— even if one of them is out of the money—or not at all. Such contingent exercise structures have become popular, and we have given them a special name, the DUOP.

SYCURVE-DUOP OPTIONS

A DUOP (dual-exercise option) structure is a portfolio of a put option and a call option on two different underlying securities, linked by a contingent exercise provision that requires that both options be exercised together or not at all. A SYCURVE-DUOP structure is very similar to a cash-settled SYCURVE option, except that a SYCURVE-DUOP put or call option has a payoff based on the price spread between the two underlying securities and requires a physical exchange of the underlying securities at the strike price spread if the SYCURVE-DUOP option expires in the money.[11]

In two cases, the SYCURVE-DUOP structure is superior to cash-settled SYCURVE options: (1) when the spread option must have strike levels based on prices rather than yields, because the yield of the underlying securities is ambiguous or difficult to measure, and (2) when an

---

[11] Strictly speaking, because the DUOP structure's payoff is dependent on a spread while the SYCURVE option's payoff is dependent on a yield spread, the payoff from a DUOP structure will usually differ from the payoff of a SYCURVE option because of the convexity of the underlying securities. Only when the underlying securities have approximately equal convexities will the DUOP structure's payoff approximately equal the SYCURVE option's payoff.

investor prefers to settle by physical delivery. An example of the first case occurs in the Japanese market when an investor wishes to take a position on the spread between 90-day Euroyen time deposits and 10-year Japanese government bonds and prefers a DUOP structure based on futures contract prices for which yield is not well defined. An example of the second case occurs when a portfolio manager, rather than receiving a SYCURVE option's cash payoff, wishes to physically swap out of one sector of the yield curve and into another sector at a target price spread.

Let us return to the example of an option on the spread between a 30-year Treasury bond and a 2-year Treasury note. Suppose an investor has purchased a SYCURVE-DUOP structure containing the following portfolio of options expiring on September 15, 1991: long call options on $8.9 million face amount of the 8⅛s of August 15, 2021, with a strike price of 100, and long put options on $54.8 million face amount of the 6⅞s of July 31, 1993, with a strike price of 100¹⁴⁄₃₂, with the provision that both options must be exercised together or not at all. We would say that the investor is long a SYCURVE-DUOP 2/30 put.

The mechanics of calculating the strike price spread, break-even price spread, and SYCURVE-DUOP payoff at expiration are straightforward but more complex than in the case of a SYCURVE option. For example, the SYCURVE-DUOP 2/30 put has the following strike price spread:

Flat price of $54.8MM 2-year notes at 100¹⁴⁄₃₂	$55,039,750
Less: Flat price of $8.9MM 30-year bonds at 100	− 8,900,000
Strike price spread	$46,139,750

The strike price spread represents the cash that the owner of the SYCURVE-DUOP 2/30 put would receive if the SYCURVE-DUOP put were exercised and $54.8 million face amount of 2-year Treasury notes were exchanged for $8.9 million face amount of 30-year Treasury bonds.

If the flat price of $54.8 million face amount of the 6⅞s of July 1993 minus the flat price of $8.9 million face amount of the 8⅛s of August 2021 is less than $46,139,750 at the expiration date, the SYCURVE-DUOP 2/30 put is in the money, and both of the options in the DUOP structure should be exercised.[12] Otherwise, the SYCURVE-

---

[12] We require the price spread to be less than the break-even price spread only because we have structured the DUOP portfolio as a 2/30 put option. If the DUOP portfolio were composed of a put option on the 8⅛s of August 2021 with a strike price of 100 and a call option on the 6⅞s of July 1993 with a strike price of 100¹⁴⁄₃₂, we would have formed a DUOP 2/30 call that would be in the money if the price spread were greater than the break-even price spread on the expiration date.

DUOP 2/30 put will be out of the money and should be allowed to expire worthless. Note that if the owner exercised the SYCURVE-DUOP 2/30 put, he or she would be buying 30-year bonds at 100 and selling 2-year notes at $100^{14}\!/\!_{32}$. That is, the DUOP would settle through a physical exchange of cash and securities. The DUOP structure is in the money when such a physical exchange of securities can occur at a net cost less (net cash received greater) than the market value of the exchange on the expiration date.

The contingent exercise provision means that the option premium paid for the SYCURVE-DUOP 2/30 put is less than the cost of the two options purchased separately. The SYCURVE-DUOP 2/30 put has a pay-off that is nearly identical to the payoff of the $1 million notional principal amount SYCURVE 2/30 put at 150 bp. Neglecting convexity (see footnote 11), we would expect the SYCURVE-DUOP 2/30 put to have the same $120,000 premium as the SYCURVE 2/30 put at 150 bp. The premium of the DUOP structure would be quoted in price units. In this case, the SYCURVE-DUOP 2/30 put would be quoted at a price of $1^{21}\!/\!_{64}$ per $100 face amount of the 30-year bonds. (We have rounded the price to the nearest $\frac{1}{64}$.)

One type of DUOP structure that is particularly popular is an option on the spread between mortgage securities and U.S. Treasury securities. In fact, we have assigned this structure a separate name, the MOTTO option.

MOTTO OPTIONS

MOTTO (mortgage over Treasury) spread options are designed to allow investors to profit from, or control the risk of, changes in the spread between mortgage and Treasury securities. Many investors seek efficient ways either to take a position on the future direction of the spread or to hedge their mortgage portfolios against possible future spread changes. The owner of a MOTTO call option benefits when mortgage-backed securities (MBSs) outperform Treasury securities, while the owner of a MOTTO put option benefits when MBSs underperform Treasury securities.

Structuring MOTTO Put and Call Options

MOTTO options are more complex to structure than SYCURVE options because the conversion from price to yield, and vice versa, is more complex in the mortgage securities market than in the U.S. Treasury market.

For most Treasury notes and bonds, the future cash flows to the owner of the security are known with certainty.[13] The owner of $1 million face amount of the 6s of November 15, 1994, for example, can expect to receive an interest payment of $30,000 on the 15th day of May and November in each of the years 1992 through 1994, as well as a principal payment of $1 million on November 15, 1994. If this security were priced at 100–18 for settlement on December 2, 1991, it would carry a yield of 5.789 percent. (The yield is the discount rate that would equate the security's price with the discounted present value of the future cash flows.)

For such securities, there is a one-to-one correspondence between price and yield. This one-to-one correspondence is the reason SYCURVE put and call options can be based either on yield spreads or, in a DUOP structure with a nearly identical payoff, on price spreads between the underlying securities.

Unfortunately, in the mortgage securities market, there is no one-to-one correspondence between the price of a mortgage security and its yield, because the future cash flows of a mortgage security are not known with certainty. We cannot know the future cash flows from a mortgage security principally because we do not know, with certainty, the prepayment rates of the individual mortgages backing the security (the mortgages in the pool). Government National Mortgage Association 9 percent coupon mortgage pass-through securities (GNMA 9s), for example, trading for settlement on December 17, 1991, were quoted at a price of 104–06 on November 29, 1991. Even though we know the price of these securities, the yield is ambiguous, since it depends on the prepayment rate of the underlying mortgages.

Most investors use a mortgage prepayment model to estimate the future mortgage prepayments, cash flows, and therefore the yield on an MBS.[14] A mortgage prepayment model will combine the weighted aver-

---

[13] The exceptions are 25- or 30-year Treasury bonds originally issued in the 1970s and early 1980s that are callable at par on any coupon payment date within five years of the maturity date. The 10⅜s of November 15, 2012, for example, originally issued in 1982, are callable at par on any coupon payment date on or after November 15, 2007. We cannot know with certainty whether these bonds will be called or not, and the yield on these bonds could be the yield to maturity, the yield to the first call date, or somewhere in between. When such bonds are among the underlying securities in a SYCURVE put or call option, the option agreement will explicitly specify either yield to maturity or yield to first call date.

[14] See Scott Pinkus, Susan Mara Hunter, and Richard Roll, *An Introduction to the Mortgage Market and Mortgage Analysis,* Goldman, Sachs & Co., February 1987; Scott F. Richard and Richard Roll, *Modeling Prepayments on Fixed Rate Mortgage-Backed Securities,* Goldman, Sachs & Co., September 1988; and Scott F. Richard, *Housing Prices and Prepayments for Fixed Rate Mortgage-Backed Securities,* Goldman, Sachs & Co., October 1991.

age coupon rate (WAC) of the mortgages in the pool, the weighted average loan age (WALA) in the pool, the average time since each mortgage in the pool was issued, current and prior period levels of mortgage financing rates, seasonal adjustments, and house prices to estimate future mortgage prepayment rates. Unfortunately, unlike the standard calculations that specify the relationship between price and yield for a Treasury note or bond, there is no mortgage prepayment model that has been accepted industrywide. The Public Securities Association (PSA) model, which was originally intended to be an industrywide standard prepayment model, does not explicitly account for the effect of differences between the current mortgage financing rate and the WAC of the mortgage pool.

The PSA model is now used by market participants as a reference point rather than as an industry standard. High-coupon MBSs, for example, whose underlying mortgages were issued in a much higher interest rate environment and could be profitably refinanced today, would be expected to prepay more rapidly than the PSA model would suggest. Low-coupon mortgages, whose underlying mortgages were issued in a much lower interest rate environment—so that those homeowners are now paying below-market rates of interest—would be expected to prepay more slowly than the PSA model would suggest.

While many broker/dealers have proprietary mortgage prepayment models that are improvements on the PSA model, there is no consensus about which model is the best and therefore no consensus about the yield of an MBS. For example, returning to the GNMA 9s priced at 104–06 on November 29, 1991, for settlement on December 17, 1991, the Goldman Sachs mortgage prepayment model would estimate the yield on these securities as 8.308 percent, equivalent to a prepayment speed of 142 percent PSA. This is also equivalent to an annualized conditional prepayment rate (CPR) of 8.35 percent, or a constant monthly prepayment rate (CMP) of 0.72 percent. By comparison, other broker/dealers' mortgage prepayment models generate estimates of the prepayment rates on these same GNMA 9s that range between 130 percent and 227 percent PSA, corresponding to yields of 8.340 percent to 8.075 percent.

What is more important, the prepayment rate will change with changes in the overall level of interest rates. If interest rates were to rise, the prepayment rate of the mortgage pool underlying the GNMA 9s would be expected to decrease. Conversely, if interest rates were to fall, the prepayment rate of the mortgage pool underlying the GNMA 9s would be expected to increase. While broker/dealers' proprietary mortgage prepayment models do recognize this effect, there is no consensus as to exactly how much prepayment rates rise when interest rates fall, and vice versa.

For all of these reasons, it is difficult to structure a MOTTO option based on the yield spread between MBSs and U.S. Treasury securities. We would have to agree in advance on a mortgage prepayment model to use when calculating prepayment rates, future cash flows, and therefore the yield on the MBS. For a start, we would have to agree on what prepayment rate to use at every level of U.S. Treasury yields and, indeed, for every possible shape of the U.S. Treasury yield curve. Clearly, this is not feasible.

Accordingly, a MOTTO put or call option is always formed as a DUOP structure. A MOTTO call option would permit the owner to buy a predetermined amount of MBSs and sell a predetermined amount of Treasury securities at a predetermined (strike) price spread. Similarly, a MOTTO put option would permit the owner to sell MBSs and buy Treasury securities at a strike price spread. Prices have the advantage of being unambiguous: GNMA 9s can trade in the market at 104–06, meaning that market participants agree on the value of the security, even though some market participants believe the GNMA 9s yield 8.340 percent at 130 percent PSA while others believe the GNMA 9s yield 8.075 percent at 227 percent PSA.

Choosing the Underlying Treasury and Mortgage-Backed Securities

When comparing the price performance of MBSs to that of Treasury securities, and therefore when choosing the underlying securities for MOTTO put and call options, it is important to choose securities that are "comparable." In theory, an MBS should be compared with the U.S. Treasury security whose dollar duration is closest to the dollar duration of the MBS. In practice, only on-the-run Treasury securities are used as benchmarks. Estimates of the dollar duration of MBSs require a mortgage prepayment model and are therefore uncertain, but fortunately this uncertainty is small enough that the appropriate Treasury benchmark can be assigned with confidence.

Typically, new-issue current coupon mortgages (MBSs trading at or near par value) have dollar durations similar to the dollar duration of seven-year Treasury notes. When first traded, MOTTO put and call options were often based on price spreads either between GNMA 9s and seven-year Treasury notes or between GNMA 9½s and five-year

Treasury notes. Today, when GNMA 7½s are considered the current coupon issue, MOTTO put and call options are often based on price spreads either between GNMA 7½s and seven-year Treasury notes or between GNMA 8s and five-year Treasury notes. In practice, an investor is free to choose the MBS and Treasury security that will underlie a MOTTO put or call option; those referred to above are merely the more frequent combinations.

When MBSs outperform Treasury securities, MBS prices rise relative to comparable-duration Treasury prices. Similarly, when MBSs underperform Treasury securities, MBS prices fall relative to comparable-duration Treasury prices.

Typically, the ratio of the face amount of MBSs to the face amount of Treasury securities underlying a MOTTO put or call option is one for one. On the expiration date of the option, the owner of $10 million face amount MOTTO put options on GNMA 9s versus five-year Treasury notes, for example, would have the right, but not the obligation, to sell $10 million face amount of GNMA 9s and buy $10 million face amount of five-year Treasury notes at the strike price spread. Because the face amounts of both underlying securities are equal, the payoff from a MOTTO option depends only on the price spread (when quoted for settlement on the same forward date) between the underlying MBS and Treasury security.

The MOTTO option can be structured to cash-settle or to require physical delivery. In the former case, when a MOTTO put or call option expires in the money or is exercised, the owner of the option receives a cash payment equal to the option's in-the-money value. In the latter case, the owner of a MOTTO put option has the right, but not the obligation, to exchange an MBS for an equal face amount of a Treasury security on a designated forward settlement date. Conversely, the owner of a MOTTO call option settled by physical delivery has the right, but not the obligation, to exchange a Treasury security for an equal face amount of an MBS on a designated forward settlement date. At the trade date, the Treasury security, MBS, strike price spread, source of price quotes, expiration date, and forward settlement date are all specified uniquely.

A MOTTO Option Example

Trades in the MBS markets settle at designated forward dates. GNMA pass-through securities carrying coupons of 9½ or less, for example, are classified as Class B securities and settle on a specific day each month. In September 1991, Class B securities settled on September 17, while in

August 1991, Class B securities settled on August 20. The expiration date of MOTTO put and call options is usually set at five business days prior to the mortgage settlement date to allow for a delivery notice on the MBSs. Also, the settlement date of the MOTTO options is usually set to coincide with the mortgage settlement date. With MOTTO options, it is important to pay close attention to trade dates, expiration dates, and settlement dates.

Suppose, for example, that an investor has purchased a MOTTO call option expiring on August 13, 1991, and settling on August 20, 1991, with a strike price spread of $^{30}/_{32}$nds. Suppose further that the underlying securities are GNMA 9s and seven-year U.S. Treasury notes (the 7⅞s of April 15, 1998). We say that the investor is long an August MOTTO call at 0–30.

Exhibit 4–5 shows recent price spreads. On July 2, 1991, the 7⅞s of April 1998 were quoted at 98$^{17}/_{32}$ for settlement on July 3, 1991. GNMA 9s were quoted at 99$^{14}/_{32}$ for settlement on July 16, 1991. The price spread of $^{29}/_{32}$nds (equal to 99$^{14}/_{32}$ less 98$^{17}/_{32}$) is not meaningful to the holder of the August MOTTO call at 0–30, since neither the GNMA 9s nor the seven-year Treasury notes have been priced for settlement on the MOTTO call option's August 20, 1991, settlement date. The investor needs to ask for forward prices.

E X H I B I T   4–5

Price Spread: GNMA 9s versus Seven-Year U.S. Treasury
(GNMA 9s and Treasury 7⁷/₈s of 1998, Quoted for Settlement on August 20, 1991)

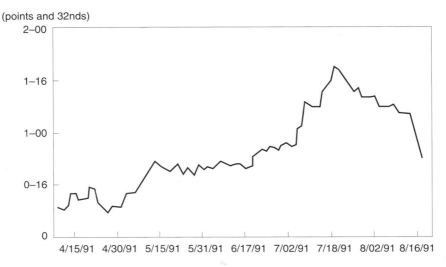

(points and 32nds)

The forward price of the GNMA 9s is $99\frac{5}{32}$ for settlement on August 20, 1991, and the forward price of the 7⅞s of April 1998 is $98\frac{3}{32}$ for settlement on August 20, 1991. Therefore, the forward price spread is $\frac{30}{32}$nds at the option settlement date. Note that the MOTTO call option's strike price spread is at the money on a forward basis.

The investor's MOTTO call option will finish in the money if the price of GNMA 9s for August delivery is more than $\frac{30}{32}$nds higher than the forward price of the 7⅞s of April 1998 on the expiration date, August 13, 1991. Assuming that on the expiration date GNMA 9s were quoted at $100\frac{13}{32}$ and the 7⅞s of April 1998 were quoted at $99\frac{5}{32}$, both for settlement on August 20, 1991, the August MOTTO call at 0–30 will finish in the money by $\frac{10}{32}$nds. Assuming the investor had purchased $10 million face amount of August MOTTO calls at 0–30, the payoff value would be equal to

GNMA 9s over 7-year notes price spread at expiration (32nds)	40
Less: Strike price spread of August MOTTO call option (32nds)	– 30
In-the-money amount (32nds)	10
Notional principal amount of August MOTTO call at 0–30	$10,000,000
Multiply by: In-the-money amount (decimal)	× 0.003125
Net option value at the expiration date	$31,250

If the investor purchased the $10 million notional principal amount August MOTTO call at 0–30 on a cash-settled basis, the investor would be entitled to receive the net option value in cash. If the investor purchased the MOTTO call on a physical-delivery basis, the investor would be entitled to sell $10 million face amount of the 7⅞s of April 1998 and simultaneously purchase an equal face amount of GNMA 9s at a net cost of $\frac{30}{32}$nds, at a time when the market price of such an exchange is $\frac{40}{32}$nds.

The premium for a MOTTO put or call option is quoted in $\frac{1}{32}$nds, which is the same unit in which the price spread between the underlying MBS and Treasury security is denominated. Therefore, the break-even price spread at expiration is easy to calculate. In this case, the August MOTTO call at 0–30 was quoted at a $\frac{7}{32}$nds premium, and the break-even price spread is

Strike price spread of MOTTO call option (32nds)	30
Add: Quoted option premium (32nds)	+ 7
Break-even price spread at the expiration date (32nds)	37

In this example, the investor made a net profit of ³⁄₃₂nds on the MOTTO call option, equal to a dollar profit of $9,375 on a $10 million notional principal amount.

As with the SYCURVE option, the MOTTO option's premium will be based on the forward price spread between the option's underlying securities, where the forward date is the option's expiration date. The forward price spread will usually differ from the quoted price spread at the trade date, if only because U.S. Treasury security prices are normally quoted for next-day settlement rather than for forward settlement. Investors will form their opinions by studying forward price spreads. Investors who believe that MBSs will underperform Treasury securities will be natural buyers of MOTTO put options and sellers of MOTTO call options. Conversely, investors who believe that MBSs will outperform Treasury securities will be natural buyers of MOTTO call options and sellers of MOTTO put options.

The payoff from MOTTO put and call options depends directly on the price spread between the underlying MBS and Treasury security at the expiration date and only indirectly on overall market levels.[15] Like SYCURVE options, MOTTO put and call options can be synthetically reproduced by dynamic hedging of an equivalent portfolio. In the case of a MOTTO call option, the equivalent portfolio consists of MBSs purchased forward combined with Treasury securities sold forward, and the notional amount of the equivalent portfolio owned would have to be continuously adjusted to match changes in the MOTTO call option's hedge ratio (the option's delta). Most investors would find such dynamic hedging tedious, expensive, and difficult to reproduce in practice. These investors prefer over-the-counter MOTTO options when hedging a mortgage portfolio's spread exposure or establishing a position that will profit in the event of spread widening or narrowing.

ISO OPTIONS

Virtually all international investors closely monitor yield spreads between different government bond markets. For the international fund manager, yield spreads are often the primary criterion for asset allocation decisions.

---

[15] The MBS and Treasury security underlying a MOTTO put or call option are chosen to have approximately equal dollar durations, so the dollar duration of the MOTTO option itself is approximately zero. However, the two underlying securities will not have equal dollar convexity, so the convexity of a MOTTO option is nonzero. In this sense, MOTTO put and call options retain an exposure to overall market levels. MOTTO call options have negative convexity, while MOTTO put options have positive convexity.

For the arbitrageur, international yield spreads have historically been a significant source of trading profits. The ISO (international spread option) provides investors with a flexible way to alter a portfolio's exposure to international markets, hedge that exposure, and take a position in international yield spreads that will profit when spreads change.

ISOs are similar to SYCURVE options in that both are options on the yield spread between two specific bonds. But the bonds that underlie ISO put and call options are drawn from two different government bond markets and are denominated in different currencies. Typically, each bond's yield is quoted according to the convention that applies in its domestic market, with the exception that Japanese government bond yields are typically quoted on a semiannually compounded basis. ISO call options represent the right to "buy" the yield spread, and they increase in value when the yield spread increases. ISO put options represent the right to "sell" the yield spread, and they increase in value when yield spreads decrease. Goldman, Sachs & Co. first introduced ISOs in mid-1990.[16]

Like SYCURVE options, ISO put and call options are typically cash-settled. The currency in which the owner of the option is paid when the option expires in the money is specified in advance, and that is the currency in which the option is said to be denominated. Since each of the underlying bonds is denominated in a different currency, the ISO option is typically denominated in one or the other, whichever the investor prefers. Alternatively, the ISO option can be denominated in a third currency, which is usually the domestic currency in which the investor's performance is measured. At the trade date, the underlying bonds, yield convention, strike yield spread, source of yield quotes, expiration date, settlement date, currency of denomination, and notional principal amount of an ISO put or call option are all specified uniquely.

Also like SYCURVE options, ISO put and call options can be formed as a DUOP structure that would settle through a physical exchange of securities. ISO-DUOP structures, for example, would allow international portfolio managers to physically reallocate their portfolios among different international bond markets at target price spreads.

As of the close of trading on August 9, 1991, the French government OAT 8⅛s of March 28, 2000, were quoted at a price of 96.25 (decimal) to

---

[16] See Richard Thomasson, "International Spread Options," *The International Fixed-Income Analyst*, Goldman, Sachs & Co., November 16, 1990.

yield 9.132 percent, and the German government Bund 9s of October 20, 2000, were quoted at 102.12 (decimal) to yield 8.647 percent (see Exhibit 4–6). The spot OAT versus Bund yield spread is therefore 48.5 bp. Suppose an investor has purchased F1 million notional principal amount of ISO put options on the yield spread between the OAT 8 ⅛s of March 2000 and the Bund 9s of October 2000. Suppose the options have a strike yield spread of 45 bp. We would say the investor is long F1 million ISO OAT/Bund puts at 45 bp.

In this example, we have chosen to denominate the ISO put options in French francs, but the ISO put options could just as easily have been denominated in German marks or even, if the investor was a U.S.-based portfolio manager, in U.S. dollars. As with SYCURVE options, the premiums and payoffs of ISO put and call options are quoted in basis points, with each basis point representing 1 percent of the notional principal amount of the option. For example, if an ISO OAT/Bund put at 45 bp was quoted at a premium of 10 bp, the net cost to the investor to purchase F1 million notional principal amount of ISO OAT/Bund puts at 45 bp would be calculated as follows:

E X H I B I T   4–6

International Yield Curves
(Based on Quoted Prices as of August 9, 1991)

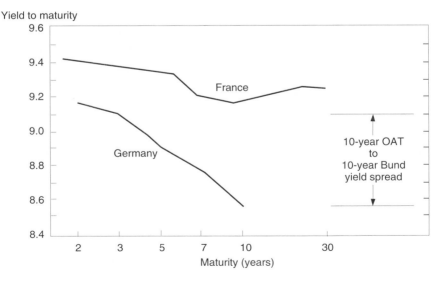

Quoted premium of ISO OAT/Bund put at 45 bp	10 bp
Multiply by: Cost per F1 notional principal per bp	× 0.01 per bp
French franc cost per F1 notional principal	0.10
Notional principal amount of ISO OAT/Bund put at 45 bp	F1 million
Multiply by: French franc cost per F1 notional principal	× 0.10
Net option cost at the trade date	F100,000

We have intentionally chosen to quote the ISO option premium in the same units as the strike yield spread so that the break-even yield spread at expiration is easy to calculate. Note that the break-even yield spread does not depend on the currency in which the ISO put or call option is denominated. For the investor who paid a 10 bp premium for an ISO OAT/Bund put at 45 bp, the break-even yield spread is

Strike yield spread of ISO OAT/Bund put option	45 bp
Less: Quoted option premium	− 10 bp
Break-even yield spread at the expiration date	35 bp

The ISO OAT/Bund put at 45 bp will finish in the money if the yield at the quoted price of the OAT 8⅛s of March 2000 minus the yield at the quoted price of the Bund 9s of October 2000 is less than 45 bp on the option's expiration date. The ISO OAT/Bund put therefore increases in value when the French government bond market outperforms the German government bond market. Assuming that the yield spread at the expiration date is 30 bp, the owner of F1 million ISO OAT/Bund puts at 45 bp would receive a payoff equal to

Strike yield spread of ISO OAT/Bund put option	45 bp
Less: Yield spread at the expiration date	− 30 bp
In-the-money amount	15 bp
Multiply by: Payoff per F1 notional principal per bp	× 0.01 per bp
French franc payoff per F1 notional principal	0.15
Notional principal amount of ISO OAT/Bund put at 45 bp	F1 million
Multiply by: French franc payoff per F1 notional principal	× 0.15
Net option payoff at the expiration date	F150,000

In this case, the investor has paid a F100,000 premium for the option and received a F150,000 payoff at the option expiration date for a net profit of F50,000.

The ISO Option's Equivalent Portfolio

An ISO put option on the OAT/Bund yield spread increases in value as the French government bond market outperforms the German government bond market. The ISO OAT/Bund put at 45 bp is at the money at the expiration date when the yield at the quoted price of the OAT 8½s of March 2000 minus the yield at the quoted price of the Bund 9s of October 2000 is equal to 45 bp. For each basis point by which the yield spread at the expiration date is below 45 bp, the F1 million notional principal amount of the ISO OAT/Bund put at 45 bp will increase in value by F10,000.

Suppose we form the following model portfolio on August 9, 1991: long F17.7 million face amount of the OAT 8½s of March 2000 and short DM 5.05 million face amount of the Bund 9s of October 2000. Assuming an August 9, 1991, French franc versus deutsche mark cross rate of 3.4015, this portfolio increases in value by F10,000 per each basis point by which the yield spread between the OAT 8½s of March 2000 and the Bund 9s of October 2000 decreases. Notice that if the yield of the OAT 8½s of March 2000 and the yield of the Bund 9s of October 2000 both increased or decreased by the same amount so that the yield spread did not change, and if the French franc versus deutsche mark cross rate did not change, the value of the model portfolio would not change.[17]

We can use this model portfolio to reproduce synthetically the returns from an ISO OAT/Bund put option at 45 bp. At the expiration date, we would want to own the model portfolio if the yield spread between the OAT 8½s of March 2000 and the Bund 9s of October 2000 was less than 45 bp. Otherwise, the put option would be out of the money, and we would not want to own the model portfolio at all.

Prior to the expiration date, we would want to own only a fraction of the model portfolio. In fact, we would want to own a fraction of the model portfolio equal to the hedge ratio (the delta) of the ISO OAT/Bund

---

[17] For the OAT 8½s of March 2000, we assume a French franc duration of F565.80 per F1 million face amount per basis point, and for the Bund 9s of October 2000, we assume a deutsche mark duration of DM 582.59 per DM 1 million face amount per basis point. In the example, the portfolio French franc sensitivity to changes in yield spread has been rounded to the nearest F100.

put option at 45 bp. If the delta of the put option was 0.20, we would want to own only a fifth of the model portfolio: long F3.54 million face amount of the OAT 8½s of March 2000 and short DM 1.01 million face amount of the Bund 9s of October 2000. By continuously adjusting the amount of the model portfolio that we own and continuously rebalancing the portfolio to keep the portfolio's exposure to yield spread changes at F10,000 per basis point, we can synthetically reproduce the returns from an ISO OAT/Bund put option at 45 bp.

Most investors would find such dynamic hedging tedious, expensive, and difficult to reproduce in practice. These investors would prefer over-the-counter ISO put and call options as a simple and convenient substitute.

Applications of ISO Put and Call Options

An international portfolio manager is bullish on French government bonds and bearish on German government bonds. As a result, the manager's portfolio is overweighted in OATs and underweighted in Bunds. As we have seen, on August 9, 1991, the yield spread between the OAT 8½s of March 2000 and the Bund 9s of October 2000 is 48.5 bp. Suppose the manager's performance is measured against the returns from an international government bond index. If the yield spread between French government bonds and Bunds tightens to 45 bp, the manager intends to return to a neutral weighting relative to the index by selling approximately F18 million in French government bonds and buying DM 5 million in Bunds.

The portfolio manager might choose to hedge his or her investment view by writing an ISO-DUOP OAT/Bund put at 45 bp. The portfolio manager prefers the DUOP structure since, if the yield spread between French government bonds and Bunds tightens to less than 40 bp and the put option expires in the money, the manager will automatically be swapped out of French government bonds into Bunds, and therefore into a neutral weighting relative to the index.

Suppose that on the trade date of August 9, 1991, an ISO-DUOP OAT/Bund put at 45 bp could be sold at a premium of 10 bp. In order to swap out of approximately F18 million face amount of OATs into approximately DM 5 million face amount of Bunds, the portfolio manager would sell short F1 million notional principal amount of ISO-DUOP OAT/Bund puts at 45 bp and receive a premium of F100,000.

Now consider what happens at the expiration date. If the portfolio manager's view is correct, and the yield spread between the OAT 8½s of March 2000 and the Bund 9s of October 2000 is less than 45 bp on the expiration date, the ISO-DUOP put at 45 bp will be in the money. The manager's portfolio will have benefited from the 3.5 bp narrowing of the yield spread to 45 bp and from the F100,000 option premium received. Finally, when the ISO-DUOP put option is exercised, the manager will have been swapped out of F17.7 million face amount of the OAT 8⅛s of March 2000 and into DM 5.05 million face amount of the Bund 9s of October 2000, returning the manager's portfolio to a neutral weighting with respect to the index. In effect, the manager will have swapped out of French government bonds and into German government bonds at a yield spread of 35 bp.

Otherwise, if the yield spread between the OAT 8⅛s and the Bund 9s were greater than 45 bp on the expiration date, the ISO-DUOP put at 45 bp would be out of the money and expire worthless. The manager's portfolio would still benefit from the F100,000 premium received on the ISO-DUOP OAT/Bund puts at 45 bp sold short.

In summary, ISO put and call options offer portfolio managers a convenient way to alter a portfolio's exposure to international markets. ISO put and call options on the OAT versus Bund, U.K. gilt versus Bund, Japanese government bond versus U.S. Treasury, and Canadian government bond versus U.S. Treasury spreads have been particularly popular.

CROSS OPTIONS

CROSS put and call options are options on bonds whose premium, strike price, and payoff are denominated in a currency different from the currency in which the bonds' coupons and principal are paid. We include CROSS put and call options in this chapter because they share an important characteristic with the spread options that we described earlier. The payoff from a CROSS put or call option is dependent on two (risky) market prices: bond prices and currency exchange rates.

Managers of international fixed-income portfolios have used CROSS put and call options to hedge risks or achieve market exposures that cannot be hedged or achieved efficiently using traditional option products. International portfolio managers are inevitably judged on the basis of their portfolios' total returns when measured in the managers' domestic currency. These managers are exposed to a combination of both foreign interest rate risk and exchange rate risk. CROSS put and call options help investors manage this risk.

CROSS put and call options were first used by Japanese insurance companies that held U.S. Treasury notes and bonds in yen-based portfolios. These investors wanted either (1) to buy put options to protect the yen value of their portfolios or (2) to sell call options in buy-write programs. Traditional, dollar-denominated put and call options could not meet their needs. If these investors sold dollar-denominated call options against their Treasury bond portfolios in a buy-write program, for example, they risked a loss if U.S. Treasury bond prices rose while the dollar simultaneously fell sharply against the yen.

Suppose, for example, that a Japanese investor purchased $1 million face amount of U.S. Treasury bonds (the 7⅞s of February 15, 2021) at 97, and paid ¥135 per dollar for the dollars required to buy the bond (see Exhibit 4–7).[18] The cost basis for the Japanese investor is therefore ¥13,095 per $100 face amount of bonds owned, for a total of ¥130.95 million. Suppose the Japanese investor pursues a buy-write strategy and sells traditional, dollar-denominated call options with a strike price of 98 on the entire $1 million face amount of bonds owned. Note that when sold, the call options were 1 point out of the money.

E X H I B I T   4–7

U.S. Treasury Bond Prices
(Flat Price of $1 Million Face Amount of the 7⅞s of 2021)

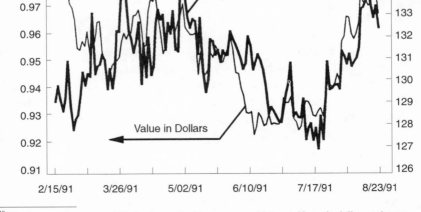

For a U.S.-based investor, such a strategy would effectively guarantee a capital gain in the event that the call option expired in the money. The calculation below shows the net capital gain or loss on this buy-write strategy if the call option sold short expires in the money and is exercised. In this case, the dollar-based investor will always realize a capital gain.

Sale price of 7⅞s of February 2021 (option strike price)	$980,000
Less: Purchase price of 7⅞s of February 2021	− 970,000
Net capital gain at the option expiration date	$10,000

If the call options expired out of the money, and therefore worthless, the U.S.-based investor would not be required to sell the bonds to the option holder. The investor would retain the bonds, though with an unrealized gain or loss. In any case, the investor retains the call option premium and accrued interest on the bonds between the purchase date and the option expiration date. Thus, an investor might pursue a buy-write strategy to enhance the current income from his or her portfolio. A buy-write strategy can be very successful, in particular, whenever actual market volatility over the term of the option is less than the call option's implied volatility on the date the option is sold short.

In contrast to the U.S.-based investor, a Japanese investor pursuing a buy-write strategy would be exposed to currency risk. If the call option expired in the money and was exercised, the Japanese investor could realize either a capital gain or loss, depending on the yen-dollar exchange rate in effect on the option expiration date. If the exchange rate was unchanged at ¥135 per dollar, the Japanese investor's capital gain would be a simple multiple of the U.S.-based investors's capital gain. In this example, it would be ¥1.35 million. Unfortunately, foreign exchange rates are quite volatile, and even modest changes in the exchange rate could turn the Japanese investor's capital gain into a capital loss.

As we show in the following calculation, if the exchange rate at the option expiration date had increased to ¥140 per dollar, the Japanese investor would realize a capital gain of ¥6.25 million. If the exchange rate at the option expiration date had decreased to ¥130 per dollar, the Japanese investor would face a capital loss of ¥3.55 million.

In the latter case, even when the bonds appreciated so that the U.S.-based investor realized a capital gain of $10,000, the fall in the value of the dollar against the yen caused the Japanese investor to realize a substantial capital loss. Because of this uncertainty, the Japanese investor faces difficulty in using a buy-write strategy with traditional option products to enhance the portfolio's current income.

Sale price of 7⅞s of February 2021
  (option strike price) $980,000 $980,000
Multiply by: Exchange rate (yen per dollar)   × 140   × 130

Net yen received (millions of yen)   137.20   127.40

Less: Purchase price
  (millions of yen at ¥135 per dollar)   − 130.95   − 130.95

Net capital gain or (loss) (millions of yen)   6.25   (3.55)

Suppose instead that the Japanese investor had sold CROSS call options on $1 million face amount of the 7⅞s of February 2021 at a strike price of ¥13,230 per $100 face amount. We would say the investor is short $1 million face amount CROSS call options on the 7⅞s of February 2021 at ¥13,230.

By selling yen-denominated CROSS call options instead of traditional dollar-denominated options, the Japanese investor is effectively guaranteed a capital gain in the event that the call options expire in the money. The calculations below show the net capital gain or loss on a CROSS option buy-write strategy if the CROSS call options sold short expire in the money and the options are exercised. Like the dollar-based investor selling dollar-denominated call options, a Japanese investor selling yen-denominated CROSS call options will always realize a capital gain.

Sale price of 7⅞s of February 2021
(CROSS option strike price)   ¥132,300,000
Less: Purchase price (at ¥135 per dollar)   − ¥130,950,000

Net capital gain at the option expiration date   ¥1,350,000

Just as with the U.S.-based investor, if the call options sold short expired out of the money and therefore worthless, the Japanese investor would not be required to sell the bonds to the option holder. The Japanese investor would retain the bonds, though with an unrealized gain or loss. The investor would also retain the call option premium and accrued interest on the bonds between the purchase date and the option expiration date.

In this example, a Japanese investor used CROSS call options to execute a buy-write strategy on U.S. Treasury securities. The Japanese investor chose CROSS options because they minimize the strategy's exposure to currency fluctuations. By using CROSS put and call options, portfolio managers can invest in foreign securities and pursue the same option strategies open to them in their domestic markets, while minimizing currency risk and exchange rate exposures.

Does a Portfolio of Options Equal a CROSS Option?

The Japanese investor pursuing a buy-write strategy with dollar-denominated options could try to hedge the strategy's currency risk by using currency options. Suppose that a Japanese investor purchases $1 million face amount of U.S. Treasury bonds (the 7⅞s of February 2021) at 97 and pays ¥135 per dollar for the dollars required to buy the bonds. Suppose, again, that the Japanese investor pursues a buy-write strategy and sells dollar-denominated call options with a strike price of 98 on the entire $1 million face amount of bonds owned.

We saw earlier that this strategy leaves the Japanese investor exposed to currency risk. Suppose the Japanese investor tries to hedge that currency risk by purchasing a currency option giving the investor the right, but not the obligation, to buy $980,000 worth of yen at an exchange rate of ¥135 per dollar. Now the Japanese investor has a portfolio of options: short a dollar-denominated call option on $1 million face amount of the 7⅞s of February 2021 at 98 and long an option to buy $980,000 worth of yen at an exchange rate of ¥135 per dollar. Both options expire on the same date.

With this portfolio, the Japanese investor is effectively guaranteed a gain in the event that the call option on the 7⅞s of February 2021 expires in the money. For example, if the exchange rate at the call option expiration date has increased to ¥140 per dollar, the Japanese investor would realize a capital gain of ¥6.25 million (though the currency option held long would expire worthless). But if the exchange rate at the option expiration date has decreased to ¥130 per dollar, the Japanese investor would choose to exercise the currency option and purchase yen at an exchange rate of ¥135 per dollar, leading to a net gain of ¥1.35 million.

Sale price of 7⅞s of February 2021 (CROSS option strike price)	$980,000	$980,000
Multiply by: Exchange rate, yen per dollar (higher of market rate or ¥135 per dollar option strike)	× 140	× 135
Net yen received (millions of yen)	137.20	132.30
Less: Purchase price (millions of yen at ¥135/$)	− 130.95	− 130.95
Net capital gain or (loss) (millions of yen)	6.25	1.35

In the event that the call option on the 7⅞s of February 2021 expires in the money, the currency option protects the Japanese investor from a capital loss. However, the portfolio of options—the call option sold short and currency option held long—is not equivalent to a CROSS option sold short. For one thing, the portfolio of options gives the Japanese investor more flexibility than the CROSS option. In particular, the options in the portfolio can be exercised independently of each other. The call option sold short, for example, could expire worthless, while the currency option held long could expire in the money. This added flexibility means that the portfolio of options is more valuable than the CROSS option, and that is reflected in the portfolio's cost.

The portfolio of options—the call option on the 7⅞s of February 2021 sold short and the currency option held long—will behave like a CROSS call option when, and only when, all of the options in the portfolio are exercised simultaneously (even when one of the options is out of the money) or not at all. If the portfolio of options contained a contingent exercise provision—requiring that all of the options be exercised together or not at all—only then would the portfolio be equivalent to a CROSS option.

It is easy to see why an investor pursuing a buy-write strategy would prefer to use CROSS options. If the CROSS option expired out of the money, a Japanese investor pursuing a buy-write strategy with CROSS options would retain the entire option premium. The option premium would enhance the portfolio's current income. In contrast, a Japanese investor pursuing a buy-write strategy with traditional dollar-denominated options would spend a substantial portion of the option premium to purchase the currency options needed to hedge the portfolio against the possibility of a capital loss. In this example, a Japanese investor could use CROSS options to eliminate exchange rate risk without reducing the premium income received.

SPREAD-LOCK OPTIONS

No survey of spread options would be complete without a description of over-the-counter options on interest rate swap spreads. Interest rate swaps are normally quoted in terms of a spread over the comparable maturity U.S. Treasury security (see Exhibit 4–8), so options on swap spreads are a natural extension of the interest rate swap market. On the option's expiration date, the owner of a SPREAD-LOCK call option has the right, but not the obligation, to buy an interest rate swap (receive a fixed rate and pay a floating rate) at a predetermined swap spread. Conversely, the owner of a SPREAD-LOCK put option has the right, but not the obligation, to sell an interest rate swap (pay fixed and receive floating) at a pre-

EXHIBIT 4-8

Interest Rate Swap Spreads
(Pay fixed, receive six-month LIBOR floating)

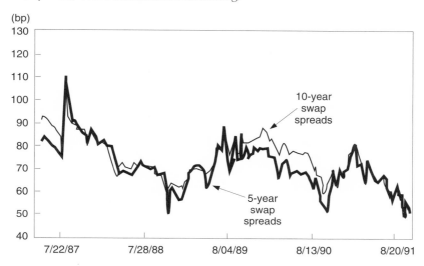

determined swap spread. SPREAD-LOCK call options increase in value as swap spreads decrease, while SPREAD-LOCK put options increase in value as swap spreads increase.

SPREAD-LOCK put and call options are different from more traditional options contracts in the interest rate swap market, such as swaptions, caps, and floors. The latter options are all options on interest rate levels rather than on interest rate spreads. For example, on the option's expiration date, the owner of a call swaption has the right, but not the obligation, to buy an interest rate swap at a predetermined swap rate.

Note that swaptions specify the entire fixed-rate side of the swap in advance, while SPREAD-LOCK put and call options specify only the swap spread in advance. For SPREAD-LOCK put and call options, the fixed-rate side of the swap is equal to a sum of the prespecified swap spread plus the yield, as of the exercise date of the option, of the comparable-maturity U.S. Treasury security.

Suppose, for example, that on August 21, 1991, an investor had purchased a SPREAD-LOCK put option on a five-year interest rate swap (fixed versus six-month LIBOR floating) at a strike swap spread of 55 bp. The SPREAD-LOCK put option expires on September 21, 1991. We say that the investor is long a five-year SPREAD-LOCK put at 55 bp. On the expiration date, the investor has the right, but not the obligation, to sell a five-year interest rate swap (pay fixed and receive six-month LIBOR floating). The fixed-rate side of the swap would equal the sum of 55 bp plus the yield, on the expiration date, of the outstanding five-year U.S. Treasury note.

Consistent with the conventions used in the interest rate swap market itself, the underlying U.S. Treasury security is not usually identified in advance. For example, with the five-year SPREAD-LOCK put at 55 bp, the fixed-rate side of the underlying swap would equal the sum of 55 bp plus the yield, on the expiration date, of the outstanding five-year U.S. Treasury note, even though that Treasury note may have been issued after the SPREAD-LOCK option's trade date.

The premium of SPREAD-LOCK put and call options is quoted in basis points, which represent a decimal fraction of the notional principal amount of the swap. For example, suppose the investor has purchased $100 million notional principal amount of the five-year SPREAD-LOCK puts at 55 bp for a premium of 9 bp. The dollar cost to the investor would be $90,000.

Notional principal amount of five-year SPREAD-LOCK put at 55 bp	$100 million
Multiply by: Option premium in basis points (decimal)	× 0.0009
Dollar cost of the option	$90,000

The five-year SPREAD-LOCK put option will be in the money if, on the expiration date, the five-year swap rate (fixed versus six-month LIBOR floating) is greater than 55 bp. Suppose that on the expiration date, the five-year swap rate is quoted in the market at 65 bp. In that case, the five-year SPREAD-LOCK put option will be 10 bp in-the-money. The owner of the SPREAD-LOCK option would be entitled to sell a five-year swap (pay fixed and receive six-month LIBOR floating), paying a fixed rate of 55 bp over the yield on the outstanding five-year U.S. Treasury note, at a time when the market swap rate is 65 bp over the yield on the outstanding five-year U.S. Treasury note.

The SPREAD-LOCK put option's break-even swap rate can be estimated from the dollar duration of the underlying interest rate swap contract. For example, the $100 million notional amount, five-year SPREAD-LOCK put at 55 bp has a break-even swap spread of approximately 57.2 bp.[19]

---

[19] We assume that the five-year swap has a dollar duration of $415 per $1 million notional principal amount per bp.

Dollar cost of $100 million five-year
SPREAD-LOCK put at 55 bp $90,000
Divide by: Dollar duration of $100 million 5-year swap   ÷ $41,500 per bp

Break-even in-the-money amount   2.2 bp
Add: SPREAD-LOCK strike spread   + 55.0 bp

Break-even swap spread on the expiration date   57.2 bp

In the example shown above, the SPREAD-LOCK put option was structured for physical settlement: The owner of the SPREAD-LOCK option had the right, but not the obligation, to sell a five-year swap contract (pay fixed and receive six-month LIBOR floating). Alternatively, SPREAD-LOCK options can be structured to cash-settle. For example, the investor could have purchased $100 million notional principal amount of five-year SPREAD-LOCK put options at a strike spread of 55 bp and strike dollar duration of $415 per $1 million notional principal amount per basis point. In this case, the investor would be entitled to receive $41,500 for each basis point by which the five-year swap spread exceeds 55 bp on the option expiration date. If the swap rate is 65 bp on the option expiration date, the investor would be entitled to receive a cash payment of $415,000.

5-year swap spread on the option expiration date   65 bp
Less: SPREAD-LOCK strike swap spread   – 55 bp

In-the-money amount   10 bp
Multiply by: SPREAD-LOCK strike dollar duration   × $41,500 per bp

Dollar payoff at the option expiration date $415,000

Applications of SPREAD-LOCK Put and Call Options

Portfolio managers and institutions use SPREAD-LOCK put and call options to ensure a favorable asset-liability balance. A financial institution, for example, may own a portfolio of mortgage assets yielding approximately 90 bp over seven-year U.S. Treasury notes and having a dollar duration approximately equal to that of the Treasury notes. Assuming the financial institution can fund at LIBOR flat, and assuming servicing and operating costs are 25 bp, this financial institution can be profitable if it can swap LIBOR-based floating-rate liabilities into fixed-rate liabilities at a spread of less than 65 bp over seven-year Treasury notes.

The financial institution anticipates purchasing an additional $100 million in assets and wants to ensure that these assets can be funded profitably. The financial institution plans to raise capital, with a floating-rate issue, in one month. Assume that seven-year interest rate swap spreads are quoted at 57 bp. If the floating-rate issue and asset purchase occurred today, the financial institution would be profitable, and its profit margin, after operating and servicing costs, would be 8 bp. Since the financial institution intends to raise funding and purchase assets one month from now, it can hedge against a possible widening of swap spreads by purchasing a seven-year SPREAD-LOCK put option expiring in one month.

SUMMARY OF SPREAD OPTIONS FOR FIXED-INCOME INVESTORS

This chapter has described a wide variety of over-the-counter options on interest rate spreads between different fixed-income classes:

- SYCURVE options, which are put and call options on the slope of the yield curve.
- MOTTO options, which are put and call options on the spread between the mortgage and Treasury markets.
- ISO options, which are put and call options on the spread between foreign fixed-income markets and other foreign fixed-income markets or the U.S. Treasury market.
- CROSS options, which are put and call options on fixed-income securities in which the option's strike price is established in a currency that is different from the currency in which the fixed-income security itself is denominated.
- SPREAD-LOCK options, which are put and call options on interest rate swap spreads.

These option products allow investors (1) to alter a portfolio's exposure to interest rate spreads, (2) to hedge interest rate spread exposures, and (3) to profit from changes in interest rate spreads. These options can be structured either for a cash settlement or for the physical exchange of securities. With a cash-settled structure, the owner of the spread option receives a cash payment equal to the in-the-money value when the option expires or is exercised. Alternatively, the owner can use a DUOP structure, which involves the physical exchange of the underlying securities if the options expire in the money or are exercised.

Merely purchasing and holding a portfolio of options on individual securities does not replicate the payoff from an option on interest rate spreads. Moreover, a portfolio of options on individual securities that minimally meets an investor's hedging requirements is often more expensive (the investor is overhedged) than the alternative of a single, over-the-counter spread option. Over-the-counter interest rate spread options can be simple, convenient, and well matched to investors' needs.

APPENDIX 4–A

An Analytic Formula for Valuing European SYCURVE Put and Call Options

In this chapter, we intentionally did not include a detailed description of how to calculate the dollar value of SYCURVE put and call options, nor did we describe how to determine an option's hedge ratio (the option's delta). Such a description is complex and may not be of interest to all readers. Rather than place such calculations in the body of the text, we develop in this appendix the formulas required to value SYCURVE put and call options. Throughout the discussion that follows, we will assume that the SYCURVE options are European and can be exercised only on the option's expiration date.

Determinants of Value

On the trade date, the value of SYCURVE put and call options is determined by a combination of at least five ingredients: (1) the strike yield spread, (2) the expiration date, (3) the discount factor between the trade date and the expiration date, (4) the forward yield spread between the SYCURVE option's two underlying securities, and (5) the volatility of the forward yield spread. Before developing the option pricing formulas, we will briefly examine each of these components.

The Strike Yield Spread and Expiration Date
The strike yield spread and option expiration date are easy to determine, as they are always specified on the trade date. Option premiums are settled on the business day following the trade date. If the option buyer elects to exercise the option and the option is cash-settled, the option's payoff settles on the business day following the option's expiration date.

The Discount Factor
The value of a SYCURVE put or call option is determined by the expected value of the payoff on the option's expiration date, discounted to the trade date. Normally, we use the financing cost of the underlying securities (either the repo rate, LIBOR, or spread over LIBOR, as appropriate) to determine the discount factor.

The Forward Yield Spread

The payoff from SYCURVE put and call options is based on the forward yield spread—the difference in yield between the two underlying securities—where the forward date is the option's expiration date. For each of the two underlying securities, we can obtain an estimate of the forward price, based on the security's price today, coupon rate, and repo rate until the forward date. Given the expected forward price for each security, the expected forward yield follows. The difference between the expected forward yields is the expected forward yield spread.[20]

Assume, for example, that on September 17, 1991, we wish to determine the expected forward yield spread to an October 17, 1991, option expiration date (an October 18, 1991, forward settlement date) between the 8⅛s of May 15, 2021 (a 30-year bond), and the 6⅞s of July 31, 1993 (a 2-year note). Assume that the 30-year bond and 2-year note are trading at prices of 101³¹⁄₃₂ and 101⁷⁄₃₂nds, respectively, for settlement on September 18, 1991. Finally, assume that both securities can be financed at a term repo rate of 5.40 percent.

Exhibit 4–9 shows our calculation of forward prices and forward yields for both the 30-year bond and the 2-year note. We find the expected forward yield spread to be 178.0 bp.[21] Note that the expected forward yield spread is less than the 179.1 bp yield spread between the 30-year bond and 2-year note on the trade date. This is typical of an upward-sloping yield curve environment (see footnote 10).

E X H I B I T   4–9

Forward Yield Spreads (30-Year Bond versus 2-Year Note)

		For Settlement on September 18, 1991			For Forward Settlement on October 18, 1991	
Coupon Rate	Maturity Date	Quoted Price (decimal)	Yield (%)	Term Financing Rate (%)	Forward Price (decimal)	Yield at the Forward Price (%)
8.125	05/15/21	101.96875	7.950	5.400	101.77776	7.967
6.875	07/31/93	101.234375	6.159	5.400	101.13359	6.187
Expected forward yield spread (bp)						178.0

---

[20] Strictly speaking, the expected forward yield is not exactly equal to the security's yield at the forward price if the security has a nonzero convexity. Fortunately, however, the difference is small for short-dated options, so we neglect it in the example that follows.

[21] In this example, the correction to the forward yield spread due to the nonzero convexity of the underlying securities (see footnote 20) is approximately 0.4 bp.

The Volatility of the Yield Spread

We use the word volatility as a shorthand notation for variability—in this case the likely variability of the forward yield spread between the underlying securities from the trade date until the expiration date of the option. The volatility is important because of its effect on option values: the larger the volatility, the higher the probability that a put or call option will finish in the money, and therefore the more valuable the option.

At first glance, the volatility of the forward yield spread seems difficult to determine. Going back to our earlier example, since the forward yield spread is the difference between the forward yield of the 30-year bond and the forward yield of the 2-year note, the volatility of the forward yield spread could in principle be found from the volatility of 30-year bond yields, the volatility of 2-year note yields, and the correlation between the two. Fortunately, there is an easier approach.

In the discussion that follows, we assume that the forward yield spread itself is a volatile security. SYCURVE put and call options can then be thought of as put and call options on a single security rather than (complex) options on the spread between two independently volatile (risky) securities. However, if we use the former approach, we need to recognize that the way changes in yield spreads behave is not the same as the way note and bond yields change.

We usually assume that note and bond yields are lognormally distributed, meaning that the quantity $\ln(y_{t+\Delta t}/y_t)$ is assumed to be normally distributed, where y_t is the note's or bond's yield today and $y_{t+\Delta t}$ is the note's or bond's yield at some future date. The yield volatility, then, would be the (annualized) standard deviation of the quantity $\ln(y_{t+\Delta t}/y_t)$. The forward yield spread, however, has a different property.

For example, Exhibit 4–10 shows a histogram of month-to-month changes in the yield spread between the on-the-run 30-year bond and the on-the-run 2-year note from January 31, 1985, through September 13, 1991. As the chart shows, changes in the yield spread are, to a good approximation, normally distributed. Over this period, the volatility of the yield spread was 70.1 bp per year. This means that changes in forward yield spreads, $S_{t+\Delta t} - S_t$, are normally distributed, where S_t is the forward yield spread today and $S_{t+\Delta t}$ is the forward yield spread at some future date. The volatility of the yield spread, then, is the (annualized) standard deviation of the quantity $S_{t+\Delta t} - S_t$.

Returning to the yield spread between the 8⅛s of May 2021 and the 6⅞s of July 1993, we show in Exhibit 4–11 a history of the yield of each security and a history of the yield spread from July 31, 1991, when the 2-

EXHIBIT 4–10

Histogram of 2- to 30-Year Yield Spread
(1,694 trading days, 21 trading days per month, January 31, 1985,
through September 13, 1991)

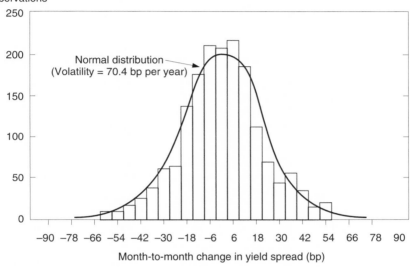

year note was issued, through September 17, 1991. During this period,
the historical yield spread volatility was 69.6 bp.

Exhibit 4–11 also shows an alternative way of estimating the yield
spread volatility, namely

$$\sigma \approx \sqrt{(\sigma_2 y_2)^2 + (\sigma_{30} y_{30})^2 - 2\rho_{2,30}\sigma_2 y_2 \sigma_{30} y_{30}} \qquad (1)$$

where σ is the volatility of the yield spread between the 30-year bond and
2-year note, y_{30} is the 30-year bond yield, σ_{30} is the volatility of the 30-
year bond yield, y_2 is the 2-year note yield, σ_2 is the volatility of the 2-
year note yield, and $\rho_{2,30}$ is the correlation coefficient. The estimated yield
spread volatility, found by using Equation 1 and the historical yield
volatilities, average yields, and the historical correlation coefficient, is
70.2 bp (see Exhibit 4–11).

In Exhibits 4–10 and 4–11, we have used historical changes in the
yield spread as a proxy for changes in the forward yield spread and historical yield spread volatility as a proxy for expected future yield spread
volatility. This is a good approximation only when future market behav-

E X H I B I T   4–11

Yield Spread Volatility

	8 1/8s of 5/15/21 30-Year Treasury Bond		6 7/8s of 7/31/93 2-Year Treasury Note		2/30 Yield Spread	
Date	Yield (%)	Log Change	Yield (%)	Log Change	Spread (%)	Change (%)
07/30/91	8.384%	–	6.832%	–	1.552%	–
07/31/91	8.352%	–0.0039	6.798%	0.0050	1.554%	0.002%
08/01/91	8.378%	0.0031	6.849%	0.0074	1.529%	–0.024%
08/02/91	8.248%	–0.0157	6.687%	–0.0240	1.561%	0.032%
08/05/91	8.233%	–0.0017	6.678%	–0.0013	1.556%	–0.005%
08/06/91	8.171%	–0.0076	6.566%	–0.0168	1.605%	0.049%
08/07/91	8.171%	0.0000	6.532%	–0.0053	1.639%	0.035%
08/08/91	8.222%	0.0062	6.489%	–0.0066	1.733%	0.094%
08/09/91	8.242%	0.0024	6.470%	–0.0029	1.772%	0.039%
08/12/91	8.222%	–0.0024	6.469%	–0.0001	1.753%	–0.019%
08/13/91	8.188%	–0.0042	6.460%	–0.0014	1.728%	–0.025%
08/14/91	8.092%	–0.0117	6.356%	–0.0161	1.736%	0.008%
08/15/91	8.123%	0.0038	6.321%	–0.0055	1.802%	0.066%
08/16/91	8.118%	–0.0007	6.284%	–0.0059	1.833%	0.031%
08/19/91	8.132%	0.0017	6.206%	–0.0125	1.925%	0.092%
08/20/91	8.120%	–0.0014	6.137%	–0.0113	1.984%	0.058%
08/21/91	8.095%	–0.0031	6.247%	0.0179	1.848%	–0.136%
08/22/91	8.079%	–0.0021	6.246%	–0.0002	1.832%	–0.016%
08/23/91	8.163%	0.0103	6.408%	0.0256	1.754%	–0.078%
08/26/91	8.182%	0.0024	6.442%	0.0053	1.740%	–0.014%
08/27/91	8.163%	–0.0024	6.398%	–0.0069	1.765%	0.024%
08/28/91	8.087%	–0.0093	6.293%	–0.0166	1.794%	0.030%
08/29/91	8.021%	–0.0082	6.240%	–0.0085	1.781%	–0.013%
08/30/91	8.087%	0.0082	6.323%	0.0133	1.764%	–0.017%
09/03/91	8.079%	–0.0010	6.305%	–0.0029	1.774%	0.010%
09/04/91	8.090%	0.0014	6.287%	–0.0029	1.803%	0.030%
09/05/91	8.115%	0.0031	6.295%	0.0013	1.820%	0.017%
09/06/91	8.045%	–0.0086	6.230%	–0.0103	1.815%	–0.005%
09/09/91	8.029%	–0.0021	6.212%	–0.0030	1.817%	0.002%
09/10/91	8.040%	0.0014	6.202%	–0.0016	1.838%	0.021%
09/11/91	8.048%	0.0010	6.218%	0.0027	1.830%	–0.008%
09/12/91	7.980%	–0.0086	6.182%	–0.0059	1.798%	–0.032%
09/13/91	7.985%	0.0007	6.170%	–0.0019	1.815%	0.0017%
09/16/91	7.961%	–0.0031	6.160%	–0.0016	1.800%	–0.015%
09/17/91	7.950%	–0.0038	6.159%	–0.0002	1.791%	–0.010%
Average	8.124%		6.362%		1.762%	
Historical yield volatility		9.114%		15.980%		
Historical covariance			1.054%			
Historical correlation coefficient			72.4%			
Estimated yield spread volatility			0.702%			
Historical yield spread volatility						0.696%

ior is expected to closely resemble past market behavior. In practice, this is rarely the case. Often an option will trade in the market at an implied volatility (an expected future volatility implied by the option's price) different from the historical volatility of the underlying security. Moreover, an option's implied volatility may differ for different option expiration dates (there is a term structure of volatility). This does not mean that the option is mispriced. Instead, it means that market participants expect future conditions to differ from those of the immediate past.

We can use Equation 1 to approximate the estimated future volatility of the yield spread by using the implied volatility of options on individual securities. For example, on September 17, 1991, the 8⅛s of May 2021 were priced to yield 7.950 percent and the 6⅞s of July 1993 were priced to yield 6.159 percent (see Exhibit 4–11). On the same date, one-month put and call options on the 30-year bond were trading at an implied volatility of approximately 9.0 percent, and one-month put and call options on the 2-year note were trading at an implied volatility of approximately 16.5 percent. Using Equation 1 and assuming a correlation coefficient of 70 percent, we find that the expected future volatility of the yield spread between the 30-year bond and 2-year note would be approximately 72.6 bp.

So far, we have used four different methods to determine the expected future volatility of the yield spread between the 8⅛s of May 2021 and the 6⅞s of July 1993: (1) the historical volatility, 70.4 bp, of the yield spread between on-the-run 30-year bonds and on-the-run 2-year notes; (2) the historical volatility, 69.6 bp, of the yield spread between the 8⅛s of May 2021 and the 6⅞s of July 1993, specifically; (3) the estimated yield spread volatility, 70.2 bp, based on the average yield of each security, the historical yield volatility of each security, and the historical correlation coefficient; and (4) an estimate of the expected future yield spread volatility, 72.6 bp, based on the actual yield of each security on the trade date, the implied yield volatility of put and call options on each security on the trade date, and an estimate of the expected future correlation coefficient. All of these estimates of the expected future yield spread volatility are very close to each other, though that may not be true in general. They can be used to value, or to establish a range of values for, SYCURVE put and call options.

Now that we have developed estimates of all of the elements that determine the value of SYCURVE put or call options, we can proceed to calculate an option's value using an option pricing formula. Unfortunately, because changes in the forward yield spread are not lognormally distributed, we cannot use the usual option pricing tools, such as the Black-Scholes model, to value SYCURVE put and call options. Instead, we need to develop an entirely new option pricing model for securities whose changes follow a normal distribution.

The SYCURVE Option Pricing Formula

To value a SYCURVE put or call option, we assume that forward yield spreads obey the following process:

$$S_{t+\Delta t} = S_t + \sigma \sqrt{\Delta t} Z$$

(2)

where:

S_t = Forward yield spread at time t

$S_{t+\Delta t}$ = Forward yield spread at time $t + \Delta t$,

σ = Standard deviation of the yield spread per unit time

Z = Standard normal random variable with

   mean = 0 and standard deviation = 1

The standard normal random variable, Z, will probably look more familiar to readers when it is operated on by the probability operator, $\text{Prob}\{\cdots\}$. For example,

$$\text{Prob}\{x \le Z \le x + dx\} = \frac{1}{\sqrt{2\pi}} e^{-x^2/2} dx$$
$$= N'(x)dx$$

$$\text{Prob}\{Z \le y\} = \frac{1}{\sqrt{2\pi}} \int_{-\infty}^{y} e^{-x^2/2} dx$$
$$= N(y)$$

$$\text{Prob}\{Z \ge y\} = \text{Prob}\{Z \le -y\}$$
$$= N(-y)$$
$$= 1 - N(y)$$

and it follows that $E\{Z\} = 0$, $\text{Var}\{Z\} = 1$, and $E\{Z^2\} = 1$, where $E\{\cdots\}$ is the expected value operator and $\text{Var}\{\cdots\}$ is the variance operator.

Based on Equation 2 and the properties of the standard normal random variable, we find the expected value and variance of the forward yield spread to be

$$E\{S_{t+\Delta\tau}\} = S_t$$
$$Var\{S_{t+\Delta t}\} = \sigma^2 \Delta t$$

This means that the expected value of the forward yield spread is, sensibly, the forward yield spread itself and that changes in the forward yield spread are normally distributed.

Now suppose that we wish to know the value at time t (today) of a European SYCURVE call option on the yield spread with a strike yield spread K. Also suppose that the call option expires at time T (the option's expiration date). In this case, C_t is the value of the SYCURVE call option and S_t is the expected value, at time t, of the forward yield spread. At expiration, the SYCURVE call option will have a value $C_T = \text{Max}(0, S_T - K)$, where S_T is the yield spread on the option expiration date and the operator $\text{Max}(\cdots)$ selects the largest item in the list. The value of the SYCURVE call option today is equal to the expected value of C_T discounted to today, namely

$$C_t = e^{-r\tau} E\{\text{Max}(0, S_T - K)\} \tag{3}$$

where $\tau = T - t$ is the time to expiration of the option and $e^{-r\tau}$ is the discount factor between today and the option's expiration date.[22]

If $p = \text{Prob}\{S_T > K\}$ is the probability that the SYCURVE call option will expire in the money, and $E\{S_T \mid S_T > K\}$ is the expected value of the yield spread given that the SYCURVE call option expires in the money, Equation 3 becomes

$$
\begin{aligned}
C_t &= (1-p)e^{-r\tau}(0) + pe^{-r\tau}(E\{S_T \mid S_T > K\} - K) \\
&= e^{-r\tau}(pE\{S_T \mid S_T > K\} - K)
\end{aligned}
\tag{4}
$$

---

[22] Here r is the continuously compounded risk-free rate. Normally, we would use LIBOR or the repo rate, R, as a proxy for the risk-free rate and make the substitution

$$e^{-r\tau} \to \left(1 + R\frac{\tau}{360}\right)^{-1}$$

Step 1: Evaluation of p

$$p = \text{Prob}\{S_T > K\}$$
$$= \text{Prob}\{S_T + \sigma\sqrt{\tau}Z > K\}$$
$$= \text{Prob}\left\{Z > \frac{1}{\sigma\sqrt{\tau}}(K - S_t)\right\}$$
$$= \text{Prob}\left\{Z > \frac{1}{\sigma\sqrt{\tau}}(S_t - K)\right\}$$
$$= N(h)$$

where

$$h = \frac{1}{\sigma\sqrt{\tau}}(S_t - K)$$

Step 2: Evaluation of $pE\{S_T \mid S_T > K\}$

$$pE\{S_T \mid S_T > K\} = \frac{1}{\sqrt{2\pi}} \int_{S_T > K} S_T e^{-x^2/2} dx$$

$$= \frac{1}{\sqrt{2\pi}} \int_{S_T + \sigma\sqrt{\tau}x > K} (S_T + \sigma\sqrt{\tau}x) e^{-x^2/2} dx$$

$$= \frac{1}{\sqrt{2\pi}} \int_{x > \frac{1}{\sigma\sqrt{\tau}}(K - S_t)} (S_T + \sigma\sqrt{\tau}x) e^{-x^2/2} dx$$

$$= S_T \frac{1}{\sqrt{2\pi}} \int_{x = \frac{1}{\sigma\sqrt{\tau}}(K - S_t)}^{+\infty} e^{-x^2/2} dx + \sigma\sqrt{\tau}\frac{1}{\sqrt{2\pi}} \int_{x = \frac{1}{\sigma\sqrt{\tau}}(K - S_t)}^{+\infty} x e^{-x^2/2} dx$$

$$= S_T \frac{1}{\sqrt{2\pi}} \int_{-\infty}^{x = \frac{1}{\sigma\sqrt{\tau}}(S_t - K)} e^{-x^2/2} dx + \sigma\sqrt{\tau}\frac{1}{\sqrt{2\pi}} \int_{y = \frac{1}{2}\left[\frac{1}{\sigma\sqrt{\tau}}(S_t - K)\right]^2}^{+\infty} e^{-y} dy$$

$$= S_t N(h) - \sigma\sqrt{\tau}\frac{1}{\sqrt{2\pi}}\left[e^{-y}\right]_{y = h^2/2}^{+\infty}$$

$$= S_t N(h) + \sigma\sqrt{\tau}\frac{1}{\sqrt{2\pi}} e^{-h^2/2}$$

$$= S_t N(h) - \sigma\sqrt{\tau} N'(h)$$

Substituting these results into Equation 4 gives the formula for the value of a SYCURVE call option:

$$C_t = e^{-rt}\left[(S_t - K)N(h) + \sigma\sqrt{\tau}N'(h)\right] \qquad (5)$$

where

$$h = \frac{1}{\sigma\sqrt{\tau}}(S_t - K)$$

This completes our derivation of the SYCURVE call option formula. The only other formula that may be of interest is the hedge ratio (the delta, Δ_C) of the SYCURVE call option. The delta is equal to the sensitivity of the SYCURVE call option value to changes in the forward yield spread. In particular,

$$\Delta_C = \frac{\partial C_t}{\partial S_t} \qquad (6)$$

$$= e^{-r\tau}N(h)$$

Most spreadsheet programs and hand-held calculators do not have the ability to solve directly for the standard normal distribution, $N(h)$. Fortunately, there is a reasonably accurate polynomial approximation of $N(h)$ valid for $h \geq 0$, which is[23]

$$N(h) = 1 - N'(h)(b_1 z + b_2 z^2 + b_3 z^3 + b_4 z^4 + b_5 z^5)$$

where

$$z = \frac{1}{1 + ah}$$
$$a = 0.2316419$$
$$b_1 = 0.319381530$$
$$b_2 = -0.356563782$$
$$b_3 = 1.781477937$$
$$b_4 = -1.821255978$$
$$b_5 = 1.330274429$$

For $h < 0$, we invoke the identity $N(h) = 1 - N(-h)$ and use the above polynomial approximation to solve for $N(-h)$.

---

[23] Milton Abramowitz and Irene A. Stegun, *Handbook of Mathematical Functions* (Washington, DC: National Bureau of Standards, 1972), Equation 26.2.17.

Though we will not reproduce the derivation here, we can use put-call parity to find the formula for a SYCURVE put option, P_t:

$$P_t = e^{rt}\left[(K - S_t)(1 - N(h)) + \sigma\sqrt{\tau}N'(h)\right] \tag{7}$$

where, again

$$h = \frac{1}{\sigma\sqrt{\tau}}(S_t - K)$$

Finally, the hedge ratio (the delta, Δ_p) of a SYCURVE put option is equal to

$$\Delta_p = \frac{\partial P_t}{\partial S_t} \tag{8}$$

$$= e^{-r\tau}(N(h) - 1)$$

Example: Value of a 30-Day SYCURVE 2/30 Call Option

Now, at last, we are able to value a SYCURVE call option on the yield spread between the 8⅛s of May 2021 and the 6⅞s of July 1993. Suppose, on September 17, 1991, we wish to determine the value of a SYCURVE call option expiring on October 17, 1991. We saw earlier that the forward yield spread is 178.0 bp. Suppose we choose the strike yield spread also to be 178.0 bp (we say the option is at the money on a forward basis) and we use 72.6 bp as the (annualized) expected future volatility of the forward yield spread over the life of the option. To review,

Trade date, t = September 17, 1991

Expiration date, T = October 17, 1991

t = 30 calendar days

= 23 trading days

= 0.08984375 years

s = 72.6 bp

S_t = 178.0 bp

K = 178.0 bp

and therefore

$$e^{-rt} = 0.99552016$$

$$h = 0$$

$$N'(h) = 0.3989422804$$

$$N(h) = 0.5$$

where we have assumed a (continuously compounded) risk-free rate of 4.9975 percent, equivalent to a term repo rate of 5.40 percent (see footnote 21). After substituting these factors into Equation 5, we find that the value of a 30-day SYCURVE 2/30 call option is

$$C_t = 8.6425 \text{ bp}$$
$$\simeq 9 \text{ bp}$$

where we have rounded the result to the nearest basis point. In dollar terms, SYCURVE put and call options are priced at $10,000 per basis point per $1 million notional principal amount. If we assume a notional principal amount of $1 million, the premium of the 30-day SYCURVE 2/30 call at 178 bp would be $90,000. Exhibit 4–12 displays a graph of the value of the SYCURVE call option for several values of the forward yield spread.

E X H I B I T   4–12

Value of 30-Day SYCURVE 2/30 Call Option

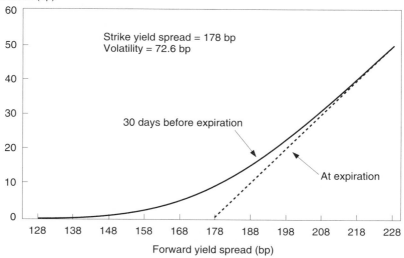

⑥ # OPTIONS ON MORTGAGE-BACKED SECURITIES

William A. Barr
Vice President
Fuji Securities Inc.

INTRODUCTION

Over-the-counter (OTC) options on mortgage-backed securities (MBSs) are a well-developed, long-established market. Sophisticated mortgage bankers use the market to hedge their pipeline, which is subject to fallout risk. Investors in MBSs enhance their returns by writing covered calls and puts on their mortgage portfolios. Market making in mortgage options is one of the services major dealers in MBSs offer their customers. With options on mortgages being a significant part of the general MBS market, understanding some of the unique features of this options market is important.

This chapter will discuss the conventions of the mortgage options market, the differences between Treasury options and mortgage options, the influence of prepayments on mortgage options, mortgage pipeline hedging, and split fee options. The chapter will conclude with two comments on mortgage options as a return-enhancing tool for portfolio managers.

This chapter was written when Mr. Barr was associate director of the Mortgage Department at Bear
Stearns & Co. Reprinted from *The Handbook of Mortgage Backed Securities,* 4th ed., ed. Frank
J. Fabozzi (Burr Ridge, IL: Irwin Professional Publishing, 1995), pp. 827–40.

MARKET CONVENTIONS: OTC OPTIONS ON MORTGAGE-BACKED SECURITIES

Options require specification of five items: (1) the underlying security, (2) the strike price, (3) the expiration date, (4) whether the option is a put or a call, and (5) whether the option is American or European. Following are the conventions the OTC mortgage options market uses to specify these items.

1. The underlying security is a TBA (the pools to be announced) MBS (GNMA, FNMA, FHLMC). The delivery month must also be specified for that security. The mortgage market prices forward delivery. If a mortgage option is exercised, the underlying mortgage must be delivered in the month specified by the option agreement. The option is valued using the price associated with the underlying security's delivery month.

2. The strike price is usually quoted as a price difference to the underlying price of the delivery month. For example, a dealer bidding at the money calls would set a strike price that is the bid price of the underlying security. A dealer offering a 1-point out-of-the-money call would set a strike price 1-point above the security's offer price. Finally, a dealer bidding a 1½ point out-of-the-money put would set the strike 1½ points down from the offer side of the market. Of course, a customer can ask a dealer to bid or offer an option with a specific strike.

3. Expiration dates for OTC mortgage options are also known as notification dates. Expiration/notification dates can be any business day prior to one week before delivery; the week before delivery allows time for inventory adjustments and allocations. Mortgage bankers seem to prefer expiration dates two weeks prior to the mortgage delivery date. The dealer community trades with expiration dates one week prior to mortgage delivery. If a customer does not specify the expiration date, the option is priced to the same date as is the dealer convention, that is, one week prior to mortgage delivery.

4. The option must be a put or a call.

5. The American or European designation of the option is not relevant. The dealer convention is that mortgage options are always European. The delivery of the underlying mortgage security and the delivery of the mortgage if the option is exercised are on the

same date, and therefore there is virtually no carry component in the option value that could induce an early exercise.

DIFFERENCES AMONG TREASURY OPTIONS, OTC AND EXCHANGE-TRADED OPTIONS, AND OTC MORTGAGE OPTIONS

The primary difference between mortgage options and Treasury options is the underlying securities. To choose between one and the other is to take a position in the relative pricing of mortgages versus Treasuries. Also, depending on the maturity of the Treasury underlying the option, there could be yield curve risk as well. (Mortgage options versus options on a 10-year Treasury note would entail mortgage/Treasury pricing risk and little yield curve risk. Mortgage options versus options on a 30-year Treasury bond or 2-year Treasury note would include yield curve risk.) To choose between options on mortgages and options on Treasuries is therefore to make a market sector position decision.

INSTITUTIONAL DIFFERENCES BETWEEN EXCHANGE-TRADED TREASURY OPTIONS AND OTC MORTGAGE OPTIONS

The institutional distinction between the OTC mortgage options and OTC Treasury options markets is nominal. However, the institutional difference between the OTC options market and the exchange-traded options market is great. What are the differences between these two markets? Should positions ever be taken in exchange-traded Treasury options for institutional reasons when a position in mortgage options is preferred? The seven most important differences are as follows:

1. *Underlying security:* A Treasury futures contract is the underlying instrument for the exchange-traded option. A specific MBS is the underlying security for an OTC mortgage option. Since an exchange-traded option is in lieu of a mortgage option, there is relative price risk of the futures contract to the mortgage market. In particular, the price risk of a position in exchange-traded options incorporates cash/futures relative price risk, potential yield curve risk, and mortgage/Treasury relative price risk. No relative price risk is associated with mortgage options, since the underlying security is a mortgage.

2. *Strikes:* There is only a set number of strikes to choose from in the exchange-traded options market. With OTC mortgage options, the customer can choose any strike. There is no restriction on the strike of an OTC mortgage option.

3. *Expiration dates:* There is only a set number of expiration dates to choose from in the exchange-traded options market. The expiration dates are one day a month, and the months with expirations dates are the current month and March, June, September, and December. With OTC mortgage options, the customer can choose any expiration date up to one week prior to the mortgage delivery date. There is no restriction on the expiration date of an OTC mortgage option.

4. *Option liquidity:* With exchange-traded options the bid-ask spread is $\frac{3}{64}$ths for front month expiration dates and $\frac{6}{64}$ths to $\frac{10}{64}$ths for back month expiration dates. Generally, $100 million par amount (1,000 contracts) can trade at these prices. The bid-ask spread for mortgage options across the dealer market for front month expiration dates is $\frac{3}{64}$ths to $\frac{6}{64}$ths (often the option price market is locked, with the only distinction being the strike). For back month options, the bid-ask spread is $\frac{4}{64}$ths to $\frac{8}{64}$ths. Exactly as with the exchange-traded options, $100 million par amount can trade at these prices. The option bid-ask spreads in both markets incorporate the price spread in the underlying security, and therefore are comparable. No liquidity is lost in trading OTC mortgage options.

5. *Pricing information:* Pricing information is readily available from price vendors for exchange-traded options. This information can be supplied real-time. For OTC mortgage options, access to pricing information requires calling dealers for quotes. With a pricing service, price information is more readily available for exchange-traded options than for OTC mortgage options. Without a price service, there is no difference between OTC mortgage options and exchange-traded options in the accessibility of price information.

6. *Commissions:* Commissions are associated with trading exchange-traded options. The prices quoted in the market are gross prices and not net commissions paid. In the OTC mortgage market, the prices quoted are net. No additional fees are paid with an OTC mortgage option trade.

7. *Credit:* When buying options at an exchange, the contraparty credit exposure is with the exchange's clearing corporation. There is also credit exposure to the clearing member with whom the option position is held. The credit exposure of an OTC mortgage option is with the dealer from whom the option is bought.

There is no reason to position exchange-traded Treasury options when the preferred trade position is mortgage options. The only significant institutional distinction between OTC mortgage options and exchange-traded options is with respect to credit exposure. If the OTC option is purchased from a well-capitalized dealer, this distinction is nominal. The decision to position in OTC mortgage options versus exchange-traded options should be purely an economic one.

THE IMPACT OF PREPAYMENTS ON MORTGAGE OPTION PRICING

Mortgage option pricing is affected by the underlying mortgage's prepayment expectations. In particular, the faster the expected prepayment speeds of an option's underlying MBS, the lower the implied volatility used to value the option.

Prepayment of principal is a characteristic of MBSs. The prepayment of principal will shorten the life/maturity of an MBS. Modified duration is determined in part by the maturity of a security. With MBSs, it is estimated using the best guess of the mortgage's future prepayments.

When yields change, the change in a security's price is a function of the security's modified duration. The larger the modified duration, the greater a security's price change for a given change in yields. Price volatility is therefore a function of modified duration.

Prepayment speeds determine the maturity of an MBS, maturity determines the security's modified duration, and modified duration determines price volatility. Therefore, prepayments and the market's best estimates of future prepayment speeds influence the price volatility of an MBS. Since expected volatility is a fundamental part of option pricing and positioning, estimates of future mortgage prepayment speeds significantly influence option prices.

The likelihood of prepayment speeds being high or low is in part a function of alternative financing opportunities in the mortgage market. If an existing MBS has a high coupon relative to the current market mortgage origination rates (the price of the security would be above par), the prepayment speed is expected to be high. If an existing MBS has a low coupon relative to the current market mortgage origination rates (the price of the security would be below par), the prepayment speed is expected to be low. Therefore, MBSs priced above par have shorter expected maturities, shorter modified durations, and lower price volatilities (given equal yield volatilities) than MBSs priced below par.

The impact of prepayment speeds on option pricing is significant. The higher the coupon of the MBS, the lower the option-implied price volatility. Exhibit 5–1 lists at-the-money option prices and implied price volatilities for GNMA securities expiring in May 1991. One can see how the implied volatilities fall as the coupons increase.

Also, for MBSs that are priced in the market near par and above, the strike price of an option will affect an option's implied price volatility. For these securities, out-of-the-money puts (and in-the-money calls) will have higher implied price volatilities than out-of-the-money calls (and in-the-money puts). Currently (April 11, 1991), the options market values strikes that are different from at the money with a change in implied price volatility of 0.3 percent per point. For options with strikes below at the money, implied volatility increases 0.3 percent per point compared with the at-the-money implied volatility. For options with strikes above at the money, implied volatility decreases 0.3 percent per point. (For example, if at-the-money options are valued at 5.0 percent implied price volatility, 2-point out-of-the-money puts will be valued at 5.6 percent implied price volatility. One-point out-of-the-money calls will be valued at 4.7 percent implied price volatility.)

E X H I B I T   5–1

At-the-Money Option Prices for GNMA Securities, Trade Date
March 25, 1991

Coupon	May Price	Implied Volatility	Option Price	Expiration Date
8.00	94:03	5.78	0:24	5/07
9.50	96:25	5:48	0:23+	5/07
9.00	99:14	5.07	0:22	5/07
10.00	103:75	4.01	0:19+	5/13
10.50	105:15	3.20	0:15+	5/13
11.00	107:10	2.59	0:13	5/13

The fact that the strike price influences the implied volatility of an option for current- and premium-priced MBSs is not surprising. Existing prepayment expectations are embedded in at-the-money options. For out-of-the-money options, not only are existing prepayment expectations accounted for in the option pricing; the change in prepayment expectations if the option moved closer to being at the money is also incorporated (i.e., the market price of the underlying security moved toward the strike price). If, for example, an MBS is priced at 99:00 and a call option on the MBS with a 102:00 strike is priced, the implied volatility to price the option will incorporate both the prepayment expectations currently in the market with the 99:00 price and the expected prepayment speeds consistent with a 102:00 price level.

To summarize, prepayments influence option pricing in two ways. First, across MBSs, the higher the price of an MBS is, the faster its expected prepayment speed will be; the faster expected prepayment speeds are, the lower the implied price volatility used to value options on that MBS will be. Second, with a particular MBS, the higher (lower) the strike relative to at the money is, the lower (higher) the implied price volatility used to value the option will be. This option pricing adjustment is due to changes in expected prepayment speeds associated with the market moving to a price level that would make the strike at the money.

HEDGING THE OPTION EMBEDDED IN THE MORTGAGE PIPELINE

The management of mortgage pipeline risk is one of the primary determinants of a mortgage banker's profitability. The key to managing this risk efficiently and effectively is to understand that a major component of this risk is option risk. A mortgage banker who issues a commitment letter or who guarantees a firm rate when accepting a mortgage application has sold a put option to the potential borrower. After a commitment is made, the homeowner has the right, but not the obligation, to "take out the loan," that is, the option to sell or to put the mortgage loan to the mortgage banker. If rates fall or the home sale falls through, the homeowner may decide not to take out the mortgage. Thus, the mortgage pipeline manager has effectively sold a mortgage put option to the potential homeowner.

Managing the mortgage pipeline's implicit put option is critical to successful mortgage banking. In the following sections, pipeline risk is described and its put option component identified. Next, two ways to hedge the option embedded in mortgage origination are discussed. Finally, the way to choose between the two hedging methods is suggested.

Pipeline Risk–Price Risk and Fallout Risk

Price Risk

Mortgage pipeline price risk arises from the difference between the terms of the borrower's mortgage loan and the terms available in the market where the loan is sold, that is, the price paid and the price received (sold) for the mortgage. The longer the period between the time a commitment is made to a borrower and the time the mortgage is sold in the market, the greater the price risk.

Mortgage bankers can deal with this risk by selling and delivering mortgage loans as soon as they are originated. Mortgages, though, are costly to sell in small lots; better execution is obtained if the mortgages are grouped and sold in fairly large amounts. To group the mortgages into large amounts, the mortgage banker has to hold mortgages in inventory, and waiting to accumulate large amounts of mortgages in inventory exposes the mortgage banker to changing interest rates. Selling mortgages for future delivery is a way to hedge inventory risk while accumulating large blocks. However, the availability of future inventory to be delivered against the forward sale must be known with certainty. Selling forward against mortgage commitments subject to fallout can leave the mortgage banker short if the mortgages do not close. How does the mortgage banker hedge commitments subject to fallout risk? Hedging the fallout risk is hedging the option component of mortgage origination.

Fallout Risk

Fallout risk arises from the fact that the borrower can choose to close or not to close after the mortgage banker has made a mortgage loan commitment. Falling interest rates with cheaper alternative mortgage financing will cause closings on mortgage commitments to decrease. On the other hand, if mortgage rates rise, commitments with "locked-in rates" will have a high likelihood of closing, since alternative financing is more expensive. Rates up, the mortgage banker owns inventory; rates down, the mortgage banker is flat inventory. From the mortgage banker's viewpoint, he or she is in a lose/neutral situation. The fallout risk profile is exactly the same as the risk profile of a short put option.

Managing Fallout Risk: Two Alternatives

The solution to the fallout risk problem is to acquire a position that offsets the risk profile of commitments subject to fallout risk. There are two ways to acquire such a position: using OTC mortgage options or self-hedging.

Hedging with Options

OTC mortgage put options generate the same but opposite risk profile of the commitment fallout risk. Therefore, buying put options is one solution to the fallout risk problem. When interest rates go up, the owner of the put is short the MBS underlying the put. When interest rates go down, the put owner has no position in the put's underlying MBS. The mortgage banker has a win/neutral position that offsets the lose/neutral position of the fallout subject mortgage commitments.

What are the costs and benefits of owning put options? The cost is the price paid for the option; this fee is lost if the option is held to expiration. The benefit is that the price risk of the pipeline subject to fallout is known for certain and with at-the-money puts eliminated.

Self-Hedging

How does a mortgage banker deal with the lose/neutral characteristics of the mortgage origination fallout risk without using options? If the mortgage banker does nothing and sells only forward pipeline that will certainly close, he or she then faces the lose/neutral position for interest rates going up or down. When interest rates go up, the mortgage banker will experience a loss as he or she becomes long inventory that was subject to fallout risk but is not yet sold. When interest rates come down, the mortgage banker loses nothing, since he or she never sold inventory forward that subsequently fell out. Alternatively, the mortgage banker could create a neutral/lose situation for interest rates up or down by selling all commitments forward, including commitments subject to fallout risk. If interest rates go up, he or she loses nothing, since the mortgages that are subject to fallout risk close and are delivered against the forward sells. On the other hand, if interest rates go down, the mortgage banker experiences fallout and ends up being short with the forward sells that were against the pipeline subject to fallout. The mortgage banker is betting on interest rates by following either course of action.

To self-hedge and not bet on interest rates, the mortgage banker can sell forward a "50 percent" hedge against the pipeline subject to fallout risk. The 50 percent hedge ensures that he or she is exposed only to half the fallout risk. If interest rates go up and all the pipeline subject to fallout closes, the mortgage banker is long only half the inventory subject to fallout risk. If interest rates come down and none of the fallout pipeline closes, the mortgage banker is short only half the inventory subject to fallout risk. The mortgage banker loses in both scenarios, but the losses are less than if he or she either does nothing or sells all the commitments and is wrong.

What are the benefits and costs of self-hedging? The benefit is that there is no fee. Unlike with a put option, where a fee is paid to own the right to sell mortgages, no fee is paid for self-hedging. The cost of self-hedging is the unlimited loss potential that is embedded in the hedge position. If interest rates rise or fall dramatically (such as in April 1987 and October 1987), the losses from hedging only 50 percent of the pipeline subject to fallout can be substantial. Also, since the loses are potential at the time the self-hedge is implemented, the uncertainty associated with a self-hedging program is a source of anxiety, and this anxiety could also be considered a cost of self-hedging.

How to Choose between Hedging with Options and Self-Hedging

The mortgage banker must compare the costs and benefits of the two hedging methods in the context of his or her future outlook on interest rate changes.

- Hedging with options
    Cost: The fee
    Benefit: No price risk and no anxiety
- Self-hedging
    Cost: Unlimited price risk and the associated anxiety
    Benefit: No fee

Hedging with at-the-money put options is the more cost-effective hedge if, by the option's expiration date, the market price of the MBS underlying the option is expected to move by more than twice the option fee. Self-hedging is the more cost-effective hedging method if the market price of the MBS is expected to change by less than twice the amount of the option fee. The mortgage banker must decide how much MBS prices will move over the term of the option and compare that movement with the option price. The mortgage banker must also decide on the value of anxiety associated with the unlimited loss potential of self-hedging.

No matter which hedging method is chosen, there is a cost to hedging. The best result the mortgage banker can achieve is zero cost (which results from self-hedging with no subsequent price movement and buying back the hedge at the original sell price). The cost of the implicit put that is a part of mortgage origination cannot be escaped. The mortgage banker can minimize that cost only by choosing the best hedging strategy.

SPLIT FEE OPTIONS

A split fee option is an option on an option. Split fee options are a commonly sold instrument in the OTC mortgage options market. The customers generally are mortgage bankers, who purchase them as an alternative to purchasing traditional OTC mortgage options when hedging their pipeline risk. Split fee options are also known as *compound options, calls on puts,* or *calls on calls.* This discussion will describe the characteristics of split fee options and give a framework for deciding whether or not to position them relative to traditional option positions.

Traditional options require five characteristics to be specified: a strike, an expiration date, an underlying security, whether the option is a put or a call, and whether the option is American or European. With traditional options, the option owner will decide on the expiration date whether or not to exercise the option. There is only one decision for the option owner after the option is purchased.

Split fee options require the above five characteristics and two more, a second fee and a second fee expiration date (the window date). A fee is paid today for the split fee option. Then, on the window date, the split fee option owner decides whether or not to pay the second fee. If the second fee is not paid, the option becomes void; if the second fee is paid, the option continues to be valid. Then the option owner must decide on the expiration date whether or not to exercise the option. With split fee options, there are potentially two decisions to make after the option is purchased.

With traditional options, the purchaser will specify the option characteristics and then ask what the fee or price is for the option. With split fee options, the purchaser will specify the five items of a traditional option, and then will specify the fee that will be paid today for the split fee option and the window date. The purchaser then asks what will be the second fee payable on the window date. The second fee is the decision variable with split fee options.

How is the second fee affected by the variables unique to split fee options and by implied volatility? The variables unique to split fee options are the window date and the amount that is set for the first fee (i.e., the fee paid today). The window date can be any day between today and the expiration date; the first fee can be any amount. How does changing the window date and first fee affect the second fee? Do different levels of implied volatility affect the sensitivities of the window date and first fee?

Exhibits 5–2, 5–3, and 5–4 compare a split fee pricing with a traditional option and show the sensitivities of the second fee to the first fee,

E X H I B I T   5–2

Fee Comparison: Split Fee Option to Corresponding Traditional Option

	Total Fee	First Fee	Second Fee
Traditional	1:04+	—	—
Split fee option window:			
3/28/91	1:09	0:16	0:25
4/26/91	1:17	0:16	1:01
5/28/91	1:29+	0:16	1:13+
Trade date:	February 26,1991		
Strike and underlying price:	97:17		
Implied volatility:	5.5%		
Expiration date:	June 11, 1991		
European put			

the window date, and the implied volatility. The price of a traditional option is also shown. The split fee option is on a GNMA 8.5 to be delivered if exercised on the regular PSA settlement date in June 1991. The date on which the split fee option is evaluated (trade date) is February 26, 1991. The strike price is at the money, which is 97:17. The expiration date is June 11, 1991. The split fee option is a put and is European. The window dates for the second fee are March 28, 1991, April 26, 1991, and May 28, 1991.

Exhibit 5–2 shows that the sum of the first and second fees is always greater than the fee of the traditional option. This relationship will hold for all window dates and for all combinations of first and second fees where the first fee is less than the fee of the corresponding traditional option.

Exhibit 5–3 shows the relationship of the first fee to the second fee for the split fee option with a March 28, 1991, window date. The first observation to be made from the exhibit is that the higher the first fee is, the lower the second fee will be. The second observation is that this relationship between fees is not linear. For a 32nd change ($312.50/million par amount) in the first fee, changes in the second fee vary depending on the initial level of the first fee. For a set change in the first fee, the smaller the initial level of the first fee, the larger the change in the second fee. The third observation is that the higher the implied volatility, the higher the second fee, and this relationship is linear.

E X H I B I T   5–3

Second Fee Sensitivity to Implied Volatilities and First Fee

	Implied Volatilities		
First Fee	**4.5**	**5.5**	**6.5**
0:04	1:12	1:26	2:08+
0:08	0:30+	1:10	1:22+
0:12	0:22	1:00	1:11
0:16	0:16	0:25	1:02+
0:20	0:10+	0:18+	0:27+
0:24	0:06	0:13+	0:21+

Trade date: February 26, 1991
Underlying security: GNMA 8.50 June
Strike and underlying price: 97:17
Expiration date: June 11, 1991
Window date: March 28, 1991
European put

Exhibit 5–4 shows the relationship of the second fee to the window date. The three window dates are March 28, April 26, and May 28. The relationship between the window and the second fee is not linear. The days between March 28 and April 26 are cheaper in terms of the second fee than the days between April 26 and May 28.

To summarize the sensitivities, the higher the implied volatility is, the higher the second fee will be. The lower the first fee, the higher the second fee, which will increase at a geometric rate. Finally, the farther into the future the window date is, the higher the second fee will be, which again will increase at a geometric rate.

Mortgage bankers use split fee options to attempt to reduce the fees they pay for their pipeline hedging. Instead of buying traditional options to cover their pipeline subject to fallout, the mortgage banker will purchase split fee options. The first fee of the split fee is less than the fee of the traditional option, and therefore initially the cost of hedging the pipeline is less than it would be using traditional options.

Now, if one of two events happens by the window date, the mortgage banker will be better off owning split fees than buying traditional options. First, the mortgage banker will benefit from split fee options if, by the window date, the amount of pipeline subject to fallout is reduced

EXHIBIT   5–4

Second Fee Sensitivities to the Window Date

First Fee	Window Date		
	3/28/91	**4/26/91**	**5/28/91**
0:04	1:26	2:18	3:11+
0:08	1:10	1:27	2:14+
0:12	1:00	1:12	1:27+
0:16	0:25	1:01	1:13+
0:20	0:18+	0:24	1:01
0:24	0:13+	0:16+	0:23

Trade date: February 26, 1991
Underlying security: GNMA 8.50 June
Strike and underlying price: 97:17
Expiration date: June 11, 1991
European put

from original estimates. By purchasing split fee options, the mortgage banker reduces the cost of his or her insurance by not paying traditional options fees for pipeline hedging that is subsequently not needed. Second, if implied volatility falls, the cost of the identical option in the market could be cheaper than the second fee. The mortgage banker, instead of paying the second fee, could replace the split fee with the same option more cheaply from the market. If the implied volatility fell sharply enough, the combination of the first fee and the price of replacing the option on the window date from the market could be less than the initial traditional option fee.

The cost of a split fee is the additional price that is paid over and above the price of the identical put that is a traditional option when combining the first and second fees. If the mortgage banker finally decides to exercise the second fee, he or she would have been better off purchasing the traditional option.

MORTGAGE OPTIONS TO ENHANCE
PORTFOLIO RETURNS

Options as a return-enhancing device is a frequently discussed topic. Therefore, only two points will be mentioned concerning mortgage options for enhancing returns.

First, total-return investors attempt to capture all the potential value that can be generated from a collateral investment. With securities, returns are generated from coupon income, price appreciation, financing specials, and price volatility. To capture the value derived from price volatility, the total-return investor must be involved with options. Investors can enhance returns by both buying and selling options; choosing which to do and when is the difficult part. When the investor does not think interest rates will change significantly over a time period, selling options over the same time period will increase returns by the amount of the option fee less any price movement. On the other hand, when the investor expects interest rates to change significantly, options are a way of creating leverage to benefit from the price move while limiting risk. Without participating in options, the total-return investor is leaving a major contributor of value out of his or her collection of investment tools.

Second, the mortgage options market is unique among short-dated options markets. For other options markets, the net sum of long and short option positions in the investor and dealer community is zero. For every option long in the investment community, there is an option short. With these options, no net value is created or lost in the investment community; only the price risk of the underlying security has been redistributed.

Mortgage options are different. Homebuyers receive from mortgage bankers puts as a part of the mortgage origination process. Mortgage bankers, in turn, buy puts from the dealer community to hedge the homeowner put position they are short. The dealers either stay short options or purchase options from mortgage investors. Unlike in other security markets, the investor and dealer community is net short options, with homebuyers net long options. To induce the investment community to accept the net short option position, homebuyers must pay a price for purchasing and taking away their options. By supplying a service to the consuming public, returns to the investment community from being short options on mortgages are probably higher than those from being short options on other securities, where the net investment community position is zero.

SUMMARY

Over-the-counter mortgage options are an integral part of the market for MBSs. Mortgage bankers need to look at the mortgage options market to determine the value of the option embedded in their mortgage pipeline, and to hedge that pipeline. Investors in MBSs can use options to enhance the returns on their mortgage portfolios. Knowledge of the mortgage options market is important to achieve these goals.

6

INTEREST-RATE CAPS, FLOORS, AND COMPOUND OPTIONS

Anand K. Bhattacharya, PhD
Managing Director
Manager, Taxable Fixed-Income Research
Prudential Securities Inc.

Interest-rate caps and floors provide asymmetric interest-rate risk management capabilities similar to those provided by options, except that protection can be customized to a much greater degree. As indicated by the nomenclature, *interest-rate caps,* also referred to as *interest-rate ceilings,* allow the purchaser to "cap" the contractual rate associated with a liability. Alternatively, *interest-rate floors* allow the purchaser to protect the total rate of return of an asset. The seller of the cap pays the purchaser any amount above the periodic capped rate on the settlement date. Conversely, the purchaser of the floor receives from the seller any amount below the periodic protected rate on the relevant date. The protection provided by caps and floors is asymmetric, in that the purchaser is protected from adverse moves in the market but maintains the advantage of beneficial moves in market rates. In this respect, caps and floors differ from interest-rate swaps. Recall that interest-rate swaps seek to insulate the user from the economic effects of interest-rate volatility, regardless of the direction of interest rates.

Interest-rate protection obtained by purchasing caps and floors can be customized by selecting various contractual features. The following decision variables are commonly used in determining the parameters of either interest-rate caps or floors.

FEATURES OF INTEREST-RATE CAPS AND FLOORS

The *underlying index* from which the contractual payments will be determined can be chosen from a set of indexes based on LIBOR, commercial paper, prime rate, Treasury bills, or certificates of deposit. Because these instruments are originated along several maturities, an additional variable associated with the index concerns the maturity of the index.

The *strike rate* is the rate at which the cash flows will be exchanged between the purchaser and seller of the customized interest-rate protection instrument. Caps with a higher strike rate have lower up-front premiums, although the trade-off between the premium and the strike rate is not directly proportional. Similarly, the purchase of floors with a lower strike rate does not result in a proportionate decrease in the up-front fee.

The term of the protection may range from several months to about 30 years, although the liquidity of longer dated instruments is not sufficiently high.

The *settlement frequency* refers to the frequency with which the strike rate will be compared to the underlying index to determine the periodic contractual rate for the interest-rate protection agreement. The most common frequencies are monthly, quarterly, and semiannually. At settlement, the cash flows exchanged could be determined on either the average daily rate prevalent during the repricing interval or the spot rate on the settlement date.

The *notional amount* of the agreement on which the cash flows are exchanged is usually fixed, unless the terms of the agreement call for the amortization of the notional amount. For instance, in "spread enhancement" strategies, which involve the purchase of an amortizing asset, such as a fixed-rate mortgage-backed security funded by floating-rate capped liabilities, amortization of the cap notional amount may be necessary to maintain the spread. Unless the amortization feature is included in the design of the cap, the spread between the asset cash flows and the liability costs will be eroded.

PRICING OF CAPS AND FLOORS

The *up-front premium* is the fee paid by the purchaser to the seller of the interest-rate agreement at the inception of the contract. This fee is similar to the premium paid to purchase options and is determined by factors such as the strike rate, the volatility of the underlying index, the length of the agreement, the notional amount, and any special features such as amortization of the notional principal.

The pricing of both caps and floors draws heavily on option pricing theory; for instance, an increase in market volatility results in a higher premium for both the cap and the floor. The strike rate for a cap is inversely related to the premium paid for the cap, because rates have to advance before the cap is in the money for the payoff to be positive. On the other hand, the strike rate for interest-rate floors is directly related to the up-front premium. A higher strike indicates that the likelihood of the index falling below this rate is greater, which indicates a higher likelihood of positive payoff from the floor. The longer the term to maturity, the greater the premium, because optional protection is available for a longer period of time. Hence, there is a higher probability that the payoff associated with these instruments will be positive. With respect to the payment frequency, the agreement with a shorter payment frequency will command a higher premium, because there is a greater likelihood of payoff and the payments are determined only on the settlement date. This may be an important determinant of cash flows, especially in highly volatile markets. Any advantageous changes in market volatility for interest-rate agreements with longer settlement frequencies may not result in a payoff for the purchaser of the agreement because the option-like characteristics of caps and floors are European rather than American in design.

There also may be additional contractual features, such as variable premiums, cost of termination options prior to stated maturity, conversion privileges from one program to another, and purchase of a combination of programs, such as *interest-rate collars* and *corridors.*

INTEREST-RATE CAPS

As noted above, an interest-rate cap can be used to create an upper limit on the cost of floating-rate liabilities. The purchaser of the cap pays an up-front fee to establish a ceiling on a particular funding rate. If the market rate exceeds the strike rate of the cap on the settlement date, the seller of the cap pays the difference. As an illustration, consider the following example, where an institution purchases an interest-rate cap to hedge the coupon rate of LIBOR-indexed liabilities, which reprice every three months.

Notional amount:	$10,000,000
Underlying index:	3-month LIBOR
Maturity:	3 years
Cap strike level:	10%
Premium:	145 basis points or 1.45% of $10,000,000 = $145,000
Settlement frequency:	Quarterly
Day count:	Actual/360

The up-front premium can be converted to an annual basis point equivalent by treating $145,000 as the present value of a stream of equal quarterly payments with a future value of zero at the maturity of the cap. Ideally, this should be computed at the rate at which the up-front premium can be funded for three years. Assuming that this premium can be funded at a rate of 9 percent and the cap has 12 reset periods, the annual basis-point equivalent of the up-front premium is 56 basis points.[1]

In this example, the payments to the purchaser of the cap by the seller can be determined as the quarterly difference between the three-month LIBOR index and the cap strike rate of 10 percent times the notional amount of the agreement. Specifically, the cap payments are computed as follows:

$$(\text{Index rate} - \text{Strike rate}) \times (\text{Days in settlement period}/360)$$
$$\times \text{Notional amount}$$

For instance, where three-month LIBOR is 11 percent, the payments made by the cap seller, assuming 90 days in the settlement period, would be determined as follows:

$$(11\% - 10\%) \times (90/360) \times 10,000,000 = \$25,000$$

The purchaser does not receive any payments when the reference rate, as indicated by the value of three-month LIBOR, is below the strike rate of 10 percent. The payoff pattern of this capped liability is illustrated in Exhibit 6–1. Because the annual amortized premium of the cap is 56 basis points, the maximum rate associated with the capped liability at a strike of 10 percent is 10.56 percent. In interest-rate scenarios where the value of three-month LIBOR is below 10 percent, the interest expense of the capped liability is higher than the unhedged interest expense by the amount of the amortization of the up-front premium. Given that the maximum risk associated with the purchase of the cap is limited to the up-front premium, the dynamics of caps are similar to those of debt options. On a more specific basis, because the purchaser of the cap benefits in rising-rate scenarios, the conceptual options analog is a strip of put options. However, caps can be purchased for maturities longer than those associated with a strip of puts. By increasing the strike rate of the cap, say, from 10 percent to 10.5 percent, the up-front premium (and hence the annual amortized premium) can be reduced. However, as illustrated in Exhibit

---

[1] This represents the annuity over three years, which when discounted quarterly at an annual rate of 9 percent equals the up-front premium of 145 basis points.

E X H I B I T   6–1

Effective Interest Expense of a Capped Liability

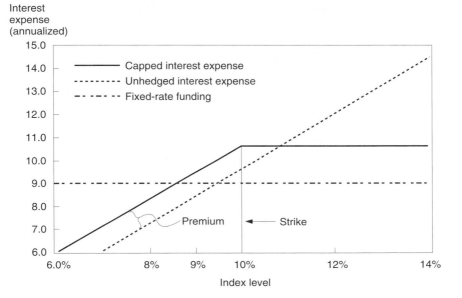

6–2, the maximum interest expense of the capped liability increases with a higher cap strike rate.

Several advantages are associated with the use of the cap in protecting the interest expense of a floating-rate liability. The purchaser of the cap can obtain protection against higher rates and also fund the liabilities as a floating rate to take advantage of lower interest rates. In this respect, the capped liability strategy can result in a lower cost of funds than certain fixed-rate alternatives.

In addition to capping the cost of liabilities, interest-rate caps can also be used to synthetically strip embedded caps in floating-rate instruments such as CMO floaters and adjustable-rate mortgages. For instance, consider an institution that owns a CMO floater bond that reprices monthly at a spread of 60 basis points over LIBOR, with a cap of 600 basis points over the initial coupon rate. If the initial coupon rate is 9.60 percent, the coupon is capped at 15.60 percent. Because the only sources of cash flow available to CMO bonds are the principal, interest, and prepayment streams of the underlying mortgages, CMO floaters are, by definition, capped. In this respect, CMO floaters are different from other LIBOR-indexed bonds, such as floating-rate notes. The institution could

E X H I B I T   6–2

Effective Interest Cost under Two Cap Levels

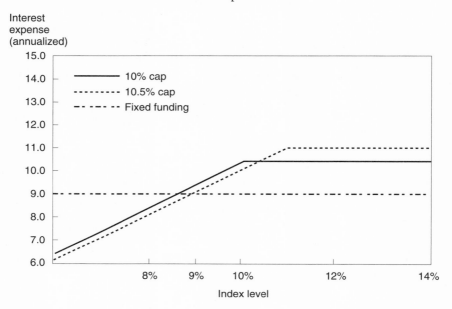

Interest
expense
(annualized)

strip off the embedded cap in the CMO floater by buying a cap at a strike rate of 15 or 16 percent. With a strike rate about 600 to 700 basis points out of the money, the cap could be purchased quite inexpensively. As interest rates increase, the loss in coupon by the embedded cap feature of the CMO bonds would be compensated by the cash inflows from the cap. The same strategy could be applied to strip caps inherent in adjustable-rate mortgages. However, the exercise of stripping caps associated with adjustable-rate mortgages is somewhat more difficult because of the existence of periodic lifetime caps.

PARTICIPATING CAPS

It is difficult to pinpoint the exact nature of financial instruments labeled as participating caps. A common theme in the definition of such instruments is the absence of an up-front fee used to purchase the cap. The confusion in definition arises from the variations of the term *participating*. One type of participating cap involves the purchase of cap protection where the buyer obtains full protection in the event that interest rates rise. However, to compensate the seller of the cap for this bearish protection, the buyer shares a percentage (the participation) of the difference between the capped rate and the level of the floating-rate index in the event that interest rates fall.

For illustrative purposes, assume that a firm purchases a LIBOR participating cap at a strike rate of 10 percent with a participation rate of 60 percent. If LIBOR increases to levels greater than 10 percent, the firm will receive cash flows analogous to a nonparticipating cap. However, if LIBOR is below the capped rate, say 8 percent, the firm gives up 60 percent of the difference between LIBOR and the capped rate, that is, $(10\% - 8\%) \times 0.6 = 1.2$ percent. In this case, the effective interest expense would be 9.20 percent (8.00% + 1.20%) instead of LIBOR plus the annual amortized premium, as in a nonparticipating cap. In bullish interest-rate scenarios, the effective interest expense using a participating cap would be higher than that for a nonparticipating cap owing to the participation feature. However, in bearish interest-rate scenarios, the effective interest cost of the floating-rate liability would be higher for a nonparticipating cap owing to the annualized cost of the up-front premium. An illustration of the effective interest costs using both hedging alternatives is presented in Exhibit 6–3.

E X H I B I T   6–3

Effective Interest Expense for Participating Cap

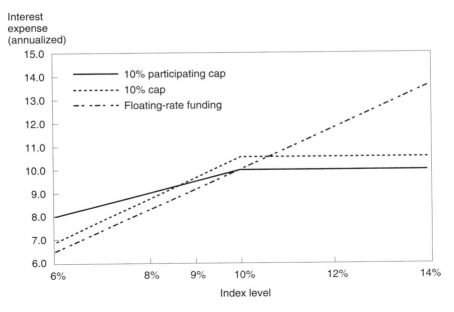

Other participating caps, also known as *participating swaps,* combine the analytical elements of interest-rate swaps and caps to create a hedge for floating-rate liability costs. In a participating cap structure, the firm uses interest-rate swaps to convert the floating liability rate to a fixed rate and uses caps to create a maximum upper limit on the remainder of the interest expense of the floating-rate liability. However, what distinguishes this structure is that the caps are purchased without paying an upfront fee. The purchase is funded by executing the swap (fixed-rate payer/floating-rate receiver) at an off-market rate involving a higher spread than the current market rate for equivalent-maturity swaps. Such participations can be structured in one of the following ways:

- The buyer decides the maximum rate on the floating-rate liability, which leads to the problem of determining the mixture of notional amounts of caps and swaps.
- The buyer decides on the relative mix of swaps and caps, which leads to the problem of determining the maximum rate level that can be attained with this combination.

Regardless of the choice by the buyer, the following relationship should hold in this type of participating structure:

$$\text{(Present value of annuity at } r_o - r_m, t) \times (\% \text{ of swap)}$$
$$= \text{Cap premium} \times (\% \text{ of cap)}$$

or

$$\text{(Present value of annuity at } r_o - r_m, t) \times (\% \text{ of swap)}$$
$$= \text{Cap premium} \times (1 - \% \text{ of swap)}$$

or

$$\% \text{ of cap} = \frac{\text{Present value of annuity at } r_o - r_m, t}{\text{Cap premium} + \text{Present value of annuity at } r_o - r_m, t}$$

where

$$r_m = \text{Current market swap fixed rate for } t \text{ periods}$$
$$r_o = \text{Off-market swap fixed rate for } t \text{ periods}$$

As an example, consider an institution that desires to cap a floating-rate liability expense that floats at a spread of 10 basis points over three-month LIBOR at a maximum rate of around 10 percent for a period of five years using this type of participating cap structure. The current market rate on a five-year pay-fixed and receive-floating (three-month LIBOR) swap is 80 basis points over the five-year Treasury yield at a rate of 9.40 percent. The current level of LIBOR is 9 percent, and off-market five-year swaps are priced at a fixed rate of 10 percent. The cap premium for a five-year cap indexed off three-month LIBOR at a strike rate of 10 percent is 200 basis points, or 2 percent of the notional amount.

The value of the annuity for five years is the difference between the off-market and the current market swap rate (that is, 10% – 9.40% = 0.60%). The present value of this annuity for five years at a discount rate of 9.4 percent (current swap rate) is 2.37185 percent. Therefore, using the above equation for participating structures, the amount of the caps is defined as [2.37185/(2.37185 + 2.0000)] = 54 percent. Hence, the amount of the swap is (1 – 0.54) = 0.46, or 46 percent. Using this structure, the effective liability expense in various interest-rate scenarios is presented in Exhibit 6–4. In this example, the synthetic fixed rate using swaps is based on the higher off-market rate, whereas the blended rate is determined as a weighted average of the cap and the swap fixed rate.

In bullish interest rate scenarios, the blended rate is higher than the unhedged expense owing to the existence of the swap. The full benefit of the fall in rates is attained only partially by the portion of the liability mix that is capped. As interest rates increase, the blended rate is also higher than current market swaps owing to the existence of the higher-priced off-market swap that is used to fund the cap premium.

INTEREST-RATE FLOORS

Interest-rate floors are used to protect the overall rate of return associated with a floating-rate asset. As an example, consider the case of a financial institution that owns adjustable-rate mortgages in its portfolio. In the event that interest rates decrease, the coupon payments on the floating-rate assets will be lower, because the repricing of variable-coupon assets is based on a floating-rate index. To protect the asset rate of return in bullish interest-rate scenarios, the firm could purchase an interest-rate floor. Analogous to

E X H I B I T   6–4

Effective Interest Expense Using Participating Cap Structure

LIBOR	Unhedged	Synthetic Fixed Rate 54% Caps	Capped Rate 46% Swaps	Blended Rate
11.0%	11.10%	10.10%	10.00%	10.046%
9.0	9.10	10.10	9.00	9.506
7.0	7.10	10.10	7.00	8.426

caps, the protective features of a floor can be customized by choosing various attributes of interest-rate protection.

As an illustration, consider the following interest-rate floor purchased by an institution to protect the return on Treasury bill–indexed floating-rate assets:

Notional amount:	$10,000,000
Underlying index:	3-month Treasury bill
Maturity:	3 years
Floor strike level:	8%
Premium:	85 basis points or 0.85% of $10,000,000 = $85,000
Settlement frequency:	Quarterly
Day count:	Actual/360

The cash flow dynamics of interest-rate floors are opposite to those of interest-rate caps, as illustrated in Exhibit 6–5. As can be seen in this illustration, a floor is beneficial in bullish interest-rate scenarios. Hence, purchasing a floor is analogous to buying a strip of call options. In bearish interest-rate scenarios, the floating-rate asset earns returns constrained only by the contractual features of such instrument (if any), such as

EXHIBIT 6–5

Effective Return of a Floored Asset

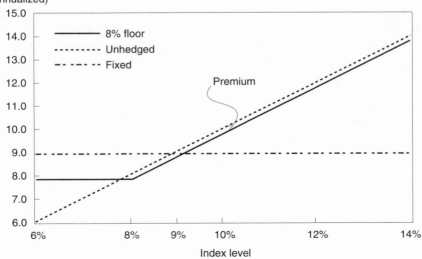

embedded caps. However, the asset return is reduced marginally by the amortization of the floor premium. In bullish interest-rate scenarios, where the asset returns are subject to erosion, the seller of the floor pays the buyer the difference between the strike rate of the floor and the value of the underlying index, adjusted for the days in the settlement period to compensate for the loss in asset coupon.

INTEREST-RATE COLLARS

Interest-rate collars involve the purchase of a cap to hedge a floating-rate liability at a higher strike rate and the sale of a floor at a lower strike rate to offset the cost of purchasing the cap. If the underlying index rate exceeds the capped rate on the reference date, the seller of the cap pays the firm the amount above the capped rate; if the market rate is less than the floor strike rate, the firm pays the buyer the difference between the floor rate and the index level. If the market rate is between the strike rate of the cap and the strike rate of the floor, the effective interest costs of the firm are normal floating-rate funding costs plus the amortized cap premium (outflow) less the amortized floor premium (inflow). The net effect of this strategy is to limit the coupon rate of the floating-rate liability between the floor strike rate and the cap strike rate. The coupon liability rate is adjusted by the net amount of the amortized cap premium paid and the amortized floor premium received to determine the effect interest cost.

For example, assume that a firm has floating-rate liabilities that are indexed at three-month LIBOR. In order to cap this floating-rate liability for one year, the firm purchases an interest-rate cap at a strike rate of 11 percent for a premium of 85 basis points. In order to offset this cost, the firm sells a cap at a strike rate of 8 percent for a premium of 60 basis points. The profit and loss profile of this strategy is presented in Exhibit 6–6. As interest rates rise above the cap strike rate, the firm receives cash flows from the seller of the cap, offsetting the higher outflow on the floating-rate liability. As interest rates fall below the floor strike rate, the falling interest expenses associated with the floating-rate liability are offset by the cash outflows to the buyer of the floor. In interest-rate scenarios between the floor and cap strike rate, no cash outflows or inflows are associated with the hedges. This results in interest expenses associated with the floating-rate liability equal to normal borrowing costs. However, effective interest costs will be slightly higher to account for the net cap less floor premium, unless the collar is structured with a zero premium.

E X H I B I T   6–6

Interest-Rate Collar

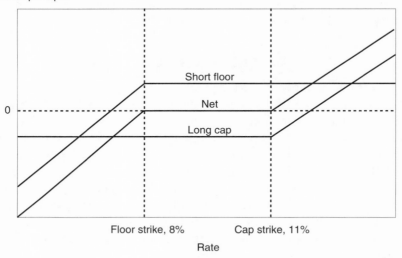

P&L per $ amount
of notional principal

The main benefit from an interest-rate collar is that the firm obtains protection from interest-rate increases at a considerably lower cost than with the purchase of a cap. However, in return for the benefit of the lower-cost interest-rate protection, the firm gives up the benefit from market rallies below the floor strike rate. Because the interest-rate protection is obtained without fixing rates, interest-rate collars are sometimes also described as *swapping into a bond*. However, this is an inefficient form of creating a collar because of the bid-ask volatility spread[2] associated with the structure. Given that the strategy involves buying a cap and selling a floor, the premium paid for the cap is based on a higher offer volatility, whereas the premium received for the floor is based on a lower bid volatility.

INTEREST-RATE CORRIDORS

An alternative strategy to reduce the cost of the cap premium is to buy a cap at a particular strike rate and sell a cap at a higher strike rate, reducing the cost of the lower strike cap and hedging the interest expense of a

---

[2] See the section "Termination of Caps and Floors."

floating-rate liability. In contrast to an interest-rate collar, the firm maintains all the benefits of falling interest rates, because there is no sale of a floor. As long as rates are below the strike rate of the lower strike cap, the effective interest expense of the firm is limited to the normal borrowing cost plus the amortized net cap premium. As interest rates increase above the lower strike rate, the interest cost to the firm is capped until market rates are above the higher strike cap. As interest rates rise above the strike rate of the second cap, interest costs increase by the amount of the outflow of the cap.

As an illustration, consider a firm that purchases a cap at a strike rate of 11 percent and sells a cap at a strike rate of 15 percent to offset the cost of the first cap. The profit and loss profile of this strategy is presented in Exhibit 6–7. At market rates below 11 percent, the caps are out of the money, and the firm's effective interest cost floats at normal borrowing costs plus the net amortized cap premium. As interest rates increase above 11 percent, the first cap is in the money and starts paying cash flows to the firm to offset the higher coupon associated with the floating-rate liability. This allows the firm to cap the effective interest expense at 11 percent plus the net amortized cap premium. However, at rates higher

E X H I B I T   6–7

Interest-Rate Corridor

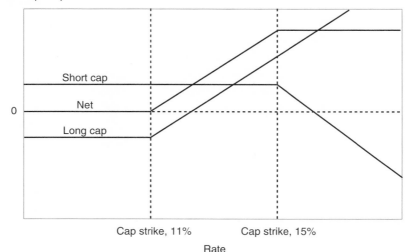

P&L per $ amount
of notional principal

0

Short cap

Net

Long cap

Cap strike, 11%   Cap strike, 15%

Rate

than 15 percent, the second cap becomes in the money and the firm has to start paying cash flows to the cap buyer. The net effect of this development is to increase the liability costs by the amount of the cash outflows associated with the second cap.

Although interest-rate collars allow the firm to offset the cost of capping floating-rate liabilities, a word of caution is in order, especially if the caps are struck under the auspices of a zero-premium strategy. Cap premiums are determined by principles of option pricing theory; consequently, the premium received for a 15 percent cap will be less than the premium paid for the 11 percent cap because of the higher strike rate and bid-offer volatility spreads. Therefore, in a zero-premium strategy, to equate the premium received for the higher strike cap to that paid for the lower strike cap, the notional amount of caps sold must be larger than the notional amount of caps purchased. Although this allows the firm to cap the liability rate at zero cost up to the strike rate of 15 percent, the firm is exposed to tremendous risk in a high–interest-rate, or "doomsday," scenario. As market interest rates increase to over 15 percent, the cash outflows paid to the buyer of the higher strike cap may negate any cash flows received from the lower strike cap and result in much higher interest costs than the lower strike cap rate. The extent of this offsetting effect will be an inverse function of the ratio of the notional amount of higher strike to lower strike caps: The greater this ratio, the smaller will be the effect of the cash inflows of the lower-strike cap and the higher will be the effective interest cost.

CAP/FLOOR PARITY

Similarly to put/call parity for options, which essentially specifies the relationship between these types of options and the price of the underlying security, caps and floors are related to interest-rate swaps. As an example, consider a strategy that involves buying a cap at 9.50 percent and selling a floor at 9.50 percent, both based off the same index, for example, LIBOR. This is equivalent to entering into an interest-rate swap, paying fixed at 9.5 percent, and receiving floating payments based on LIBOR. If interest rates increase to above the cap level, say 11 percent, the cap will pay 1.5 percent. At the same level, the holder of the swap will receive LIBOR at 11 percent. This translates into a positive cash flow of the difference between LIBOR and the fixed rate of the swap, that is, 11 percent – 9.5 percent = 1.5 percent. If the interest rates decrease to below the floor level, say, 7.5 percent, the holder of the floor pays the difference between the index and the floor strike rate, that is, 9.5 percent – 7.5 percent = 2 percent. At the same level, the swap holder loses the difference between the swap fixed rate and LIBOR, that is, 2 percent. Therefore, the cap/floor swap parity may be stated as

Long cap + Short floor = Fixed swap

However, for cap/floor swap parity to hold, the fixed rate of the swap should be paid on the same basis (actual/360 days, 30/360 days, or actual/365 days) as the floating rate, not a varying basis on the two rates. A graphical illustration of cap/floor swap parity is presented in Exhibit 6–8.

The cost of a market swap is zero because no premium cash flows are exchanged at inception. Therefore, using cap/floor swap parity, the cost of a cap should be the same as the cost of a floor struck at the same rate on an identical index. This relationship should hold irrespective of the pricing model used to value the caps and floors. Unless this relationship is true at every point, an arbitrage opportunity exists in these markets that could be used to emulate the characteristics of the overpriced instrument. For instance, if caps are overpriced, a synthetic cap could be created by buying a floor and entering into an interest-rate swap, paying fixed at the floor strike rate and receiving floating using the same underlying

E X H I B I T   6–8

Synthetic Swap Cap/Floor Swap Parity

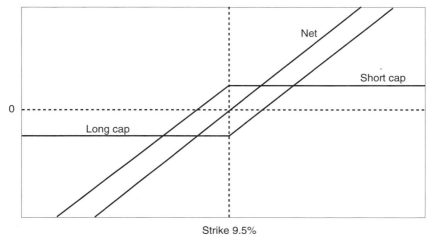

Strike 9.5%

Rate

index as the floor. Such arbitrage possibilities due to deviation from cap/floor swap parity also ensure efficient pricing in these markets.

TERMINATION OF CAPS AND FLOORS

As is apparent from the discussion of the characteristics of caps (floors), these instruments are essentially a strip of put (call) options on forward interest rates. Hence, caps and floors are priced using the same theoretical and analytical concepts involved in pricing options. The termination value of caps and floors can be determined using concepts similar to those involved in determining the market value of options (premium) prior to expiration; in interest-rate swaps, where the termination of swaps is based on the bid-ask spread to the Treasury yield, the bid-ask spread for caps and floors is stated in terms of volatility. On a practical basis, this is a much "cleaner" method of determining bid-ask spreads in the cap and floor market than deriving forward curves using bid and ask yield spreads. To compensate the financial intermediary for the market-making function, the offer volatility is higher than the bid volatility. Because option premiums are directly related to volatility, the difference between the offer premium and bid premium for either a cap or a floor prior to maturity will be directly related to the magnitude of the spread between bid and offer volatility.

COMPOUND OPTIONS

Interest-rate protection provided by conventional options, such as puts and calls, and derivative optionlike instruments, such as caps and floors, extends over a specified period of time. During this time period, the option may be either "exercised," terminated prior to maturity, or allowed to expire worthless. The exercise (or lack thereof) is triggered by movements either in the price of the underlying security (as in the case of debt options) or in the underlying index (as in the case of caps and floors). However, any termination of the optional contract prior to maturity is incurred at the expense of the bid-offer spread. Given that swaps, caps, and floors are usually longer in maturity than conventional put and call options, termination costs are likely to be higher for such instruments. Additionally, the interest-rate protection provided by swaps, caps, and floors falls more in the category of passive hedging because, with the exception of the exchange of cash flows, there is no ongoing active management of the hedge.

For a shorter time horizon where the holding (outstanding) period of the asset (liability) is subject to change, firms can use interest-rate debt options. Such options can be used to manage asset/liability spreads or off-set short-term opportunity losses associated with long-term interest-rate protection instruments. For instance, in rising interest-rate scenarios, where liability costs rise more quickly than the return on assets or the return on assets is fixed, put options can be used to offset the erosion in spread. The benefit of falling rates is still maintained as the loss on puts is limited to the up-front premium. Entities paying fixed in an interest-rate swap would be able to offset the opportunity loss in falling-rate scenarios by purchasing calls on Treasuries. In recent years, an important innovation known as *compound options* or *split-fee options* has allowed investors to limit losses of such short-term option strategies by permitting them to assess market conditions before purchasing additional optional coverage.

Compound options, which are essentially options on options, allow the firm to purchase a window on the market by paying a premium that is less than the premium on a conventional option on the same underlying instrument. The optional coverage can be extended at expiration of the window period by paying another premium. In essence, compound options provide an additional element of risk management by providing the opportunity to further limit downside losses associated with asymmetric coverage without sacrificing the essential ingredients of optional coverage.

Compound options allow the investor to purchase an option to exercise another option by paying a fee known as the *up-front premium* for a specified period of time. At the end of this period, known as the *window date,* the investor may exercise the option by paying another fee known as the *back-end fee.* Therefore, the label *split-fee* stems from the dichotomous nature of the fees paid for the combined option. Split-fee options also have been labeled *up and on* options; this terminology refers to the up-front fee and the back-end fee paid on the window date.

Comparison with Conventional Option Strategies

Compound options offer several advantages over conventional options, such as additional leverage and greater risk-management capabilities. This point is illustrated by contrasting the coverage provided by compound puts and calls with conventional options. The graphical representation of the profit profile of a long put versus a compound put is illustrated in Exhibit 6–9. As indicated in the graph, the net profit profile of a long put is the standard textbook representation. As interest rates decline, causing increases in the value of the underlying security, the losses associated with the purchase of an at-the-money conventional put are limited to the up-front premium (*CE*). As interest rates increase, resulting in a fall in the price of the underlying security, the option can be exercised and the underlying security sold at the higher strike price. The net profit from exercising the option is the difference between the strike price and the value of the underlying security less the cost of the option. the net profit profile of the conventional put option in bullish and bearish interest-rate scenarios is denoted by *HEA*.

However, with the compound put option, the same degree of protection afforded by the conventional put is available in bullish interest-rate scenarios at a much lower cost, as indicated by the up-front premium of *CD* in Exhibit 6–9. In the event that interest rates continue to decline, the compound option can be allowed to expire unexercised. On the other hand, if interest rates are expected to increase, the optional coverage can be extended by exercising the second leg of the compound option. The total profit from the exercise of the compound option may be less than that obtained from exercising the conventional put if the sum of the up-front fee and the back-end fee is greater than the up-front put premium. In the event that the

EXHIBIT   6–9

Long Put versus Split-Fee Option

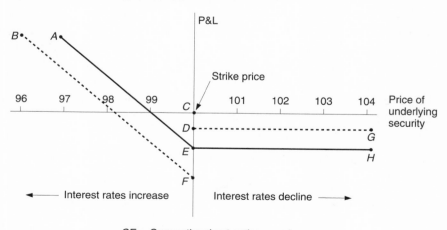

CE = Conventional put option premium
CD = Front-end fee for compound put option
DF = Back-end fee for compound put option

compound option is not exercised at the window date, the profit profile of the split-fee option strategy will be discontinuous, as indicated by *GD* in the graph. If the back-end fee is paid and the option is exercised on the window date, the profit profile of the compound put is *HEFB*.

Portfolio managers frequently will purchase call options to profit from impending bullish changes in the market. The rationale underlying this strategy is based on the expectation that if interest rates decline, leading to an increase in the price of the underlying security, the portfolio manager will be able to purchase the asset at the lower strike price. The profit profile of this conventional call option is compared to that of a compound call in Exhibit 6–10. As indicated in the illustration, if interest rates remain unchanged or increase, the losses of a conventional call strategy are limited to the up-front call premium. The profit profile of the call is labeled *QNJ* in the graph; the call strategy is profitable in bullish interest-rate scenarios. In bearish interest-rate scenarios, the use of split-fee options results in losses lower than those associated with the conventional call strategy because of the lower up-front premium. However, if at the window date interest rates are lower, resulting in the exercise of the compound option, the profit profile of the compound call is denoted by *PMOK*. If the compound call is not exercised, the profit profile of the split-fee option will be denoted by *PM*.

E X H I B I T   6–10

Long Call versus Split-Fee Option

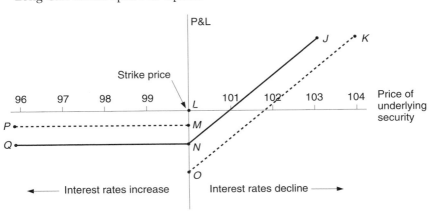

LN = Conventional call option premium
LM = Front-end fee for compound call option
MO = Back-end fee for compound call option

Uses of Compound Options

Compound options have been used mainly to hedge mortgage pipeline risk, especially the risk of applicants seeking alternative sources of financing or canceling the loan. This risk, known as *fallout risk,* is usually hedged by purchasing put options. The ramifications of fallout risk are especially severe if the expected mortgage production has already been sold forward. If interest rates fall and mortgage loans fall out of the pipeline, the mortgage lender can let the option expire unexercised. On the other hand, if rates increase, the lender can participate in the upside movement of the market by selling originated loans at the higher put strike price. With a compound put option, the mortgage lender can obtain the same optional protection at a much lower cost and retain the flexibility of extending the protection after assessing market conditions. If at the window date there is no need for put protection, the loss is lower than that of the premium of a conventional put. On the other hand, if additional protection is required, it can be purchased by either extending the compound option or by purchasing a conventional put option. For instance, it is possible that if forward market prices are higher (lower) on the window date, the purchase of a put (call) may be cheaper than exercising the option on the option.

Portfolios using active call-buying programs as yield-enhancement vehicles may purchase compound calls when there is uncertainty regarding an impending fall in interest rates. Instead of purchasing a higher-premium conventional call, the compound call allows the portfolio manager to purchase a window on the market for a lower cost. At the window date, if there is a greater degree of certainty regarding bullish market conditions, the compound options can be extended. However, if the degree of uncertainty increases, the loss is limited to the lower up-front premium.

Compound options, such as calls, can also be used in conjunction with longer-term instruments, such as fixed interest-rate swaps, to offset short-term opportunity losses caused by a fall in interest rates. However, perhaps the largest potential use of compound option technology lies in the application of these concepts to the cap and floor market in designing long-term options on options. Recall that caps (floors) are essentially a package of European puts (calls) on forward interest rates. The market for options on caps and floors, which allow the buyer to either cancel or initiate customized interest-rate protection, is still fairly undeveloped, but the potential uses of such instruments are enormous. As with any optional coverage, the development of such options on a series of options will add another element of flexibility provided by customized risk-management instruments.

SUMMARY

Swaps, floors and compound options are customized risk-management instruments. Whereas interest-rate swaps are intended to insulate the user from changes in interest-rate volatility, caps and floors are designed to provide asymmetric coverage in capping liability costs and protecting the rate of return on assets. In either case, the user retains the right to participate in upside movements of the market. To reduce the up-front cost of purchasing caps and floors, the user can either enter into participating agreements that involve giving up a proportional share of beneficial market moves or enter into agreements, such as collars and corridors, that are analogous to option spread strategies.

Because the termination of such agreements involves exit costs, these instruments may prove beneficial for passive hedging where interest-rate protection is desired for longer periods of time. By the same token, these agreements also should not be used if the holding period of either the asset or the liability is flexible or subject to change. For shorter periods of time, the user may decide to use split-fee options, which provide greater leverage and risk-management capabilities similar to conventional options, although contemporary use of split-fee options has been mainly in mortgage pipeline hedging. However, compound option technology can be applied readily to develop options on caps and floors, thereby adding an additional element of flexibility to these instruments in designing customized interest-rate protection.

OPTION PRICING

ⓖ # AN OVERVIEW OF FIXED-INCOME OPTION MODELS

Lawrence J. Dyer
Kidder Peabody & Co.

David P. Jacob*
Managing Director
Nomura Securities International, Inc.

$\mathbf{F}$ixed-income option pricing has evolved from an esoteric specialty into an important analytic tool in the fixed-income market. In addition to its obvious application in the large and expanding over-the-counter and exchange-traded fixed-income options markets, option pricing theory has been successfully applied to a variety of fixed-income securities and instruments with embedded options, including callable bonds, mortgage pass-throughs, and more recently commercial mortgage-backed securities, and complex liability streams such as single premium deferred Annuities (SPDAs) issued by insurers. Over time, researchers have developed increasingly complex option pricing models to represent the behavior of fixed-income securities. This chapter provides a critical guide to option pricing models in the fixed-income area. It reviews the theoretical basis of option pricing for fixed-income securities and appropriateness of commonly used option pricing models—modified Black-Scholes, binomial-on-yield, and yield-curve, or arbitrage-free models—for various practical option pricing situations. The comments on appropriateness of these models for option pricing are equally valid for the measurement of the duration of the interest-rate sensitivity of an option.

* David P. Jacob was with Morgan Stanley when the first draft of this chapter was prepared. Reprinted from *The Handbook of Fixed Income Securities,* 4th ed., ed. Frank J. Fabozzi and T. Dessa Fabozzi (Burr Ridge, IL: Irwin Professional Publishing, 1995), pp. 1171–1203.

Investors must choose the model they believe is appropriate for a given application. At a practical level, the choice of an option pricing model involves a trade-off between the degree to which the model approximates reasonable behavior assumptions for fixed-income securities and the costs of developing and using the model. Two criteria are used to judge a model. The first is how well the price process of the model matches historical and theoretical models of interest-rate behavior; for example, negative interest rates should be precluded or occur with negligible probability. The second is that the model should not allow risk-free arbitrage between option prices and security prices. The mathematical description of this condition may appear daunting. Its practical implication, however, is easy to understand: An option pricing model should not produce prices that allow the creation of an options position that will always produce a profit when hedged with an offsetting security position, or vice versa.

The most advanced models yield results that exhibit the nonarbitrage principle throughout the life of the security underlying the option. This may require thousands or even millions of calculations to ensure that the model does not allow arbitrage over the 30-year life of a long corporate bond or mortgage. Thus, while the most complex models require considerable resources to develop and use, they ensure that the results are reasonable. Using an inappropriate model can lead to incorrect value and duration estimates for the options under consideration. The cost of such errors can greatly exceed the cost of developing an appropriate model. Less complex models apply a more lenient standard for eliminating arbitrage opportunities, such as examining only a short-term rate rather than the entire yield curve. This produces acceptable results in some cases, but not all.

For example, a Black-Scholes model modified to price short-term options on bond futures or coupon bonds provides options prices that, for practical purposes, are not significantly different from those derived from the more complex fixed-income option pricing models that are available. Although these models may produce slightly different prices for similar assumptions, these differences probably would not allow a trader or an investor to earn a profit consistently. However, a Black-Scholes–like fixed-income option pricing model gives prices for long-term options on fixed-income securities that are inaccurate. It assigns high prices to some types of options on fixed-income securities that are easily shown to be worthless. Therefore, using such a model to value or hedge long-term options or securities with embedded long-term options, such as callable bonds, may lead to poor results.

This chapter reviews the fundamentals of option pricing and then discusses the assumptions and the theoretical merits of various models that have been used in fixed-income option pricing. The discussion is on a nontechnical level, relying on examples instead of equations to illustrate relevant points. The purpose of this chapter is to provide an overview of the various models and help practitioners decide which model is the most appropriate in a particular situation.

The next section reviews the basic components and principles common to all models. Three basic categories of models that have been used in pricing fixed-income options are then discussed. The assumptions underlying each model are stated and their theoretical merits are compared. Then the practical implications of those assumptions are addressed, and we answer the question "Which model should we use?"

THE BASICS OF OPTION PRICING

In principle, finding the price of a fixed-income option is a straightforward process. First, the price of the underlying security is projected forward to the expiration date of the option, and each price is assigned a probability of occurring based on a process that makes the expected returns from holding the bond equal to the risk-free interest rate. Then the payoffs for the option at expiration are determined by the security's price, the type of option, and the option's strike price. Finally, the current value of the option is determined by calculating the expected present value of its payoffs at expiration. Alternatively, a self-financing, dynamically adjusted portfolio that combines a position in the underlying security and either borrowing or lending at the risk-free rate of interest may be used to determine the value of the option.

Options come in a variety of flavors. Call options give their owner a payoff equal to the larger of the difference between the price of a bond and the option's strike price or zero. Exhibit 7–1 shows the value of a call option with a strike price of 100 at expiration and one month and three months to expiration for various bond prices. Put options also give their owner a payoff equal to the larger of the difference between the strike price of the option and the bond's price or zero. Exhibit 7–2 shows the value of a put option with a strike of 100 at expiration and one month and three months to expiration for various bond prices. In addition, an option may be a European-style option that cannot be exercised before maturity, an American-style option that may be exercised at any time before its expiration, or some combination of the two.

E X H I B I T 7–1

Value of an American Call Option with a Strike Price of 100

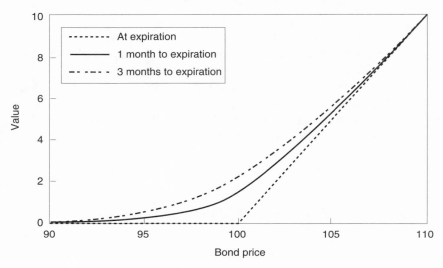

In practice, fixed-income securities present a number of complications that must be carefully examined if an option pricing model is to provide reasonable values. For example, the discounting rate used to find the present value of an option on a fixed-income security and the interest rate of the bond underlying the option ought to be correlated. This correlation significantly increases the complexity of finding the present value of a fixed-income security's payoffs and is ignored in many option pricing models. In many models, the discount rate is fixed. This can lead to inconsistencies. For example, if the short-term rate is fixed at 10 percent, and this rate is always above the return from holding the risky security, the pricing process provides no incentive for investors to hold long-term securities. These models result in option prices that would allow riskless profits if they were available in the marketplace. Eliminating this problem requires specifying the short- and long-term rates in the model carefully and thus introducing a correlation between them. Another complication is that a model may incorrectly define a process that drives a security price, for example, by allowing negative interest rates. In this case, the model may provide option prices that appear reasonable—for example, they would satisfy put/call parity—but will systematically misprice options.

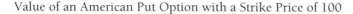

E X H I B I T   7–2

Value of an American Put Option with a Strike Price of 100

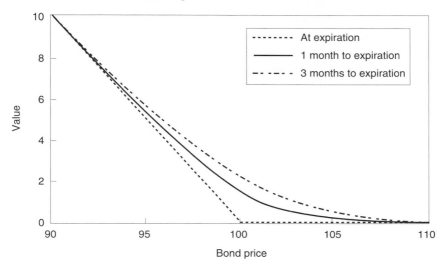

Bond price

The first part of this section discusses the principle of arbitrage pricing, which is the basis of analytical option valuation techniques. This
principle states that if two different investments or investment strategies
have identical cash flows, they must be assigned the same value by the
market. The option models discussed here use this principle to find the
cost of a dynamic, self-financing investment strategy that replicates the
payoff of an option; the value of the option must be the expected cost of
executing the strategy. The second part of this section discusses the
importance of correctly modeling the stochastic process governing the
behavior of security prices when constructing an option pricing model.

Arbitrage Pricing

If two investments produce identical cash flows with identical risks,
investors should assign them the same price. If this is not the case, a rational investor will simultaneously buy the cheap security and short the
expensive security. Because the future payoffs for the two securities
exactly offset each other, such an investor will earn the difference
between the securities' prices without incurring risk or investing any

cash. Of course, we have ignored many practical factors, such as taxes, liquidity, and transaction costs, that can cause prices to diverge between two otherwise identical investments. Including these factors results in a fuzzy zone where the prices of the securities may differ, but either the difference is too small to allow a profit to be locked in or institutional factors fully account for the price difference. If the price difference were to move outside this zone, arbitrage would be possible.

The following example illustrates how arbitrage arguments are applied to determine the price of an option. This approach is based on the insight that the value of an option may be hedged over a range of prices by following a particular trading strategy. With this strategy, the option is hedged by an offsetting position in the underlying security. This position is chosen in such a way that, for certain assumptions, it offsets the price change in the option for a given price change in the underlying security. This technique is also known as *delta-neutral hedging*. Though this technique mimics the price changes of an option that are due to changes in the underlying security's price, it must also include the effect of the leverage implicit in an option contract. This leverage, or borrowing, is designed to make the payoffs for a delta-neutral hedge exactly match those of the option. Because the payoff of the option is exactly matched at expiration, the cost of creating the hedge—that is, the cash investment required to set up the delta-neutral hedge—must be the value of the option for the assumptions in use.

Consider a security that has two possible future values: If state 1 occurs, the security is worth $100; if state 2 occurs, the security is worth $70. A risk-free security exists that costs $90 today and pays $100 in both future states. This translates into a risk-free rate of 11.11 percent. A call option on the security with a strike price of $80 is offered. The call would pay $20 in state 1 and $0 in state 2. Exhibit 7–3 finds the value of this option.

The first section of Exhibit 7–3 shows the equations that relate the option payoff in each future state to the payoff from a delta-neutral hedging strategy that combines holdings in the security and cash borrowed at the risk-free rate. The second section shows that holding two-thirds of a unit of the security and borrowing $42 in cash exactly replicates the option payoff. Note that the option replication strategy is independent of the probability of a particular state occurring and the current price of the security. The last section finds the value of the call option assuming that the current price of the security is $80. The value of the call option is the cost of the strategy that replicates its payoffs, namely, $11.33.

E X H I B I T   7–3

Delta-Neutral Investment Strategy That Replicates the Performance
of a Call Option with a Strike Price of $80

Section 1

The Option payoffs replicate the security payoffs and borrowing.

$$\text{State security payoff} \times \text{Amount of security} - \text{Borrowing} \times \left(1 + \frac{\text{Risk-free rate}}{}\right) = \text{Option payoff}$$

State	security payoff		Amount of security		Borrowing		Risk-free rate		Option payoff
1	$100	×	Amount	−	Borrowing	×	(1 .1111)	=	max (100 − 80, 0) = $20
2	$70	×	Amount	−	Borrowing	×	(1 .1111)	=	max (70 − 80, 0) = $0

Section 2

Holding 2/3 of a unit of the security and borrowing $42 replicates the option payoff.

$$\text{State security payoff} \times \text{Amount of security} - \text{Borrowing} \times \left(1 + \frac{\text{Risk-free rate}}{}\right) = \text{Option payoff}$$

State	security payoff		Amount of security		Borrowing		Risk-free rate		Option payoff
1	$100	×	2/3	−	$42	×	(1 .1111)	=	$20
2	$70	×	2/3	−	$42	×	(1 .1111)	=	$0

Section 3

The value of the option is the cost of creating the replacement portfolio.

$$\text{Current price of security} \times \text{Amount of security} - \text{Borrowing} = \text{Option value}$$

Current price of security		Amount of security		Borrowing		Option value
$80	×	2/3	−	$42	=	$11.33

The theory of modern finance requires that equilibrium prices among
all securities not allow riskless arbitrage among securities.[1] The preceding
example considered only the call option, the short-term rate, and the security underlying the call option. To eliminate arbitrage, a large number of
securities must be examined. For example, a 30-year Treasury bond may
be stripped into 59 coupon payments before maturity, along with a coupon
and principal payment at maturity. Each payment must be considered a

---

[1] For a complete discussion on arbitrage and option pricing, see Richard Bookstaber, David P. Jacob,
and Joseph Langsam, "The Arbitrage Free Pricing of Options on Interest-Sensitive
Instruments," *Advances in Futures and Options Research* 1, part A (1986).

separate security to rule out all arbitrage opportunities. Because of the large number of possible arbitrage situations, many models in use do not rule out all arbitrage opportunities. This is acceptable in applications where the violations of arbitrage are not so severe as to warrant the added complexity of an arbitrage-free model.

The insights from arbitrage pricing are used in another option pricing technique. Exhibit 7–3 shows that the price of the option does not depend on the probability of the underlying security's price moving up or down and that the option's price is independent of the expected return of the bond. Therefore, the option's price is determined relative to the bond price solely by arbitrage considerations. The implications of this is that investors can value options as though they were risk neutral. This technical consideration of financial theory implies that the option can be priced as if the expected return of the security underlying the option were equal to the risk-free rate, allowing the price of the option to be determined without solving the arbitrage equations.

Volatility

Stated simply, volatility is a measure of how much a security's price is likely to move in a given unit of time.[2] By convention, volatility is quoted on an annualized percentage basis. This section discusses the effect of an increase in volatility on the value of an option and also discusses the effect of alternative processes on volatility.

Volatility affects the value of an option through its effect on the underlying security's distribution of payoffs. Volatility may also affect the discounting process in models that incorporate yield curve dynamics. We will discuss the discounting process in the next part of this section as well as in our discussion of the various models.

An increase in volatility does not always cause the price of an option to rise, and a decrease does not always cause the price to fall. For example, the price of an in-the-money option may decrease as volatility increases because the increase in volatility increases the price range of the payoff distribution. If the new payoff distribution sufficiently increases the probability of the option expiring out of the money, the price of the option will fall. Volatility changes may also have nonobvious effects on fixed-income securities or strategies with explicit or implicit price caps

---

[2] Volatility measures are discussed in Chapter 16.

and/or floors. These include callable bonds, mortgages, and various option strategies (such as price spreads).

It is important to realize that intuition based on knowledge of traditional equity options pricing models can lead to false conclusions when dealing with the more complicated payoffs found in fixed-income securities, such as those from interest-only or principal-only strips of mortgage-backed securities or options on CMOs.

Discounting Procedure

The risk-free rate used in the discounting procedures in the preceding examples expresses the time value of money, which is obviously essential in valuing cash flows that are to be received in the future. In the more advanced option pricing models, this rate plays a central role in option pricing through its relationship to the nonarbitrage-pricing principle, because the replicating portfolio requires that some amount of money be borrowed or lent at the short-term riskless rate. If this risk-free rate is not specified carefully, the model will allow arbitrage. In the context of fixed-income option pricing, the proper handling of the risk-free rate is critical for the elimination of put/call parity arbitrage. This will be examined in detail in the next section.

To illustrate how the risk-free rate can affect the value of an option, we will examine the effect of a change in the risk-free rate in the example of Exhibit 7–3. The value of a call option on this security with a strike price of $80 and a riskless rate of 11.11 percent is $11.33. If we retain all the other assumptions but raise the riskless rate of interest to 17.65 percent, the value of the option will be $13.67, which is $2.34 higher than the price for the initial risk-free rate.

For options on fixed-income securities, a change in one interest rate is likely to be accompanied by changes in the interest rates of other maturities. For example, a change in the short-term rate would be likely to cause a similar shift in the direction of longer-term rates, and vice versa. Although modeling such interactions so that arbitrage opportunities are excluded is complex, it greatly affects the pricing of options whose expiration dates are near the maturity dates of the underlying securities. For short-term options on long-term bonds, such careful modeling of the discount process leads to only minor changes in option prices; in this case, the extra precision in the model is not worth the extra effort.

Representation of the Underlying Security's Price Process

In the preceding examples, the security could achieve only two possible values at the end of each period. These examples provide little detail on the process driving the price of the security or the relationship between the price of the security and other investments. In practice, discrete representations such as binomial or multinomial lattices, as well as continuous representations of security price behavior, are used to model securities' price behavior. In these models, the process by which security prices change is carefully constructed, though the different models may use different processes. While theorists search for the process that best represents reality, the practitioner should ask, "Are there simpler representations that will suffice in my situation?"

Obviously, a process that allows the yield curve to take on a multitude of shapes is more realistic than a simple binomial model of a bond's yield-to-maturity, where the yield of a security can move to only two possible levels from any point in time. However, the added complexity of a full yield-curve model will not result in any practical advantage in modeling a three-month option on a noncallable 30-year coupon bond when compared with simple models, because the effect of the bond's volatility will dominate the effect of any yield-curve reshaping. However, a more complicated option, such as one that pays off on the basis of the difference between two rates, may require a more complete model of yield-curve behavior or some other change in the modeling approach.

In the next section, we will show that many of the currently employed fixed-income option models assume an interest-rate process rather than a price process for the underlying security. The reasons for this will become apparent later; however, it is obvious that this approach leads to a host of questions that are not addressed by the equity models. For example, can one assume the yield curve moves in a parallel fashion? Should all rates along the yield curve be assumed to be perfectly correlated? Do volatilities differ systematically along the yield curve? Do reasonable processes admit differently shaped yield curves The answers to these questions will be discussed later in this chapter.

In evaluating alternative option pricing models, our approach is to compare the results with an eye to the differences in the underlying processes of the models. Two similar processes should provide similar prices. Although it would seem puzzling if different processes that appeared to be reasonable representations of reality produced radically different option values or option characteristics, in theory such an effect can occur.

Recent work has examined the effect of different interest-rate processes on the pricing of callable bonds.[3] In essence, the results of this modeling show that the value of an option may be significantly affected by the underlying process, particularly if the process assumes that rates are mean reverting. Differences in the theoretical value assigned to an option for different distributions are not unexpected in this case, because mean reversion significantly reduces the probability of a large change in interest rates. The good news is that the relative value among bonds is far less affected than is the absolute value assigned to the embedded option.

COMPARISON OF MAJOR MODELS

The Black-Scholes formula and its binomial counterpart, the Cox-Ross-Rubinstein binomial pricing model, have been well known among Wall Street quantitative analysts since their creation. Thus, it has been natural for analysts who find themselves involved in fixed-income applications to use these models to price fixed-income options. However, as the characteristics of fixed-income options have become better understood, new models have been developed that more accurately represent the pricing process of fixed-income securities.

This section discusses three basic categories of fixed-income option models. The first category includes applications of variations of the Black-Scholes model for fixed-income securities. The discussion of the characteristics of Black-Scholes also applies to binomial models, such as the Cox-Ross-Rubinstein binomial model, that are based on the same assumptions. Next, we consider a binomial model based on yield-to-maturity of bonds. As we will see, the main reason for the development of this model was to address concerns about the applicability of the log-normal assumption for bond returns in Black-Scholes–like models. The final category of models is composed of what we call yield-curve models. The common theme among these models is that, in one way or another, they specify the interest-rate dynamics along the entire yield curve. These specifications restrict the changes in shape of the yield curve both over time and for different interest-rate movements so that arbitrage opportunities in the model are eliminated. This increases the computational complexity and thus the cost of using such a model.

---

[3] See M. Hogan and S. Breidbart, "The Long-Term Behavior of Interest Rates and Options Pricing" New York: (Morgan Stanley, November 1989).

The discussion in this section centers on the major elements of each model and some of the models' relative strengths and weaknesses. The models' usefulness for valuing various types of options and securities will be discussed in the next section.

Black-Scholes

Fischer Black and Myron Scholes were the first to derive an analytic solution for the price of a European option on a non-dividend-paying stock. Their solution showed that the value of an option on a stock was determined by arbitrage considerations rather than by an investor's risk preferences or expectations about the future performance of the stock. The value of an option depends on five parameters: (1) the stock price, (2) the exercise price of the option, (3) the volatility of the stock's return, (4) the time to expiration of the option, and (5) the continuously compounded short-term interest rate for borrowing and lending. Their solution assumed that the logarithm of the stock's returns followed a normal distribution. An example of the price distribution is shown in Exhibit 7–4; this model assumes that the distribution of security prices is skewed so that higher prices are more likely to occur than lower prices.

E X H I B I T   7–4

Price Distribution Projected One Year Forward Based on an Initial Bond Price of 100 and a 10% Annual Price Volatility

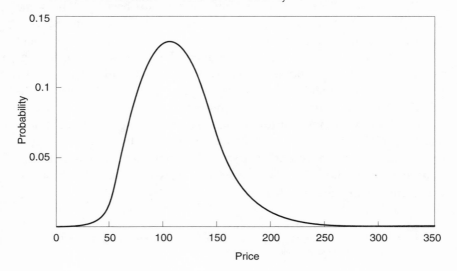

The following discussion illustrates a number of ways in which this model breaks down when applied to options on fixed-income securities and discusses some of the common "fixes" for these problems. The fixes are appropriate in some circumstances but not in others.

The Appropriate Price Volatility Changes over Time

Blindly applying Black-Scholes can lead to trouble. Suppose that the formula is used to price a three-year European call option on a three-year zero-coupon bond. Because the bond matures at the end of three years, its price at expiration must be $100; therefore, the value of this option must be the maximum of zero or the discounted value of par minus the strike price. Thus, its value depends only on the strike price. The option payoff in this case is independent of the process, volatility, short-term riskless rates, and the current value of the security, because the price of the underlying security at the expiration of the option is known with certainty. The first two rows of Exhibit 7–5 show how the arbitrage value of this option differs from the Black-Scholes prices for different strike prices. What went wrong with Black-Scholes in this case?

The most obvious problem is the volatility assumption of Black-Scholes as it applies to bonds. Because bonds have a finite maturity, the price volatility of a bond falls toward zero as time passes, whereas the Black-Scholes model assumes that price volatility is constant over time.[4]

E X H I B I T   7–5

Value of a 3-Year Call Option on a 3-Year Zero-Coupon Bond

	Strike Price				
	80	**90**	**100**	**110**	**120**
Arbitrage value[*]	$15.02	$ 7.51	$ 0.00	$ 0.00	$ 0.00
Black-Scholes value[†]	19.22	14.49	10.70	7.78	5.60
Black-Scholes value as volatility goes to zero[‡]	15.02	7.51	0.00	0.00	0.00

[*] Assumes that the three-year risk-free rate is 10% annual.

[†] Assumes a 4% price volatility, risk-free rate of 10% annual, and current bond price of 75.13.

[‡] Assumes a risk-free rate of 10% and current bond price of 75.13.

---

[4] Modifications of the model to allow for volatility changing as a function of the stock price were derived by John Cox and Stephen Ross in "The Valuation of Options for Alternative Stochastic Processes," *Journal of Financial Economics* 3, no. 1/2 (1976), pp. 145–66.

Is there any way to correct this deficiency? Taking the limit of the Black-Scholes value as the volatility approaches zero, as shown in Exhibit 7–5, gives the same values as the arbitrage-based argument. Note that this example uses the correct riskless rate for the Black-Scholes model—the zero-coupon bond rate corresponding to the expiration date of the option—not an overnight rate as is sometimes used. This approach does not, however, resolve the question of what volatility to use for other expiration dates.

Possibility of Negative Interest Rates
Even with the available quick fixes and adjustments, problems remain with using Black-Scholes in the fixed-income area. One of these problems can be demonstrated through the following example of an out-of-the-money call. Consider a 5-year European call option on a 30-year zero-coupon bond. If the 5-year riskless rate is 8 percent and the yield of the 30-year zero is 6 percent, the bond is worth $17.41 today. Further, assume that the price volatility for this option is 25 percent and the strike price is $102. The value of this option must be 0, because the bond can never be worth more than $100 unless interest rates are negative. Yet the Black-Scholes model assigns this option a value of $1.80. This is over 10 percent of the underlying bond's price of $17.41.

This error is due to the lognormal assumption for bond prices in Black-Scholes. Bonds have a minimum and a maximum price: The minimum price is 0 and the maximum price is the sum of the remaining cash flows associated with the bond (assuming interest rates are nonnegative). According to the lognormal price assumption, there is some probability that a bond will reach any positive price.

Adjusting for Coupon Payments
So far we have restricted our examples to zero-coupon bonds; in reality, most bonds pay coupons. Black-Scholes must be adjusted to reflect the effects of both coupon payments and changes in accrued interest for the underlying bond over the life of an option. The modification of Black-Scholes used in this case is the same approximation that is used for stocks with known dividend payments.

This modification results in the replacement of the current bond price in the Black-Scholes model with the price of the bond less the present value of any coupons paid and its change in accrued interest from the settlement date to the expiration date. Consider a six-month European call option struck at par on a 30-year, 10 percent semiannual coupon priced at par. The six-month riskless rate is 8 percent on a bond-equivalent basis.

The price volatility is 10 percent. The present value of the coupon payment (before the option's expiration date) in six months given the riskless rate of 8 percent (BEY) is $4.81 ($5/1.04). The value of the underlying security in Black-Scholes is therefore $95.19 (100 − 4.81). Substituting this price in the Black-Scholes equation gives a call option value of $8.06. This technique also adjusts for the pull toward par of both premium and discount bonds. Premium bonds tend to fall in price and discount bonds tend to rise in price because both will be priced at par when they mature. Note that we use the short-term rate for discounting; using the long-term rate would allow an investor to risklessly earn the long-term rate over a short-term period.

American Options

The final issue with regard to the Black-Scholes model is what to do in the case of an American-style option. Recall that American options, in contrast to European options, permit exercise prior to their expiration. Many fixed-income options fall into this category. The Black-Scholes model was developed for European options on non-dividend-paying stocks. Although American-style calls on non-dividend-paying stocks have the same value as a European call, in general an American option is worth more than a European option. This is because it is often optimal to exercise an American option before expiration.

The binomial option pricing methodology allows American-type options to be valued. This method was first presented by Cox, Ross, and Rubinstein.[5] In contrast to the Black-Scholes model, which is a closed-form solution to the option pricing problem, the binomial model is a numerical method. This approach parallels the examples in our first section; however, the price movements of the underlying security are specified in such a way that, for large binomial lattices, they follow the same lognormal process as the Black-Scholes model. Moreover, the binomial model can be used to solve the problems for which the Black-Scholes model is inappropriate, such as American calls on a dividend-paying security or American-style put options. But because the assumptions for the price distribution in this model are the same as in Black-Scholes, the binomial model requires the same modifications previously discussed and is subject to the same criticisms. The next subsection discusses how a binomial model can be adapted to solve for option values when the yield

---

[5] John Cox, Stephen Ross, and Mark Rubinstein, "Option Pricing: A Simplified Approach," *Journal of Financial Economics,* September 1979, pp. 229–63.

of a bond is assumed to be lognormally distributed. This approach answers the main criticisms of the Black-Scholes model for pricing short-term options on bonds.

Binomial Model Based on Yield to Maturity[6]

Exhibit 7–6(a) shows a lognormal yield distribution assuming a bond with an initial yield of 10 percent and an annual yield volatility of 10 percent after one year. The lognormal yield distribution is skewed; increases in yield are more likely than decreases, as shown by the tail to the right in Exhibit 7–6(a). Exhibit 7–6(b) shows the price distributions that result from this yield distribution assuming bonds with a 10 percent coupon and 1, 10, and 30 years to maturity. Comparing these figures with Exhibit 7–4 shows how the lognormal yield process model differs from the lognormal price process in the Black-Scholes model. Though the lognormal price distribution results in prices for all bonds that are positively skewed, the lognormal yield process does not. When yields follow a lognormal distribution, the maximum price of a bond must be less than the sum of its cash flows, and the minimum price is zero. The shape of the price distribution is determined by the effects of the yield distribution, the difference between the maximum price and the current price of the bond, and the convexity of the bond, Exhibit 7–6(b) illustrates that the combination is likely to result in a negatively skewed price distribution for short-maturity bonds that have a low maximum price and low convexity and a positively skewed price distribution for long-maturity bonds that have a higher maximum price and larger convexity.

The lognormal yield-to-maturity model offers a number of attractive characteristics relative to the Black-Scholes model. By definition, there is no possibility of negative interest rates, because the yields follow a lognormal distribution. Further, because the bond prices are calculated from a yield distribution for each period, they will reflect both the decrease in price volatility and the pull toward par as the bond ages. This was not true in the price volatility models discussed above.

The following example, shown in Exhibit 7–7, illustrates the binomial model based on yields. Consider a 1-year European call option on a 30-year zero coupon bond. In this example, both the 1- and 30-year interest rates are initially at 10 percent (BEY) and the yield volatility is 15 percent. As with the other models discussed thus far, the option's price is

---

E X H I B I T   7–6

(a) Yield Distribution Projected One Year Forward Based on an Initial
     Yield Level of 10% and a 10% Annual Yield Volatility
(b) Price Distribution Projected One Year Forward for Various-Maturity
     Bonds with 10% Coupons Based on Yield Distribution in Exhibit 7–6(a)

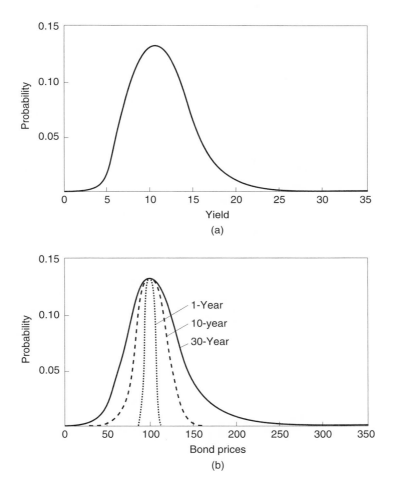

determined by arbitrage: The payoffs of the option are replicated at each
node with a portfolio containing the underlying security and borrowed
money. This requires that the yield lattice be translated into a price lattice
for the underlying bond. Section 2 of the exhibit shows the price lattice
for the 30-year zero-coupon bond in the example. Notice that the maturi-

EXHIBIT 7–7

Binomial Model Based on Yield to Maturity

Section 1

Yield lattice for a 15% yield volatility

Years forward	0	1	2
			13.50%
Projected yields	10%	11.62%	10.00%
		8.61%	7.41%

Section 2

Price lattice for a 30-year zero-coupon bond

Years forward	0	1	2
Remaining maturity	30	29	28
			$2.89
Projected prices	$5.73	$4.13	$6.93
		$9.12	$13.52

Section 3

Value of a call struck at $5.73 with the risk-free rate fixed at 10%

Years forward	0	1	2
			max (2.89 − 5.73, 0) = $0.00
Call values	$1.78	$0.45	max (6.93 − 5.73, 0) = $1.20
		$3.91	max (13.52 − 5.73, 0) = $7.79

Section 4

Value of a put struck at $5.73 with the risk-free rate fixed at 10%

Years forward	0	1	2
			max (5.73 − 2.89, 0) = $2.84
Put values	$0.78	$1.53	max (5.73 − 6.93, 0) = $0.00
		$0.00	max (5.73 − 13.52, 0) = $0.00

---

ty of the bond decreases as the lattice progresses through time. The option price is found following the methods illustrated in the first section of this chapter. The last two sections of the exhibit show the value of an option at each node in the lattice assuming that the short-term rate is always 10 percent. In this case, the value of an at-the-money call option is $1.78 and that of a put is $0.78.

The advantages of the lognormal yield process for bond prices over the lognormal price process are obvious. There are no adjustments to the inputs of the model to rectify its shortcomings as there are for price volatility and coupon bonds in Black-Scholes. Moreover, this model can easily value American-style options by solving the lattice equations.[7] In fact, the binomial lattice can handle the hybrid nature of options embedded in callable bonds, which are European during the call protection period and American thereafter.

Violation of Arbitrage-Free Pricing
In the above example, we assumed that the riskless rate was a constant. Aside from the lack of realism of this assumption, particularly over long periods of time, it may allow arbitrage opportunities between bonds and the riskless rate. If the riskless rate is not between the returns on the bond for the up and down lattice points, arbitrage opportunities exist. It is sometimes difficult to avoid such arbitrage opportunities. For example, as a bond approaches maturity, the returns for up and down yield shifts approach the yield on the bond; this is an identity at maturity. If the risk-free rate is fixed while the yield on the bond varies for a long-term option such as a callable bond, there must eventually be an arbitrage between the risk-free rate and the bond's return at some of the states on the lattice. As a result, these models are usually designed to have the riskless rate move along with the yield of the underlying security.

Exhibit 7–8 shows the values of the call and put in Exhibit 7–7, assuming that the risk-free rate is equal to the long-term rate in each period. This approach changes the values of both options slightly. The effect is larger for longer-term options and for higher volatilities. Although this method adjusts the short-term rate in such a way that obvious arbitrage opportunities can be avoided, it does not produce an arbitrage-free lattice. The lattice, which is based on a flat term structure and parallel yield shifts, may be shown to have arbitrage opportunities in two ways. Section 1 of Exhibit 7–9 shows that the European put and call values in Exhibit 7–8 violate put/call parity. Section 2 of Exhibit 7–9 shows that a duration-matched combination of a 1-year and a 30-year zero-coupon bond will outperform an equal investment in a 10-year bond over the first period if only parallel shifts of this yield curve are possible. Similar results may be shown for the rest of the lattice. This arbitrage between bonds on the yield curve makes

---

[7] The American feature is handled by replacing the value of the option at each point by the larger of the values of the European option or of immediate exercise.

E X H I B I T   7–8

Value of a Put and Call on the 30-Year Zero-Coupon Bond in Exhibit 7–7
When the Bond Yield and Risk-Free Rate Move in Parallel

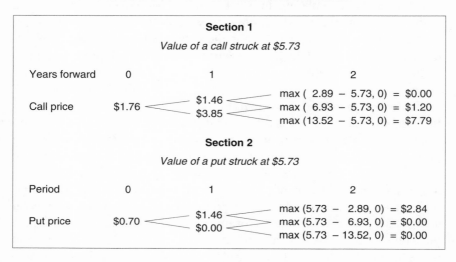

Section 1

Value of a call struck at $5.73

Years forward	0	1	2
			max (2.89 − 5.73, 0) = $0.00
Call price	$1.76	$1.46 / $3.85	max (6.93 − 5.73, 0) = $1.20
			max (13.52 − 5.73, 0) = $7.79

Section 2

Value of a put struck at $5.73

Period	0	1	2
			max (5.73 − 2.89, 0) = $2.84
Put price	$0.70	$1.46 / $0.00	max (5.73 − 6.93, 0) = $0.00
			max (5.73 − 13.52, 0) = $0.00

possible the violation of put/call parity. Another problem with this model is that the yield volatility on the lattice is constant over the life of the bond. This is reasonable for short time periods, but does not match the observed behavior of yields for different-maturity bonds. One would prefer a model in which yield volatility decreases as maturity increases. This would match the observed historical behavior of yield volatilities.

We now turn to a group of models that are internally consistent with regard to arbitrage between bonds of different maturities. Unfortunately, these models require considerably more work to define and apply than the models examined so far.

Yield-Curve Models

The two previous subsections showed that modifying equity option pricing models to price options on fixed-income securities leads to both practical and theoretical inconsistencies. The underlying cause of these difficulties has been discussed in a number of research papers[8] and can be summarized as follows: *A theoretically consistent fixed-income option pricing model must specify the dynamics of the yield curve in such a way*

---

[8] For example, see J. Harrison and D. Kreps, "Martingales and Arbitrage in Multiperiod Securities
    Markets," *Journal of Economic Theory* 20, no. 3 (June 1979), and Bookstaber, Jacob, and
    Langsam, "The Arbitrage Free Pricing of Options."

E X H I B I T   7–9

Signs of an Arbitrage-Ridden Lattice

Section 1

Violation of a put/call parity for floating short-term rate in Exhibit 7–8

Put/Call Parity Relationship

$$\begin{matrix} \text{Call} \\ \text{price} \end{matrix} - \begin{matrix} \text{Put} \\ \text{price} \end{matrix} = \begin{matrix} \text{Bond} \\ \text{price} \end{matrix} - \begin{matrix} \text{Discounted} \\ \text{strike price} \end{matrix}$$

Test for Parity

$$\$1.76 - \$0.70 \overset{?}{=} \$5.73 - \frac{\$5.73}{(1.1)^2}$$

$$\$1.06 \neq \$1.00$$

Section 2

The return of a duration-matched combination of zero-coupon bonds dominates the return of a single bond.

For parallel yield shifts in Exhibit 7–8, returns for a combination of 31% 30-year and 69% 1-year zero-coupon bonds dominate a 10-year zero-coupon bond.

Return for Bond

	1-Year	10-Year	30-Year	Combination
State 1	10.00%	(3.56%)	(27.9%)	(2.31%)
State 2	10.00%	23.34%	59.16%	25.24%

that no security or combination of securities consistently provides a higher expected rate of return than another over a short period of time. Practitioners have adopted various approaches to implementing this condition for arbitrage-free pricing.

This subsection discusses the three main methods used to build an arbitrage-free fixed-income option pricing model. They should be considered different methods of solving the same arbitrage-free pricing problem and not different models of the pricing process. As such, they should provide the same answer to any given problem, provided they are based on the same set of assumptions. Each approach offers a different set of advantages and disadvantages that makes one method or another easier to implement in a given situation. As the basic characteristics of these arbitrage-free, yield-curve models are similar, our discussion centers on their implementation in an arbitrage-free binomial model. This approach illustrates the important features of an arbitrage-free model in the most intuitive way. Two other methods commonly used to create an arbitrage-free yield-curve model (simulations of the yield-curve process and numerical solutions to the partial differential equation that describes the arbitrage-free pricing condition) are discussed briefly.

Arbitrage-Free Binomial Model

The arbitrage-free binomial model is based on a lattice of interest rates much like the binomial model based on yields discussed in the previous subsection. In this model, the yields on the lattice represent a series of possible future short-term interest rates designed to satisfy conditions preventing changes in the yield curve that would permit arbitrage opportunities. The binomial model based on yield, in contrast, uses a lattice of the underlying security's yield that may allow arbitrage. Most of the arbitrage-free binomial models assume a multiplicative binomial process that approximates a lognormal yield distribution when making the lattice of short-term rates.

A yield lattice is designed so that the period between lattice points corresponds to a short-term rate. In a model based on 90-day interest rates, the lattice would consist of three-month rates; in a model based on 30-day rates, the lattice would consist of one-month rates. The choice of the term is important, because it determines the size and number of periods of the lattice. This, in turn, determines the accuracy and cost of running the model. This model will always produce an answer, but if the lattice is too small, the answer produced is likely to be wrong. A test that is frequently used to determine whether the size of a lattice is sufficient for a given type of problem is to check for significant option value changes when the lattice size is increased. If the lattice is sufficiently large for the type of problem under consideration, the value will not change significantly. Once the size of the lattice has been tested and found to be accurate for pricing a type of option, it may be used to value similar types of options with confidence.

Exhibit 7–10 builds a two-period, arbitrage-free binomial lattice using one approach. Other methods may also be used to produce an arbitrage-free binomial lattice. The yield curve for the lattice is based on one-, two- and three-period zero-coupon bonds with yields of 8 percent, 9 percent, and 9.5 percent, respectively. Section 2 shows that the expected value of the yields from the conventional binomial lattice approach do not equal the initial yield curve. But the lattice may be adjusted such that the short-term rate volatility is unchanged and the expected value of the lattice yields equals the initial yield curve.

E X H I B I T   7–10

Constructing an Arbitrage-Free Binomial Lattice

Section 1

Initial zero-coupon bond yield curve

Maturity (years)	0	1	2
Yield	8.00%	9.00%	9.50%

Section 2

Binomial lattice of one-period forward rates based on the initial 8% one-period rate and 10% yield volatility

Maturity (years)	1	2	3
One-period forward rate lattice	8.00%	8.84% / 7.24%	9.77% / 8.00% / 6.55%
Yield curve from lattice	8.00%	8.02%	8.06%

Section 3

Lattice adjusted to provide the initial yield curve

Maturity (years) adjusted	1	2	3
One-period forward rate lattice	8.00%	11.02% / 9.02%	12.75% / 10.44% / 8.54%
Yield curve from lattice	8.00%	9.00%	9.50%

Exhibit 7–11 solves for the options prices on the lattice. The put/call parity relationship holds for the two-year European put and call on the three-year zero-coupon bond, as will be shown. As discussed in the first section of this chapter, for any contingent claim that can be priced by arbitrage, the value of the claim can be found by computing the expected discounted value of its payoffs, provided that the model adjusts the expected return of the underlying security to be equal to the riskless rate for each period in the lattice. Because the arbitrage-free binomial lattice makes this adjustment, the values of the call and put in the exhibit can be computed in this manner. Alternatively, the lattice may be used to solve for the arbitrage portfolios that mimic the behavior of the option.

E X H I B I T   7–11

Arbitrage-Free Option Prices: Arbitrage-Free Price Lattice for
Three-Period Zero-Coupon Bond

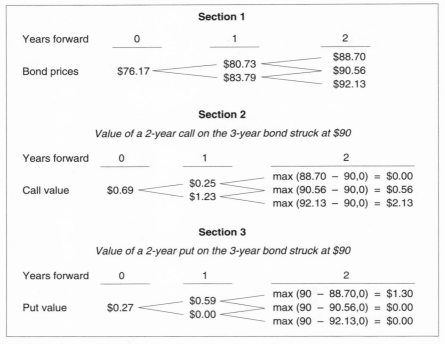

Section 1 of Exhibit 7–11 shows that the price lattice for values of
the three-period zero-coupon bond at the end of period 2 is 92.13, 90.56,
and 88.70. The payoffs for the call and put are determined by these prices,
as shown in sections 2 and 3. To value the option, these payoffs are discounted back to the beginning of the lattice, using the short-term rates for
the state in section 3 of Exhibit 7–10. The expected values of the call and
put are \$0.69 and \$0.27, respectively. If the lattice is arbitrage free,
put/call parity will hold and the difference between the values of the call
and the put will equal the difference between the values of the underlying
bond and the discounted values of the strike price for the options.[9] The
current value of the three-period zero-coupon bond is 76.17, and the discounted value of the strike price is 75.70 ($90 \div 1.09^2$). Thus, the difference between these values is \$0.42, the same as the difference between
the call and the put. Put/call parity is satisfied.

---

[9] For a discussion of put/call parity, see Bookstaber, Jacob, and Langsam, "The Arbitrage Free Pricing
of Options."

At this point, we would like to make several observations about the lattice and the procedure. The choice of the probability of rates going up, $p = \frac{1}{2}$ was arbitrary. We could instead have chosen it to be ¾. In this case, the adjustments to the lattice required for nonarbitrage condition would differ, but the procedures would remain the same.[10]

One of the attractions of this method is that only one lattice needs to be created for a given volatility and yield curve. Once this is done, all securities, regardless of whether their payoffs are certain or uncertain, can be priced with the same lattice in a similar manner by discounting back along the lattice and computing expected values. Moreover, because it is a lattice model, it easily handles American options.

Other than the extra work that is necessary to build the arbitrage-free binomial lattice, this model seems to have addressed all of the theoretical problems that we have encountered. Nevertheless, there are reasons to develop alternative models. Certain types of assets and liabilities have payoffs that depend not only on the interest rate at the time of payoff (this is the case for a European call or put) but also on the entire path of rates until the time of payoff—for example, a mortgage-backed security or a single-premium deferred annuity issued by an insurance company.

Although the lattice of interest rates remains connected for these problems, the cash flows on the lattice depend on the path of interest rates. This results in a cash flow lattice that is disconnected; the cash flows along every path through the lattice are different. This significantly increases the number of calculations needed to solve a problem on the lattice. For a connected lattice there are $n(n + 1)/2$ systems of equations that must be solved, where n is the number of periods in the lattice. Therefore, the solution for a 30-period lattice contains 465 equations. For a disconnected lattice, however, there are 2^n systems of equations to solve: The solution for the 30-period lattice contains a system of over 1 billion equations. To make the problem tractable, practitioners use sampling procedures that examine a limited number of paths through the payoff lattice. The sampling efficiency of these procedures may be increased by applying variance reduction techniques that improve the sampling efficiency.[11]

An alternative to sampling from the binomial lattice is the use of Monte Carlo simulation techniques to solve the continuous time model of

---

[10] However, in this case, to maintain the same volatility one would have to change the size of the up-and-down move.

[11] For a description of this technique, see David P. Jacob, Graham Lord, and James Tilley, "A Generalized Framework for Pricing Interest-Sensitive Cash Flows," *Financial Management,* Winter 1987.

the options pricing equation. This technique is discussed in the following subsection, along with other numerical techniques.

Monte Carlo Simulation

In practice, the Monte Carlo simulation technique works as follows. First, a large sample of short-term interest-rate paths is generated from the current short-term rate; these short-term rates are generated in such a way that they follow a lognormal distribution. However, these interest-rate paths will not, in general, price back to the current yield curve because their expected values are approximately the short-term rate. Therefore, the short-term rates are adjusted following a procedure similar to that illustrated in our discussion of the arbitrage-free binomial model. The adjustment makes the expected value of a zero-coupon bond priced on the set of paths equal to the price for the bond from the current spot-rate curve. The adjustments should also maintain the volatility of the changes in the short-term rate. Given a set of arbitrage-free paths, any security or option with payoffs that can be defined on the interest-rate paths may be valued by first determining the payoffs associated with the instrument along each of the paths and then discounting these payoffs back along the paths at the short-term rates. The initial yield curve should, however, be appropriate for the security being priced. This requires an adjustment to the Treasury yield curve, usually made by adding a spread to the curve. The spread that provides the market's price for a security is called an *option-adjusted spread*.

Monte Carlo simulation has been particularly useful for valuing mortgage-backed securities. The payoffs for a mortgage-backed security will, in general, have different values along each path at each point in time.[12] The advantage of this method over a binomial model for valuing mortgages is that a large number of different paths are generated. In contrast, all of the sample paths from the binomial model share one of two nodes in the first period, one of three nodes in the second period, and so on. This reduces the number of unique states at a given point in time, and thus decreases the accuracy of the mortgage price estimated along the paths.

Differential Equation Approach

In some cases, the value of the payoff can be obtained by numerically solving a differential equation. The techniques are beyond the scope of

---

[12] For a description of the mortgage-backed example, see David P. Jacob and Alden L. Toevs, "An Analysis of the New Valuation, Duration and Convexity Models for Mortgage-Backed Securities," in *The Handbook of Mortgage-Backed Securities:* Revised Edition, ed. Frank J. Fabozzi (Chicago: Probus Publishing, 1988).

this chapter, but they are fairly standard and can be found in any good book on numerical methods. This method applies a more rigorous mathematical approach to the valuation of an option and therefore reduces its computational complexity. One should be aware, however, that even with this approach, adjustments are made to the projected yields in the model so that bonds are priced in accordance with their market values.

WHICH MODEL SHOULD BE USED?

None of the option pricing models described is perfect for all situations. Users must choose between those models that are easy to implement but do not capture all of the special characteristics of fixed-income securities and those that adhere to arbitrage-free pricing principles but are expensive to build and cumbersome to use. One might think that the added accuracy would always be worth the extra expense. However, some of the yield-curve models require large amounts of computer resources and take a great deal of time to produce results. Obviously, a trader who must manage a position's risk exposure in a rapidly changing market would be willing to sacrifice some theoretical nicety in favor of speed.

In other circumstances, such as pricing complex securities, the results from a model must be judged relative to the realities of the marketplace. Frequently the markets for such securities do not fully reflect the assumptions of perfect liquidity, no transaction costs, and perfect information made in the pricing models. Under these circumstances, no model can be used to risklessly arbitrage mispricing, but a model may provide reasonable indications of value. The choice in a specific situation ought to be dictated by the performance of the models available for the application. If two models lead to the same investment or trading decisions from the user's perspective, the approach that is easier to use and/or most cost effective is the logical choice.

In this section, we summarize our views on which model or models appear to provide reasonable performance in specific situations. We begin by discussing the relative merits of the models for pricing short-term fixed-income options; we then discuss long-term fixed-income options.

Options with Short Terms to Expiration

Short-term options on fixed-income securities trade both in the over-the-counter market and on the futures exchanges. These options typically have one year or less to expiration.

Options on Fixed-Income Securities and Futures Contracts

In practice, options on fixed-income securities are priced by a modified version of the Black-Scholes model, its binomial equivalent, or a binomial model on yields. Options on fixed-income futures contracts are usually priced by the Black commodity level, which is a modification of the Black-Scholes model, though a binomial model in yield may be adapted to this case. Options on money market instruments, such as Eurodollar futures, are usually priced with a Black commodity model modified to represent a security's yield instead of its price. Of course, one could use an arbitrage-free binomial model to evaluate short-term options on any of these securities but the results from this complex model would be unlikely to be worth the extra work.

One would expect both the Black-Scholes and binomial yield models to produce similar results for European options with short terms to expiration to long-maturity bonds and notes that are nearly in the money. This conclusion is based both on the similarity of the long-term bond price distributions for the Black-Scholes model and the binomial model in yield (discussed in the previous section) and on the assumption that the differences in discounting procedures between these models should not have a significant effect on the resulting option prices due to the short time to expiration. However, the differences in the distributions may affect the pricing of out-of-the-money options.

Many practitioners prefer the binomial model based on yields for these options because Black-Scholes may neither produce reliable results for American-style options nor reliably price options on securities with short terms to maturity. In Exhibits 7–4 and 7–6 the differences in the skewness of the price distribution for these models illustrate the potential for mispricing.

The binomial yield model has an additional advantage in that the yield volatilities of a bond are comparable over time. In contrast, the price volatilities used in Black-Scholes models are sensitive to changes in the bond's duration, which in turn is sensitive to yield changes, coupon effects, and aging. Therefore, price volatilities may not be comparable over time for bonds and notes. This is particularly true for bond and note futures where changes in the cheapest-to-deliver bond may significantly change the duration of the contract. Consequently, yield volatilities are a better measure of the market's volatility and therefore of the relative value of options. In our view, they should be used as relative historical volatility measures even if options are priced and hedged based on the Black-Scholes model.

The distinction between pricing options on cash bonds and pricing options on futures is of limited importance because of the close tracking of prices between the cash and futures markets. One should also remember that the price of a futures contract reflects financing considerations, whereas the price of a cash bond does not. This may cause some confusion. For example, an at-the-money call option on a futures contract would be an in-the-money call on a cash security in a positively sloped yield curve. The exception to this is when the cheapest-to-deliver bond is likely to change as rates change. In this case, there may be a significant change in the duration of the bond or note contract that should not be measured by the models discussed here.[13] Modeling this effect is possible using a binomial yield lattice, but it is beyond the scope of this chapter.

The preceding comments refer to using the models to determine the value of short-term fixed-income options, but for many applications, hedging an option is equally important. Although we believe that the Black-Scholes model may leave something to be desired in measuring value, it offers some advantages over the other models in hedging applications. Because the Black-Scholes model is continuous, the prices and risk measures for options, such as delta, kappa, theta, and so on, change smoothly. For the binomial model, numerical differences due to the coarseness of the lattice can make the risk measures coarse. This causes the risk measure to change in an abrupt and therefore unnatural way. An approach that smooths these values uses a series of lattices measuring different option parameters to compute a price curve and then uses analytic approximations to facilitate the calculation of the derivatives. Alternatively, larger lattices may be used to increase the accuracy of the binomial approach.

Short-Term Options on Mortgage-Backed Forwards

Options on mortgage-backed forwards are often evaluated using Black's commodity model. However, this approach will tend to overstate the true value of calls and understate the true value of puts unless the volatility input is adjusted for the negative convexity of the mortgage. The embedded prepayment feature of the mortgage-backed security is the source of this effect. Although a more complex approach (such as a technique based on a yield-curve model) can be created to incorporate this effect, such a model would be much more expensive than the Black commodity model.

---

[13] The effect of such a change is discussed in the *Financial Futures Handbook* (Morgan Stanley, February 1989).

Alternatively, a binomial model may be created that incorporates the effect of price compression on the pricing of mortgage options.[14] It is interesting to note that the Black commodity model is the standard model used in this market.

Long-Term Options

Recently the attention of Wall Street analysts has focused on the pricing of long-term options. This is because of the rapid development of the mortgage market and the effect of volatile interest rates on callable corporate debt. The nearly universal conclusion is that consistent pricing for long-term options can be obtained only through an arbitrage-free yield-curve model.

Callable and Putable Bonds

Corporate bonds are frequently issued with a call feature. For example, telephone bonds are issued with maturities as long as 40 years and with a call option that is typically European for the first 5 years and American thereafter. Further, the call price declines over time according to a schedule. Originally many practitioners used the binomial model based on yields to value these options, but this model sometimes produced values for the options that did not make sense. To a large extent, this was due to the arbitrary nature of the risk-free rate chosen for the model. Changes in this rate could produce very different conclusions on the value of these options. Unfortunately, this model could not provide a method for determining a reasonable risk-free rate. More recently, arbitrage-free models that provide appropriate discount rates have been used to value these securities. These models specify the risk-free, or discounting, rate over the life of the option, which allows more consistent valuations of these securities.

However, these models do not guarantee the user a profit when they suggest that a particular option is cheap or rich. To extract the profit implied by the model, an investor would have to purchase or sell the callable bond and then effectively hedge it dynamically for the life of the option or until the market reaches a "fair value" for the option. Therefore, the performance of the model must be tested under real market conditions. The same test should be applied to any option trading strategy.

---

[14] For more information, see David P. Jacob and M. Sitte, *Price Compression and the Pricing of Options on Mortgage-Backed Securities* (Morgan Stanley, March 1989).

Mortgage-Backed Securities

Another major area where yield-curve models have been applied and proved their worth is the evaluation of mortgage-backed securities. The embedded option for these securities is the interest-sensitive prepayment component of the mortgage. This makes the cash flows for these securities quite dependent on the path of interest rates. Because of the path dependence of the cash flows and long term of the securities, Black-Scholes and binomial models on yields are not well suited for analyzing these securities. Therefore, a yield-curve model is necessary to obtain consistent option values.

Most practitioners favor the Monte Carlo simulation approach because of its flexibility and relative simplicity, as discussed in the previous section. However, numerical solutions to partial differential equations or the arbitrage-free binomial lattice may also be used.

When creating a mortgage model, remember that the prepayment function is very important in determining the option's characteristics. If it is estimated on unrepresentative data (for example, if you believe that homeowners have changed their prepayment behavior relative to the history used in an estimate), or if it is estimated over a small amount of data, its results should be treated with suspicion. As with callable bonds, those who understand the assumptions realize that the mispricings suggested by the model are usually not arbitrageable without risk. However, the results of empirical tests of this approach show that the model is quite useful in discerning relative value.[15]

Other Applications

Yield-curve models have been applied extensively to the analysis of interest-sensitive insurance company liabilities. In fact, some of the earliest theoretical work on these models was done to evaluate insurance company liabilities such as single-premium deferred annuities.[16] These liabilities are similar to mortgage-backed securities in that their cash flows are interest sensitive with a large degree of path dependence. Therefore, most analysts favor a simulation approach in modeling these instruments. The pricing of these securities may depend on the slop of the yield curve; because of investors' and competing insurers' behavior, a two-factor model may represent this process better than a one-factor model.

---

[15] See David P. Jacob, Gary Latainer, and Alden L. Toevs, *Value and Performance of Mortgage-Backed Securities* (Morgan Stanley, 1987).

[16] See Peter D. Noris and Sheldon Epstein, "Finding the Immunizing Investment for Insurance Liabilities: The Case of the SPDA," in *Fixed-Income Portfolio Strategies: State-of-the-Art Technologies and Innovations,* ed. Frank J. Fabozzi (Chicago: Probus Publishing, 1989).

Closing Thoughts

At this point, we would like to look forward to the next generation of models and then summarize our view of practical option pricing.

What Will the Next Generation of Models Look Like?

Despite the time and effort expended to develop the option pricing models discussed above, the future will probably produce new, more complex models. This is because more complex securities and strategies will be developed. For example, an investor may desire an option that provides a payoff based on the difference between the 90-day Treasury bill rate and the yield on the long bond. In this situation, one might build a model that allows some independence among the different parts of the yield curve. The arbitrage-free models currently available have nearly perfect correlation between the short-term and long-term rates. However, as long as the option does not depend on the difference between two rates, one might want first to test to see how well a non-arbitrage-free model works before attempting a two-factor model. Two-factor models will be necessary to price instruments such as commercial mortgage-backed securities which have embedded options related to interest rates and credit.

As we mentioned earlier, the appropriateness of distributional and volatility assumptions used in the model may come under more study. Although the history of the levels of interest rates and the shape of the yield curve are frequently studied, the historical behavior of volatility is not. Given the importance of these parameters in valuing securities with embedded options, more empirical work would be useful.

The Real Test of Option Pricing Models

The true test of a model—whether it works in practice—is an important point that is often missed in the quest for "better" models. If a model does not accomplish what you want, all of its complexity is worthless. It should therefore be tested to see how well it can reproduce the payoffs that it promises. This is accomplished by dynamically adjusting a hedge portfolio recommended by the model. If the hedge's ability to reproduce the option's payoffs is poor, the model will not be useful for arbitrage. On the other hand, it may still be useful for answering relative value questions or as an indication of a security's duration and convexity; these aspects should be tested as well.

In some situations, one may have to work with models that provide prices that have relatively large confidence intervals. For example, some of the derivative mortgage-backed securities, such as interest-only and principal-only strips, have cash flows that are extremely sensitive to the path of interest rates; thus, imperfections in the prepayment model used to generate the mortgage's cash flows are magnified. Moreover, there is very little price history with which to test a model's usefulness. In this case, one must be cautious in the application of the technology. However, one should not be deluded into believing that by ignoring the problems and using a simpler model more useful answers can be obtained. In summary, users should work with the most cost-effective model that has been successfully tested for their particular application. In situations where testing is not feasible, they should go with the most theoretically correct model that their resources permit.

SUMMARY

The characteristics of fixed-income securities differ from those of equities. Therefore, the option pricing models designed for stocks are inappropriate for valuing and analyzing the characteristics of fixed-income securities in many situations. But we have shown that the basic principles of pricing via arbitrage and the ability to replicate the payoffs of an option that are the basis of the equity models can be applied to fixed-income securities. given the added complexity and costs associated with the best theoretical answer, it is interesting to note that it is not required for all applications.

In some situations, such as with short-term European options on bonds or futures, one can (and, from a cost standpoint, probably should) consider models that, though not theoretically pure, produce results that are close enough to those produced with the more complex models. In other situations, such as pricing mortgage-backed securities, more complicated models are usually necessary. Exhibit 7–12 summarizes our recommendations and offers caveats for the models for a variety of applications. The most important point is that all models should be tested with real data before being adopted. This will provide the only true indication to practitioners as to how useful a model can be.

E X H I B I T   7–12

Summary and Recommended Applications for the Models

Model	Recommended Application	Advantages	Disadvantages	Caveats
Black-Scholes/ Cox-Ross-Rubinstein binomial models	Short-term options on bonds, notes, and interest rates Short-term options on futures Short-term options on mortgage-backed forwards	Easy to implement Low cost "Standard model"	Does not model early exercise for American-style options The short-term rate in the model is fixed Adjustments are required for interest payments and accrual price volatility changes over the life of an option The mortgages' price volatility must be adjusted to reflect convexity	Inappropriate for long-term options and, potentially, short-term options on short-term bonds
Binomial in yield	Short-term options on bonds, notes, and interest rates Short-term options on futures	Better model of price, yield, and pull-to-par process for bonds and notes Prices American-style options Allows floating short-term rate	Violates put/call parity More expensive to run than Black-Scholes	May be used for long-term options such as callable bonds, but the results should be carefully checked for reasonableness
Yield-curve models	Long-term options on bonds, notes, and interest rates Callable bonds Mortgage-backed securities Complex assets and liabilities, e.g., single premium deferred annuities for insurance companies	Satisfies put/call parity Better model of long-term interest-rate behavior Can price American-style options (binomial and numerical solution of differential equations) Yield volatility behavior is consistent with empirical observations, i.e., short-term rate volatility is greater than long-term rate volatility	Most expensive models to develop and run	Highly correlated short-and long-term rates make this inappropriate for options on the difference between two rates Differences between market value and model's value for long-term options may not be realizable through arbitrage trading due to transaction costs and mistracking Accuracy of mortgage model depends on prepayment rate estimates

⑥ THE BINOMIAL MODEL FOR VALUING OPTIONS AND BONDS WITH EMBEDDED OPTIONS

Frank J. Fabozzi, PhD, CFA
Adjunct Professor of Finance
School of Management
Yale University

The previous chapter discussed option pricing models and explained the limitations of employing the Black-Scholes option pricing model to value interest rate options. The proper way to value options on interest rate instruments is to use an arbitrage-free model that takes the yield curve into account. Such a model can incorporate different volatility assumptions along the yield curve.

This chapter presents and illustrates one such arbitrage-free model: the binomial interest rate model, or simply binomial model. This model is used to value both stand-alone options and options embedded in bonds. The binomial model presented here was first developed by three practitioners from Goldman Sachs—Fischer Black, Emanuel Derman, and William Toy—and is sometimes referred to as the *Black-Derman-Toy model*.[1] The extension of the binomial model to value options embedded in bonds was first presented in an article by Andrew Kalotay, George Williams, and Frank Fabozzi.[2] The next chapter demonstrates how the binomial model can be used to value caps and floors.

---

[1] Fischer Black, Emanuel Derman, and William Toy, "A One-Factor Model of Interest Rates and Its Application to Treasury Bond Options," *Financial Analysts Journal,* January–February 1990, pp. 24–32.

[2] Andrew J. Kalotay, George O. Williams, and Frank J. Fabozzi, "A Model for the Valuation of Bonds and Embedded Options," *Financial Analysts Journal,* May–June 1993, pp. 35–46. Parts of this chapter are adapted from this article.

The binomial model involves generating a tree of interest rates that can be used to value any bond or option. The tree is constructed so that the value generated for on-the-run issues is equal to the market value for each on-the-run issue. The assumption is that the on-the-run issues are fairly priced. We begin this chapter with an explanation of how to value an option-free bond.

VALUING OPTION-FREE BONDS: A REVIEW

The value of any bond is equal to the present value of the expected cash flow. The discount rate used to determine the present value of each cash flow should be the theoretical zero-coupon rate, also called the *theoretical spot rate*. The theoretical spot rates are generated from the on-the-run Treasuries using a procedure called *bootstrapping*.

To illustrate this procedure, assume the following on-the-run Treasury yield curve:

Maturity	Yield to Maturity	Market Price
1 year	3.5%	100
2 years	4.2	100
3 years	4.7	100
4 years	5.2	100

Each bond is trading at par value (100), so the coupon rate is equal to the yield to maturity. We will simplify the illustration by assuming annual-pay bonds.

Using \$100 as par, the present value of the cash flow for the 2-year coupon Treasury is

$$\frac{4.20}{(1+z_1)^1} + \frac{104.20}{(1+z_2)^2}$$

where

$$z_1 = \text{1-year spot rate}$$
$$z_2 = \text{2-year spot rate}$$

In our example, $z_1 = 0.035$. Therefore, the present value of the 2-year Treasury security is

$$\frac{4.20}{(1.035)^1} + \frac{104.20}{(1+z_2)^2}$$

Since the price of the 2-year coupon Treasury security is \$100, the following relationship must hold:

$$\frac{4.20}{(1.035)^1} + \frac{104.20}{(1+z_2)^2} = 100$$

Solving for the theoretical 2-year spot rate, we get $z_2 = 4.2147\%$.

Given the theoretical 2-year spot rate, we can obtain the 3-year theoretical spot rate. The present value of the 2-year coupon Treasury security is

$$\frac{4.70}{(1.035)^1} + \frac{4.70}{(1.042147)^2} + \frac{104.70}{(1+z_3)^3}$$

Since the price of the 3-year coupon Treasury security is $100, the following relationship must hold:

$$\frac{4.70}{(1.035)^1} + \frac{4.70}{(1.042147)^2} + \frac{104.70}{(1+z_3)^3} = 100$$

Solving, we get $z_3 = 4.7345\%$

Similarly, the 4-year theoretical spot rate is found to be 5.2707 percent. The four theoretical spot rates are as follows:

Year	Spot Rate
1	3.5000%
2	4.2147
3	4.7345
4	5.2707

Given the four spot rates, the value of any Treasury security can be calculated. For example, consider a 4-year Treasury with a coupon rate of 6.5 percent. The value of this Treasury security is found by discounting the coupon payments at the spot rates as follows:

$$\frac{\$6.5}{(1.035)} + \frac{\$6.5}{(1.042147)^2} + \frac{\$6.5}{(1.047345)^3} + \frac{\$100+\$6.5}{(1.052707)^4} = \$104.643$$

An alternative but equivalent procedure is to value a security by discounting at the implied forward rates, or simply forward rates. Assuming that the yield curve is derived purely from the expectations of future interest rates, based on arbitrage arguments, the market's consensus of future interest rates can be extrapolated from the Treasury yield curve. These rates are called *forward rates*. The simple arbitrage approach for deriving forward rates will not be described here.[3] The 1-year forward rates for the

---

[3] The interested reader is referred to Chapter 3 of Frank J. Fabozzi, *Valuation of Fixed Income Securities and Derivatives* (New Hope, PA: Frank J. Fabozzi Associates, 1995).

on-the-run Treasury yield curve used earlier to derive the theoretical spot
rates are

Current 1-year forward rate	3.500%
1-year forward rate 1 year from now	4.935
1-year forward rate 2 years from now	5.784
1-year forward rate 3 years from now	6.893

The 1-period forward rates are often called the *short rates*.

Spot rates and forward rates are related, since they are derived from
the yield curve. The 1-period spot rate j periods from now is related to the
j-period spot rate as follows:

$$z_j = [(1 + f_1)(1 + f_2)(1 + f_3) \ldots (1 + f_j)]^{1/j} - 1$$

where

f_j = 1-period forward rate for period j

For example, the 4-year spot rate is found from the forward rates as
follows:

$$z_4 = [(1.035)(1.04935)(1.05784)(1.06893)]^{1/4} - 1$$
$$= 5.2707\%$$

This agrees with the 4-year spot rate found earlier.

Because of the relationship between spot and forward rates, forward
rates can be used to value a bond. Consider once again the 4-year
Treasury with a 6.5 percent coupon. Using forward rates, the value of this
Treasury is found as follows:

$$\frac{\$6.5}{(1.035)} + \frac{\$6.5}{(1.035)(1.04935)} + \frac{\$6.5}{(1.035)(1.04935)(1.05784)} +$$
$$\frac{\$100 + \$6.5}{(1.035)(1.04935)(1.05784)(1.06893)} = \$104.643$$

This agrees with the value found using spot rates.

THE BINOMIAL INTEREST RATE TREE

When valuing an option or a bond with an embedded option, consideration must be given to interest rate volatility. This can be done by introducing a *binomial interest rate tree*. This tree is nothing more than a
graphical depiction of the one-period or short rates over time based on

some assumption about interest rate volatility. The construction of this tree is illustrated next.

Exhibit 8–1 shows an example of a binomial interest rate tree. In this tree, each node (bold circle) represents a time period that is equal to one year from the node to its left. Each node is labeled with an N and a subscript that indicates the path the 1-year rate took to get to that node. L represents the lower of the two 1-year rates, and H represents the higher of the two 1-year rates. For example, node N_{HH} means that to get to that node, the following path for 1-year rates occurred: The 1-year rate realized is the higher of the two rates in the first year and then the higher of the 1-year rates in the second year.[4]

Look first at the point denoted by just N in Exhibit 8–1. This is the root of the tree and is nothing more than the current 1-year spot rate or equivalently, the current 1-year rate, which we denote by r_0. In creating

E X H I B I T   8–1

4-Year Binomial Interest Rate Tree

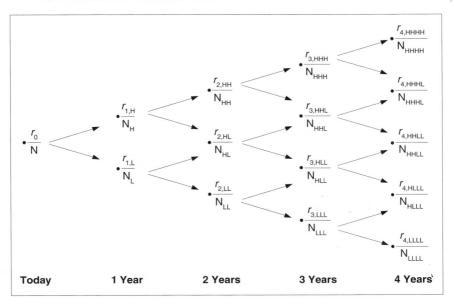

| Today | 1 Year | 2 Years | 3 Years | 4 Years |

---

[4] Note that N_{HL} is equivalent to N_{LH} in the second year, N_{HHL} is equivalent to N_{HLH} and N_{LHH} in the third year, and N_{HLL} is equivalent to N_{LLH}. We have simply selected one label for a node rather than clutter up the figure with unnecessary information.

this tree, we have assumed that the 1-year rate can take on two possible values in the next period and the two rates have the same probability of occurring. One rate will be higher than the other. We assume that the 1-year rate can evolve over time based on a random process called a *lognormal random walk* with a certain volatility.

We use the following notation to describe the tree in the first year. Let

$$\sigma = \text{Assumed volatility of the 1-year rate}$$
$$r_{1,L} = \text{Lower 1-year rate one year from now}$$
$$r_{1,H} = \text{Higher 1-year rate one year from now}$$

The relationship between $r_{1,L}$ and $r_{1,H}$ is as follows:

$$r_{1,H} = r_{1,L}(e^{2\sigma})$$

where e is the base of the natural logarithm 2.71828.

For example, suppose $r_{1,L}$ is 4.4448 percent and σ is 10 percent per year. Then

$$r_{1,H} = 4.4448\% \ (e^{2 \times 0.10}) = 5.4289\%$$

In the second year, there are three possible values for the 1-year rate, which we will denote as follows:

$r_{2,LL} = $ 1-year rate in second year assuming the lower rate in the first year and the lower rate in the second year

$r_{2,HH} = $ 1-year rate in second year assuming the higher rate in the first year and the higher rate in the second year

$r_{2,HL} = $ 1-year rate in second year assuming the higher rate in the first year and the lower rate in the second year *or*, equivalently, the lower rate in the first year and the higher rate in the second year

The relationship between $r_{2,LL}$ and the other two 1-year rates is as follows:

$$r_{2,HH} = r_{2,LL}(e^{4\sigma})$$

and

$$r_{2,HL} = r_{2,LL}(e^{2\sigma})$$

So, for example, if $r_{2,LL}$ is 4.6958 percent, then, assuming once again that σ is 10 percent,

$$r_{2,HH} = 4.6958\% \ (e^{4 \times 0.10}) = 7.0053\%$$

and

$$r_{2,HL} = 4.6958\% \ (e^{2 \times 0.10}) = 5.7354\%$$

In the third year there are four possible values for the 1-year rate, which are denoted as follows—$r_{3,HHH}$, $r_{3,HHL}$, $r_{3,HLL}$, and $r_{3,LLL}$—and whose first three values are related to the last as follows:

$$r_{3,HHH} = (e^{6\sigma}) \, r_{3,LLL}$$
$$r_{3,HHL} = (e^{4\sigma}) \, r_{3,LLL}$$
$$r_{3,HLL} = (e^{2\sigma}) \, r_{3,LLL}$$

Exhibit 8–1 shows the notation for a 4-year binomial interest rate tree. We can simplify the notation by letting r_t be the 1-year rate t years from now for the lower rate, since all the other short rates t years from now depend on that rate. Exhibit 8–2 shows the interest rate tree using this simplified notation.

E X H I B I T   8–2

4-Year Binomial Interest Rate Tree with 1-Year Rates[*]

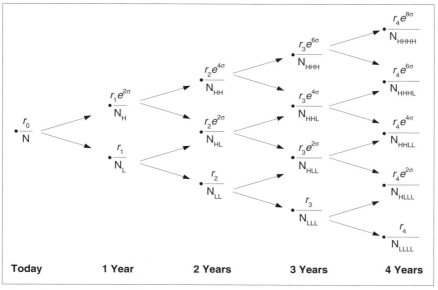

* r_t equals the forward 1-year lower rate.

Before we go on to show how to use this binomial interest rate tree to value bonds, let's focus on two issues here. First, what does the volatility parameter σ in the expression $e^{2\sigma}$ represent? Second, how do we find the value of the bond at each node?

Volatility and the Standard Deviation

We can show that the standard deviation of the 1-year rate is equal to $r_0\sigma$.[5] The standard deviation is a statistical measure of volatility. It is important to see that the process we assumed generates the binomial interest rate tree (or, equivalently, the short rates) implies that volatility is measured relative to the current level of rates. For example, if σ is 10 percent and the 1-year rate (r_0) is 4 percent, the standard deviation of the 1-year rate is $4\% \times 10\% = 0.4\%$, or 40 basis points. However, if the current 1-year rate is 12 percent, the standard deviation of the 1-year rate is $12\% \times 10\%$, or 120 basis points.

Determining the Value at a Node

To find the value of the bond at a node, we first calculate the bond's value at the two nodes to the right of the node we are interested in. For example, in Exhibit 8–3, suppose we want to determine the bond's value at node N_H. The bond's value at node N_{HH} and N_{HL} must be determined. Hold aside for now how we get these two values because, as we will see, the process involves starting from the last year in the tree and working backward to get the final solution we want, so these two values will be known.

Effectively, we are saying that if we are at some node, the value at that node will depend on the future cash flows. In turn, the future cash flows will depend on (1) the bond's value one year from now and (2) the coupon payment one year from now. The latter is known. The former depends on whether the 1-year rate is the higher or lower rate. The bond's value based on whether the rate is the higher or lower rate is reported at the two nodes to the right of the node that is the focus of our attention. Thus, the cash flow at a node will be either (1) the bond's value if the short rate is the higher rate plus the coupon payment or (2) the bond's value if the short rate is the lower rate plus the coupon payment. For

---

[5] This can be seen by noting that $e^{2\sigma} \approx 1 + 2\sigma$. Then the standard deviation of the 1-period rate is

$$\frac{re^{2\sigma} - r}{2} \approx \frac{r + 2\sigma r - r}{2} = \sigma r$$

E X H I B I T   8–3

Calculating a Value at a Node

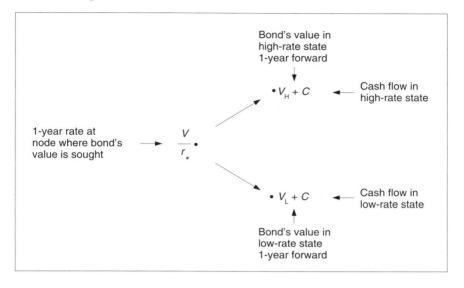

example, suppose we are interested in the bond's value at N_H. The cash flow will be either the bond's value at N_{HH} plus the coupon payment or the bond's value at N_{HL} plus the coupon payment.

To get the bond's value at a node, we follow the fundamental rule for valuation: The value is the present value of the expected cash flows. The appropriate discount rate to use is the 1-year rate at the node. Now there are two present values in this case: the present value if the 1-year rate is the higher rate and the present value if it is the lower rate. Since we assume that the probability of both outcomes is equal, we compute an average of the two present values. This process is illustrated in Exhibit 8–3 for any node, assuming that the 1-year rate is r_* at the node where the valuation is sought and letting

V_H = Bond's value for the higher 1-year rate
V_L = Bond's value for the lower 1-year rate
C = Coupon payment

Using our notation, the cash flow at a node is either

$V_H + C$ for the higher 1-year rate
$V_L + C$ for the lower 1-year rate

The present value of these two cash flows using the 1-year rate at the node, r_*, is

$$\frac{V_H + C}{(1+r_*)} \text{ present value for the higher 1-year rate}$$

$$\frac{V_L + C}{(1+r_*)} \text{ present value for the lower 1-year rate}$$

Then the value of the bond at the node is found as follows:

$$\text{Value at a node} = \frac{1}{2}\left[\frac{V_H + C}{(1+r_*)} + \frac{V_L + C}{(1+r_*)}\right]$$

CONSTRUCTING THE BINOMIAL INTEREST RATE TREE

To see how to construct the binomial interest rate tree, let's use the assumed on-the-run yields we used earlier. We will assume that volatility, σ, is 10 percent and construct a 2-year tree using the 2-year bond with a coupon rate of 4.2 percent.

Exhibit 8–4 shows a more detailed binomial interest rate tree with the cash flow shown at each node. We'll see how all the values reported in the exhibit are obtained. The root rate for the tree, r_0, is simply the current 1-year rate, 3.5 percent.

In the first year, there are two possible 1-year rates: the higher rate and the lower rate. What we want to find is the two 1-year rates that will be consistent with the volatility assumption, the process that is assumed to generate the short rates, and the observed market value of the bond. There is no simple formula for this. It must be found by an iterative process (i.e., trial and error). The steps are as follows.

Step 1: Select a value for r_1. Recall that r_1 is the lower 1-year rate. In this first trial, we *arbitrarily* selected a value of 4.75 percent.

Step 2: Determine the corresponding value for the higher 1-year rate. As explained earlier, this rate is related to the lower 1-year rate as follows: r_1 $e^{2\sigma}$. Since r_1 is 4.75 percent, the higher 1-year rate is 5.8017 percent ($= 4.75\% \ e^{2 \times 0.10}$). This value is reported in Exhibit 8–5 at node N_H.

Step 3: Compute the bond value's one year from now. This value is determined as follows.

E X H I B I T 8–4

The 1-Year Rates for Year 1 Using the 2-Year 4.2%
On-the-Run Issue: First Trial

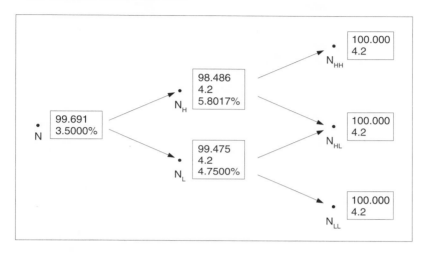

3a. Determine the bond's value two years from now. In our example, this is simple. Since we are using a 2-year bond, the bond's value is its maturity value ($100) plus its final coupon payment ($4.2). Thus, it is $104.2.

3b. Calculate the present value of the bond's value found in 3a for the higher rate in the second year. The appropriate discount rate is the higher 1-year rate—5.8017 percent in our example. The present value is $98.456 (= $104.2/1.058017). This is the value of V_H that we referred to earlier.

3c. Calculate the present value of the bond's value assumed in 3a for the lower rate. The discount rate assumed for the lower 1-year rate is 4.75 percent. The present value is $99.475 (= $104.2/1.0475) and is the value of V_L.

3d. Add the coupon to both V_H and V_L to get the cash flow at N_H and N_L, respectively. In our example, we have $102.686 for the higher rate and $103.675 for the lower rate.

3e. Calculate the present value of the two values using the 1-year rate r_*. At this point in the valuation, r_* is the root rate, 3.50 percent. Therefore,

$$\frac{V_{\mathrm{H}}+C}{(1+r_*)}=\frac{\$102.686}{1.035}=\$99.213$$

and

$$\frac{V_{\mathrm{L}}+C}{(1+r_*)}=\frac{\$103.675}{1.035}=\$100.169$$

Step 4: Calculate the average present value of the two cash flows in step 3. This is the value we referred to earlier as

$$\text{Value at a node} = \frac{1}{2}\left[\frac{V_{\mathrm{H}}+C}{(1+r_*)}+\frac{V_{\mathrm{L}}+C}{(1+r_*)}\right]$$

In our example, we have

$$\text{Value at a node} = \frac{1}{2}[\$99.213+\$100.169]=\$99.691$$

Step 5: Compare the value in step 4 to the bond's market value. If the two values are the same, the r_1 used in this trial is the one we seek. This is the 1-year rate that would then be used in the binomial interest rate tree for the lower rate and the corresponding higher rate. If instead the value found in step 4 is not equal to the market value of the bond, the value r_1 in this trial is not the 1-year rate that is consistent with (1) the volatility assumption of 10 percent, (2) the process assumed to generate the 1-year rate, and (3) the observed market value of the bond. In this case, the five steps are repeated with a different value for r_1.

When r_1 is 4.75 percent, a value of $99.691 results in step 4, which is less than the observed market price of $100. Therefore, 4.75 percent is too large and the five steps must be repeated trying a lower rate for r_1.

Let's jump right to the correct rate for r_1 in this example and rework steps 1 through 5. This occurs when r_1 is 4.4448 percent. The corresponding binomial interest rate tree is shown in Exhibit 8–5.

Step 1: In this trial, we select a value of 4.4448 percent for r_1, the lower 1-year rate.

Step 2: The corresponding value for the higher 1-year rate is 5.4289 percent ($= 4.4448\% \, e^{2 \times 0.10}$).

Step 3: The bond's value one year from now is determined as follows:

    3a. The bond's value two years from now is $104.2, just as in the first trial.

EXHIBIT 8–5

1-Year Rates for Year 1 Using the 2-Year 4.2% On-the-Run Issue

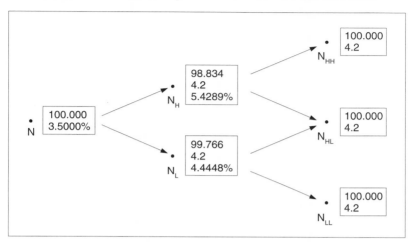

3b. The present value of the bond's value found in 3a for the higher 1-year rate, V_H, is \$98.8344 (= \$104.2/1.054289).

3c. The present value of the bond's value found in 3a for the lower 1-year rate, V_L, is \$99.7656 (= \$104.2/1.044448).

3d. Adding the coupon to V_H and V_L, we get \$103.0344 as the cash flow for the higher rate and \$103.9656 as the cash flow for the lower rate.

3e. The present value of the two cash flows using the 1-year rate at the node to the left, 3.5 percent, gives

$$\frac{V_H + C}{(1 + r_*)} = \frac{\$103.0344}{1.035} = \$99.5501$$

and

$$\frac{V_L + C}{(1 + r_*)} = \frac{\$103.9656}{1.035} = \$100.4498$$

Step 4: The average present value is \$100, which is the value at the node.

Step 5: Since the average present value is equal to the observed market price of \$100, r_1 or $r_{1,L}$ is 4.4448 percent and $r_{1,H}$ is 5.4289 percent.

We can "grow" this tree for one more year by determining r_2. Now we will use the three-year on-the-run issue, the 4.7 percent coupon bond, to get r_2. The same five steps are used in an iterative process to find the 1-year rates in the tree two years from now. Our objective now is to find the value of r_2 that will produce a bond value of \$100 (since the 3-year on-the-run issue has a market price of $100) and is consistent with (1) a volatility assumption of 10 percent, (2) a current 1-year rate of 3.5 percent, and (3) the two rates one year from now of 4.4448 percent (the lower rate) and 5.4289 percent (the higher rate).

We can see how this is done using Exhibit 8–6. Let's look at how we get the information in the exhibit. The maturity value and coupon payment are shown in the boxes at the four nodes three years from now. Since the 3-year on-the-run issue has a maturity value of $100 and a coupon payment of $4.7, these values are the same in the box shown at each node. For the three nodes two years from now, the coupon payment of $4.7 is shown. Unknown at these three nodes are (1) the three rates two years from now and (2) the value of the bond two years from now. For the two nodes one year from now, the coupon payment is known, as are the 1-year rates one year from now. These are the rates found earlier. The value of the bond, which depends on the bond values at the nodes to the right, is unknown at these two nodes.

Exhibit 8–7 is the same as Exhibit 8–6 complete with the values previously unknown. As can be seen from Exhibit 8–7, the value of r_2, or, equivalently, $r_{2,LL}$, that will produce the desired result is 4.6958 percent.

E X H I B I T   8–6

Information for Deriving the 1-Year Rates for Year 2 Using the 3-Year 4.7% On-the-Run Issue

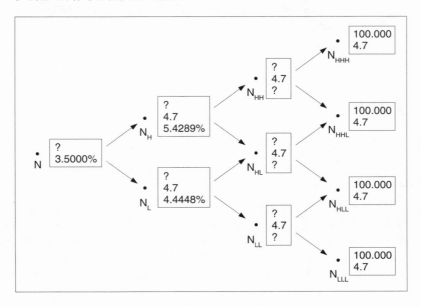

We showed earlier that the corresponding rates $r_{2,HL}$ and $r_{2,HH}$ would be 5.7354 and 7.0053 percent, respectively. To verify that these are the 1-year rates two years from now, we work backward from the four nodes at the right of the tree in Exhibit 8–7. For example, the value in the box at N_{HH} is found by taking the value of $104.7 at the two nodes to its right and discounting at 7.0053 percent. The value is $97.8456. (Since it is the same value for both nodes to the right, it is also the average value.) Similarly, the value in the box at N_{HL} is found by discounting $104.7 by 5.7354 percent and at N_{LL} by discounting at 4.6958 percent. The same procedure used in Exhibits 8–4 and 8–5 is used to get the values at the other nodes.

VALUING AN OPTION-FREE BOND WITH THE BINOMIAL TREE

Exhibit 8–8 shows the 1-year rates or binomial interest rate tree that can then be used to value any Treasury security with a maturity up to four years. To illustrate how to use the binomial interest rate tree, consider one more time the 6.5 percent coupon, 4-year Treasury. Also assume that the on-the-run yield curve is the one given earlier, and hence the appropriate binomi-

E X H I B I T   8–7

The 1-Year Rates for Year 2 Using the 3-Year 4.7% On-the-Run Issue

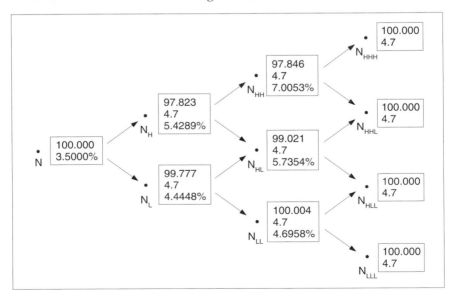

al interest rate tree is the one in Exhibit 8–8. Exhibit 8–9 shows the various values in the discounting process and produces a bond value of $104.643.

It is important to note that this value is identical to the value found earlier when we discounted at either the spot rates or the 1-year forward rates. We should expect to find this result, since our bond is option free. This clearly demonstrates that the valuation model is consistent with the standard valuation model for an option-free bond.

USING THE BINOMIAL TREE TO VALUE AN OPTION[6]

Our initial goal was to construct the binomial interest rate tree to value an option. Now that we have the binomial tree, let's illustrate how it can be used to value an option. Consider a 2-year call option on a 6.5 percent, 4-year Treasury bond with a strike price of 100.25. We will assume that the yield for the on-the-run Treasuries is the one given earlier and that the volatility assumption is 10 percent per year. Exhibit 8–9 shows the binomial interest rate tree, along with the value of the Treasury bond at each node.

E X H I B I T   8–8

Binomial Interest Rate Tree for Valuing Up to a 4-Year Treasury Security (10% Volatility Assumed)

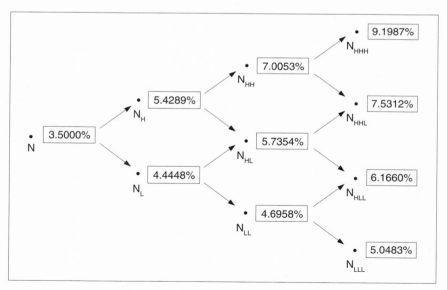

---

[6] This section draws from Chapter 11 of Fabozzi, *Valuation of Fixed Income Securities and Derivatives*.

We use a portion of Exhibit 8–9 to value the call option. Specifically, Exhibit 8–10 shows the value of our Treasury (excluding coupon interest) at each node at the end of the second year. Three values are shown: 97.9249, 100.4184, and 102.5335. Given these three values, the value of a call option struck at 100.25 can be determined at each node. For example, if in two years the price of this Treasury bond is 97.9249, then, since the strike price is 100.25, the value of the call option will be zero. In the other two cases, since the price two years from now is greater than the strike price, the value of the call option is the difference between the price of the bond and 100.25.

Exhibit 8–10 shows the value of the call option two years from now (the option expiration date) for each of the three nodes. Given these values, the binomial interest rate tree is used to find the present value of the call option. The backward induction procedure is used. The discount rates are those from the binomial interest rate tree. For years 0 and 1, the discount rate is the second number shown at each node. The first number at each

E X H I B I T   8–9

Valuing a 4-Year Treasury with a Coupon Rate of 6.5%
(10% Volatility Assumed)

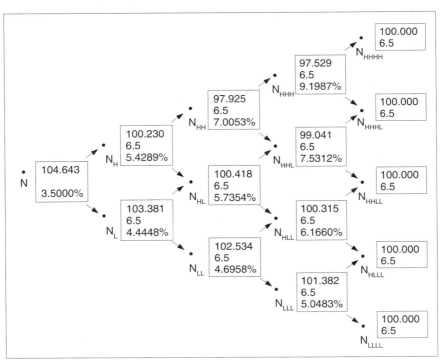

E X H I B I T   8–10

Valuing a Call Option Using the Binomial Method

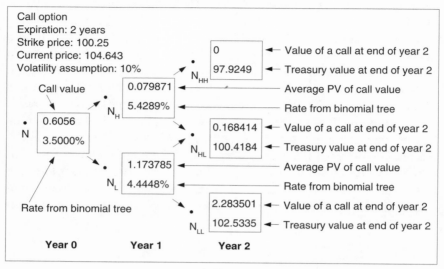

Call option
Expiration: 2 years
Strike price: 100.25
Current price: 104.643
Volatility assumption: 10%

node for year 1 is the average present value found by discounting the call option value of the two nodes to the right using the discount rate at the node. The value of the option is the first number shown at the root, $0.6056.

The same procedure is used to value a put option. This is illustrated in Exhibit 8–11 assuming that the put option has two years to expiration and the strike price is 100.25. The value of the put option two years from now is shown at each of the three nodes in year 2. The present value of the put is $0.5327.

Satisfaction of the Put-Call Parity Relationship

A relationship exists between the price of a call option and the price of a put option on the same underlying instrument, with the same strike price and the same expiration date. This relationship is commonly referred to as the *put/call parity relationship.* For European options on coupon bearing bonds, the relationship is

> Put price = Call price + Present value of strike price + Present
> value of coupon payments – Price of underlying bond

To demonstrate that the arbitrage-free binomial model satisfies the put/call parity relationship for European options, let's use the values from our illustration. We just found that

E X H I B I T   8–11

Valuing a Put Option Using the Binomial Method

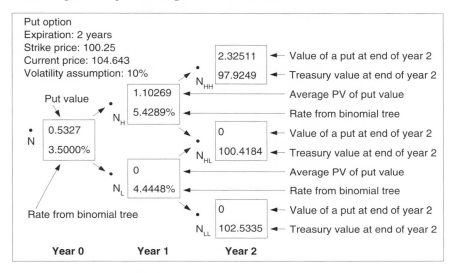

Put price = 0.6056
Call price = 0.5327

We showed that the theoretical price for the 6.5 percent, 4-year option-free bond is 104.643. Also, we showed the spot rates for each year. The spot rate for year 2 is 4.2147 percent. Therefore,

$$\text{Present value of coupon payments} = \frac{100.25}{(1.042147)^2} = 92.3053$$

The present value of the coupon payments is found by discounting the two coupon payments of 6.5 by the spot rates. As just noted, the spot rate for year 2 is 4.2147 percent and the spot rate for year 1 is 3.5 percent. Therefore,

$$\text{Present value of coupon payments} = \frac{6.5}{(1.035)} + \frac{6.5}{(1.042147)^2} = 12.2650$$

Substituting the values into the right-hand side of the put/call parity relationship, we find

$$0.6056 + 92.3053 + 12.2650 - 104.643 = 0.5319$$

The put value that we found is 0.5327. The discrepancy is due simply to rounding error. Therefore, put/call parity holds.

VALUING A BOND WITH AN EMBEDDED OPTION[7]

Now we will demonstrate how the binomial interest rate tree can be applied to value a bond with an embedded option. The valuation process proceeds in the same fashion as in the case of an option-free bond, but with one exception: When the embedded option may be exercised by either the issuer (in the case of a callable bond) or the investor (in the case of a putable bond), the bond value at a node must be changed to reflect what would happen if the option were exercised.

Valuing a Callable Bond

In the case of a callable bond, the value at a node must be changed to reflect the lesser of its value if it is not called (i.e., the value obtained by applying the recursive valuation formula described above) and the call price.

For example, consider a 6.5 percent corporate bond with four years remaining to maturity that is callable in one year at $100. Let's assume that the on-the-run Treasury yield curve is as follows:

Maturity	Yield to Maturity	Market Price
1 year	3.0%	100
2 years	3.7	100
3 years	4.2	100
4 years	4.7	100

Suppose the appropriate credit spread for this corporate bond issue is 50 basis points. Then the on-the-run yield curve for this issuer is the same as the one used earlier to obtain the binomial interest rate tree shown in Exhibit 8–8. Therefore, we will use the binomial interest rate tree in Exhibit 8–8 to value this callable bond.

Exhibit 8–12 shows two values at each node of the binomial interest rate tree. The discounting process explained earlier is used to calculate the first of the two values at each node. The second value is the value based on whether the issue will be called. For example, at nodes N_L, N_H, N_{LL}, N_{HH}, N_{LLL}, and N_{HLL} in Exhibit 8–12, the values from the recursive valuation formula are $101.968, $100.032, $101.723, $100.270, $101.382, and $100.315, respectively. These values exceed the assumed call price ($100), and therefore the second value is $100 rather than the calculated value. It is

---

[7] This section draws from Chapter 6 of Fabozzi, *Valuation of Fixed Income Securities and Derivatives*.

E X H I B I T 8–12

Valuing a Callable Corporate Bond with 4 Years to Maturity, a Coupon
Rate of 6.5%, and Callable in 1 Year at 100 (10% Volatility Assumed)

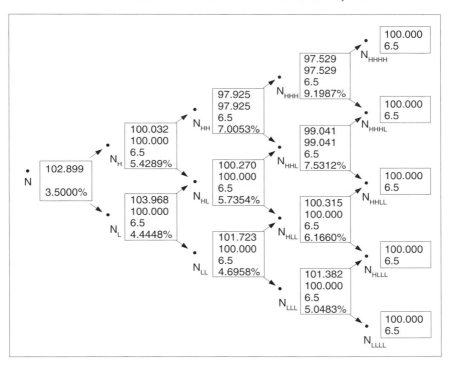

the second value that is used in subsequent calculations. The root of the tree
indicates that the value for this callable bond is $102.899.

The question that we have not addressed in our illustration, which is
nonetheless important, is the circumstances under which the issuer will
call the bond. A detailed explanation of the call rule is beyond the scope
of this chapter. Basically, it involves determining when it would be economical for the issuer on an after-tax basis to call the issue.

The valuation procedure can be accommodated to handle a call
schedule in which the call price varies for each year.[8]

The value of the embedded call option can be found as follows. The
value of a callable bond is equal to the value of a noncallable bond minus
the value of the call option. This means that

---

[8] For an illustration, see Chapter 6 of Fabozzi, *Valuation of Fixed Income Securities and Derivatives*.

Value of a call option = Value of a noncallable bond −
                        Value of a callable bond

We saw earlier that the value of a noncallable bond using the binomial tree in Exhibit 8–8 is $104.643. We just found that the value of the callable bond if the call price is $100 in each year is $102.899. The value of the call option is therefore $1.744.

Valuing a Putable Bond

To illustrate how to value a putable bond, consider a 6.5% corporate bond with four years remaining to maturity that is putable in one year at par ($100). Also, assume that the appropriate binomial interest rate tree for this issuer is the one in Exhibit 8–8.

Exhibit 8–13 shows the binomial interest rate tree with the bond values altered at three nodes (N_{HH}, N_{HHH}, and N_{HHL}) because the bond values at these nodes exceed $100, the assumed value at which the bond can be put. The value of this putable bond is $105.327.

Since the value of a nonputable bond can be expressed as the value of a putable bond minus the value of a put option on that bond, this means that

Value of a put option = Value of a nonputable bond −
                        Value of a putable bond

In our example, since the value of the putable bond is $105.327 and the value of the corresponding nonputable bond (i.e., option-free bond) is $104.643, the value of the put option is −$0.684. The negative sign indicates the issuer has sold the option or, equivalently, the investor has purchased the option.

Extension to Other Embedded Options

The bond valuation framework presented here can be used to analyze other embedded options such as caps and floors on floating-rate notes, range notes, step-up notes, and the optional accelerated redemption granted to an issuer in fulfilling its sinking fund requirement.[9] The framework can also be used to value a bond with multiple or interrelated embedded

---

[9] Some of these options are illustrated in Chapter 12 of Richard W. Wilson and Frank J. Fabozzi, *Corporate Bonds: Structures and Analysis* (New Hope, PA: Frank J. Fabozzi Associates, 1996).

E X H I B I T   8–13

Valuing a Putable Corporate Bond with 4 Years to Maturity, a Coupon
Rate of 6.5%, and Putable in 1 Year at 100 (10% Volatility Assumed)

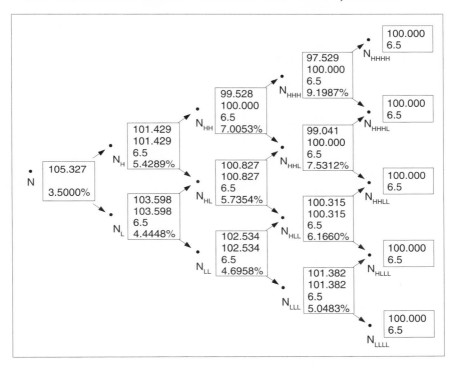

options. The bond values on each node are altered based on whether one
of the options is exercised.

SUMMARY

The binomial method can be used to value options and bonds with
embedded options. The valuation method involves generating a binomial
interest rate tree based on (1) the on-the-run yield curve, (2) an assumed
interest rate generation process, and (3) an assumed interest rate volatility. The tree provides the appropriate volatility-dependent one-period rates
that should be used to discount future option values and the cash flows of
a bond.

9

⑥ ## VALUING EMBEDDED OPTIONS IN INTEREST RATE CAPS, FLOORS, AND COLLARS

Mark J. P. Anson, PhD
Vice President
Salomon Brothers Inc

INTRODUCTION

Interest rate options are more difficult to value than stock or index options because a whole term structure must be modeled instead of a single variable. In addition, the behavior of interest rates can be somewhat complicated. In recent years, a whole range of economic models has been developed to predict the future term structure of interest rates. These models choose parameters such that the model resembles the market data as closely as possible. From among these economic term structures we may choose a mean reversion model, proportional volatility, or a normal distribution.[1]

---

[1] For mean reversion, see Richard Rendelman and Brit Bartter, "The Pricing of Options on Debt Securities," *Journal of Financial and Quantitative Analysis,* March 1980, pp. 11–24; for proportional volatility, see John Cox, Jonathan Ingersoll, and Stephen Ross, "A Theory of the Term Structure of Interest Rates," *Econometrica,* March 1985, pp. 385–407; for normal distribution, see Farshid Jamshidian, "An Exact Bond Option Pricing Formula," *Journal of Finance,* March 1989, pp. 21–25.

These models assume some underlying stochastic description of interest rate movement. For example, the Cox, Ingersoll, and Ross model, assumes the following equation to describe interest rates:

$$dr = a(b - r)dt + \sigma\sqrt{r}\ dz$$

where dz is a Weiner process distributed $\phi(0, \sqrt{dt})$. This model allows for mean reversion where the short rate is pulled to a level b at rate a. Superimposed on this pull is a normally distributed stochastic term, $\sigma\sqrt{r}\ dz$. A problem with prior stochastic models is that interest rates could become negative (in the economic world of the models). To correct for this, Cox, Ingersoll, and Ross set the standard deviation of the stochastic term proportional to the square root of r. This means that the short-term interest rate increases as its standard deviation increases.

This chapter presents a different approach to describing yield curve movements. Starting with the current term structure of interest rates, we construct a binomial, no-arbitrage model that is consistent with the current observed yield curve. A binomial tree is a discrete representation of the continuous time movement of interest rates.[2] An advantage of this model is its simplicity and iteration; that is, it is easy to program a computer to run a number of iterations to construct a binomial representation of the term structure. Further, the resulting term structure will be consistent with the current yield curve and volatility estimates.

This chapter first demonstrates how to use a binomial term structure to value embedded options in interest rate caps, floors, and collars. Next, it presents a modified option pricing model for valuing interest rate cap options based on Black's model for commodity options.[3] Finally, the chapter compares the two independently derived cap option values and attempts to explain any discrepancies in pricing.

INTEREST RATE CAPS

An *interest rate cap* is a contract that places a maximum value on a floating rate of interest. The buyer of a cap seeks to place a maximum limit on the interest rate to be paid. On the other side of the transaction, the seller of a cap accepts a limitation on the amount of interest he or she can receive on the underlying floating-rate interest instrument in return for a cap premium.

If the market benchmark rate rises above the cap strike interest rate, the cap contract can provide either for an embedded rate equal to the cap strike or for payments from the seller to the buyer of the cap. Both methods of compensating the cap buyer will accomplish the same result. For purposes of this chapter, we will assume that the cap buyer receives a payment from the seller as compensation for the benchmark rate rising in excess of the cap rate.

For financial managers, caps are designed to provide insurance against the rate of interest on a floating-debt instrument loan rising above a certain level. When a cap on a loan and the loan itself are both provid-

---

[2] See, for example, Fischer Black, Emanuel Derman and William Toy, "A One-Factor Model of Interest Rates and Its Application to Treasury Bond Options," *Financial Analysts Journal,* January–February 1990, 33–39; Andrew Kalotay, George Williams and Frank J. Fabozzi, "A Model for Valuing Bonds and Embedded Options," *Financial Analysts Journal,* May–June 1993, 35–46; Fischer Black and Piotr Karansinki, "Bond and Option Pricing When Short Rates are Lognormal," *Financial Analysts Journal,* July–August 1991, 52–59.

[3] See Fischer Black, "The Pricing of Commodity Contracts," *Journal of Financial Economics*, March 1976, pp. 167–79.

ed by the same financial institution, the cost of the options underlying the cap is often incorporated into the interest rate charged. When the cap is provided by a different financial institution, an up-front payment for the cap is required.

The mechanics of a cap are as follows. The buyer and seller agree on the cap strike rate (e.g., 5.0 percent), the term of the cap, the starting date for the cap, the reset frequency (quarterly, semiannual, etc.), the reference benchmark rate and the cap premium. Exhibit 9–1 illustrates the operation of a cap.

A cap guarantees that the rate charged on a loan at any point in time will be the lesser of the market rate or the cap rate. Consider a cap rate on a $1 million loan of 5 percent where the cap rate is reset every six months. To fulfill his or her obligations under the cap agreement, the seller of the cap must pay to the buyer of the cap the following amount at the end of every six months:[4]

$$0.5 \bullet \$1,000,000 \bullet \max (R - 0.05, 0) \tag{1}$$

where R is the floating benchmark rate at the beginning of the reset period. The individual reset periods are sometimes referred to as *caplets*.

E X H I B I T   9–1

The Effective Interest Rate with a Cap of 5.0%

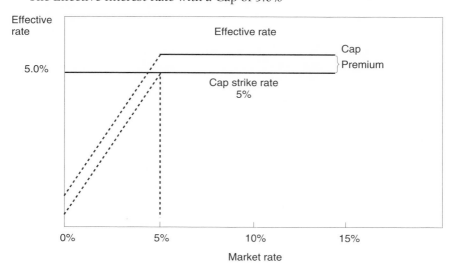

----
[4] Cap payments are usually made at the end of each reset period; that is, the payoff from a capped rate is usually made in arrears. Therefore, the cap payment must be discounted back to the current period to determine its present value.

To see the embedded options in a cap, note that the expression $\max(R - 0.05, 0)$ represents the payoff from a call option on the floating benchmark (R). Therefore, the buyer of a cap has a series of call options on the floating rate R for each reset period. Thus, each caplet represents a call option on the benchmark rate.

To provide a general framework, if the cap rate is R_c, the amount of the loan or underlying notional is P, and the interest payments are made at times $t, 2t, \ldots nt$, the cap agreement requires the seller to make a payment at time $(j + 1)t$ equal to the following:

$$t \bullet P \bullet \max\ (R_j - R_c, 0) \tag{2}$$

where R_j is the value at time jt of the floating rate that is being capped.

PRICING EMBEDDED OPTIONS IN INTEREST RATE CAPS, FLOORS, AND COLLARS

The Term Structure of Interest Rates

To develop a binomial term structure, we must start with the on-the-run Treasury yield curve. The on-the-run yield curve represents the yields to maturity on securities selling at par with the same credit quality but different maturities. In addition, to apply a more formal option pricing model, we must be able to derive the expected forward rates that will apply to each reset period of the cap.

For our example in this chapter, we use the yield curve presented in Exhibit 9–2, from which we can derive the spot and forward rates presented in Exhibit 9–3. The interested reader should consult Chapter 8 for a complete discussion of spot rates, forward rates, and the term structure of interest rates.

E X H I B I T   9–2

Yield to Maturity for Coupon-Bearing Bonds

Security	Maturity	Yield to Maturity	Value
1	0.5 year	4.00%	100
2	1.0 year	4.50	100
3	1.5 years	5.00	100

EXHIBIT 9–3

Spot and Forward Rates

Time Period	Spot Rate	Forward Rate
0.5 year	4.000%	4.000%
1.0 year	4.556	5.012
1.5 years	5.144	5.604

Now that we have a description of the term structure of interest rates, we must still develop a random structure of interest rate movements. If the term structure could be predicted with certainty, there would be no need for interest rate caps. It is exactly this randomness that makes caps valuable.

Constructing a Binomial Term Structure

If we know the current term structure of interest rates and have an estimate of the volatility of interest rates we can construct a binomial term structure tree by allowing the six-month interest rate to increase to R_u or decrease to R_d with equal probability.[5] The resulting tree will be a discrete representation of the possible evolution over time of the six-month interest rate based on an estimate of interest rate volatility.[6]

For the purposes of this chapter, we assume the estimated volatility of the six-month forward interest rate is 15 percent ($\sigma = 15\%$). To construct a binomial term structure tree, we must find forward rates that are

---

[5] For simplicity we assume an equal probability of an interest rate increase or decrease, but we could just as easily construct a binomial tree with any set of probabilities that sums to 1.

[6] If we take the time period during which we wish to model interest rates and subdivide it into T periods, with each period corresponding to a move in interest rates, we will construct a tree describing all possible interest rates prevailing at the end of each period n, where $n = 1, 2, \ldots$ T. In each nth period, there will be $n + 1$ possible interest rate outcomes. If we determine that an upward movement in interest rates has a probability of p, and a downward movement of interest rates has a probability of $(1 - p)$, the general form of the probabilities of each interest rate movement is

$$B(n \mid T, p) = \frac{T!}{(T-n)!n!} \times p^n (1-p)^{T-n}$$

See J. Cox, Stephen Ross, and Mark Rubinstein, "Option Pricing: A Simplified Approach," *Journal of Financial Economics,* September 1979, pp. 229–63, for a thorough discussion of applying a binomial option pricing model.

consistent with our estimated volatility and our existing on-the-run yield curve.[7] Therefore, the security values and yields to maturity presented in Exhibit 9–2 are used to determine the random binomial rates presented in Exhibit 9–4.

Exhibit 9–4 displays at each node of the tree the value of the three-period bond based on the random binomial interest rates. In our simple term structure, we know the final value of the three-period bond is $102.50, which equals a face value payment of $100 and a coupon of $2.50. In addition, we know the value of the bond today is $100. Therefore, using the binomial tree, we may work backward to find the random interest rates consistent with our estimate of volatility and probability of an interest rate increase that will equate current value to final value.

For instance, at node N_u, the bond value of $98.74 equals the expected value of the bond next period ($98.59 and $99.57 weighted with equal probability) plus the coupon of $2.50, discounted back to node N_u at a rate of interest equal to 5.74 percent. 5.74 percent is the exact solution, given a volatility estimate of 15 percent and an equal probability of interest rate increases and declines that will allow a bond value to be calculated at node N_u which is consistent with the initial and final bond values. A complete discussion of how to construct a binomial tree is presented in Chapter 8.

These rates need not necessarily be higher or lower than the six-month rate in the preceding period. Further, the constructed tree is a discrete representation of a lognormal distribution over time of the six-month interest rates. If we could define the periods instantaneously, we would achieve the continuous time concept of the term structure.[8]

---

[7] The volatility between the six-month forward rates can be measured as

$$\sigma = \ln (R_{1,u}/R_{1,d}) / 2$$

which in turn implies that

$$R_{1,u} = R_{1,d} (e^{2\sigma})$$

See Kalotay, Williams, and Fabozzi, "A Model for Valuing Bonds and Embedded Options," for a complete discussion on how to derive a binomial tree using the estimated volatility and the existing term structure. The idea is to determine the value of an n-period bond at each node of the binomial tree, where the value at each node is equal to the present value of the expected future cash flows and the future cash flows are discounted by the random implied forward rates, $R_{1,u}$ and $R_{1,d}$.

[8] See Black and Karasinski, "Bond and Option Pricing," for a discussion of the lognormal model. They define their model as

$$dr = a(b - r)dt + dz$$

where dz is a Weiner process that is distributed $\phi\left(0, \sqrt{dt}\right)$.

EXHIBIT 9–4

Binomial Forward Rates for Two Periods Given the Three-Period
On-the-Run Yield-to-Maturity of 5.0% and Estimated Volatility of 15%

$$
\begin{array}{l}
\text{(tree diagram)}
\end{array}
$$

- $V_0 = 100$
  - N_u
    - $V_u = 98.74$
    - $C = 2.5$
    - $R_{1,u} = 5.74\%$
      - N_{uu}
        - $V_{uu} = 98.59$
        - $C = 2.5$
        - $R_{2,uu} = 7.93\%$
          - 102.5
          - 102.5
      - N_{ud}
        - $V_{ud} = 99.57$
        - $C = 2.5$
        - $R_{2,ud} = 5.87\%$
          - 102.5
  - N_d
    - $V_d = 100.29$
    - $C = 2.5$
    - $R_{1,d} = 4.25\%$
      - N_{ud}
      - N_{dd}
        - $V_{dd} = 100.32$
        - $C = 2.5$
        - $R_{2,dd} = 4.35\%$
          - 102.5
          - 102.5

Valuing Embedded Options in Caps

Once we have constructed a binomial term structure tree, we can apply it
to determine the value of an embedded option in an interest rate cap. We
begin by returning to our original parameters for the cap; that is, we
assume a notional value of $1 million, a capped rate of 5.0 percent, a reset
period of every six months, a starting date for the cap of $t = 0.5$, and a cap
maturity of two periods.[9]

By working backward through the nodes of the tree, we can arrive
at a value of the embedded option in the cap at time 0. We know that at
the beginning of the final cap reset period ($t = 1$ year to $t = 1.5$ years) the
value of the cap at each node of the tree is given by:

$$\text{Cap}_{2,uu} = [0.5 \bullet \$1,000,000 \bullet \max(0.07926 - 0.05, 0)] \div (1 + 0.07926/2)$$
$$\text{Cap}_{2,ud} = [0.5 \bullet \$1,000,000 \bullet \max(0.0587 - 0.05, 0)] \div (1 + 0.0587/2) \quad (3)$$
$$\text{Cap}_{2,uu} = [0.5 \bullet \$1,000,000 \bullet \max(0.0425 - 0.05, 0)] \div (1 + .0425/2)$$

where each caplet is discounted by the forward rate over the time period
$t = 1.0$ to $t = 1.5$ years as determined by the binomial tree. The value of
the cap at each node in period 3 ($t = 1.5$ years) is also the final value of
the option associated with the cap. Since there are no further reset periods, at the end of period 3 the embedded option expires. Therefore, the
value of the option at expiration is also the final value of the cap. Solving

---

[9] We also assume that the benchmark interest rate follows the on-the-run yield curve presented in
Exhibit 9–2.

the above equations, we get terminal option values equivalent to $Cap_{2,uu}$ = $14,072; $Cap_{2,ud}$ = $4,226; and $Cap_{2,dd}$ = $0.[10]

As we proceed backward through the nodes of the binomial tree, the embedded option value over reset periods other than the final period is valued differently than in equation 3. At these interim nodes, the value of the embedded cap option is equal to the sum of (1) the discounted intrinsic cap value for the current reset period as measured by equation 3 *plus* (2) the expected value of the embedded option for the next reset period discounted back to the current period. For example, at node N_u,

$$\text{Option value} = [0.5 \bullet \$1,000,000 \bullet \max(0.0574 - 0.05, 0) \quad (4)$$
$$\div (1 + 0.0574/2)] + [\tfrac{1}{2}(\$14,072 + \$4,226)$$
$$\div (1 + 0.0574/2)]$$

which reduces to

$$\text{Option value} = \$3,597 + \$8,894 = \$12,491$$

At node N_u, the option value is the sum of the current period's discounted intrinsic value of $3,597 plus the present value of the expected cap value for the next period of $8,894. Therefore, the total value of the embedded option at time $t = 0.5$ and node N_u is $12,491.[11] Similarly, at node N_d, the intrinsic value of the cap is $0.00 (because 4.35 percent is less than 5.0 percent), and the present value of the expected value of the embedded option for the next period is $2,069. Therefore, the value of the embedded option at $t = 0.5$ and node N_d is the sum of $0 plus $2,069, or $2,069.

Finally, we need to determine the value of the embedded option at time 0. Since the cap does not begin until after six months, the value is the embedded option at $t = 0$ is simply the present value of the expected option value at time $t = 0.5$ years. Therefore, the value of the embedded option at time 0 equals

$$\tfrac{1}{2} [\$12,496 + \$2,069] \div [1 + 0.04/2] = \$7,137$$

[10] Recall that in our scenario, the cap payment is made *at the end of the period.* Since the cap payment is made in arrears, it must be discounted back to the beginning of the period in which the cap begins. The discount rate is chosen to be consistent with the on-the-run term structure.

[11] We remind the reader that we constructed our binomial tree based on the assumption that there was an equal probability of an interest rate increase as well as an interest rate decrease. Therefore, the expected value of next period's embedded option is the simple average of $Cap_{2,uu}$ and $Cap_{2,ud}$. However, the binomial model is general enough to allow for different probability estimates. For instance, we could have modeled the probability of an interest rate increase to be 0.6 and the probability of an interest rate decrease to be 0.4.

$7,137 represents the value today of the embedded option of the cap for all reset periods given our binomial term structure. This value is consistent with the observed term structure in Exhibit 9–2 as well as with our volatility estimates. Exhibit 9–5 displays the option values.

Valuing Embedded Options in Floors and Collars

While this approach has been used to value embedded options in interest rate caps, it is general enough to be applied to interest rate floors and collars. For example, using our same term structure and the binomial tree developed in Exhibit 9–4, we can determine the value of the embedded option for an interest rate floor and an interest rate collar.

An interest rate floor provides a lower bound on a floating rate. Thus, a lender may want to maintain a minimum level of interest income on a floating-rate loan. A floor can provide a guarantee to a lender that it will receive no less than a certain interest rate, even if the floating rate declines.

For our example, suppose a lender requests an interest rate floor of 4.5 percent; that is, for any reset period, the annual rate of interest paid to the lender cannot fall below 4.5 percent. To receive this benefit, the lender will be willing to pay the borrower the value of the embedded option associated with the interest rate floor. In return for this payment, the borrower must agree to pay to the lender (in addition to the floating rate of interest) the following amount at the end of each reset period:

$$0.5 \bullet \$1,000,000 \bullet \max\,(0.045 - R,\, 0) \tag{5}$$

E X H I B I T   9–5

Valuing the Embedded Option in a Two-Period Interest Rate Cap of 5.0%

Option = $14,072
$Cap_{2,uu}$ = $14,072
$R_{2,uu}$ = 7.93%

Option = $12,491
Cap_u = $3,597
$R_{1,u}$ = 5.74%

N_{uu}

N_{ud}

Option = $7,137
R_0 = 4.0%

N_u

N_d

Option = $4,226
$Cap_{2,ud}$ = $4,226
$R_{2,ud}$ = 5.87%

Option = $2,069
Cap_d = $0
$R_{1,d}$ = 4.25%

N_{du}

N_{dd}

Option = $0.00
$Cap_{2,dd}$ = $0.00
$R_{2,dd}$ = 4.35%

where R is the floating benchmark rate at the beginning of the reset period. The interest rate floor has value to the lender only when the floating benchmark rate falls below 4.5 percent.

If we compare equation 5 to equation 1 at the beginning of the chapter, we quickly see that the expression max $(0.045 - R)$ represents the payoff from a put option on the floating rate, R. In effect, with an interest rate floor, the borrower sells a put option back to the lender, whereas with an interest rate cap, the borrower buys a call option from the lender. When the floor (or cap) on a loan and the loan itself are both provided by the same lender, the value of the floor (or cap) is usually incorporated into the interest rate charged to the borrower.

Using our existing binomial tree from Exhibit 9–4, we can establish the value of the interest rate floor at the terminal nodes of the tree as

$$\text{Floor}_{2,uu} = [\ 0.5 \bullet \$1,000,000 \bullet \max (0.045 - 0.07926, 0)\ ] \quad (6)$$
$$\div (\ 1 + 0.07926/2)$$
$$\text{Floor}_{2,ud} = [\ 0.5 \bullet \$1,000,000 \bullet \max (0.045 - 0.0587, 0)\ ]$$
$$\div (\ 1 + 0.0587/2)$$
$$\text{Floor}_{2,uu} = [\ 0.5 \bullet \$1,000,000 \bullet \max (0.045 - 0.0435, 0)\ ]$$
$$\div (1 + 0.0435/2)$$

Once again, since there are no further reset periods, at the end of period 3 ($t = 1.5$ years), the floor expires, and the value of the embedded option at expiration is also the final value of the floor. Solving the above equations, we get terminal option values equivalent to $\text{Floor}_{2,uu} = \$0$, $\text{Floor}_{2,ud} = \$0$, and $\text{Floor}_{2,dd} = \$734$.

Similarly to valuing caps, we work backward through the binomial tree to determine the value at time $t = 0$ of the floor. Again, we remind the reader that the value of the embedded floor option at the interim nodes is the sum of (1) the intrinsic floor value as measured by equation 6, *plus* (2) the expected value of the next period's embedded option discounted back to the current period. For example, at node N_d, the value of the floor is

$$\text{Option value} = [0.5 \bullet \$1,000,000 \bullet \max (\ 0.045 - 0.0425, 0) \quad (7)$$
$$\div (1 + 0.0425/2)] + [\ \tfrac{1}{2}\ (\text{Floor}_{2,dd} + \text{Floor}_{2,du})$$
$$\div (\ 1 + 0.0425/2)\ ]$$

which reduces to

$$\text{Option value} = \$1,224 + \$359 = \$1,583$$

To summarize, at node N_d, the value of the floor is the sum of the intrinsic value of the option for the current reset period plus the present value of the expected value of the floor in future periods. Therefore, the value of the embedded option at time $t = 0.5$ years and node N_d is \$1,583. Note that at node N_u, the value of the floor and the present value of the expected value of the embedded option for the next period are both \$0.00. This is because at Nodes N_u, N_{uu} and N_{ud}, the binomial floating rate exceeds the interest rate floor of 4.5 percent.

Finally, at time $t = 0$, the value of the embedded floor option is the present value of the expected option value at time $t = 0.5$ years. Similarly to the cap calculation above, our calculation is

$$\tfrac{1}{2} [\; \$1,583 + \$0.00 \;] \div (\; 1 + 0.04/2) = \$776$$

Exhibit 9–6 demonstrates the binomial pricing for the interest rate floor; \$776 represents the value today of the interest rate floor for all reset periods given our binomial term structure. We note that the value of the floor (\$776) is much less than the value of the cap (\$7,137). The reason is twofold.

First, the interest rate floor of 4.5 percent is set at a rate that is below the three-period on-the-run yield of 5.0 percent. Thus, the floor is established below the current market rate for a three-period investment. Second, our term structure of interest rates, as presented in Exhibit 9–2, is upward sloping; that is, interest rates are expected to rise over time, not

EXHIBIT 9–6

Valuing the Embedded Option in a Two-Period Interest Rate Floor of 4.5%

			Option = \$0.00 $Floor_{2,uu}$ = \$0.00 $R_{2,uu}$ = 7.93%
	Option = \$0.00 $Floor_{1,u}$ = \$0.00 $R_{1,u}$ = 5.74%	N_{uu} N_{ud}	
Option = \$776 R_0 = 4.0%	N_u N_d		Option = \$0.00 $Floor_{2,ud}$ = \$0.00 $R_{2,ud}$ = 5.87%
	Option = \$1,583 $Floor_{1,d}$ = \$1,224 $R_{1,d}$ = 4.25%	N_{du} N_{dd}	
			Option = \$734 $Floor_{2,dd}$ = \$734 $R_{2,dd}$ = 4.35%

decline. Consequently, the expectation is that the cap will be more valu-able than the floor.

We can draw some similarities among the floor option, the cap option, and equity options. In the Black-Scholes environment for pricing equity options, it is assumed that the underlying stock has a positive drift term; that is, over time, the price of the stock is expected to increase. Therefore, an at-the-money equity call option will be worth more than an at-the-money equity put option because investors expect the stock price to increase in value over the life of the option. Consequently, the call option will have greater value because of the greater likelihood that the underlying stock price will increase rather than decrease over the life of the option.

Similarly, with our interest rate options, the floor/put option value is less than that of the cap/call option value because investors expect that interest rates will increase over time. However, in a downward-sloping yield curve environment, we would predict the opposite result. The value of the interest rate floor would be greater than the value of the interest rate cap because investors would expect short-term interest rates to decline over time.

Finally, we examine an interest rate collar. A collar establishes a range in which a floating rate may fluctuate but not exceed. In other words, a collar is a combination of a long position in an interest rate cap and a short position in an interest rate floor.

In our example, the borrower would buy the 5.0 percent cap from the lender and sell back to the lender the 4.5 percent floor. In fact, the sale of the floor by the borrower helps to finance the purchase of the cap. In addition, since the market expectation is that interest rates will increase rather than decrease, the sale of the floor is a reasonable way to reduce the cost of the cap.

In our example, the cost of the collar is simply the net of the cost of the cap and the floor:

$$\text{Value of the collar} = \$7,137 - \$776 = \$6,361$$

In practice, the collar is usually constructed so that the price of the cap equals the price of the floor. In other words, the sale of the put/floor option provides the revenue with which to purchase the call/cap option. The net cost of the collar is then zero.

A MODIFIED OPTIONS PRICING APPROACH TO PRICING EMBEDDED OPTIONS IN CAPS

In this section, we present an alternative pricing method to the binomial tree to value the individual embedded options in each caplet. We modify a model first presented by Black to value options on commodity futures contracts.[12] His model is as follows:

$$c = e^{-r(T-t)} \bullet [FN(d_1) - XN(d_2)] \tag{8}$$

where

$$d_1 = [\ln(F/X) + (\sigma^2/2)(T - t)] \div [\sigma\sqrt{(T-t)}]$$

$$d_2 = d_1 - \sigma\sqrt{(T-t)}$$

To see how this model may be applied to an embedded cap option, recall the general valuation of equation 2 where R_j is the value at time jt of the benchmark rate being capped. Also, let F_j equal the forward rate between time jt and $j(t + 1)$. Given our assumptions about unbiased expectations, we can use the forward rate, F_j, as a discount rate over the period jt to $j(t + 1)$. Since the cap is paid at the end of the period, the value of the cap at time jt is

$$t \bullet P \bullet \max(R_j - R_c) \div (1 + (t)F_j) \tag{9}$$

Equation 9 is the present value of an end-of-period payment on each caplet embedded in the interest rate cap. We now note that the forward rate, F_j, is the expectation today of the one-period interest rate at time jt. If we assume unbiased expectations, then

$$F_j = R_j \tag{10}$$

---

[12] See Black, "The Pricing of Commodity Contracts." Black derives his model by noting that the futures price, F, is related to the spot price, S, by the following relationship:

$$F = Se^{\alpha(T-t)}$$

where α equals the risk-free rate of interest less the yield on the asset if S represents a financial asset, α equals the risk-free rate of interest plus storage costs per dollar less convenience yield if S is a storable commodity, and α equals the risk-free rate of interest less the risk-free rate of interest on a foreign denomination if S is a currency.

We can then regard the option on the caplet between time jt and $j(t + 1)$ as a call option on F_j instead of R_j.[13] This insight allows us to use Black's model in equation 8. Assuming constant volatility, we can substitute equations 9 and 10 into equation 8 to yield the following valuation formula for the embedded option in each individual caplet:

$$t \bullet P \bullet e^{-rjt} \bullet [F_j N(d_1) - R_c N(d_2)] \div (1 + (t)F_j) \tag{11}$$

where

$$d_1 = [\ln(F_j/R_c) + \sigma^2 jt/2] \div [\sigma\sqrt{jt}]$$

$$d_2 = d_1 - \sigma\sqrt{jt}$$

In our example, there are only two reset periods, and therefore, only two caplets. For the first caplet, $t = 0.5$ years, $P = \$1,000,000$, $jt = 0.5$ years, $F_j = 5.012\%$, $R_c = 5.0\%$, $\sigma = 15\%$, and $r = 4.0\%$. Solving equation 11 we get a value for the first-period caplet of $\$1,365$. For the second caplet, $t = 0.5$ years, $P = \$1,000,000$, $jt = 1$ year, $F_j = 5.604\%$, $R_c = 5.0\%$, $\sigma = 15\%$, and $r = 4.5\ \%$. Plugging these figures into equation 11 results in a value of $\$3,283$. Together the present value of the two caplets under our modified Black model is $\$4,648$. Compare this value with that derived by our binomial model of $\$7,137$.

The difference in option values may be traced to the nature of the stochastic distribution underlying the two models. The modified Black model assumes a continuous-time environment; that is, the incremental time periods between interest rate movements are very small (in fact, instantaneous). In our binomial tree, the time period between interest rate movements is six months. The difference between discrete time interest rate movements and continuous movements may be a likely culprit for the

---

[13] Each caplet may also be valued as a European put option on a discount bond if we view the discounted payoff from a caplet to be equal to

$$(1 + R_c dt) \bullet \max[\ 1/(1 + R_c dt) - 1/(1 + R_j dt),\ 0]$$

If we consider $1/(1+R_j dt)$ as the value at time t_0 of a bond maturing at time t_1, this expression is the same as $1 + R_c dt$ European puts on a discount bond with an option exercise price of $1/(1 + R_c dt)$. When viewed in this manner, an interest rate cap is a portfolio of put options on discount bonds. See See John Hull and Alan White, "Pricing Interest-Rate-Derivative Securities," *Review of Financial Studies*, 3, no. 4 (1990), pp. 573–92, and; John Hull, *Options, Futures and Other Derivative Securities* (Englewood Cliffs, NJ: Prentice Hall, 1993).

discrepancy in option values. However, the discrete time movement is more realistic because with an interest rate cap, only the interest rate at the beginning of the reset period matters. In this sense, embedded cap options are similar to Bermuda equity options where there are discrete exercise dates over the life of the option.

However, if we make the reset intervals over the life of the cap very short and increase the branches on our tree, in the limit our binomial model should approximate the continuous-time-modified Black model. This is because, in the limit, as the number of intervals increases over a fixed time period, the binomial distribution will equal the lognormal distribution that underlies the modified Black model. Therefore, the two models should converge to the same value. See Appendix 9–A for a demonstration of this proof.

In addition, Black's model assumes a constant volatility over the life of the option contract. Although our binomial model makes a similar assumption for ease of calculation, it is general enough to allow for changing the volatility during each cap reset period. Furthermore, the binomial tree was designed to be completely consistent with today's term structure as detailed in Exhibit 9–2. One disadvantage of some of the continuous-time models is that they do not automatically fit the observed term structure of interest rates.

Finally, prior theoretical models make assumptions about the mean reversion of interest rates and choose parameters in an attempt to reflect this phenomenon. The binomial model presented here does not need to model mean reversion. This is because whatever mean reversion exists, it is already embedded in the current term structure of interest rates. Since our binomial model was constructed to be consistent with the current term structure, it must also be consistent with the existing mean reversion.

SUMMARY

This chapter demonstrated how a binomial model of the forward rate term structure may be used to value embedded options in interest rate caps, floors, and collars. This model was shown to be consistent with the current Treasury term structure and estimates of volatility. Furthermore, the binomial model is general enough to be adapted to any observable term structure and volatility measure.

When comparing interest rate caps (calls) and floors (puts) to equity options, we noted some similarities. Given an upward-sloping yield curve, an interest rate cap will be more valuable than an interest rate floor because investors expect short-term interest rates to increase over time. Similarly, with respect to equity options, an at-the-money call option will be more valuable than an at-the-money put option because investors expect the underlying stock to increase in value over time.

When the value of the embedded cap option as derived from our binomial tree was compared to the value of the cap option derived from the modified Black model, the Black model indicated a lower option value. This is because the Black model assumes a continuous-time interest rate environment where the reset periods on the cap are very short. However, caps typically have longer reset periods, up to six months, much like Bermuda equity options. Consequently, we find the binomial model to be a more accurate measure of the option value.

Extending the Binomial Formula to Continuous Time

In this appendix, we demonstrate that in the limit, the binomial formula for pricing embedded options approximates the Black continuous-time solution. Consider the binomial pricing equation established by Cox, Ross, and Rubinstein.[14] The general form of the binomial payoff at time T is

$$\max [\ 0,\ u^n d^{T-n} R - R_c] \tag{1A}$$

where T is the total number of time periods and n is the number of upward movements in interest rates ($n = 0, 1, 2 \ldots T$). The general form of probabilities of each potential payoff given by the binomial distribution is

$$B(n \mid T, p) = \frac{T!}{(T-n)! n!} \times p^n (1-p)^{T-n} \tag{2A}$$

$B(n \mid T, p)$ represents the probability of observing n upward movements in interest rates out of T trials given a probability, p, of an upward movement. Multiplying the payoffs in equation 1A by the probabilities in equation 2A and summing across all possible payoffs and discounting back to the current period, we get the following binomial option pricing formula:

$$c = \left\{ \sum_{n=0}^{T} \frac{T!}{(T-n)! n!} \bullet p^n (1-p)^{T-n} \max \left[0, u^n d^{T-n} R - R_c \right] \right\} \div \left(1 + R_f \right)^T \tag{3A}$$

To compare the discrete-time binomial model to the continuous-time modified Black model, we define a as the boundary of the n states of nature where the option has positive value. This allows us to drop the expression $\max [0,\ u^n d^{T-n} R - R_c]$ because we are considering only non-negative states of nature. In addition, we can reduce the states of nature over which we summate from $n = 0, \ldots T$ to $n = a, \ldots T$. Then equation 3A reduces to

---

[14] Cox, Ross, and Rubinstein, "Option Pricing."

$$c = R \bullet \left\{ \sum_{n=a}^{T} \frac{T!}{(T-n)!n!} \bullet p^n (1-p)^{T-n} \bullet u^n d^{t-n} \right\} \div \left(1 + R_f\right)^T \qquad (4A)$$

$$-R_c \bullet \left\{ \sum_{n=a}^{T} \frac{T!}{(T-n)!n!} \bullet p^n (1-p)^{T-n} \right\} \div \left(1 + R_f\right)^T$$

The second expression is the discounted value of the cap rate multiplied by a binomial probability applicable to the hedging probabilities determined by the risk-free hedged portfolio. The first bracketed expression is the interest rate R multiplied by a binomial probability. It may be interpreted in the same way if we set

$$p' = \frac{up}{1 + R_f} \qquad \text{and} \qquad 1 - p' = \frac{d(1-p)}{1 + R_f}$$

We can then write the following equation:

$$p^n (1-p)^{T-n} \frac{\left(u^n d^{T-n}\right)}{\left(1 + R_f\right)^T} = \frac{[up]^n}{\left[1 + R_f\right]^n} \bullet \frac{\left[d(1-p)\right]^{T-n}}{\left[1 + R_f\right]^{T-n}} = (p')^n \bullet (1-p')^{T-n}$$

Using this notation, the binomial model for pricing a European call option can be summarized as follows:

$$c = R \bullet B(n \geq a \mid T, p') - R_c \bullet B(n \geq a \mid T, p) \qquad (5A)$$

where
$$p = \frac{\left(1 + R_f\right) - d}{u - d}$$

It has been demonstrated that as n, the number of binomial intervals per year, becomes very large, the binomial distribution converges to a normal distribution.[15] Mathematically, this means

$$\lim_{n \to \infty} B(n \geq a \mid T, p') \to N(d_1) \quad \text{and} \quad \lim_{n \to \infty} B(n \geq a \mid T, p) \to N(d_2)$$

---

[15] Cox, Ross, and Rubinstein, "Option Pricing."

Consequently, equation 5A, in the limit, may be written as

$$c = RN(d_1) - R_c N(d_2) \div (1 + R_f)$$

This is the same as equation 11 for the modified Black approach. Further, it has been demonstrated that the Black-Scholes approach (and therefore the modified Black approach) tends to price call options below the prices of the binomial valuation method.[16] However, as we have indicated, the binomial method is most appropriate for pricing interest rate cap options because of the discrete reset periods, and therefore it provides the most accurate option valuation.

---

[16] See Thomas Copeland and Fred Weston, *Financial Theory and Corporate Policy* (New York: Addison-Wesley, 1988).

⑥ # A MODEL FOR THE VALUATION OF CALLABLE BONDS

Ehud I. Ronn, PhD
Associate Professor of Finance
University of Texas at Austin

INTRODUCTION

The pricing of callable Treasury, agency, and corporate securities requires modeling several aspects of interest rate valuation that are specific to these securities. The model proposed in this chapter uses as inputs a "bullet" term structure of interest rates, appropriate credit spreads, and market-implied volatilities to value the bond with embedded options in an arbitrage-free framework.[1] The model implements a specific interest rate model, that of lognormally distributed rates of interest.

The literature on interest rate models originated with the Cox-Ingersoll-Ross model.[2] Ho and Lee were the first to offer a stochastic interest rate model that exactly matched the observable term structure of interest rates.[3] Black, Derman, and Toy, Black and Karasinsky, and Hull and

---

This chapter is based in part on the author's work while serving as vice president, Trading Research Group, at Merrill Lynch & Co. Numerous current and former officers of Merrill Lynch & Co. contributed to the development of this model. However, this chapter does not represent the view of Merrill Lynch & Co.

[1] The term *embedded option* refers to a security that incorporates an implicit option within its provision. Examples include callable bonds, putable bonds, and bonds with sinking fund provisions that permit an acceleration of the amount sunk.

[2] John C. Cox, Jonathan E. Ingersoll, Jr., and Stephen Ross, "A Theory of the Term Structure of Interest Rates," *Econometrica*, March 1985, pp. 385–407.

[3] Thomas S. Y. Ho and Sang-Bin Lee, "Term Structure Movements and Pricing Interest Rate Contingent Claims," *Journal of Finance*, December 1986, pp. 1011–29.

White extended the Ho-Lee model to match a term structure of volatility curves in addition to the term structure of interest rates.[4] An important contribution to rendering models computationally efficient was made by Jamshidian, who provided the forward-induction procedures used for the efficient construction of a binomial tree for the short-term rate of interest.[5]

The lognormally distributed model is one of the commonly used interest rate models proposed in the financial economics literature. Thus, this analysis is a specific application of the one-factor interest rate to the valuation of Treasury, agency, and corporate bonds with embedded options.

The model begins by capturing the form of the credit risk–adjusted term structure of interest rates; that is, for a specific issuer, the model adds a term structure of credit spreads to the Treasury's "bullet" term structure. These credit spreads represent the interest rate differential above the corresponding Treasury par rate that a specific issuer, such as FNMA, must pay for its bonds to be priced at par. Then, for a specific interest rate volatility, the model proceeds to build an interest rate "tree," or lattice, that exactly matches that Treasury yield curve. Once constructed, this lattice permits the valuation of bonds with embedded options.

In exemplifying the model, the chapter provides an analysis of implied volatilities in the Treasury and agency markets. For bonds with embedded options, this latter input is crucial for the calculation of option-adjusted duration and convexity as well as for richness/cheapness analysis.

CRITERIA FOR SELECTION OF INTEREST RATE MODELS FOR THE VALUATION OF CALLABLE BONDS

The valuation of bonds with known cash flows, or "bullet" bonds, is a straightforward calculation of the relevant present values of these cash flows and their summation. In contrast, many interest rate-dependent securities, such as bond and swaps, frequently contain option-like features, including call, put, or sinking fund provisions. Whenever a bond's cash flows are not deterministic, an interest rate model is required to value the option features. Further, the purchaser or seller of such interest rate–dependent securities can be motivated by speculation or hedging

---

[4] Fischer Black, Emanuel Derman, and William Toy, "A One-Factor Model of Interest Rates and Its Application to Treasury Bond Options," *Financial Analysts Journal*, January–February 1990, pp. 33–39; Fischer Black and Piotr Karasinski, "Bond and Option Pricing when Short Rates Are Lognormal," *Financial Analysts Journal*, July–August 1991, pp. 52–59, and; John Hull and Alan White, "Pricing Interest-Rate-Derivative Securities," *Review of Financial Studies*, Vol. 3, No. 4, 1990, pp. 573–92.

[5] Farshid Jamshidian, "Forward Induction and Construction of Yield Curve Diffusion Models," *Journal of Fixed Income*, June 1991, pp. 62–74.

interests. The availability of interest rate models permits the user to value and hedge his or her exposure to interest rate risk.

Clearly the Black-Scholes formula is one candidate model for the valuation of interest rate–dependent securities. Unfortunately, it is poorly suited for the valuation of bonds with embedded options. The Black-Scholes model was originally derived to calculate the no-arbitrage value for options written on common stocks. Specifically, the model assumes that: (1) the stock price follows the lognormal distribution, which implies that the logarithm of the stock price is normally distributed; (2) the stock's volatility is constant; and (3) the rate of interest is constant. In applying the model to interest rate securities, these key assumptions give rise to several problems:

1. Absent default, the bond matures at par.[6] This violates the Black-Scholes statistical assumption of lognormal distribution.

2. As the bond matures, volatility declines. This violates the Black-Scholes assumption of constant volatility.

3. Black-Scholes posits a constant rate of interest, which in turn implies that bond prices are *nonrandom;* that is, bond prices at any future dates are known with certainty. Thus, a fundamental inconsistency is present in the model: Interest rates cannot simultaneously be constant and stochastic.

These problems notwithstanding, ad hoc modifications of Black-Scholes are frequently applied to options on bonds when (1) the option of interest is European and (2) the option's maturity is short relative to that of the underlying bond.

Clearly, however, these conditions are not satisfied in the case of callable bonds. First, the option is not of the European type; it can be exercised any time the bond has moved beyond the call protection period. Second, since the option is theoretically exercisable up to the bond's maturity date, the option's expiration period is clearly not small relative to the bond's maturity.

Thus, for these types of embedded options, we require a model that is tailored to the specific characteristics of interest rate–dependent securities. An interest rate model that is able to value option-like payoffs requires explicit specification of the relevant *interest rate volatility.* Hence we require that such interest rate models

- Be arbitrage free.
- Match the observable term structure of interest rates.

---

[6] The phenomenon of the bond price approaching par as the maturity date nears is known as *pull-to-par.*

- Be computationally efficient
- Be able to handle American-style payoffs.

The model described in this chapter satisfies these key requirements.

THE MODEL'S INPUTS

Market Data

The model requires three types of market information:

1. The Treasury's "bullet" yield curve. As estimated by traders, these are the par yields of noncallable "bullet" Treasury securities.
2. Credit spreads of lower-rated issues to the Treasury curve. These values are added to the Treasury's yields to obtain a credit risk–adjusted par yield curve.[7] To obtain an economically correct valuation, we require the estimation of discount factors or, equivalently, the term structure of interest rates. Thus, using these par yields, the term structure of zero-coupon, credit-specific rates is "bootstrapped" from these par yields.[8] Exhibit 10–1 presents two yield curves for December 29, 1994, the

---

[7] These credit spreads are carefully monitored by traders, who typically quote an entire term structure of credit spreads, from short-term spreads through a 30-year maturity. This eliminates the necessity of estimating these spreads from the traded prices of these issuers' noncallable bonds.

[8] This is one of the common methods by which the present value function, or the term structure of so-called "spot" rates of interest, is constructed from the coupon rates on par bonds. Specifically, assume we observe the par rates c_T for all maturities T, $T = 0.5, 1, \ldots, 29.5, 30$. (As a practical matter, we typically observe the rates of the eight on-the-run Treasury instruments: bills with maturities of 0.25, 0.5, and 1 years, notes with maturities of 2, 3, 5, and 10 years, and 30-year bonds. However, a linear interpolation among these rates provides the par rates for all maturities extending out to 30 years.) Then we consider the present value equation relating a $100 par bond with maturity T to the present value of its properly discounted cash flows:

$$100 = 100 \frac{c_T}{2} \sum_{t=0.5}^{T} DF_t + 100 DF_t$$

where DF_t is the present value factor for maturity t. Next we separate out the expression for the annuity factor $\sum_{t=0.5}^{T} DF_t$ into two parts:

$$\sum_{t=0.5}^{T} DF_t = \sum_{t=0.5}^{T-0.5} DF_t + DF_t$$

Finally, we substitute the result into the previous equation and simplify, to obtain the solution for DF_T:

$$DF_t = \frac{1 - \left(c_T \sum_{t=0.5}^{T-0.5} DF_t \right)/2}{1 + c_T/2}$$

This provides a recursive procedure for estimating DF_T using c_T and the previously calculated DF_t, $t = 1, \ldots, T - 1$. The recursive procedure is initiated at $T = 0.5$ using $DF_{0.5} = 1/(1 + c_{0.5}/2)$.

Term Structures of Par Rates, December 29, 1994

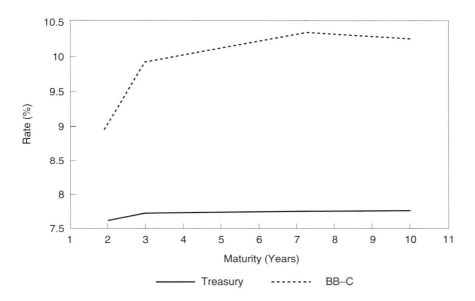

riskless Treasury on-the-run par yields and the risky BB-C curve lying above the Treasury curve.

3. Yield volatility. This is the long-run volatility of the short-term rate of interest used in the interest rate model. The next section provides a complete description of the use of this volatility measure in constructing the interest rate model and "tree" and in the valuation of callable bonds.

Bond Indicatives

The model requires three types of bond-indicative information:

1. Maturity date of the bond.
2. Coupon rate.
3. Call protection period and call schedule past the call protection period.

For example, a typical call structure on an issue of 30-year bonds might contain the following provisions. The first 10 years constitute the call protection period, during which the bond cannot be called. For the next 10

years, the bond may be callable, but at a premium that declines monotoni-
cally to par. The initial premium is equal to par plus one-half the coupon
rate.[9] For the last 10 years of its life, the bond remains callable at par.

VALUATION OF CALLABLE BONDS

This section demonstrates the model's valuation of a two-year bond
callable in one year, including the model's one-factor interest rate "engine."

Step 1: Calculation of Present Value Factors

As noted earlier, the model "bootstraps" the yield curve from the coupon
rates on part bonds. In this example, assume the following Treasury yield
curve:

Yield for par bond maturing at year 1, $c_1 = 4.59\%$
Yield for par bond maturing at year 2, $c_2 = 5.23\%$

If we assume, for simplicity, annual payments of coupon,[10] these
parameters imply

$$\begin{cases} 100 = (100 + 4.59)DF_1 \\ 100 = 5.23\,DF_1 + (100 + 5.23)DF_2 \end{cases}$$

where DF_T is the discount (present value) factor for maturity T implied by
the current yield curve.[11] Solving these two equations yields

$$DF_1 = 0.9561$$
$$DF_2 = 0.9028$$

Note that the implied one-year forward rate equals

---

[9] Thus, for a bond with a coupon of 9 percent, the initial call price is $104.50.

[10] This assumption is made only for illustrive purposes. The actual model accurately accounts for
bonds' semiannual pay feature.

[11] As noted above, the issuer-specific credit spread is added to the rates of the on-the-run Treasuries.
For example, if the trader quoted a credit spread of 20 bp for year 1 and 25 bp for year 2, the
appropriate issuer-specific par rates would be $4.59\% + 0.2\% = 4.79\%$ for year 1 and $5.23\% +
0.25\% = 5.48\%$ for year 2, and the solution for the discount factors would be found from

$$\begin{cases} 100 = (100 + 4.59)DF_1 \\ 100 = 5.23\,DF_1 + (100 + 5.23)DF_2 \end{cases}$$

resulting in
$$DF_1 = 0.9543$$
$$DF_2 = 0.8985$$

$$\frac{DF_1}{DF_2} - 1 = \frac{0.9561}{0.9028} - 1 = 5.90\%$$

Step 2: Construction of the Arbitrage-Free Interest Rate Tree

The lattice approach constitutes an efficient procedure for the valuation of options. To implement this approach, we require the specification of an interest rate model. The model used here is a lognormally distributed interest rate model, with constant interest rate volatility, that precisely matches the observable term structure of (credit-adjusted) interest rates.[12]

Based on this interest rate, we define an interest rate "tree" as one that enumerates all possible interest rates at future periods, as depicted in Exhibit 10–2.

The objective here is to create a tree that exactly matches the observable yield curve of interest rate; this means matching the $DF_1 = 0.9561$ and $DF_2 = 0.9028$ calculated above. At this juncture, we require the additional input of the interest rate volatility, σ. This measure of uncertainty is analogous to the stock price variability in the computation of Black-Scholes equity option values. Using a 9 percent volatility input, the model now specifies that the interest rate moves in a binomial fashion as shown in Exhibit 10–3.

E X H I B I T   10–2

The Components of an Interest Rate Tree

Today	Year 1	Year 2
		?
	?	
4.59%		?
	?	
		?

---

[12] Formally, if the short-term rate of interest is r, then

$$\frac{dr}{r} = \mu_t dt + \sigma dz$$

where μ_t is the time-dependent drift term chosen to match the term structure, σ is the constant interest rate volatility, and dz is a normally distributed variable with mean zero and variance dt.

E X H I B I T   10–3

Construction of the Interest Rate Tree

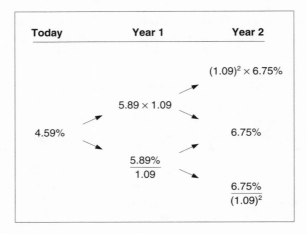

Today	Year 1	Year 2
		$(1.09)^2 \times 6.75\%$
	5.89×1.09	
4.59%		6.75%
	$\dfrac{5.89\%}{1.09}$	
		$\dfrac{6.75\%}{(1.09)^2}$

The averages of future interest rates—5.89 percent at year 1, 6.75 percent at year 2 and so on—are, to a good approximation, equal to today's forward rates.[13]

Step 3: Valuation of Two-Year Callable Bond

Our objective here is to obtain the fair, no-arbitrage value of a two-year, 6 percent bond callable at par in one year. Given the interest rate process described in Exhibit 10–3, the price behavior of the callable two-year, 6 percent coupon bond is shown in Exhibit 10–4.

Hence the bond is called at year 1 if rates decline to 5.40 percent. The current bond value, B, is given by

$$B = \frac{1}{1.0459}(0.5 \times 105.61 \times 0.5 \times 106) = 101.16$$

With current yield rates of $y_1 = 4.59\%$ and $y_2 = 5.23\%$, the value of a noncallable two-year, 6 percent bond is given by the present value of the cash flows:

$$6 \times P_1 + 106 \times P_2 = 6 \times 0.9561 + 106 \times 0.9028 = 101.43$$

Thus, the value of the one-year call is

Call option = Bullet bond – Callable bond = 101.43 – 101.16 = .27

---

[13] For more details on the construction of an arbitrage-free interest rate "tree," see Appendix 10–A.

E X H I B I T   10–4

Valuation of the Callable Bond

Today	Year 1	Year 2
	$6 + \min\left\{\dfrac{106}{1.0642}, 100\right\} = 6 + 99.61$ ⟶	106
B		
	$6 + \min\left\{\dfrac{106}{1.054}, 100\right\} = 6 + 100$	

The principle of step 3 called *backward induction*, is applied to the valuation of bonds with embedded options.[14] Note that the use of a binomial tree permits the valuation of any structure of embedded calls, including a given date–specific schedule of call prices.

Exhibit 10–5 describes the evolution over time of the interest rate, as well as the prices of the callable bullet bonds.

Note that at year 1, when interest rates have gone up to 6.42 percent, the prices of the callable and bullet bonds are identical: Both are priced to maturity. In contrast, when interest rates have declined to 5.40 percent, the prices of the callable and bullet bonds diverge, since the former can be called whereas the latter cannot.

RICHNESS/CHEAPNESS ANALYSIS: THE CALIBRATION OF INTEREST RATE VOLATILITY

As anticipated in the models of Black, Derman, and Toy, Black and Karasiniski, and Hull and White, the volatility, σ, is unlikely to be con-

---

[14] This backward induction procedure can be easily modified to price a two-year bond *putable* at par at year 1. Modifying Exhibit 10–4, the price behavior of the putable two-year, 6 percent coupon bond is

Today	Year 1	Year 2
	$6 + \max\left\{\dfrac{106}{1.0642}, 100\right\} = 6 + 100$	
P		
	$6 + \max\left\{\dfrac{106}{1.054}, 100\right\} = 6 + 100.57$ ⟶	106

The bond is put at year 1 if rates rise to 6.42 percent. The current bond value, P, is given by

$$P = \frac{1}{1.0459}(0.5 \times 106 + 0.5 \times 106.57) = 101.62$$

With the bullet bond priced at \$101.43, the value of the one-year put is 101.62–101.43 = 0.19.

E X H I B I T   10–5

Bond and Interest Rate Tree

	Today	Year 1	Year 2
			6 + 100
			6 + 100
			8.02%
		6 + 99.61	
		6 + 99.61	
Noncallable bond	101.43	6.42%	6 + 100
Callable bond	101.16		6 + 100
Interest rate	4.59%		6.75%
		6 + 100.57	
		6 + 100	
		5.40%	6 + 100
			—
			5.68%

stant. Ideally, one would seek to estimate a term structure of volatility $\sigma(t)$. As a practical alternative, consider the following proposed procedure to identify "fair" volatilities:[15]

1. Collect a set of bond prices and indicatives, a Treasury yield curve, and credit spreads.

2. Use the above interest rate model to estimate bond i's implied volatility, σ_i.[16]

3. Specify predetermined "factors": time to first call, T_C; time from first call to maturity, $T_M - T_C$; in-the-money forward, $\max\{F-100, 0\}$; and out of-the-money forward, $\max\{100-F, 0\}$;

4. Regress $\ln \sigma_i$ on constant plus T_C, $T_M - T_C$, $\max\{F - 100, 0\}$, and $\max\{100 - F, 0\}$ to determine "statistically significant" factors.[17]

---

[15] For a detailed presentation of the theory underlying the following discussion and an empirical implementation to callable Treasury securities, see Robert R. Bliss and Ehud I. Ronn, "The Implied Volatility of U.S. Interest Rates: Evidence from Callable U.S. Treasuries," (working paper, University of Texas at Austin, November 1995).

[16] The implied volatility is that interest rate volatility at which the bond's model value equals its market price.

[17] In the estimation procedure, we wish to give more weights to those implied volatilities that contain more "information." Hence we use weighted least squares using the bond's volatility sensitivity—known as *vegas* and given analytically by the bond value-change for a given increase in volatility—as weights.

$$\ln \sigma_i = a_1 + a_2 T_{Ci} + a_3 \left(T_{Mi} - T_{Ci} \right) + a_4 \max\{ F_i - 100, 0 \}$$
$$+ a_5 \max\{ 100 - F_i, 0 \} \tag{1}$$

There are essentially two types of regressors in equation 1: calendar times and moneyness effects. The time effect is captured by time to call and time from call to maturity. We would expect both of these to depress the market-determined implied volatility. The greater the time from call to maturity, the greater the "residual bond's" length, and we know empirically that yield volatilities decline with time to maturity. Further, if there is mean reversion in interest rates, a greater time-to-first-call date would also lower the impled (average) volatility. The motivation for the moneyness effects is "borrowed" from the results in the equity markets; that is, volatilities from options away from the money differ from at-the-money options, and this specification permits the data to reflect this empirical phenomenon.

Using market prices and credit spreads provided by the government trading desk at Merrill Lynch & Co., this procedure was applied on a weekly basis to a set of actively-traded securities issued by government-sponsored enterprises (GSEs) such as FNMA and SLMA. The results of the regressions are provided in Exhibit 10–6.

We can draw several conclusions from this exhibit. First, note that while the coefficient on T_{Mi}–T_{Ci} is, as expected, reliably negative, the coefficient on T_{Ci} varies in sign. Further, while the out-of-the-money effect is reliably positive, the in-the-money effect is unstable and occasionally insignificantly different from zero. Note the relevance of updating these regression analyses to reflect the prevailing "term structure of volatility" at different points in time.

Analyses such as the above are useful to bond investors due to their use as intramarket richness/cheapness indicators.[18] Specifically, a callable bond will be considered cheap to its callable brethren if its implied volatility, σ_i, exceeds the volatility obtained from substituting the bond's indicatives into the regression equation 1; hence the importance of such ongoing calibration efforts. For issuers of bonds, such calibration efforts can assist in the determination of "fair" market volatilities for the new issues they bring to market.

---

[18] The extension of this approach to an intermarket comparison of richness/cheapness, such as a contrast of callable corporate and callable agencies, is a subject for future practitioner and academic research.

E X H I B I T   10–6

Regression Results for Equation 1

$$\ln \sigma_i = a_1 + a_2 T_{Ci} + a_3 (T_{Mi} - T_{Ci}) + a_4 \max\{F_i - 100, 0\} + a_5 \max\{100 - F_i, 0\}$$

Prior expectations on coefficients:

$$a_2 < 0,\ a_3 < 0,\ a_4 > 0,\ a_5 > 0$$

Date	N	a_1	a_2	a_3	a_4	a_5
June 28, 1993	13	3.256	−0.0245	−0.0786	−0.0597	0.0226
		(11.53)	(−0.53)	(−2.50)	(−1.09)	(0.41)
Dec. 23, 1993	13	2.906	−0.0529	−0.0178	−0.0267	0.2048
		(25.72)	(−2.82)	(−1.37)	(−1.71)	(6.94)
Dec. 30, 1993	13	2.739	−0.0193	0.0142	0.0071	0.1014
		(34.19)	(−1.48)	(1.52)	(0.63)	(3.51)
Jan. 6, 1994	13	2.920	−0.0215	−0.0806	0.0698	0.1899
		(8.07)	(−0.35)	(−1.96)	(1.32)	(2.88)
Jan. 13, 1994	15	2.491	0.0762	−0.0210	−0.0251	0.1150
		(17.24)	(2.96)	(−1.00)	(−1.29)	(1.35)
Jan. 20, 1994	15	2.844	0.0225	−0.0672	0.0044	0.1678
		(19.73)	(0.89)	(−3.31)	(0.21)	(3.77)
Jan. 27, 1994	15	2.750	0.0087	−0.0381	−0.0027	0.1321
		(12.67)	(0.24)	(−1.21)	(−0.08)	(2.30)
Dec. 23, 1993– Jan. 27, 1994	84	2.844	0.0022	−0.0482	0.0061	0.1426
		(27.95)	(0.13)	(−3.40)	(0.48)	(4.85)

Note: Numbers in parentheses are *t*-statistics.

SUMMARY

This chapter has presented the theory and empirical results dealing with the implementation of a lognormally distributed interest rate model to the valuation of callable bonds. The key issues the model demonstrates relate to interest rate modeling and calibration:

1. The use of a one-factor interest rate model, and its attendant numerical implementation in a recombining binomial tree, to the valuation of bonds with embedded options.

2. The calibration of this model to the term structures of interest rates, credit spreads, and, above all, volatility.

In turn, the use of this model facilitates the determination of the richness or cheapness of bonds with embedded options.

APPENDIX 10–A

Matching the Term Structure in a No-Arbitrage Recombining Interest Rate Lattice: A Numerical Example

A simple numerical example will demonstrate the lattice, or tree, approach to the valuation of callable bonds. Suppose $\Delta = 1$ year and the present value factors have been calculated to be

$$PV_1 = 0.9561$$
$$PV_2 = 0.9028$$

Thus, $r_1 = 1/0.9561 - 1 = 4.59\%$. Note that the forward rate here is $0.9561/0.9028 - 1 = 5.90\%$. Assume further that $\sigma = 9\%$.

Using a volatility of 9 percent, the interest rate tree specifies that the short-term rate moves in a binomial fashion as shown in Exhibit 10–7.[19]

EXHIBIT 10–7

The Interest Rate Tree

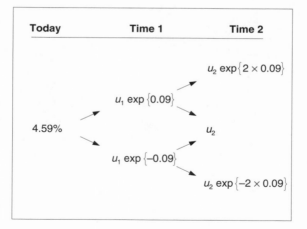

---

[19] Note that in this numerical example, we use the accurate continuously compounded expression $\exp\{0.09\} = e^{.09}$ rather than the discrete approximation used in the text, 1.09.

We seek to find a parameter, designated u_1, such that the price of $100 in two years' time conforms to the current yield curve's implied value of $90.28. The price behavior of the two-year zero-coupon bond is

Today	Time 1	Time 2
P_2	$\dfrac{100}{1 + u_1 \exp\{0.09\}}$	100
	$\dfrac{100}{1 + u_1 \exp\{0.09\}}$	100

The no-arb properties of the model imply that the price of the zero-coupon bond must equal the discounted expected value, using probabilities of 0.5, of the cash flows next period. In other words, P_2 must satisfy

$$P_2 = \frac{1}{1.0459}\left(0.5\frac{100}{1+u_1\exp\{0.09\}} + 0.5\frac{100}{1+u_1\exp\{-0.09\}}\right)$$

Since we know $P_2 = 90.28$ from the current yield curve, we can solve for $u_1 = 5.89$ percent. (Note that this u_1 is appropriately equal to the forward rate, 5.90%.) This procedure can then be used to derive the interest rate tree out to 30 or more years.

VALUING OPTIONS ON TREASURY BOND FUTURES CONTRACTS

Ehud I. Ronn, PhD
Associate Professor of Finance
University of Texas at Austin

Klaus Bjerre Toft, PhD
Assistant Professor of Finance
University of Texas at Austin

INTRODUCTION

Options on Treasury bond futures contracts have emerged as one of the most popular exchange-listed option contracts in the world. Since the T-bond futures option's initial listing on the Chicago Board of Trade (CBT) in October 1982, the trading volume grew to more than 28 million contracts in 1994.[1] The T-bond futures option contract is by far the world's most successful exchange-traded option on a long-term fixed income instrument. On the CBT alone, it accounts for 75 percent of the volume in financial options. Exhibit 11–1 shows volumes for the underlying T-bond futures contracts (panel A) and the options on T-bond futures contracts (panel B) from 1977 through 1994.

The phenomenal growth in trading volumes shown in Exhibit 11–1 can be attributed to numerous factors. As interest rate volatility increased during the 1970s and 1980s, the need for tools to manage this financial risk became apparent. In addition, the large U.S. federal budget deficit over the last two decades was financed in part by the issuance of long-term Treasury

---

[1] Market Information Inquiry System, Chicago Board of Trade, 1995.

E X H I B I T   11-1

Annual Total Trading Volume of T-bond Futures Contracts
and Options on T-bond Futures Contracts Listed on the
Chicago Board of Trade, 1977–94

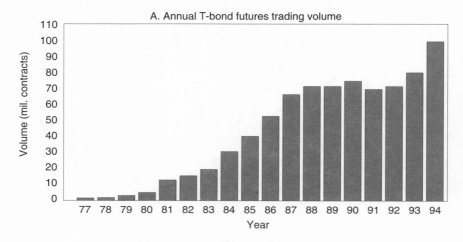

A. Annual T-bond futures trading volume

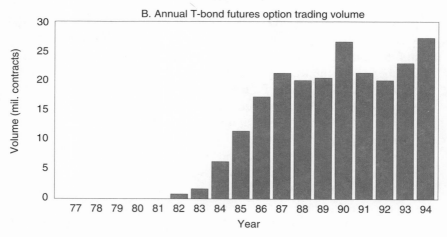

B. Annual T-bond futures option trading volume

Sources: Chicago Board of Trade, *Financial Instrument Guide*, 1994; and
The CBT Market Information Inquiry System, 1995.

bonds. This contributed significantly to the demand for instruments to
hedge and express views about the long end of the term structure of interest rates. Exchange-traded T-bond futures contracts and options on these
contracts provided investment managers with precisely such tools.

This chapter describes and analyzes exchange-traded options on T-
bond futures contracts. In the first section, we review the contract speci-

fications and introduce the flexible Treasury bond futures option. This type of option, which first traded on the CBT in January 1994, allows clients to tailor contract specifications to fit their needs while maintaining many of the attractive features characterizing exchange-traded option contracts. Then we describe several important trading strategies that can be implemented using these options.

Next, we discuss different theoretical approaches to valuing T-bond futures options. Black's model provides a simple method to price European options on futures contracts.[2] However, since the standard T-bond futures option is of the American type, Black's model is often inadequate when the probability of early exercise is significant. Barone-Adesi and Whaley's approximation to the value of an American option is a quick and reliable alternative to Black's model.[3] In fact, this model is used by the CBT to settle nontraded American flexible options.

Finally, because both Black's and Barone-Adesi and Whaley's models are theoretically inconsistent for pricing options on fixed-income instruments, we include a discussion of yield curve-based interest rate models. While these models require more computational power and are harder to calibrate, they are necessary when consistent modeling of T-bonds, T-bond futures, and options on T-bond futures is required.

OPTIONS ON TREASURY BOND FUTURES CONTRACTS

It is instructive to discuss the option's underlying asset, the Treasury bond futures contract. In principle, this is simply a futures contract on a long Treasury bond with a face value of $100,000. However, institutional features make the T-bond futures contract much more complicated. First, the T-bond futures contract stipulates that a Treasury bond is eligible for delivery if it has at least 15 years to maturity on the first business day of the delivery month. Furthermore, if the bond is callable, the time to the first call date must be at least 15 years. The right to select the deliverable asset, the *quality option,* is a valuable option for the short position; this option tends to reduce the futures price.

Second, the short position holds the right to choose the delivery date within the delivery month, the *timing option.* If the term structure of interest rates is upward sloping, the bond's negative cost of carry tends to

---

[2] Fischer Black, "The Pricing of Commodity Contracts," *Journal of Financial Economics*, March 1976, pp. 161–79.

[3] Giovanni Barone-Adesi and Robert E. Whaley, "Efficient Analytic Approximation of American Option Values," *Journal of Finance*, June 1987, pp. 301–20.

result in delivery toward the end of the delivery period. On the other hand, a negatively sloped term structure of interest rates may make it optimal to deliver the bond earlier in the delivery month.

Third, the T-bond futures contract contains a *wildcard option;* that is, the notice of intent to deliver can be submitted as late as 8 P.M. Central time, while the settlement price is determined at 2 P.M. Consequently, on each day on which delivery can be initiated, between 2 and 8 P.M. the short position retains the option to deliver a U.S. Treasury bond at a settlement price that was determined at 2 P.M. If interest rates increase significantly between 2 and 8 P.M., the value of this option can be significant.

Finally, during the delivery month, trading of the futures contract ceases on the seventh business day preceding the last business day of the delivery month. All futures contracts outstanding at that time require delivery. However, the short holds one more option, denoted the *switching option,* that permits him or her to determine which bond to deliver at the end of the month at the settlement price determined on the last day of trading.

Despite the complexities in T-bond futures contracts, we can for most purposes treat the T-bond futures contract as a forward on the bond that is currently the cheapest to deliver. The T-bond futures contract is thus a suitable tool for hedging risk factors that are highly correlated with the value of U.S. Treasury bonds. While T-bond futures contracts are appropriate hedging vehicles for risk that is linear in the value of U.S. Treasury bonds, options on T-bond futures contracts provide investors with additional tools to construct nonlinear exposures to long-term government bond prices.

Contract Specification and Delivery Procedure

The *buyer* of a call option on a T-bond futures contract has the right, but not the obligation, to enter into a *long* T-bond futures contract of a specific maturity at any time prior to the option's expiration. If the option is exercised, the futures position is entered at the strike price. Conversely, the *buyer* of a put option has the right, but not the obligation, to enter into a *short* futures contract at a price equal to the strike price. It is the buyer of the option, the long position, who has the right to exercise the option if he or she wishes to do so. For this privilege the buyer pays an option premium that is determined by competitive forces on the floor of the CBT.

T-bond futures contracts' quarterly delivery cycle determines the options' expiration and trading dates. Currently T-bond futures contracts on the regular quarterly cycle expire during the months of March, June,

September, and December. The CBT lists options on the T-bond futures contracts with expirations during the next three regular quarterly expiration months. Trading of each of these options ceases in the month prior to the underlying futures contract's delivery month at 12 P.M. on the first Friday preceding, by at least five business days, the first notice day for the corresponding T-bond futures contract.[4] The options expire on the first Saturday following the last day of trading. For example, trading of options on the September 1995 T-bond futures contract ceased on Friday, August 18, 1995, at 12.00 P.M., while the options expired on Saturday, August 19, 1995, at 10 A.M.

In addition to listings determined by the quarterly cycle, options are listed for the current front month. The underlying futures contract for this front-month option is the next futures contract on the regular quarterly cycle. Front-month options are listed only if no T-bond futures contract on the regular cycle expires during the front month of the current quarter. For example, at the beginning of January, four option maturities are traded: one front-month option (February) and three options on the quarterly cycle (March, June, and September). This is illustrated in Exhibit 11–2. February and March options exercise into a March futures contract, while the June and September options exercise into June and September futures contracts, respectively. Thus, it is not possible to trade a short-term option on a futures contract with a distant delivery month.

T-bond futures options are of the American type: During any trading day before the option's expiration, the long position can choose to exercise the option. If the investor chooses to sell the option, he or she receives the current option premium and the position is closed. On the other hand, an investor who wishes to exercise the option notifies the clearing corporation of his or her intent to exercise the option. When the notification of exercise is received, the clearing corporation randomly selects another clearing member with a short position in the same option series. This clearing member then assigns the exercise to one of its customers with a short position. The exercise is finalized by assigning, by book entry, a long (short) futures position to the call owner (put owner) and a short (long) futures position to the call writer (put writer). The futures position is entered at a settlement price equal to the striking price

---

[4] The first notice day is the business day before the first day on which delivery on the T-bond futures contract is possible. The T-bond futures contract's first delivery day is the first business day in the delivery month. Consequently, the first notice day is the last business day prior to the delivery month.

E X H I B I T   11–2

Options on U.S. Treasury Bond Futures Contracts Listed at
the Beginning of January 1995

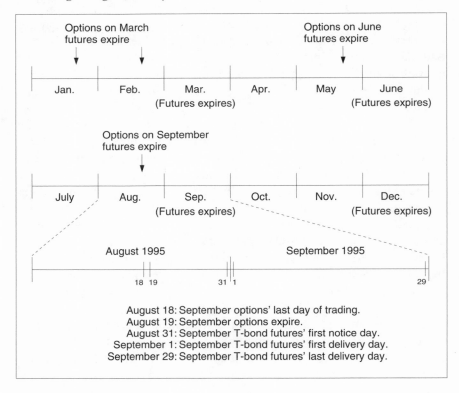

August 18: September options' last day of trading.
August 19: September options expire.
August 31: September T-bond futures' first notice day.
September 1: September T-bond futures' first delivery day.
September 29: September T-bond futures' last delivery day.

and marked to market immediately. In other words, exercise is accomplished simply by substituting an option position with a futures position with no need to deliver a physical asset. This eliminates problems that may be caused by illiquidity and potential market interruptions when a physical asset must be delivered. Of course, the assigned T-bond futures contract may eventually result in the delivery of a Treasury bond. The entire procedure is easily accomplished, since both options on T-bond futures contracts and the T-bond futures themselves are cleared by the same clearing system.

Currently front-month options are available with strike prices in increments of 1 point, and back-month options are available in increments of 2 points. For example, as of June 6, 1995, September put options with strike prices ranging from 102 to 116 in increments of 2 points were actively traded. However, as is usually the case, at-the-money or slightly out-of-the-money options have the largest trading volume. On this particular date, with the September T-bond futures contract settling at 114–22, the September 112 put option had a trading volume equal to 10,213 contracts.[5] Note that T-bond futures contracts are quoted in whole points plus ½₂ of a point, while options on T-bond futures are quoted in whole points plus ¼₄ of a point. A point is equivalent to $1,000. Exhibit 11–3 summarizes the T-bond futures option's contract specifications discussed in this section.

Flexible Treasury Futures Option

In January 1994, the Chicago Board of Trade introduced flexible options on U.S. Treasury futures contracts. During the first year of trading, a total of 174,295 flexible T-bond option contracts changed hands. While this number is dwarfed by the trading volume of the standard T-bond futures option contract, the flexible Treasury futures option is nevertheless an interesting innovation designed to bridge the gap between over-the-counter deals and exchange-traded standard contracts. An investor who wishes to trade the flexible option determines key specifications of the contract. He or she may, with certain restrictions,[6] choose the strike price, expiration date, exercise style (European or American), and underlying futures contract (U.S. T-bond, 10-year, 5-year, or 2-year T-note futures contract). The flexible T-bond futures option thus allows the trader to construct a customized product that retains many of the benefits associated with exchange-listed contracts. In particular, counterparty risk is virtually eliminated, since flexible option contracts are cleared and guaranteed by the Chicago Board of Trade Clearing Corporation. Furthermore, initial requests for quotes are widely disseminated to potential traders both on and off the trading floor to attract as many competitive bidders as possible. Finally, flexible T-bond option contracts' similarity to standard exchange-traded contracts and the physical proximity of the trading pits guarantee immediate and precise information that may be used to price flexible T-bond futures options.

Exhibit 11–4 summarizes of the contract specifications. The minimum size requirement to initiate a trade is 100 contracts. For most practical purposes, this limits the use of the flexible options to institutional

---

[5] Source: Bloomberg, *Financial Markets Commodities News.*
[6] The most important restriction in these flexible contracts precludes the purchase of options whose expiration dates exceed that of a traded standard option.

E X H I B I T   11–3

Specifications for Options on U.S. Treasury Bond Futures Contracts

Trading unit	One $100,000 face value CBT U.S. Treasury bond futures contract of a specified contract month.
Description	At any time prior to expiration, the buyer of one T-bond futures option may exercise the option to assume a position in one T-bond futures contract (long if the option is a call and short if the option is a put) of a specified contract month at a strike price set when the option was bought. Upon exercise, the seller of one T-bond futures option assumes an opposite position in one T-bond futures contract (short if the option is a call and long if the option is a put) of a specified contract month at a strike price set when the option was sold.
Strike price	Trading is currently conducted with strike prices in multiples of 2 points ($2,000) per T-bond futures contract (108, 110, 112, etc.) However, front-month options trade with strike prices in increments of 1 point ($1,000) per T-bond futures contract.
Premium payment	The premium must be paid in full by each clearing member to the clearing corporation, and by each option customer to his or her commission merchant, when the option is bought.
Price quotation	Multiples of $\frac{1}{64}$ of 1% of a $100,000 T-bond futures contract ($15.625 per $\frac{1}{64}$).
Daily trading limits	Same as daily limit for T-bond futures, currently 3 points ($3,000), i.e., the option premium can move only 3 points above or below the previous day's settlement price. Variable limits are also the same as those for T-bond futures, currently 4½ points ($4,500). Limits do not apply during the option's expiration month.
Exercise	The buyer of a T-bond futures option may exercise the option on any business day prior to expiration by giving notice to the clearing corporation by 8:00 P.M. The clearing corporation, through its clearing members, then assigns the notice to an option seller. The clearing corporation will establish a futures position for the buyer (long if the option is a call and short if the option is a put) and an opposite futures position for the seller at the strike price before the opening of trading on the following business day.
Last day of trading	T-bond futures options cease trading in the month prior to the futures contract delivery month. Options stop trading at 12:00 P.M. on the first Friday preceding, by at least five business days, the first notice day for the corresponding T-bond futures contract.
Trading hours	7:20 A.M. to 2:00 P.M. (Chicago time) Monday through Friday. Evening trading hours are between 5:00 and 8:30 P.M. (Chicago time) or 6:00 P.M. and 9:30 P.M. (Chicago daylight saving time) Sunday through Thursday.
Expiration	Unexercised T-bond futures options expire at 10:00 A.M. on the first Saturday following the last day of trading.
Contract months	The front month of the current quarter plus the next three contracts of the regular quarterly cycle (March, June, September, and December). If the front month is a quarterly contracts month, no monthly contract will be listed. The monthly option contract exercises into the current quarterly futures contract. For example, a July T-bond option exercises into a September futures position.

Sources: Chicago Board of Trade, various publications.

E X H I B I T   11–4

Contract Specifications for Flexible Options on U.S. Treasury Bond and 10-Year, 5-Year, and 2-Year Treasury Note Futures

Trading unit	The minimum size to initiate a request for quote (RFQ) in a flexible Treasury option series is 100 contracts, each having a face value at maturity of $100,000 ($200,000 for 2-year T-note flexible options.)
Tick size	¹⁄₆₄ of a point ($15.625) for T-bond and 10-year and 5-year T-note flexible Treasury options; one-half of ¹⁄₆₄ of a point for 2-year T-note flexible options. Dollar values are rounded up to the nearest cent per contract.
Strike prices	For T-bond and 10-year T-note flexible options, strike prices may be expressed (1) in absolute levels, set to any ¹⁄₃₂ of a point, or (2) in levels relative to the underlying futures contract set in ¼-point increments. For 5-year and 2-year T-note flexible options, strike prices may be expressed (1) in absolute levels, set to any ¹⁄₆₄ of a point, or (2) in levels relative to the underlying futures contract, set in ¼-point increments.
Daily price limit	Three points ($3,000 per contract) above or below the previous day's settlement premium (expandable to 4½ points) for T-bond and 10-year and 5-year T-note flexible options; one point ($2,000 per contract) above or below the previous day's settlement premium (expandable to 1½ points) for 2-year T-note flexible options. Limits are lifted on the last trading day.
Last trading and expiration day	Unexercised flexible T-bond options expire on the last trading day. On the last trading/expiration day, trading ceases at noon and expiration occurs later that day at 4:30 P.M. (CST).
Expiration date	Any Monday through Friday, provided that (1) it is not an exchange holiday and (2) the date does not exceed the expiration date of the standard option whose underlying is the most deferred futures contract to have had trading activity.
Exercise style	RFQ initiators can choose either an American or European exercise style.
Exercise	The buyer of an American-style flexible Treasury bond option may exercise the option on any business day prior to expiration by giving notice to the Chicago Board of Trade Clearing Corporation by 4:10 P.M. Chicago time. For European-style options, the option is exercised on the expiration day only, prior to 4:10 P.M. At expiration, all in-the-money options are automatically exercised.
Trading hours	7:20 A.M. to 2:00 P.M. Chicago time, Monday through Friday. RFQs can be submitted to the flexible Treasury options pit reporter from 6:45 A.M. to 15 minutes prior to the close of trading for a flexible treasury options series.

Source: *Flexible Treasury Options on U.S. Treasury Bond and Note Futures* (Chicago: CBT, 1994).

investors.[7] When a trader chooses to list a new series, he or she submits a request for quote (RFQ). This RFQ is assigned an identification number (e.g., RFQ001) and disseminated on and off the exchange floor. Traders who desire to take opposite positions have 10 minutes to communicate their responses to their floor representatives. After the response time period has elapsed, an open-outcry auction similar to that conducted for standard options starts.

For most practical purposes, the initiator of the RFQ can completely customize the contract's strike price, time to maturity, and exercise type. The strike price may be specified as either an absolute number or a number relative to the underlying future's price. For example, it is possible to request a quote on an option that is ½ point out of the money. The precise strike price will be determined 10 minutes hence, when bidding on the option begins.

The flexible option's expiration day can be any trading day as long as the time to maturity does not exceed that of the currently traded standard option with the longest time to maturity. This guarantees that any trader who takes the opposite side of the transaction can effectively lay off much of the risk by entering offsetting trades in standard T-bond futures options contracts. Flexible option transactions are reported immediately to the clearing corporation and subsequently settled on a daily basis. Since a particular flexible option series cannot be expected to trade on a regular basis, settlement values must be computed using standardized models for the option prices. The clearing corporation uses Black's model to price European options and Barone-Adesi and Whaley's model to price options of the American type. These models will be discussed later in the valuation section.

Option Strategies

T-bond futures option contracts make it possible to express views about long-term interest rates while avoiding some of the disadvantages of entering T-bond futures contracts. Whereas a position in T-bond futures contracts may lead to virtually unlimited losses, the downside of a long option position is limited to the initial premium paid for the option.

---

[7] A lot size of 100 contracts is equivalent to an option on futures that calls for the delivery of bonds with a face value of $10 million.

As an example, consider an investor who on May 31, 1995, believes that interest rates are going to decrease during the next three months. A long position in a call option on the September 1995 T-bond futures contract is consistent with this view. On May 31, 1995, the futures contract settled at 112–21; in decimal numbers, this settlement price equals 112.65625 points. The price of the September call option with a strike price of 112 closed at 2–15; this is equivalent to 2.234375. If we assume that the investor traded at the close, he paid $2,234.38 for the option to enter one T-bond futures contract. If interest rates subsequently increase significantly, the option may expire worthless but the losses are limited to the premium of $2,234.38. On the other hand, in a scenario of decreasing interest rates, and thus increasing T-bond futures prices, the long option position retains the full upside potential.

Long call and put positions provide investors with relatively safe ways to express views about the direction of long-term interest rate movements. Short positions, on the other hand, are riskier if left uncovered. Consider an investor who believes that interest rates will either increase or stabilize at the current level. Consistent with these beliefs, he or she writes out-of-the-money call options and thus receives current income equal to the option premium. While current income is an appealing feature, the downside risk is enormous: If interest rates plunge and T-bond futures prices increase significantly, the losses may become very large.

T-bond futures options can also be used in conjunction with an existing long fixed-income portfolio. An appropriately selected put position provides a floor under the value of the portfolio: If the fixed-income portfolio's value plunges because of higher interest rates, the put position finishes in the money and thus provides insurance against major losses. Whereas the protective put portfolio's current yield is reduced by the put premium, call writing can be used to enhance the portfolio's current yield. In return, the covered call writer gives up a portion of the upside potential. This limits portfolio returns in scenarios where interest rates decrease significantly.

T-bond options may also be used to enhance the yield of a portfolio of short-term money market instruments during periods of decreasing interest rates. Buying call options on T-bond futures contracts makes it possible for money market investors to participate in a rally of long-term bonds without incurring significant downside risk.

The strategies just discussed are tailored to beliefs about the direction of the long-term rates of interest. Other strategies implement views about the volatility of the T-bond futures prices and therefore also the volatility of the long end of the term structure of interest rates. For example, if the market believes interest rates are unlikely to change significantly in the near future—that is, volatility is cheap—investors may find it advantageous to "buy volatility" while not expressing any views on the direction of interest rates. This can be accomplished by simultaneously buying at-the-money call and put options on a T-bond futures contract. If interest rates change significantly, this strategy, a straddle, may return large profits. On the other hand, if the T-bond futures price exhibits low volatility and stays at the same level, the straddle expires worthless.[8] Volatility may be sold simply by simultaneously writing at-the-money call and put options. This strategy yields a high current income, but the downside potential is very large. If one desires to limit the downside on the short straddle, one can cap potential losses by adding out-of-the-money call and out-of-the-money put options to the straddle. The current income received from this butterfly spread is naturally less than that received from a short straddle.

We have discussed only a few possible strategies, but the number of different positions is, for all practical purposes, unlimited. Portfolios of Treasury futures contracts and options on these contracts make it possible to tailor a fixed-income portfolio's long-term interest rate exposure to fit virtually any investor preference or belief.

VALUATION

Several methods may be used to value options on Treasury bond futures contracts. Simple yet powerful models are based on an assumption about the distribution of the futures price. Ease of use and intuitive appeal make Black's and Barone-Adesi and Whaley's models strong candidates for a first attempt to value T-bond futures options. However, these formulas ignore options embedded in the T-bond futures contract, and they have theoretical deficiencies that can be solved only by a more elaborate modeling of the entire term structure of interest rates.

---

[8] Volatility can be traded in a number of ways using combinations of T-bond futures and options on T-bond futures contracts. As previously discussed, the holder of the short T-bond futures position receives several embedded options. Consequently, the T-bond futures contract's basis reflects, in addition to the cost of carry, the volatility-dependent values of these options. Thus, volatility trades can also be constructed using T-bond futures contracts.

Black's Price-Based Model

Valuation of options on Treasury bond futures contracts is most easily accomplished using Black's model for the value of a European option on a futures contract. Thus, for the moment we will ignore the possibility of early exercise. Black's model is rooted in modern option valuation theory, which essentially began with Black and Scholes.[9] Black and Scholes derived the value of a European call option on equity as a function of the underlying stock price, strike price, time to expiration, rate of interest, and volatility of the stock's rate of return. Merton extended the Black-Scholes formula to account for proportional dividend payments as well as time-dependent volatility.[10] Black adapted the derivation to value European options on futures contracts when the futures price follows a geometric Brownian motion. He identified the partial differential equation the option price must satisfy and solved this equation subject to boundary conditions determined by the option's payoff at maturity. The following formula shows Black's pricing result expressed in a way general enough to encompass the valuation of both European call and put options:

$$c = \phi e^{-rT}\left[FN(\phi d) - KN\big(\phi(d - \sigma\sqrt{T})\big)\right] \tag{1}$$

where

$$d \equiv \frac{\log(F/K)}{\sigma\sqrt{T}} + \tfrac{1}{2}\sigma\sqrt{T} \tag{2}$$

and

$\qquad c$ = Current value of the contingent claim (call or put option)

$\qquad \phi$ = Call-put indicator: $\phi = 1$ for calls, $\phi = -1$ for puts

$\qquad F$ = Current futures price

$\qquad K$ = Strike price

$\qquad N(\cdot)$ = Cumulative standard normal distribution function

$\qquad r$ = Risk-free rate of interest

---

[9] Fischer Black and Myron Scholes, "The Pricing of Options and Corporate Liabilities," *Journal of Political Economy*, May–June 1973, pp. 637–59.

[10] Robert C. Merton, "Theory of Rational Option Pricing," *Bell Journal of Economics and Management Science*, Spring 1973, pp.141–83.

T = Time to option expiration

σ = Futures price volatility

A brief discussion of this formula may be helpful. First, note that although the futures contract is itself a complex derivative security, the option valuation problem is greatly simplified by imposing an assumption about the distribution of the futures price. This makes it possible to derive the value of the option directly from the dynamics of the futures price. Second, although the risk-free rate of interest is written as a constant, it should be interpreted as the zero-coupon rate for a period equal to the option's time to expiration. Third, a time-dependent volatility can be easily accommodated by using the average futures price volatility over the option's lifetime; that is,

$$\sigma = \sqrt{\frac{1}{T}\int_0^T \sigma_F^2(t)dt}$$

where $\sigma_F(t)$ is the instantaneous volatility expressed as a function of time t. Finally, equation 1 is simply the Black-Scholes formula for an option on a dividend-paying asset where the dividend yield equals the risk-free rate of interest.

American-Style Options

The simplicity of Black's model makes it an often-used formula for the valuation of futures options and for the calculation of volatilities implied from these options.[11] However, the CBT's option on the Treasury bond futures contract is of the American type. In particular, if the option is deep-in-the-money, the long position has a strong incentive to exercise the option early. To see this, consider a call option where F is large relative to the strike price, K, and only one day remains to expiration.[12] Thus, for all practical purposes, we can ignore the possibility that the option will expire out of the money. If the option is exercised immediately, the option hold-

---

[11] For a given option valuation formula (e.g., Black's), the implied volatility is the volatility that sets the model value equal to the option's market price. Mathematically, given an option's market price c^M, the implied volatility σ is implicitly defined by the equation $c(\sigma) = c^M$, where $c(\cdot)$ is the option model's value expressed as a function of the volatility.

[12] For the following example, we assume that the last day of trading and the expiration date are identical.

er receives $F - K$ in addition to a long futures position.[13] The total value of this portfolio one day later is

$$(F - K)e^{r\Delta t} + \left(F_e - F\right) \tag{3}$$

where Δt is a one-day time period and F_e equals the futures settlement price on the option's last day of trading. The first term represents the mark-to-market payment when the option is exercised early plus accrued interest, while the second term equals the futures contract's mark-to-market payment on the option's expiration date. Contrast this amount to the case where exercise is postponed to the last day of trading. In this case, the exercise value equals

$$F_e - K \tag{4}$$

Since equation 3 is strictly greater than 4, optimally one should never keep this option to maturity; doing so would forgo one day's interest on $F - K$.[14]

Hence we require an alternative valuation method that takes early exercise into account. There are several approaches to the valuation of American options, including the Cox, Ross, and Rubinstein binomial model and the finite difference approach of Brennan and Schwartz.[15] While an arbitrary degree of precision can be obtained by either of these methods, they may not be fast enough for real-time systems where a large number of option values and sensitivities must be calculated simultaneously. One frequently-employed alternative was developed by Barone-Adesi and Whaley. This model approximates the partial differential equation for the early-exercise premium with a second-order ordinary differential equation. As applied to options on futures contracts, the approximate value of the American option, expressed in a way general enough to encompass valuation of both calls and puts, is given by

---

[13] Recall that the option is exercised into a futures contract that is immediately marked to market.

[14] Analogous arguments hold for the American put option.

[15] See John C. Cox, Stephen Ross, and Mark Rubinstein, "Option Pricing: A Simplified Approach," *Journal of Financial Economics,* September 1979, pp. 229–63, and Michael J. Brennan and Eduardo S. Schwartz, "Finite Difference Methods and Jump Processes Arising in the Pricing of Contingent Claims: A Synthesis," *Journal of Financial and Quantitative Analysis,* September 1978, pp. 462–74. For an extensive bibliography on the valuation of American options, see Peter Carr and Dmitri Faguet, "Fast, Accurate Valuation of American Options" (working paper, Cornell University, 1994).

$$C = \begin{cases} c + A\left(\dfrac{F}{F^*}\right)^{\gamma} & \text{when } \phi F < \phi F^* \\ \phi(F - K) & \text{when } \phi F \geq \phi F^* \end{cases} \tag{5}$$

where

C = Current value of the American contingent claim (call or put option)

c = Current value of the American option's European counterpart

ϕ = Call-put indicator, $\phi = 1$ for calls, $\phi = -1$ for puts

F^* = Critical futures price above (below) which the call (put) option should be exercised

F^* is found by solving the equation

$$\phi\left(F^* - K\right) = c + \phi\left[1 - e^{-rT} N\left(\phi d\left(F^*\right)\right)\right]\frac{F^*}{\gamma} \tag{6}$$

with relevant parameters given by

$$\gamma = \tfrac{1}{2}\left[1 + \phi\sqrt{1 + \frac{8r}{\sigma^2\left(1 - e^{-rT}\right)}}\right]$$

$$A = \frac{\phi F^*}{\gamma}\left[1 - e^{-rT} N\left(\phi d\left(F^*\right)\right)\right]$$

$$d(F) = \frac{\log(F/K) + \tfrac{1}{2}\sigma^2 T}{\sigma\sqrt{T}}$$

Barone-Adesi and Whaley's model illustrates some of the properties of American option values. First, the value of an American option can be written as the sum of two parts: (1) the value of an otherwise equivalent European option and (2) the value of the early exercise premium, $A(F / F^*)^{\gamma}$. Second, as the underlying futures price approaches the early exercise boundary ($F \to F^*$), the theoretical value of the option approaches $\phi(F - K)$. This is guaranteed because F^* solves equation 6. Finally, American options satisfy a "smooth-pasting" condition as $F \to F^*$: The slope of the option value as a function of F approaches that of the

E X H I B I T   11–5

Barone-Adesi and Whaley and Black Call Option Prices on June 14, 1995

Strike	Last	Barone-Adesi Whaley	Black	Difference
102	NA	12.09	11.98	0.11
104	NA	10.09	10.02	0.08
106	8.13	8.13	8.09	0.04
108	6.33	6.27	6.25	0.02
110	4.58	4.58	4.57	0.01
112	3.16	3.12	3.12	0.01
114	1.95	1.97	1.97	0.00
116	1.13	1.14	1.14	0.00
118	0.58	0.60	0.60	0.00
120	0.28	0.29	0.29	0.00
122	0.11	0.12	0.12	0.00

Input parameters: $F = 114.09$, $\sigma = 10.10\%$, $T = 65$ days (0.178 years), and $r = 5.54\%$.
Data source: Bloomberg, *Financial Markets Commodities News*.

option's intrinsic value, ϕ. Indeed, the expression for A is constructed such that this condition is satisfied.

Exhibit 11–5 illustrates the use of and the differences between option values calculated using the Barone-Adesi and Whaley model and the Black model. The exhibit shows prices and values of September 1995 call options written on the T-bond futures contract. The data were collected on June 14, 1995, at 1:59 P.M. Chicago time. The last column shows the difference between option values calculated using Barone-Adesi and Whaley's model, and Black's model. The volatility used to price the option is the implied volatility that minimizes the sum of the squared deviations of the Barone-Adesi and Whaley model values from the prices for the last traded call options with strike prices of 112, 114, and 116. Note that the early exercise premiums shown in the last column are insignificant for at-the-money options. However, for lower strike prices, the early-exercise premium is significant. Indeed, Barone-Adesi and Whaley's model predicts that options with strike prices of 102 and 104 should be exercised early; this is consistent with the observation that none of these contracts traded on that particular day.

Interest Rate Models

Up until now, we have focused on bond-futures adaptations of option pricing models originally developed for stocks and in which the stochastic process for the underlying asset in the risk-neutral economy follows a geometric Brownian motion. While these models are simple to use, they are subject to criticism when applied to the entire array of interest rate-dependent securities.

Specifically, there are theoretical deficiencies in employing price-based option pricing models to interest rate-contingent claims in general, and T-bond futures options in particular. Recall that the Black-Scholes model—and its currently discussed successors, the Black model and the Barone-Adesi and Whaley model—assume that (1) the risk-neutral stock price is lognormally distributed, (2) the stock's volatility is constant, and (3) the rate of interest is constant.[16] Thus, there are several well-known criticisms of the application of such equity-based option models to the interest rate arena:

1. Absent default, the bond matures at par.[17] Therefore, the asset price cannot follow a geometric Brownian motion.

2. Lognormally distributed bond prices may result in negative future interest rates; that is, zero-coupon bonds may be priced above par in the future.

3. The Black-Scholes model posits a constant rate of interest, which in turn implies that bond prices are nonrandom; that is, bond prices at all future dates are known with certainty. Thus, there is a fundamental inconsistency in the model: Interest rates cannot simultaneously be constant and stochastic.

Therefore, if we desire to model both the T-bond futures contract and the option written on the contract in a consistent manner, we must use an interest rate model that guarantees the absence of arbitrage opportunities among all interest rate-contingent securities. Further, such an interest rate model should be able to handle all the option features within the T-bond futures option contract, including the options embedded in the futures contract itself (i.e., the quality option, the switching option, the timing, and the

---

[16] As discussed earlier, the latter two restrictions can be slightly relaxed for Black's model: The volatility and the interest rate can be well-behaved deterministic functions of time.

[17] In the absence of default, the phenomenon of "pull to par" refers to bond prices converging toward par as the maturity date approaches.

wild-card options). The financial economics literature now contains numerous models that explicitly address these concerns. These papers model the time-series process of the short-term rate of interest or, alternatively, the set of forward rates of interest, as following some specific stochastic process; further, several of these models can be "calibrated" to match the term structure of interest rates and the term structure of volatilities.[18]

The following procedure outlines an implementation of the interest rate approach to the valuation of a T-bond futures call option. For this example, we will settle on the continuous-time version of the Ho–Lee model:[19]

1. Estimate the term structure of interest rates, and calculate the instantaneous forward rates for all maturities t, $f(0, t)$. For example, coupon-STRIPS prices constitute a set of discount factors from which the term structure of interest rates, as well as the set of instantaneous forward rates $f(0, t)$, is immediately calculable as $f(0, t) = -\partial \log P(0, t)/\partial t$, where $P(0, t)$ is the price at time 0 of a zero-coupon bond with maturity t.[20]

---

[18] Broadly, these models can be divided into three types:

1. One-factor short-term interest rate models: Oldrich Vasicek, "An Equilibrium Characterization of the Term Structure," *Journal of Financial Economics,* 5, 1977, pp. 177–88; Uri L. Dothan, "On the Term Structure of Interest Rates," *Journal of Financial Economics,* 6, 1978, pp. 59–69; George Courtadon, "The Pricing of Options on Default-Free Bonds," *Journal of Financial and Quantitative Analysis,* March 1982, pp. 75–100; John C. Cox, Jonathan E. Ingersoll, Jr., and Stephen A. Ross, "A Theory of the Term Structure of Interest Rates," *Econometrica,* March 1985, pp. 385–407.

2. One-factor models that match the term structure of interest rates: Thomas S. Y. Ho and Sang-Bin Lee, "Term Structure Movements and Pricing Interest Rate Contingent Claims," *Journal of Finance,* December 1986, pp. 1011–29; Fischer Black, Emanuel Derman, and William Toy, "A One-Factor Model of Interest Rates and Its Application to Treasury Bond Options," *Financial Analysts Journal,* January–February 1990, pp. 33–39; Fischer Black and Piotr Karasinski, "Bond and Option Pricing when Short Rates Are Lognormal," *Financial Analysts Journal,* July–August 1991, 52–59; John Hull and Alan White, "Pricing Interest-Rate-Derivative Securities," *Review of Financial Studies,* 3, 1990, pp. 573–92.

3. One- and multi-factor models of the term structure of forward rates of interest: David Heath, Robert Jarrow, and Andrew Morton, "Bond Pricing and the Term Structure of Interest Rates: A Discrete Time Approach," *Journal of Financial and Quantitative Analysis,* December 1990, pp. 419–40; David Heath, Robert Jarrow, and Andrew Morton, "Bond Pricing and the Term Structure of Interest Rates: A New Method for Contingent Claims Valuation," *Econometrica,* January 1992, pp. 77–105.

[19] Unfortunately, this particular model is subject to the criticism that it permits negative rates of interest to occur.

[20] Coupon-STRIPS represent the interest payments stripped from coupon-paying Treasury notes and bonds and thus constitute a consistent set of zero-coupon bond prices. We ignore any complications arising from tax clientele effects and pricing effects caused by differences in tax treatments.

2. By selecting the interest rate process' drift terms $\mu(t)$ as a function of time, we can calibrate the model such that all zero-coupon bonds are priced correctly. For the Ho-Lee model, this yields

$$dr = \mu(t)\, dt + \sigma\, dw(t)$$

where

$$\mu(t) = f_t(0,t) + \sigma^2 t$$

$f_t(0,t)$ = Partial derivative of $f(0,t)$ with respect to t

dr = Change in the short-term rate of interest, r

σ = Constant volatility of dr

$dw(t)$ = Increment of a standard Brownian motion

3. Discretize the continuous-time process for the short rate r by constructing a binomial interest rate lattice with time-steps conforming to all points, including possibly multiple intraday exercise opportunities, at which exercise and delivery decisions must be made.

4. At each node, starting from the end of the lattice, compute the values of all zero-coupon and coupon-paying bonds.[21] From the prices of deliverable bonds, calculate the value of the futures contract by selecting the optimal delivery policy.

5. Calculate the value of the T-bond futures option as the greater of (1) the expected discounted value of the payoffs (using the risk-neutral distribution) when the option is not exercised and (2) the intrinsic value of the option.

6. Calculate the current value of the option on the T-bond futures contract by performing the above calculation for each node and working backward through the interest rate tree to the present.

---

[21] One advantage of using models with normally distributed interest rates (e.g., Ho-Lee or Hull and White) is that closed-form analytical solutions are available for discount bonds as well as bond options. For the Ho-Lee model, conditional on r, the price of a $T - t$ period zero-coupon bond, $P(t, T)$ is given by

$$P(t,T) = A(t,T)e^{-r(T-t)}$$

where

$$\log A(t,T) = \log\frac{P(0,T)}{P(0,t)} - (T-t)\frac{\partial \log P(0,t)}{\partial t} - \tfrac{1}{2}\sigma^2 t(T-t)^2$$

Naturally, we may calculate the value of any coupon bond, B, by summing across the products of zero-coupon bond prices $P(t, T)$ and the payments of coupon and principal, CF_t

$$B = \sum_t P(t,T)CF_t$$

In conclusion, one can construct interest rate models that are more appropriate for the valuation of interest rate–dependent securities than Black-Scholes. Indeed, for certain types of securities—such as callable bonds, which embed a long-term call option within the security—the Black-Scholes-type models may result in poor valuations and incorrect hedge ratios. Nevertheless, Black's and Barone-Adesi and Whaley's models are appropriate for the valuation of T-bond futures options because these options' maturities are very short relative to those of the underlying bonds. The short time to option expiration relative to the underlying bond's maturity date implies that the pull to par evidenced in bond prices does not have time to take effect and that, consequently, these price diffusion–based models yield consistent and reasonable values.

SUMMARY

This chapter discussed the options on Treasury bond futures contracts traded on the Chicago Board of Trade. The key ingredients include the option's liquidity, the institutional background, speculative and hedging uses, and no-arbitrage valuation approaches. This contract, which is among the world's most liquid option contracts, is extremely important because it constitutes a highly efficient exchange-traded mechanism for hedging and speculating on the long-term rate of interest in the United States.

12

AN INTUITIVE APPROACH TO FIXED-INCOME OPTION VALUATION

David Audley, PhD
Director of Investment Systems and Technology
Tiger Management Corporation

Richard Chin
First Vice President
Co-Director of Equity Products and Strategies Group
Prudential Securities Incorporated

Shrikant Ramamurthy
Vice President
Fixed-Income Research and Product Management
Prudential Securities Incorporated

Investors determine the value of fixed-income securities with embedded options through the use of option valuation models. The *option-adjusted spread (OAS) model* is one such valuation model; it probabilistically projects how future interest rates may be distributed and then determines the value of the option under these conditions. The process, which is computationally intensive, conceptually produces a net spread (the option-adjusted spread) to a reference yield curve (which is usually a zero-coupon curve that is derived from the U. S. Treasury curve).

The complement to the OAS is the option value, which is the approximate number of basis points of yield that must be added to or subtracted from the nominal yield spread to arrive at the OAS. If the option value may be estimated by intuitive means, an investor may also estimate the value of the OAS. This chapter addresses how option value may be approximated given the historical frequency of certain interest rate threshold levels and the use of a sector yield curve to establish a context in which the decision to exercise an option may be made.

COMPUTATIONS VERSUS INTUITION/HISTORICAL DATA

Option valuation models are sophisticated analytical tools that calculate an option's value. While myriad complex technical issues embody these models, it is not necessary to be well versed in all of the mathematical details to utilize these models effectively. Users of these models will find that market experience and common sense, in conjunction with an effective valuation model, are the keys to properly estimating an option's value. In fact, as the market makes the final judgment on value, the model ideally should be a reflection of how the option is valued in the marketplace rather than a mathematical solution alone.

An embedded option can be valued simply by estimating the likelihood that the option will be exercised. To determine the feasibility of exercising an option, the current level of interest rates and the probability that rates will move to a level that encourages the profitable exercise of the option must be evaluated. For example, let's assume that rates are at historically high levels and thus there is an intuitively derived chance that rates will fall. The question is whether rates will fall sufficiently to induce an issuer to call a set of callable bonds. If the threshold yield level for the exercise of the option is historically very low, only a small probability exists that the bonds will be called. Thus, the call options should have little value. In addition, the call option needs to be valued within the context of the yields of other, similar bonds in the callable bonds sector. If the bond is to be called for refunding purposes, the issuer needs to be concerned about the yield levels of the new issues that would replace the outstanding callable bonds. These new yield levels are dictated at the time of refunding by the yields of comparable securities within the same sector.

SECTOR YIELD CURVE

The sector yield curve represents the yields of noncallable bonds that span the various terms to maturity and are applicable for a particular sector, such as single-A-rated industrials or government agencies. Often, the sector curve is referred to as the *corporate* curve or *agency* curve and is derived from the U.S. Treasury curve and the appropriate yield spreads at each maturity point that are dictated by the marketplace. An issuer that has sufficient outstanding noncallable debt issues may have its own specific yield curve. For example, FNMA currently has more than 50 noncallable debentures, so a FNMA curve may be constructed. Generally, the sector curve encompasses a number of issuers and reflects the average yields of generic noncallable issues as a whole.

Exhibit 12–1 shows the generic yield spreads for different debt sectors, terms to maturity, and credit ratings as quoted by the Prudential Securities Corporate and Agency Trading Desks as of February 7, 1995. The exhibit shows that for any one credit rating, the yield spreads increase with maturity. Therefore, even if the Treasury curve were flat, the sector curve would be upwardly sloping. The degree of positive slope to the sector curve is driven by the supply and demand of available issues in a maturity range and the perception that default risk increases as maturity increases. Since the sector curve represents the yields for bonds within that sector, it may be used as a "local" reference for determining value. A bond that is "fairly valued" would lie directly on the sector curve, while bonds that are rich or cheap would lie below or above the sector curve, respectively. Therefore, instead of using the Treasury curve as a reference benchmark, the sector curve may now be used as the reference in determining relative value.

SECTOR CURVE AND EMBEDDED OPTIONS

The advantage of using the sector curve is that it captures the effect of varying yield spreads as a function of maturity when valuing embedded options. The sector curve defines the yield curve environment in which the economic decision to exercise the embedded option is made. For callable bonds, the sector yield curve illustrates the possible refunding costs at each maturity. For example, if a 10-year bond is callable during its last 5 years, the decision to exercise the option in any year is influenced heavily by the interest costs of the bonds that could be used to refund the issue. If the decision to refund is made, the issuer must choose between a short-term issue to the original maturity date or another 10-year callable issue. However, it is possible that the interest costs would be prohibitive, making it uneconomical to call the bond. In any case, the refunding possibilities are determined by the sector curve at that time, in addition to the issuer's financing constraints and flexibilities. A key point is that it is more appropriate to use the current sector curve as a starting point in the estimation of the possible refunding alternatives at the call date than it is to use the current Treasury curve.

SECTOR PRICE AND SECTOR OAS

The *sector price* of a bond is the bond's theoretical price in relation to the sector curve; that is, the sector value is the present value of the cash flows

EXHIBIT   12–1

Yield Spreads (BPs) to Treasuries for Generic Noncallable Corporate and Agency Issues

Corporate	1-Yr.	2-Yr.	3-Yr.	4-Yr.	5-Yr.	7-Yr.	10-Yr.	30-Yr.
Industrial:								
AAA	20	23	29	32	32	35	35	47
AA	22	28	33	37	35	43	45	55
A	32	37	47	52	50	55	55	68
BBB	42	49	54	62	77	83	85	100
Utility:								
AAA	23	28	31	30	31	33	35	50
AA	29	32	36	33	35	40	42	60
A	40	45	48	45	47	50	52	70
BBB	50	56	59	55	58	63	66	90
Finance:								
AAA	25	29	34	38	40	44	50	65
AA	30	35	42	47	52	63	68	83
A	37	47	52	67	68	72	75	108
BBB	53	57	62	72	86	88	88	158
Commercial Banks:								
AAA	27	32	37	42	50	58	65	55
AA	33	42	47	52	60	63	65	70
A	38	42	51	60	75	85	95	90
BBB	57	62	65	72	88	95	108	120
Yankee:								
AAA	28	30	33	36	38	41	44	60
AA	31	35	40	43	56	72	75	82
A	38	42	48	53	73	80	85	92
BBB	47	54	63	70	77	90	102	110
Canadian:								
AAA	31	35	38	40	42	45	51	68
AA	38	40	45	47	57	60	65	82
A	35	45	50	59	68	74	89	120
BBB	50	60	70	73	78	89	99	130
Agency:								
FNMA	18	18	20	20	19	28	30	37
FHLB	18	18	20	20	19	28	30	NA

Source: Prudential Securities' IMPACT database as of February 7, 1995.

individually discounted at the appropriate sector yield levels while taking any embedded options into account. If the market price of a bond is less than its sector value, the bond is cheap; if the market price exceeds the sector price, the bond is rich.

Generally, the OAS is interpreted as the net spread to the Treasury curve after adjusting for the effect of the embedded option. In a similar vein, a "sector OAS" may be calculated that furnishes a net spread to the sector curve.[1] A callable or putable bond is fairly valued to the sector curve if it has a sector OAS of zero, indicating that the bond has neither a net positive nor a negative yield spread to the sector curve.

The calculation of the sector OAS uses the sector curve as the backdrop for the valuation of the embedded option. This implies that the economic decision to call or put a bond is made within the yield environment for that sector. For example, if a callable bond has a nominal yield spread of 20 basis points over the sector curve but has a sector OAS of plus 5 basis points, the call option has a value of 15 basis points. This call value indicates that, given the likely course of interest rates, the callable bond theoretically should have a yield spread of about 15 basis points higher than the underlying noncallable bond that is determined by the sector curve. The remaining 5 basis points of value stems from the cheapness of the underlying bond (at the given market price).[2]

ESTIMATION OF OPTION VALUE

The two bonds shown in Exhibit 12–2 will be used to illustrate how the sector yield curve and historical interest rate levels may be used to obtain a qualitative, as opposed to quantitative, sense of the value of the embedded option. In each case, the approach is not to focus on a stochastic interest rate process or an explicit OAS or option value calculation. Instead, the "intuitive

---

[1] Technically speaking, the OAS is the constant spread to the zero-coupon curve that is derived from the coupon yield curve, and not a spread to the coupon yield curve itself. See Deniz Akkus, David Audley, Erik Carlson, Richard Chin, and Shrikant Ramamurthy, "Term Structure of Interest Rates: Fundamentals for the Pricing of Interest-Rate Derivatives" *Technology and Its Effect on Valuation Metrics: Study #26*, Financial Strategies Group, Prudential Securities Inc., July 1994.

[2] Note that an OAS to the Treasury curve (as distinct from the sector curve) may produce different values for the call option since, in the OAS-to-Treasuries case, the "sector" yield curve is defined by a single spread (OAS) to the Treasury curve. This is in contrast to the varying yield spreads that form the sector curve discussed above. Thus, two distinct sector curves may be under consideration, depending on whether the OAS is calculated relative to the Treasury curve or to the sector curve.

E X H I B I T   12–2

Sector Yield Curves for the Qualitative Analysis of Embedded Options

	Description of Bonds Used in Examples								
Issuer	Coupon (%)	Maturity	Option Type	Option Exercise Date	Option Exercise Price	Market Price	Market YTM (%)	Spread Tresury (BPs)	OAS (BPs)
Southern Bell Telephone	8.125	5/1/17	Call	2/14/95	103.92	97.13	8.41	75/30-Year Treasury	52
General Electric Capital	8.500	7/24/08	Put	7/24/95	100.00	104.40	7.96	44/10-Year Treasury	42

Sector Yield Curve for Southern Bell Telephone 8.125% (AAA-Rated Utilities)							
	1-Yr.	2-Yr.	3-Yr.	5-Yr.	7-Yr.	10-Yr.	30-Yr.
Treasury (%)	6.80	7.19	7.33	7.46	7.47	7.52	7.66
Sector spread (BPs)	23	28	32	35	37	45	59
Sector curve (%)	7.03	7.47	7.65	7.81	7.84	7.97	8.25

Sector Yield Curve for General Electric Capital 8.50% (AAA-Rated Industrials)							
	1-Yr.	2-Yr.	3-Yr.	5-Yr.	7-Yr.	10-Yr.	30-Yr.
Treasury	6.80	7.19	7.33	7.46	7.47	7.52	7.66
Sector spread (BPs)	15	20	23	25	30	35	50
Sector curve (%)	6.95	7.39	7.56	7.71	7.77	7.87	8.16

Note: Yield curves are as of the time of analysis on February 7, 1995, as quoted by the Prudential Securities Corporate Bond Trading Desk.

calculation" of an option's value is compared to the value calculated by the use of a model. By comparing the two, we can determine whether the calculated option value is consistent with intuition and historical trends.[3]

CALLABLE BOND EXAMPLE

Bond Description

The Southern Bell Telephone 8.125s of 05/01/17 are currently callable at a price of $103.92. The call price declines annually until 05/01/12, after which point the bond is callable at par until final maturity. The Southern

---

[3] This analysis assumes that the movement of future interest rates will not be significantly different from the movement of interest rates over the past 20 years.

Bell 8.125s have a market price of $97.13 to yield 8.41 percent to maturity, at a spread of 75 basis points over the 30-year Treasury bond.

On the surface, as the bond is callable for the next 22 years, the call option appears to have significant value. However, another perspective of the call option's value may be gained by considering the changes in the sector values of both the callable bond and the underlying noncallable bond as functions of downward shifts in the sector curve. By comparing the downward shift that is required for early redemption with historical yield curves, it is possible to estimate the likelihood of the bond being called by means other than through an option valuation model.

METHOD 1: SECTOR PRICE OF THE CALLABLE BOND
Likelihood of Call Today

For the current Treasury yield curve and the sector shown in Exhibit 12–2, a current sector price, which represents the theoretical price of the bond given its coupon, maturity, and call option structure, may be calculated. For each downward shift of the sector curve, it is possible to find the corresponding sector price, which is the theoretical value of the bond in the new rate environment. The downward shift that causes the sector price to be roughly equal to the current call price is approximately equivalent to the drop in rates that would have to occur for the bond to be considered a candidate for early redemption. Exhibit 12–3 shows that an immediate drop in rates of 135 basis points, assuming constant sector yield spreads, results in a sector price of $103.84, which is slight-

E X H I B I T   12–3

Historical Frequency of Required Treasury Yields for Early Redemption of Southern Bell Telephone 8.125% of 5/1/17

Redemption Date	Call Price	Required Curve Shift (BPs)	Sector Price	Benchmark Treasury	Required Treasury Yield (%)	Historical Frequency (%)
2/14/95	103.92	−135	103.84	Long bond	6.31	2
2/14/00	102.83	−120	102.72	Long bond	6.46	3
2/14/05	101.74	−100	101.60	10-year	6.52	6
2/14/10	100.65	−75	100.60	7-year	6.72	10

Note: Historical frequency from February 1975 to January 1995. Since the 30-year Treasury did not exist prior to 1977, the historical frequency reflects a composite of 20-year and 30-year Treasury bond yields. Analysis as of February 7, 1995.

ly below the current call price. A rate decrease of this magnitude would result in a yield of 6.31 percent or less for the 30-year Treasury. The yield on the long bond has dropped to 6.31 percent or less approximately 2 percent of the time since February 1975. This indicates that although it is possible for the 30-year Treasury to drop to these low levels, the probability of it doing so it limited, as is the probability that the bond will be called in the immediate future.

Likelihood of Call in the Future

Assuming that the bond is not called now, what is the probability that the bond will be called five years from now? A similar process may be undertaken assuming that five years have elapsed and that the sector yield curve is the same as it is today. (Considering that the current yield curve appears to be a "typical" upwardly sloping yield curve, this is a reasonable assumption.) At this future point in time, the bond is closer to its final maturity by five years and the call price has declined to $102.83. We found that a drop of 120 basis points from the current levels is needed to produce a sector price of $102.72, at which level it is likely that the bond will be called early. This corresponds to an interest rate environment in which the 30-year Treasury is yielding 6.46 percent or less, which has happened only 3 percent of the time since February 1975.

Jumping ahead an additional 10 years (15 in all), at which point in time the bond would be callable at 100.65, a drop in interest rates of 75 basis points from current levels is required to produce a sector price of $100.60, which is very close to the call price. Such a drop in rates would translate into a seven-year Treasury yield of 6.72 percent or less. The yield on the seven-year Treasury note has been at this level 10 percent of the time since February 1975. Thus, even at this point in time, the probability that the bond may be called early is relatively small.

The net result of this analysis is that the Southern Bell 8.125s, which are callable for the next 22 years, resemble a bond that probably will not be called for at least 15 years. Initially, it appeared that the bond's call option had significant value given the long call period. However, from a historical perspective, there is only a small probability that the bonds may be called in the near term, so the call option may have less value than initially thought.

Effect of Sector Spreads

In the analysis above, we also assumed that the sector yield spreads remained constant as the yield curve was shifted downward. In reality, it is likely that the yield spreads would tend to widen as rates fell. As issuers take advantage of the lower interest rate environment to issue new debt, the increased supply of securities in the marketplace would tend to increase the yields of outstanding debt, since the outstanding issues would now be competing with a greater number of alternative investments. Under this scenario, the cost of refunding the callable issue increases, which depresses the sector price of the callable bond. Thus, an even greater downward shift in the yield curve would be required to compensate for the effect of wider sector yield spreads, which further decreases, to some degree, the likelihood that the bonds will be called.

METHOD 2: REFUNDING COSTS VERSUS COSTS OF NONCALLABLE BOND

Another method of estimating the value of the call option is to weigh the costs of refunding the issue against the savings in interest payments. It is assumed that this cost of refunding is approximately 1 to 2 points and that the cost is added to the call price of the bond to arrive at a refunding target present value. This establishes the necessary break-even level of interest rates at which the present value of the underlying noncallable bond is equal to the refunding target. At this point, the issuer should be indifferent, from an economic point of view, whether to call the bonds or to continue the current interest payments until final maturity.[4]

Exhibit 12–4 shows the required yield curve shifts that are associated with the refunding targets and the historical frequency of such a shift for different possible redemption dates. From this standpoint, it is also unlikely that the bond will be called in the near future. Once again, the call options may not have as much value as was originally guessed, although it may have more value than anticipated from the earlier analysis in Exhibit 12–3.

For the Southern Bell 8.125s, Prudential Securities' option model calculates an option value of 20 basis points, which (considering that the bond is unlikely to be called over the next 15 years) is a reasonable yield compensation to investors for selling the call option to the issuer. Note that other option models may calculate a significantly different value for the call option, and this may be due to the particular interest rate assumption that is used in the computations.

---

[4] This analysis does not take into account the value of all future opportunities to call the bond early; instead, the analysis focuses on the choice between calling the bond immediately and not calling the bond prior to maturity.

E X H I B I T   12–4

Historical Frequency of Required Treasury Yields for Redemption Target
of Underlying Bond for Southern Bell Telephone 8.125% of 5/1/17

Redemption Date	Call Price	Approximate Refund Target	Required Curve Shift (BPs)	PV of Underlying Bond	Benchmark Treasury	Required Treasury Yield (%)	Historical Frequency (%)
2/14/95	103.92	105.92	–68	105.91	Long bond	6.98	5
2/14/00	102.83	104.83	–63	104.78	Long bond	7.03	5
2/14/05	101.74	103.49	–30	103.55	10-year	7.22	14
2/14/10	100.65	102.40	–16	102.41	7-year	7.31	24

Note: Historical frequency form February 1975 to January 1995. Since the 30-year Treasury did not exist prior to
1977, the historical frequency reflects a composite of 20-year and 30-year Treasury bond yields. Analysis as of
February 7, 1995.

EFFECT OF INTEREST RATE MODELS
ON OPTION VALUE

Many option valuation models, including some models that are com-
mercially available to investors, assume a purely lognormal interest-rate
process that does not incorporate a feature known as mean reversion.
Mean reversion assumes that there is a tendency for interest rates to
exist within a certain band over time and that interest rates are not
expected to reach extreme levels. Models that do not have the mean
reversion feature will assign a higher probability to very low interest
rates than models that do have mean reversion, all other things being
equal. For callable bonds, this results in higher call option values and
lower OASs in the models that lack this feature in comparison to the
models that do have mean reversion.[5] Prudential Securities' interest rate
model includes mean reversion.

Models that do not have mean reversion essentially allow interest
rates to propagate without constraint and do not reflect the fact that
Treasury rates historically have had upper and lower limits. Therefore, if,
as in the above example, the threshold level of interest rates is 100 basis
points lower than current levels, a model without mean reversion will calculate a higher probability for this occurrence than will a model with

---

[5] See David Audley, Richard Chin, and Vincent Pica, "The Effect of Mean Reversion on OAS,"
  Technology and Its Effect on Valuation Metrics: Study #1: Financial Strategies Group,
  Prudential Securities Inc., August 1990.

mean reversion, and thus assign a higher call option value, regardless of historical trends. When bonds with embedded options are analyzed using the model without mean reversion, one needs to determine whether the high option values are consistent with historical observations.

PUTABLE BOND EXAMPLE

The General Electric Capital 8.50s of 07/24/08 may be put at par to the issuer on 7/24/95. The bond is priced at $104.40 for a yield to maturity of 7.96 percent at a spread of 44 basis points over the 10-year Treasury note. The yield-to-put is −1.34 percent, which is through the Treasury curve.

The sector spreads and the resulting sector yield curve for General Electric Capital bonds are shown in Exhibit 12–2. Since the sector yield curve is the interest rate environment in which the decision to exercise the put option is made, an investor compares the put bond to alternative investments that are available within the same sector on the exercise date. If the coupon on the putable bond is at a premium relative to other bonds of similar final maturity on the put date, the put option will not be exercised and the bond will be kept by the investor. This may be interpreted as a call option that the investor has in choosing to keep the bond. On the other hand, if the coupon on the put bond is at a discount to other, similar, bonds on the put date, the bond will be put and the proceeds will be reinvested into higher-yielding securities.

Assume for the moment that the sector curve on the put date is the same as the current sector curve. On the exercise date, the remaining term of the put bond is 13 years and the yield of noncallable AAA-rated industrial paper of this maturity is between 7.87 percent and 8.16 percent. (See Exhibit 12–2.) Since the coupon of 8.50 percent is at a premium relative to these other bonds, the put option should not be exercised from an economic viewpoint. If the bond is not put, then, on the day immediately following the exercise date, the price on the 8.50 percent bond will reflect the price of a 13-year bullet bond.

Even though the sector yield curve is not really static, the above analysis indicates that the current sector curve does not favor the exercise of the put option. Sector yields need to rise before the coupon of the put bond is on par with those of other bonds in the AAA-industrial sector. In this particular case, since the "call" option is currently in the money, the call option would have significant value, while the put option would have limited value.

Estimating the Sector OAS

The qualitative values of the option may be translated into estimates of the OAS from the following relationships:[6]

$$\text{Sector OAS} = \text{Yield-to-put spread} + \text{``Call value''} \qquad (1)$$

or, equivalently,

$$\text{Sector OAS} = \text{Yield-to-maturity spread} + \text{Put value} \qquad (2)$$

Relative to the sector curve and yields shown in Exhibit 12–2, the yield-to-put spread is –790 basis points and the yield-to-maturity spread is approximately –3 basis points.[7] (The negative yield spreads to the sector curve indicate that the investor is receiving a yield that is less than the yields of comparable bullet bonds as a result of the put option premium being included in the price of the bond.) Since the put option was shown above to have limited value (assume roughly 5 basis points or less), the sector OAS is estimated to be in the neighborhood of zero basis points as a consequence of equation 2 (see equation 3).

$$\text{Sector OAS} \approx -3 + 5 \approx 0 \qquad (3)$$

For a sector OAS of zero, it then follows that the call value is approximately 790 basis points, as seen from equation 4.

$$0 \approx -790 + \text{Call value} \qquad (4)$$

These estimates may be compared to the Prudential Securities calculated values of zero basis points for the sector OAS, while the put and the call are calculated to be worth 3 basis points and 774 basis points, respectively, at a 12 percent yield volatility.[8] Thus, the estimated OAS and option values are very close to their actual calculated values.

ESTIMATING THE OAS TO THE TREASURY CURVE

As analysis similar to that shown in equations 1 and 2 may be performed to estimate the OAS to the Treasury curve. Relative to the Treasury curve,

---

[6] For further discussion see David Audley, Richard Chin, Shrikant Ramamurthy, and Susan Volin, "OAS and Effective Duration," *Handbook of Fixed Income Securities*, (Burr Ridge, IL: Irwin Professional Publishing, 1995, 4th ed.), Chapter 30 in Frank J. Fabozzi and T. Dessa Fabozzi (eds.), and David Audley and Richard Chin, "Bonds with Embedded Put Options," Financial Strategies Group, Prudential Securities Inc., December 1990.

[7] The yield-to-maturity spread and the yield-to-put spread are relative to the yields on comparable-maturity bonds in the same sector and not relative to the yield on the reference Treasury issue used for pricing.

[8] See Chapter 15.

the yield-to-put spread is –775 basis points and the yield-to-maturity spread is 39 basis points. Since the put option is worth roughly 5 basis points, the OAS to the Treasury curve is estimated to be in the neighborhood of 44 basis points, while the call should be worth about 819 basis points. (The Prudential Securities calculated value of the OAS is 42 basis points, while the put is calculated to be worth 5 basis points and the call to be worth 802 basis points at a 12 percent yield volatility.)

MEAN REVERSION REVISITED

The above values of OAS are calculated by Prudential Securities' option model, which factors in the effect of mean reversion. A model that does not have mean reversion will likely assign a greater probability that rates will decrease by the exercise date and thus compute higher option values and OASs than would the Prudential Securities model. To help assess whether a specific value of OAS is consistent with intuition and historical trends, it is useful to refer to the relationships shown in equations 1 and 2. If the OASs are truly as high as may be implied by option models without mean reversion, there is significant value in keeping the bond since rates are more likely to fall than they are to rise.

The average yield on the 10-year Treasury note since February 1975 is 8.16 percent with a standard deviation of 2.60 percent. At the time of the analysis, the yield on the 10-year Treasury note was 7.52 percent, which is below the average 10-year yield for the past 20 years. Thus, it appears to be more likely that rates will increase rather than decrease, which deflates the value of the call option.

However, when considering the sector yield curve for the General Electric Capital 8.50s, the sector curve needs to be shifted upward by about 60 basis points for the 8.50 percent coupon to be on par with other securities of similar maturity in the sector. An upward shift of at least this magnitude translates into a yield of 8.12 percent or more on the 10-year Treasury note, assuming constant sector yield spreads. Since February 1975, yields lower than 8.12 percent have occurred 41 percent of the time. Thus, from a historical standpoint, and especially given the current interest rate environment, it is reasonably possible that long-term rates will stay low enough for the call option to be exercised and the put option not to be exercised. Thus, it may be expected that the OAS would not be vastly different than the nominal yield-to-maturity spread and not as high as may be suggested by option models without mean reversion.

SUMMARY

Fixed-income option models, which calculate the values of embedded options, are built on a foundation of mathematical rigor. However, investors may use straightforward, intuitive approaches to estimate the value of an embedded option and hence estimate a bond's OAS without having to utilize an option model. This nontechnical approach allows investors to compare actual calculated values of OAS with their estimates and to determine if the computations are consistent with their expectations. If significant differences exist between the two values, they often can be attributed to the specific (but critical) interest rate assumptions that drive the OAS model. In particular, the presence of mean reversion in an interest rate model has a dramatic effect on the calculated value of an option.

With the multitude of OAS models that are used within the investment community, investors often face an array of OAS calculations. Here we have presented a means by which any one calculated value of OAS may be judged for its reasonableness and thereby help arrive at the "correct" OAS.[9]

---

[9] See David Audley and Richard Chin, "What is the Correct OAS?" Financial Strategies Group, Prudential Securities Inc., May 14, 1990.

13

⑥ VALUATION OF CREDIT RISK DERIVATIVES

Yiannos A. Pierides
Assistant Professor of Finance
Department of Public and Business Administration
University of Cyprus, Nicosia, Cyprus

The credit risk derivatives market has grown dramatically in the last two years. Credit risk derivatives are instruments whose payoffs are tied to the credit characteristics of a particular asset. For example, a portfolio manager holding some corporate bonds that trade at a spread of 100 basis points above Treasuries could buy a credit risk derivative that will compensate the manager if the securities start trading at a spread greater than 100 basis points above Treasuries.

There are two recent studies on credit risk derivatives. The Flesaker, Hughston, Schreiber, and Sprung (FHSS) approach is based on the assumption that the actual time of default on a corporate bond always comes as a surprise to investors and that corporate bonds of all maturities (including short ones) will be subject to nontrivial default risk.[1] As Flesaker et al. point out, this feature of their model contrasts markedly with another school of thought on the default process of corporate bonds. The latter school is represented by Merton[2] and Black and Cox[3] and models corporate debt by regarding equity as a call option on the assets of the

---

[1] B. L. Flesaker, L. Hughston, L. Schreiber, and L. Sprung, "Credit Derivatives: Taking All the Credit," Risk Magazine, September 1994.

[2] R. Merton., "On the Pricing of Corporate Debt: The Risk Structure of Interest Rates," *Journal of Finance,* May 1974.

[3] F. Black and J. Cox, "Valuing Corporate Securities: Some Effects of Bond Indenture Provisions," *Journal of Finance,* May 1976.

firm. Default is modeled as occurring on the first scheduled payment date on the corporate bond when the firm's assets are no longer high enough to make it rational for the shareholders to provide the necessary cash to make the payment. Default can occur only at maturity in the case of a zero-coupon bond and on a coupon date (or at maturity) in the case of a coupon bond. Since the value of the firm's assets is presumed to be an observable process, the default can be predicted with increasing precision as the time for payment draws near. As a result, with this approach default does not come as a surprise (unlike with the FHSS approach).

Das was the first to apply this approach by pricing derivatives on the prices of zero-coupon corporate bonds in the framework of Merton.[4] However, he does not consider credit risk derivatives on coupon corporate bonds, even though a substantial portion of the outstanding corporate debt is coupon bearing. Furthermore, he considers only options on the bond price, even though credit risk derivatives can also be structured as options on the bond spread.

This chapter deals specifically with derivatives on coupon corporate bonds that are structured as either options on the bond price or options on the bond spread. These options are structured in the context of the Black and Cox model of corporate coupon bond pricing.

THE BLACK AND COX MODEL OF COUPON CORPORATE BOND PRICING

Black and Cox make the following three assumptions:

1. The riskless interest rate (denoted r) is constant.
2. Firm value (V) dynamics: $dV = aV\,dt + sV\,dz$; where a and s are constants and dz is the increment of a Wiener process. Note that these two assumptions are the same as the assumptions of the Black-Scholes model, except that here we assume that total firm value (V), not the stock price, follows a lognormal process.
3. The firm has outstanding a single issue of debt promising B at time T_B and discrete coupons in the amount c (fixed) at times $0.2T_B$, $0.4T_B$, $0.6T_B$, and $0.8T_B$. These coupon payments must be financed by issuing new subordinated securities; that is, no asset sales are allowed. If a coupon payment is not made, the firm is in default and the promised payment of B becomes due immediately.

---

[4] S. Das, "Credit Risk Derivatives," *Journal of Derivatives,* Spring 1995.

Black and Cox show that the value of the coupon-paying debt at time t, denoted $f(V, t)$ will satisfy the following partial differential equation (PDE):

$$rvf_v + 0.5s^2V^2f_{vv} - rf + f_t + \sum_{i=1}^{4} c\delta(t - (0.2)iT_B) = 0$$

where $\delta()$ is the Dirac delta function.

This PDE is identical to the Black-Scholes PDE except that it includes an additional term (the last one) that accounts for the need to pay coupons on the debt. The boundary condition at bond maturity is that the bond value be equal to the promised amount B if the latter exceeds firm value and be equal to firm value otherwise.

In light of the preceding stopping condition on a coupon date (in case the firm goes bankrupt), no closed-form solution exists for the value of the debt. For this reason, Black and Cox advocate the use of standard numerical procedures.

It stands to reason that the ex-coupon bond price (i.e., the price of the bond after payment of the coupon) is not defined on a coupon date if the firm goes bankrupt on that coupon date. For this reason, any option contract must be based on the cum-coupon bond price. Let $G(V,t)$ be the cum-coupon bond price at t.

Credit risk derivatives protect holders of coupon bonds from a reduction in the bonds' value. Unlike zero-coupon bonds, coupon bonds can default prior to their maturity, and as a result any credit risk derivative on a coupon bond will necessarily involve a barrier option that ceases to exist in the event of bankruptcy. We consider two types of barrier options: a put on the coupon bond's price and a call on the coupon bond's spread above the risk-free rate. We begin with the put.

AN AMERICAN PUT OPTION ON THE CUM-COUPON BOND PRICE (G)

Consider the following American put: At any $t < T$, where $T =$ option maturity $< T_B$, assuming the firm is not bankrupt, the option's owner can sell the bond at a time-varying exercise price $K(t)$ equal to the cum-coupon price of the bond for a fixed spread g above the risk-free rate. For example, consider the coupon bond defined earlier: It promised B at T_B and coupons in the amount c at $0.2T_B$, $0.4T_B$, $0.6T_B$, and $0.8T_B$. Then, for example,

$$K(0.2T_B) = c + c\exp(-(r+g)(0.4T_B - 0.2T_B)) + c\exp(-(r+g)(0.6T_B - 0.2T_B))$$
$$+ c\exp(-(r+g)(0.8T_B - 0.2T_B)) + B\exp(-(r+g)(T_B - 0.2T_B))$$

Note that $K(t)$ is defined in a way consistent with the bond price on which the option is defined: both are cum-coupon.

Furthermore, the option contract provides that if the firm goes bankrupt at any time prior to option maturity, the option will be immediately exercised. This is a necessary condition to impose, since the bond will cease to exist if the firm goes bankrupt, and hence there will be no way to calculate the payoffs to the option. This provision makes this option contract a barrier option. Since the firm can go bankrupt only on a coupon date prior to bond maturity, the option can be terminated only on coupon dates.

To see why this option qualifies as a credit risk derivative, suppose we know that a Triple B credit rating implies that the bond is priced at a spread of $g = 1\%$. Furthermore, assume that a portfolio manager bought the bond when it was rated Triple B. If this portfolio manager also purchases this American put, he or she is protected from a downgrading. For example, if the bond is downgraded to Single B, its price will decrease, and hence the put will be in the money since its exercise price is equal to the price of the bond for a Triple B rating. By exercising it, the portfolio manager is guaranteed a value equal to the price at which the bond should trade if it had not been downgraded. In other words, a portfolio manager purchasing a bond rated Triple B (which is assumed to trade at a spread above r of 1 percent) and a put on the bond with an exercise price $K(T) =$ bond price for a spread above r of $g = 1\%$ is guaranteed at option maturity T a portfolio value equal to max $(G(V, T), K(T))$. It follows that the lowest portfolio value at T will be the bond value for a 1 percent spread above r, but if the actual bond price, $G(V,T)$, ends up being higher than this value, the portfolio value will be higher. So the portfolio manager insures the portfolio from a credit deterioration but benefits from a credit improvement.

We first present a no–early exercise result.

Proposition 1: This American put will never be exercised early in a voluntary way. It will be exercised early only if it is a forced exercise, that is, if the option is terminated. Hence American and European put values will be the same.

A formal proof is beyond the scope of this chapter.[5] However, we provide some intuition as to the reasoning that leads to proposition 1. The

[5] A formal proof is provided in Y.A. Pierides, *Essays on Finance,* 1994, (unpublished doctoral thesis, Sloan School, Massachusetts Institute of Technology, Cambridge, Massachusetts).

two factors against early exercise are: (1) The exercise price increases with the passage of time, and therefore the longer we wait to exercise, the higher the exercise price that we get; and (2) if we wait, we retain the option to change our mind. The one factor in favor of early exercise, is that the earlier we exercise, the earlier we start earning interest on the exercise price. It can be shown that the first factor against early exercise more than offsets the factor in favor of early exercise and, as a result, early exercise is never optimal.

We now consider the pricing of this put. Let $F[G, t]$ be the option price at time t. We assume that the option price depends on the cum-coupon bond price G and time t. Since G depends on V, we can think of option price as a function of V and t that is., $F[G, t] = N[V, t]$.

Using the usual arbitrage argument, we can show that the option price will satisfy the following PDE.

$$0.5 \, N_{vv} s^2 V^2 + N_t - rN + rN_v V = 0$$

The boundary conditions are:

$$N[V, T] = \max[0, K(T) - G(V, T)]$$
$$N[V, t] \geq \max[0, K(t) - G(V, t)]$$

This PDE is identical to the Black-Scholes PDE. This is not surprising, since we have only one source of uncertainty in the model (V) and V follows a log-normal process (as does the stock price in the Black-Scholes model).

The first boundary condition says that the option value at maturity will be the exercise value if the latter is positive and zero otherwise. The second one says that the price of an American put can never fall below the put's exercise value. The corresponding boundary conditions in the Black-Scholes model have a similar interpretation. However, a crucial difference is that the boundary conditions in the Black-Scholes model are linear in the underlying stochastic variable, whereas in this model they are nonlinear. This nonlinearity prevents us from obtaining a closed-form solution as in the Black-Scholes model.

We employ a numerical method of solution. Recall from the earlier discussion that no closed-form solution exists for the coupon bond price either. For this reason, to price the put on the coupon bond, we need two numerical schemes. The first scheme gives us the coupon bond price, G; the second scheme uses the G calculated form the first scheme to calculate the option price.

Numerical Results

The parameter values chosen were

$$T = 5$$
$$T_B = 10$$
$$r = 0.1 \text{ per year}$$
$$B = 50$$
$$g = 0.03$$
$$s = 0.2 \text{ or } 0.4$$
$$c = 3 \text{ at } t = 2, 4, 6, 8$$

Exhibit 13–1 gives bond and option prices for different firm values.

As expected, the bond price rises with increases in firm value. Furthermore, note that for the low-volatility case ($s = 0.2$), bond price is

E X H I B I T   13–1

Put on Price of Coupon Bond
$T = 5, T_B = 10, r = 0.1, g = 0.03, B = 50, c = 3$ at $t = 2, 4, 6, 8$

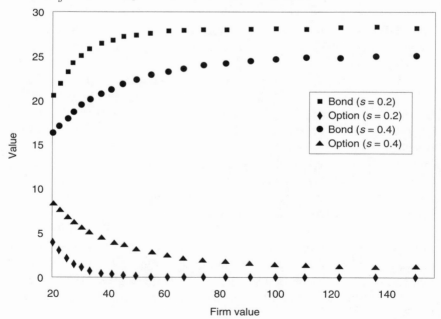

For $s = 0.2$ (0.4) option terminated at: $t = 2$ for $V < 27.3$ (18.3), $t = 4$ for $V < 30.2$ (20.2).

only slightly less than firm value when firm value is low ($V = 20$); the reason is that in such circumstances, the probability that the firm will avoid bankruptcy either on the next coupon date or at maturity is very low. As a result, the equity of the firm is not worth much.

The (cum-coupon) bond price is lower the higher the volatility. This is analogous to Merton's analytical result that higher volatility reduces zero-coupon bond prices. However, in the case of the coupon bond, no such result can be established analytically because no closed-form formula exists for the coupon bond price.

As expected, the put option price is a decreasing function of firm value. Moreover, for given firm value, the option price is higher the higher the volatility. This is the result of two separate effects. The first effect relates to the previously mentioned relation between bond price and volatility. For given firm value, the higher the volatility, the lower the bond price. Since this is a put option, a lower bond price increases the option price. The second effect is a direct impact of higher volatility on put prices that is analogous to the effect of higher volatility on the price of a put option on a common stock.

Another feature of Exhibit 13–1 is that the option becomes virtually worthless when firm value is high enough (approximately $V = 60$ for the $s = 0.2$ case) that the bond becomes effectively risk free. The risk-free bond price is

$$B \exp(-10r) + c \exp(-2r) + c \exp(-4r) + c \exp(-6r) + c \exp(-8r) = 25.86$$

This is a reasonable result because once the bond becomes risk free, it remains risk free until its maturity, and therefore there is no possibility that the option will be exercised.

Numerical analysis confirmed our earlier analytical result (proposition 1) that the put will be exercised early only if the exercise is forced, that is, if the option is terminated. Furthermore, this barrier option is terminated early as follows: (1) When $s = 0.2$, it is terminated at $t = 2$ (the first coupon date) whenever $V < 27.3$ and at $t = 4$ (the second coupon date) whenever $V < 30.2$; (2) when $s = 0.4$, it is terminated at $t = 2$ whenever $V < 18.3$ and at $t = 4$ whenever $V < 20$. Note that the default barrier is higher the lower the volatility because lower volatility increases the bond price.

Various other sensitivity results were established by varying the parameter values used as inputs. For example, it was confirmed that the option price is consistently lower for a lower maturity. As expected, a lower strike price (i.e., a higher g) lowers the option price. Finally, the influence of higher interest rates on put prices for given firm value is ambiguous.

ANOTHER CREDIT RISK DERIVATIVE: AN AMERICAN CALL ON THE BOND'S SPREAD

Consider the following American call option: At any $t \leq T$, where $T =$ option maturity $< T_B$, assuming the firm is not bankrupt, the option's owner can exercise the option and receive an amount equal to max(0, $\in$ $(V, t) - g)$ where $\in (V, t)$ is the spread above the risk-free rate at which the coupon bond trades at time t (on a cum-coupon basis) and g is a fixed exercise price. For example, consider the coupon bond defined earlier. It promised B at T_B and coupons in the amount c at $0.2T_B$, $0.4T_B$, $0.6T_B$, and $0.8T_B$. The spread on a noncoupon date—for example, when $t = 0$—defined as $\in (V, 0)$ solves the following equation:

$$
\begin{aligned}
G(V, 0) = \; & c \, \exp(-(r + \in (V, 0)) \, (0.2 \, T_B)) \\
& + c \, \exp(-(r + \in (V, 0)) \, (0.4T_B)) \\
& + c \, \exp(-(r + \in (V, 0)) \, (0.6T_B)) \\
& + c \, \exp(-(r + \in (V, 0)) \, (0.8T_B)) \\
& + B \, \exp(-(r + \in (V, 0)) \, (T_B))
\end{aligned}
$$

where $G(V, 0)$ equals the cum-coupon bond price at time 0. Hence $\in (V, 0)$ equates the right-hand side of the above equation to the numerically calculated cum-coupon bond price $G(V, 0)$. The spread on a coupon date—for example, when $t = 0.2(T_B)$, $\in (V, 0.2(T_B))$ solves the following equation:

$$
\begin{aligned}
G(V, 0.2(T_B)) = \; & c + c \, \exp(-(r + \in (V, 0.2(T_B))) \, (0.2 \, T_B)) \\
& + c \, \exp(-(r + \in (V, 0.2(T_B))) \, (0.4T_B)) \\
& + c \, \exp(-(r + \in (V, 0.2(T_B))) \, (0.6T_B)) \\
& + B \, \exp(-(r + \in (V, 0.2(T_B))) \, (0.8T_B))
\end{aligned}
$$

where $G(V, 0.2(T_B))$ equals the cum-coupon bond price at time $0.2T_B$.

These equations can be solved for $\in (V, t)$, using the Newton-Raphson root-finding scheme.

Furthermore, the option contract provides that if the firm goes bankrupt, at any time prior to option maturity, the option will be immediately terminated and the payoff will be the exercise value. This is a necessary condition to impose since the bond will cease to exist if the firm goes bankrupt, and hence there will be no way to calculate the payoffs to the option. This provision makes this option contract a barrier option. Since the firm can go bankrupt only on a coupon date prior to bond maturity, the option can be terminated only on coupon dates.

Another complication to consider is that on a coupon date, the last equation may have no root; this will happen whenever $G < c$ (as is obvious from inspection of the last equation). In such circumstances, the value of $\in (V, t)$ is set equal to an arbitrarily defined upper bound $\in^{max}$ and option payoffs are calculated using $\in^{max}$.

The equation which gives the spread on a noncoupon date will always have a root. Nevertheless, for consistency reasons, whenever the calculated value of $\in$ exceeds $\in^{max}$, $\in$ is automatically set to $\in^{max}$ and we calculate option payoffs using $\in^{max.}$

It is obvious that this option qualifies as a credit risk derivative because its value rises with increases in the bond's spread, that is, with decreases in the bond's price. However, it is less obvious how a portfolio manager holding corporate bonds would use this option. To explore this, recall from the earlier discussion that a portfolio manager purchasing a bond rated BBB (which is assumed to trade at a spread above r of 1 percent) and a put on the bond with an exercise price $K(T)$ = bond price for a spread above r of $g = 1\%$ is guaranteed at option maturity T a portfolio value equal to max $(G (V, T), K (T))$. In other words, the lowest portfolio value at T will be the bond value for a 1 percent spread above r, but if the actual bond price ends up being higher than this value, the portfolio value will be higher. So the portfolio manager insures the portfolio from a credit deterioration but benefits from a credit improvement. If instead the portfolio manager purchasing the BBB bond also buys y calls on the spread with exercise price $g = 1\%$, the portfolio value at T will be

$$G (V, T) + y \max (\in (V, T) - g, 0)$$

A portfolio manager could choose y so that the portfolio value at T is also equal to max $(G (V, T), K (T))$, since this payoff has a straightforward economic interpretation. The optimal y is therefore given by the equation

$$\max (G (V, T), K (T)) = G (V, T) + y \max (\in (V, T) - g, 0)$$

Note that irrespective of the choice of y, if $G (V, T) > K (T)$, this equation is always satisfied (since in this case $(\in (V, T) < g$). Hence, we focus on the choice of y if $G (V, T) < K (T)$. In this case,

$$K(T) = G(V, T) + y(\in(V, T) - g, 0)$$

For ease of exposition, assume that $0.8\ T_B < T < T_B$; that is, the option maturity extends beyond the last coupon payment. Then the last equation can be rewritten as

$$B\exp(-(r + g)(T_B - T)) = B\exp(-(r + \in(V, T))(T_B - T)) + y(\in(V, T) - g)$$

Using the approximation $\exp(z) = 1 + z$ for small z, we can show that the optimal y is given by

$$y = B(T_B - T)$$

This discussion is summarized in proposition 2.

Proposition 2: A portfolio manager who holds a bond trading at a spread g over r and wants to protect it against a rise in its spread above g should either (1) buy one put on the bond with exercise price equal to the bond price for a spread g over r or (2) buy y calls on the spread with exercise price g, where $y = B(T_B - T)$.

We now present an analytical pricing result.

Proposition 3: The price of the call may exceed the current value of the spread.

A formal proof is beyond the scope of this chapter. However, we sketch the proof here by showing that when the call price exceeds the spread, no arbitrage opportunity exists. Hence this can be an equilibrium situation.

Suppose that at any $t_1 < T$,

$$F[\in(V, t_1), t_1] > \in(V, t_1)$$

that is, option price $= F[\in(V, t_1), t_1]$ exceeds the spread.

To investigate whether an arbitrage opportunity exists, let us try to follow the arbitrage strategy described in Cox and Rubinstein[6] to exploit situations where the price of a call on a stock exceeds the current stock price. In our context, that strategy involves selling the call and buying $\in(V, t_1) / f(V, t_1)$ corporate bonds (note that $f(V, t_1) =$ bond price) worth $\in(V, t_1)$.

---

[6] J. Cox and M. Rubinstein, *Options Markets,* (Englewood Cliffs, NJ: Prentice Hall, 1985).

The time t_1 payoff is clearly positive. However, if the call we sold is exercised on or before the expiration date, we may be in trouble: We have to pay an amount $\in (V, t_2) - g$, where t_2 is time of exercise of the option, and it is not clear that the bonds we purchase at t_1 will be worth this much at t_2. Hence our payoff may be negative, and no arbitrage opportunity exists

We now consider the pricing of this put. Let $F[\in (V, t), t]$ be its price at t. We assume that option price depends on the spread $\in (V, t)$ and time t. Since $\in$ depends on V, we can think of option price as a function of V and t; that is, $F[\in (V, t), t] = Q[V, t]$.

Using the usual arbitrage argument, we can show that the option price will satisfy the Black-Scholes PDE. The boundary conditions are

$$Q[V, T] = \max[0, \in (V, T) - g]$$
$$Q[V, t] \geq \max[0, \in (V, t) - g]$$

No closed-form solution exists to this valuation problem because the boundary conditions are nonlinear in the state variable. For this reason, we employ a numerical method of solution.

Numerical Results

The parameter values chosen were the same as in the case of the put; furthermore, we assume that $\in^{max} = 0.3$. Exhibit 13–2 gives the bond spread and the option price for different firm values. As expected, the bond spread decreases with increases in firm value. Also, the bond spread for given firm value is higher the higher the volatility because higher volatility reduces bond prices. The call option price is a decreasing function of firm value (and an increasing function of bond spread).

When $s = 0.4$, note that for low firm values the option price exceeds the value of the spread. This provides numerical confirmation of the analytical result in proposition 3. Furthermore, Exhibit 13–2 shows that higher volatility increases option prices for given firm value. This is the result of two separate effects. The first effect relates to the previously mentioned relation between bond spread and volatility. For given firm value, the higher the volatility, the higher the bond spread. Since this is a call option, a higher bond spread increases the option price. The second effect is a direct influence of higher volatility on call prices that is analogous to the effect of higher volatility on the price of a call option on a common stock.

However, in the general case, the influence of higher volatility on the call price is ambiguous because of the capped nature of this option.

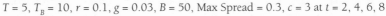

Call on Spread of Coupon Bond
$T = 5$, $T_B = 10$, $r = 0.1$, $g = 0.03$, $B = 50$, Max Spread = 0.3, $c = 3$ at $t = 2, 4, 6, 8$

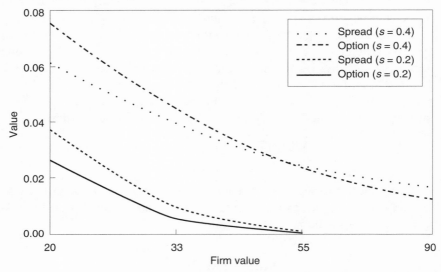

Numerical analysis showed that for particular parameter values (a key determinant is the level of $\in^{max}$), when the option is in the money or not way out of the money, higher volatility reduces the option price for given firm value. The reason is that when the option is in the money (or not way out of the money), its capped feature implies that the upside potential is limited whereas the downside risk is unlimited. In such circumstances, higher volatility reduces option prices because it implies that the option will more likely end up out of the money without providing significant upward potential to counterbalance the former effect.

Various other sensitivity results were obtained by varying the parameter values used as inputs. For example, it was confirmed that the option price is higher the higher the option maturity and the lower the exercise price. Also, a higher $\in^{max}$ (max spread) results in higher option prices.

Finally, by comparing Exhibits 13–1 and 13–2, we see that in the $s = 0.2$ case, whenever firm value reaches a level of approximately 60, the bond price reaches its risk-free level and the spread tends to zero. Under these circumstances, the prices of both the put and the call tend to zero.

SUMMARY

This chapter examined the structuring and pricing of credit risk derivatives for coupon bonds. Both a put on the bond price and a call on the bond spread can serve as credit risk derivatives. These put and call options must be of the barrier type. Furthermore, the call on the coupon bond's spread must be capped; otherwise there will be no way to calculate its price.

A number of unexpected pricing results were obtained. American puts on the coupon bond price will be exercised early only if the exercise is forced. The price of the call on the spread can exceed the current value of the spread. In some circumstances, higher volatility can reduce the price of the call option on the spread of the coupon bond.

An obvious way to extend this analysis is to consider the influence of stochastic interest rates on the pricing of these credit risk derivatives. However, Cornell and Green show empirically that low-grade corporate bonds have much lower sensitivity to interest rates than high-grade corporate bonds.[7] They also show that low-grade bonds are much more sensitive to the issuing firm's asset value changes than high-grade bonds. In light of this, the Black and Cox constant interest rate assumption is probably fairly realistic for pricing credit risk derivatives on lower-grade debt.

---

[7] B. Cornell and K. Green, "The Investment Performance of Low Grade Bond Funds," *Journal of Finance,* March 1991.

⑥ # AN OPTIONS APPROACH TO VALUING AND HEDGING MORTGAGE SERVICING RIGHTS

Robert D. Selvaggio, PhD
Director
Fixed Income & Mortgage Research Group
The Chase Manhattan Bank, N.A.

In the wake of substantial portfolio impairments suffered during the mortgage refinancing waves of 1992 and 1993, mortgage servicers are reassessing their valuation methodologies and risk management practices. While option-adjusted spread (OAS) modeling has not yet become standard practice in the servicing market, some participants are recognizing the optionality embedded in the servicing business and are acting to modify their option risks. We believe that an options-based approach to valuing and hedging mortgage servicing rights is the only viable methodology for effective risk/return management. After a brief description of the business of mortgage servicing, this chapter presents an options-analytic approach to valuation and hedging.

WHAT IS MORTGAGE SERVICING?

The mortgage servicer is an agent of the mortgagee that is hired as an intermediary between the mortgagee and the mortgagor. The servicer collects and records payments (and facilitates remittance to the mortgage owner), handles escrow, and arranges foreclosure in the event of nonper-

Robert Noskiewicz and Christine Pisani provided valuable research assistance.

formance. In return for these services, the servicer earns a negotiated fee of between 25 and 50 basis points on the mortgage balance and additional remuneration in the form of escrow earnings, float on the mortgagor's monthly principal and interest payments (during the interval between receipt of payments and remittance to the mortgagee), and late fees (indeed, it is often commented that the best customer is one who is chronically a few days delinquent). The costs borne in mortgage servicing include capital and labor, foreclosure expenses, and the interest costs of both escrow and advances of principal and interest (P&I) for delinquent mortgages.

Because the servicing fee provides the bulk of the return to mortgage servicing, the business assumes the general interest rate risk profile of an interest-only (IO) exposure (actually, the non-IO ancillary cash flows render servicing values slightly less sensitive to adverse rate changes than pure IO strips).[1] This chapter takes as a starting point servicing cash flows in the aggregate and presumes that all assumptions about, for example, non-rate-dependent defaults and future growth in nominal operating expenses are given.

HOW ARE MORTGAGE SERVICING RIGHTS VALUED?

Changes in the net cash inflows associated with servicing a given pool of mortgages are directly correlated with changes in market yields. This is a result of the impact of interest rates on current and prospective mortgage prepayments: As rates fall, mortgagors refinance their loans, curtailing servicing cash flows; as rates rise, mortgage loans and servicing cash flows are extended. Except in cases of extreme discount or extreme premium mortgage collateral and very wide interest rate swings, the direct correlation between cash flows and rates imbues mortgage servicing with *negative duration* (i.e., as rates rise [fall], servicing gains [loses] value) and *negative convexity* (i.e., as rates rise [fall], duration becomes less [more] negative). Indeed, the mortgagor's call option, the prepayment option, is the salient factor that makes both the risk profile and the valuation of servicing rights interesting. Because future servicing cash flows are not known with certainty at the valuation date but are expected to be

---

[1] An excellent description of each revenue and expense item associated with servicing portfolios is provided in Scott Brown, Lakhbir Hayre, Kenneth Lauterbach, Richard Payne, and Thomas Zimmerman, "Analysis of Mortgage Servicing Portfolios," *Journal of Fixed Income,* December 1992, pp. 60–75.

a function of the path of future interest rates through exercise of the prepayment option, a probabilistic approach is required. This means applying multiple stochastic interest rate paths (e.g., we usually run 5,000) through an econometric prepayment model to develop alternative mortgage balance levels from which cash flows are derived. Each future cash flow along each path is discounted to the present by the rate corresponding to its path and maturity plus a constant spread (the OAS) that is applied to all rates across all paths. The result is a "price" for each of the multiple paths; the "path prices" are averaged to derive the servicing valuation. Although this probabilistic approach is termed *Monte Carlo* analysis, it does not imbue option valuation with gambling-type qualities; fixed-income analysts have learned to disabuse (often alarmed) senior management of any such notion.

The interest rate paths are generated by a stochastic term structure model that, by construct, implies no arbitrage possibilities in simultaneous lending and borrowing across the maturity spectrum. The term structure model takes as its raw inputs on-the-run Treasury yields and implied yield volatilities and produces, as an intermediate product, implied zero-coupon or spot rates. In particular, two final outputs are extracted: forward short rates for modeling ancillary (i.e., non-servicing fee) income such as P&I float and escrow earnings and for discounting cash flows; and forward intermediate to long rates from which current coupon mortgage rates are modeled.[2]

Prepayment behavior is modeled as an amalgam of nonlinear functions that capture, at a minimum, seasoning (through weighted-average maturity of collateral), refinancing incentive (via the relationship between weighted-average coupon and current mortgage rates), and burnout (a function of the path of historical rates). Associated with each stochastic rate path, then, is a unique prepayment profile that, in concert with a mortgage pool's "normal" amortization schedule, determines the path of mortgage balances and thus the path of servicing fees and, ultimately, total monthly servicing cash flows. With our model in place, we identify a benchmark servicing portfolio (typically the most recent aquisition or sale for which we have details), input all the pool-specific data required, and calculate path prices given a starting OAS. If the average of the path prices lies above the observed price of our benchmark servicing portfo-

---

[2] For a full discussion of the term structure model we use, see Fischer Black, Emanuel Derman, and William Toy, "A One-Factor Model of Interest Rates and Its Application to Treasury Bond Options," *Financial Analysts Journal*, January–February 1990, pp. 33–39.

lio, we increase the OAS and calculate new path prices; if the average is below the observed price, we lower the OAS. This process concludes when we converge on the OAS that yields the correct benchmark price. We then use this OAS to value servicing portfolios that are similar to the benchmark portfolio. There are two important exceptions to this procedure. First, in formulating a reservation price for a potential servicing rights acquisition, we generally start our valuations with an OAS that provides an acceptable prospective return on equity rather than with a market-implied spread. Second, to satisfy bank regulators, we typically revalue purchased servicing rights on our balance sheet using the OAS at which the portfolio was originally booked.

HEDGING MORTGAGE SERVICING RIGHTS: AN OPTION REPLICATION APPROACH

While the potential profitability of the mortgage servicing business is well recognized, especially among firms that are large enough to realize economies of scale, institutions have grown increasingly wary of the inherent risks in mortgage servicing cash flows and market values. Chief among these risks is the possibility of a sudden and unanticipated downward innovation of the yield curve that accelerates prospective prepayments and curtails planned (net) revenues.[3] Many high-profile mortgage servicers suffered huge losses during the yield curve-induced refinancing waves of 1992 and 1993, resulting in intensified interest in hedging. *We view* hedging *as the process of modifying risk/return profiles to better reflect the preferences of senior management, regulators, and (presumably) shareholders and, toward that end, strive to mitigate but not necessarily minimize financial market risk.*

Exhibit 14–1 shows the relationship between changes in the value of a purchased mortgage servicing rights (PMSR) portfolio and immediate parallel shifts in the on-the-run Treasury yield curve.[4] Note that when

---

[3] Certainly liquidity, operating, and credit risks exist, as well as the risk arising from prepayment function inaccuracies, innovations in option volatilities, and varying OAS. Most analysts agree, however, that yield curve risk is the most important.

[4] Shumacher, Detkar, and Fabozzi show that parallel yield curve shifts capture by far the greatest portion of interest rate risk to CMO returns (and IO returns in particular) and argue that the (smaller) risk of slope changes can be managed quite independently of the former. See Michael Schumacher, Daniel Dektar, and Frank Fabozzi, "Yield Curve Risk of CMO Bonds," in Frank J. Fabozzi, (ed.), *CMO Portfolio Management* (Summit, N.J.: Frank J. Fabozzi Associates,1994). In this example we focus entirely on shift risk, but the reader should understand that the same methodology can be used to evaluate and manage exposure to yield curve twists.

E X H I B I T   14–1

Yield Curve Sensitivities: PMSR; PMSR Hedge and Net Position

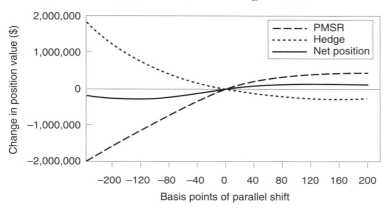

the curve shifts upward, PMSR values rise, but at a rapidly decreasing rate as the benefits of lower prospective prepayments are quickly offset by higher discount rates; conversely, when the curve shifts downward, PMSR values fall at an *increasing* rate as the potential for prepayments surges and swamps the benefits of declining discount rates. (The collateral modeled for this example is 30-year conforming mortgages at a slight discount.) The "PMSR" curve is a snapshot of the negative duration and negative convexity described above.

To create the PMSR curve, we simply value the PMSR portfolio 21 times—a "base case" valuation and a valuation for each curve shift at 20-basis-point intervals from negative 200 basis points to positive 200 basis points. Even though this implies running 105,000 stochastic rate paths (21 valuations × 5,000 paths/valuation), the entire analysis takes only a few minutes on a Sun workstation.

After being presented with the PMSR curve, the manager of the servicing portfolio describes a desired profile and decides how much he or she is willing to pay to attempt to achieve it. Intuitively, we know that the manager will be adding positive duration and positive convexity to flatten somewhat the PMSR rate exposure. An option replication approach is used to generate the desired rate exposure subject to the cost constraints imposed: Using mathematical optimization techniques, we choose from a set of potential hedge vehicles to minimize a loss function that describes how poorly we are replicating that exposure. Simple applications of this methodology, which allows us to redefine very well the durations and convexities of our servicing portfolios (in an options context, we are hedging both *delta* and *gamma*), can be implemented within a number of popular spreadsheet packages. The dashed hedge curve in Exhibit 14–1 is the exposure created by a very basic portfolio of potential hedge instruments—a 100 bp out-of-the-money, 10-year CMT (Constant-Maturity Treasuries) floor with a tenor of 5 years—the notional amount is an output of the replication model. While we typically include over-the-counter (OTC) and exchange-traded derivatives in our hedge portfolio, we advocate the use of CMT floors for institutions with less efficient access to the financial markets; in our analyses, CMT floors dominate all other OTC options in cost and effectiveness. We value the CMT floors using the same rate process used to value the servicing portfolio.

The "net position" curve represents the parallel shift exposure of the combined portfolio of servicing and CMT floors. Exhibit 14–2 shows that both duration and convexity have increased significantly toward zero. Whereas a 100-basis-point drop in yields would result in a loss of $794,000 to the servicing portfolio alone, it is associated with a $206,000 loss to the combined servicing/CMT floor portfolio. Indeed, an immediate 200-basis-point negative shift in the yield curve would exact a toll of $1.9 million on the servicing portfolio, but only $178,000 on the combined (hedged) portfolio. Note that we have not built the bid/offer spread associated with the floors into this analysis; the effect of the spread is rather small and would be captured by a slight parallel downward shift in the "hedge" and "net position" curves in Exhibit 14–1.

While controlling the servicing portfolio's sensitivity to immediate rate shocks, we are concerned primarily with managing its prospective risk/return trade-off over a meaningful holding period. After all, if delta/gamma neutralization were truly our sole objective, the easiest and most effective way to achieve that goal would be to *sell* the servicing portfolio! Exhibit 14–3 graphs the empirical density functions of the (sto-

E X H I B I T   14–2

Effective Durations and Convexities: Unhedged and Hedged
(Defined for +/– 60 bp)

	Unhedged Portfolio	Hedged Portfolio
Effective duration	(8.17)	(2.32)
Effective convexity	(549.51)	(126.78)

E X H I B I T   14–3

Stochastic 1-Year Holding Period Analysis

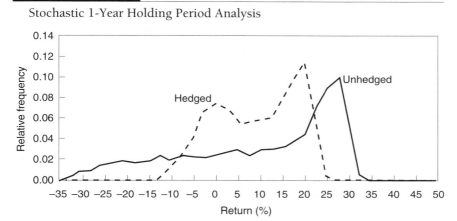

chastic) one-year holding period rates of return calculated both with and without the CMT floor position suggested by our option replication routine. To generate these curves, we start with 5,000 rate paths from our term structure model and use each path to calculate servicing and floor values 12 months into the future as well as the future values of all (i.e., reinvested) monthly cash flows over the year. The rate of return along each path is determined by starting with market-dictated initial period value and holding beginning and end-of-period OAS constant at 400 basis points.

Casual observation reveals that the return distribution of the hedged portfolio is more concentrated about its mean and less negatively skewed than the return distribution of the unhedged portfolio. Exhibit 14–4 contains statistics that describe each return distribution.

The CMT floors reduce return variability, increase the skewness of the return distribution,[5] and reduce expected return by a statistically (and economically) insignificant margin. It is clear that many servicing portfolio managers, particularly those who are most sensitive to shortfall risk, will choose to hedge.

---

[5] Levy and Sarnat show that investors tend to prefer more skewness to less, and they detail conditions of "third-degree stochastic dominance" that when applied to the example above, imply that all wealth-maximizing investors who prefer less risk to more (all else equal) and are more willing to put an extra dollar at risk as their wealth increases will prefer the "hedged" portfolio. See Hiam Levy and Marshall Sarnat, *Portfolio and Investment Selection: Theory and Practice* (Englewood Cliffs, NJ: Prentice-Hall, 1984), pp.163, 202–211.

E X H I B I T   14–4

Comparison of Prospective Return Distributions

	Unhedged Return	Hedged Return
Prob(return ≤ 0%)	30.7%	24.6%
Prob(return ≤ 5%)	24.9%	8.7%
Prob(return ≤ 10%)	19.2%	1.5%
Sample mean	10.9%	10.7%*
Sample standard deviation	17.5%	9.2%†
Sample skewness	–0.68	–0.24

* Cannot reject hypothesis of equal means at 75 percent confidence level (incorporating the bid-offer spread on the floors would increase the difference in mean returns).

† Reject hypothesis of equal variances at 99 percent confidence level.

CONCLUSIONS AND SUGGESTIONS FOR DEFENDING A HEDGE POLICY

We have shown that mortgage servicing rights can be valued and hedged using a consistent option-based methodology and that hedging creates both desirable exposures to immediate yield curve shocks and desirable risk/return profiles. In our experience, we find that many accountants and regulators do not get as excited by our duration/convexity and variance/skewness alterations as we do. They do, however, appreciate two statistics not mentioned above: (1) the high adjusted R^2 of our prepayment function (or a similar measure of our ability to capture the nonlinear relationship between CPR and explanatory variables) and (2) (in the spirit of FAS80) the –0.99 correlation coefficient between the "hedge" curve and the "PMSR" curve in Exhibit 14–1. We are always happy to provide both.

⑥ # CHOOSING THE "CORRECT" VOLATILITY FOR THE VALUATION OF EMBEDDED OPTIONS

David Audley, PhD
Director of Investment Systems and Technology
Tiger Management Corporation

Richard Chin
First Vice President
Co-Director of Equity Products and Strategies Group
Prudential Securities Incorporated

Market participants often speak about interest rate volatility without specifying the particular type of volatility being discussed, whether it is the volatility of long-term yields, short-term rates, or implied or historical yields. This chapter addresses how the "effective yield volatility" may be a more relevant measure of volatility than the short-rate volatility used by many one-factor interest rate models. In addition, we assert that when valuing embedded options, the historical volatility of a specific issuer or sector is a more pertinent yardstick of volatility than the general Treasury volatility.

Volatility is one of the most important factors that determine the "true" value of an option. As a result, investors are called on to make an assessment of an appropriate level of volatility to use in option valuation models, which commonly assume a constant level of volatility. The examples in this chapter will show that since volatility is a function of the chosen time period, more than one type and level of volatility need to be

David Audley was director in the Financial Strategies Group, Prudential Securities Incorporated, when this chapter was written.

considered. These different volatility assumptions can result in different assessments of an option's value and, therefore, the security's value.

WHAT IS VOLATILITY?

Conceptually, volatility represents uncertainty; a higher level of volatility corresponds to a wider dispersion of probable scenarios. Technically, volatility is a measurement of the amount of variation (or "noise") around a general trend. For Black-Scholes analysis of stock options, volatility is commonly calculated as the annualized standard deviation of the percentage change in price,[1] for which one standard deviation encompasses approximately two-thirds of the range of possible prices. Thus, as volatility increases, a greater range of stock prices needs to be spanned before accounting for two-thirds of the population. The effect of greater volatility can be visualized as a flattening of the familiar bell-shaped probability distribution curve, where the likely range of values is more dispersed and hence less concentrated around the mean.

Volatility in interest rates reflects a similar dispersion in the range of likely interest rates. Investors recognize that an increase in volatility leads to an increase in the value of any option, since the probability of profitable exercise grows.

Thus, in volatile interest rate environments, callable bond issuers should be willing to pay more for the increased value of the call option, and investors in these callable issues will want to be compensated for the increased likelihood that their assets may be called away.

ONE-FACTOR INTEREST RATE MODELS
AND SHORT-RATE VOLATILITY

Generally, bonds with embedded options are analyzed using one-factor interest rate models as these types of models are the most common and are easier to implement than multifactor models. One-factor models generally focus on short-term interest rate movements because cash flows are discounted over a short period of time (typically one or six months) during the computations. Consequently, users of these one-factor models specify a level of volatility for short rates that is to be used in the valuation of the embedded option.

---

[1] Assuming a lognormal price process, the volatility is calculated as the annualized standard deviation of the natural logarithms of the ratio between successive elements in the time series.

However, bonds with embedded options generally have maturities of several years or more. Further, bonds are valued by a yield spread to a benchmark Treasury issue. As Treasury yields vary, so do the yields of the bonds with embedded options. In fact, it is the level of long-term and not short-term interest rates that generally determines if an issuer will exercise a call option to refund an issue. *Thus, it is more reasonable to be concerned with the volatility of long-term yields than with short-term rates when calculating the value of an embedded option.* However, for the commonly used one-factor interest rate models, there is no allowance for the explicit specification of the volatility of long-term rates even though these volatilities may be viewed as the appropriate reference volatilities. As discussed in the next section, the concepts of *effective maturity* and *effective yield volatility* are mechanisms that allow the user-specified volatility of short rates to be translated to the volatility of long-term rates when using one-factor models.

EFFECTIVE MATURITY AND EFFECTIVE YIELD VOLATILITY

The yield of a security is defined in relation to the specific point in time at which the security is retired, either due to the exercise of a call or put option or due to final maturity. For a bond with embedded options, the date on which it will be retired is not known with certainty; thus, the bond's yield to "maturity" is not well defined. However, for a bond with embedded options, the *effective maturity,* which is the maturity of a duration-matched bullet-payment bond, may be calculated. For example, a new, par-priced 10-year issue that is callable in the last 5 years at par may have an effective maturity of 7 years. Given this, the bond with the embedded option has the price sensitivity of a seven-year bullet. The effective yield of a bullet bond with this effective maturity and quoted market price may be calculated. Once the effective yield is obtained, the *effective yield volatility* of the duration-matched bullet may be found for the associated short-rate volatility and the resultant price volatility as shown in equation 1

Effective yield volatility = Price volatility/

$$\text{(Effective duration} \times \text{Effective yield)} \qquad (1)$$

The effective yield volatility, then, allows investors to focus on the volatilities of long-term rates such as that of the benchmark Treasury instead of being limited to the volatilities of only the short rates when using one-factor interest rate models.

VOLATILITY BENCHMARKS

Investors may look to several reference points to determine the volatility level that is suitable to use in the valuation of the embedded option. For each variation, there is historical information that can be drawn on to assess an appropriate volatility level. In addition, for each variation, a comparison is made between the option-adjusted spreads (OASs) to show how each of these volatility types can influence the assessment of value. Exhibit 15–1 shows the characteristics of the bonds that are used to illustrate each type of volatility in the sections that follow.

Short-Rate Volatility

Investors who use one-factor interest rate models usually input a volatility for short rates. Frequently the level chosen is 10 or 15 percent. Exhibit 15–2 shows the effect of different volatility assumptions on OASs for FNMA 9.30s. Specifically, the FNMA 9.30s of 02/10/00, which are callable at par beginning on 02/10/95, have OASs of 80 basis points and

E X H I B I T   15–1

Characteristics of Bonds Used in Examples

Issue	FNMA Debentures	Southern California Edison (SCE)
Coupon	9.30%	10.00%
Maturity	02/10/00	01/15/20
Call date	02/10/95	Currently callable
Call price	100.00	109.20
Price*	102.125	102.493
Modified duration (years)	5.83	9.55
Yield to maturity	8.95%; +92 bps/10-year Treasury	9.74%; +153 bps/30-year Treasury

*Prudential-Bache Capital Funding quote as of close on January 23, 1991.

68 basis points for short-rate volatilities of 10 and 15 percent, respectively. If a generic 10-year FNMA noncallable bullet was spread at +34 basis points, most investors would view the bond as cheap at those volatility levels.[2] However, Exhibit 15–2 also shows that the 10 and 15 percent short-rate volatilities translate into effective yield volatilities of 7.5 and 11.1 percent, respectively. Thus, if investors focus on 10 and 15 percent volatilities because these were the historical volatility levels for longer-maturity Treasury yields, the use of these levels as input into an option valuation model may not have provided the desired results. On the other hand, if investors analyze securities on the basis of movements in the underlying benchmark Treasury issue, the historical yield volatility of Treasuries may be used.

E X H I B I T   15–2

Comparison of Computed OASs for FNMA 9.30s of 2/10/00 Using Varying Volatility Measures

Volatility Type*	(Equivalent) Short-Rate Volatility (%)	(Equivalent) Price Volatility (%)	(Effective) Yield Volatility (%)	OAS (BPs)
Short-rate volatility	**10.0**	3.0	7.5	80
Short-rate volatility	**15.0**	4.5	11.1	68
30-day Treasury volatility[†]	20.0	5.9	**14.5**	56
60-day Treasury volatility[‡]	17.0	5.1	**12.5**	63
30-day price volatility	11.5	**3.4**	8.6	77
60-day price volatility	10.0	**3.0**	7.5	80
30-day yield volatility	9.0	2.7	**6.7**	82
60-day yield volatility	7.6	2.3	**5.7**	85

* Boldface figures represent assumed volatility levels that would be entered into an option valuation model. Remaining volatility figures are either the equivalent or effective volatilities resulting from the particular input level. The effective yield volatility is the volatility of the equivalent, duration-matched bullet bond.

† Based on closing prices and yields for FNMA 9.30s and 10-year Treasury notes from 12/4/90 to 1/23/90.

‡ Based on closing prices and yields for FNMA 9.30s and 10-year Treasury notes from 10/31/90 to 1/23/90.

---

[2] See David Audley and Richard Chin, "What Is the Correct OAS?" Financial Strategies Group, Prudential-Bache Capital Funding, September 1990.

Treasury Yield Volatility

Investors may look to the historical yield volatility of a comparable Treasury benchmark to identify an effective yield volatility level to use when valuing embedded options. For example, the FNMA 9.30s at the time of the analysis were priced relative to the 10-year Treasury note. As shown in Exhibit 15–2, the 30-day and 60-day yield volatilities of the 10-year Treasury note were 14.5 and 12.5 percent, respectively. Exhibit 15–2 also shows that the FNMA 9.30s had OASs of 56 and 63 basis points at effective yield volatilities of 14.5 and 12.5 percent, respectively. Note that short-rate volatilities of 20 and 17 percent are equivalent to the targeted effective yield volatilities of 14.5 and 12.5 percent respectively.

When the volatility of the Treasury benchmark is used as the reference volatility, Exhibit 15–2 shows that the OASs of 56 and 63 basis points were less than the OASs of 80 and 68 basis points obtained by using just the short-rate volatility. Thus, if the Treasury yield volatility levels at the time were to continue, and if movements in the agency and Treasury markets were perfectly correlated, the use of Treasury yield volatilities will show that the FNMA 9.30s were not as attractive as was thought when short-rate volatilities were used. However, the next section will show that Treasury volatilities alone do not present the entire story.

Historical Price Volatility

Investors may also assess value using the historical price volatility of the specific security. Historical *price* volatility is used frequently since it is a less ambiguous term than *yield* volatility, as yield volatility may be expressed in terms of yield to put, call, stated maturity, or worse.

Historical price volatilities are used to determine the value of the embedded option when volatility is measured from the recent price performance of the security itself. The advantage of price volatility is that it incorporates both the responsiveness of the security to changes in interest rates and the forces of supply and demand that influence the value of the security in the marketplace. In general, corporate and government agency securities are not as responsive to changes in interest rates as are Treasury securities. For example, when Treasury yields fall, corporate and agency yield spreads may widen relative to Treasuries as issuers take advantage of lower rates to issue new debt. The increased supply tends to depress prices, leading to wider yield spreads. Similarly, when Treasury rates rise, yield spreads may tighten due to a decrease in the supply of new issuance.

As a result, the volatility of specific corporate and agency sectors generally is lower than that of Treasuries. When Treasury volatilities are higher than the specific sector volatility, the use of Treasury volatilities overstates the value of the embedded option and understates the OAS. Thus, for callable bonds, the use of historical price volatilities to value a security's embedded option could result in lower option values and higher OASs. Since the decision to exercise an embedded call option depends on the interest rate environment for a particular sector or issuer, the relevant volatility level for the valuation of the option is the historical volatility for the given issuer.

For FNMA 9.30s, the 30-day[3] and 60-day price volatilities for the period prior to January 23, 1991, were 3.4 and 3.0 percent, respectively. Exhibit 15–2 shows that the OASs for these historical price volatilities (and the equivalent short-rate volatilities of 11.5 and 10 percent) were 77 and 80 basis points, which were higher than the OASs calculated under the Treasury volatility assumption. This was due to the lower volatilities that had been recently observed for the FNMA 9.30s.

As was previously shown in equation 1, through the use of effective duration, the historical price volatilities of 3.4 and 3.0 percent translate into effective yield volatilities of 8.6 and 7.5 percent, respectively. The relationship between historical price volatility and historical yield volatility is discussed in the next section.

Historical Yield Volatility

The historical yield-to-maturity volatility is an equivalent expression of the volatility that is based on the movements in price. For a given security, changes in the price and yield are related through the security's modified duration. Consequently, the relationship between the yield volatility and price volatility may be estimated using a variation of equation 1:[4]

$$\text{Yield volatility} = \text{Price volatility} / (\text{Duration} \times \text{Yield}) \qquad (2)$$

---

[3] The volatility level should be calculated over a relatively short period of time so that the changing maturity of the security has only a small effect on the volatility. For example, a 10-year bond becomes a 9-year bond one year later. This may result in its being priced off a different portion of the Treasury curve and thus introduce another element into the volatility calculation.

[4] The historical yield volatility may be different from the effective yield volatility when the historical volatility calculation uses the yield to maturity and assumes that the security is retired at the stated maturity and not by optional redemption. On the other hand, the effective yield volatility uses the effective duration of the security, which takes into account the embedded option. For callable bonds at a given price volatility, the associated effective yield volatility is greater than the corresponding historical yield since the effective duration is less than the nominal duration.

For the FNMA 9.30s described in Exhibit 15–1 and a historical yield volatility of 6.7 percent, the price volatility is 3.5 percent based on equation 2. This is very close to the 3.4 percent that was found from the historical price data. Thus, similar OAS results would be obtained when the actual historical price volatility, or when the calculated price volatility (as derived form the historical yield volatility), is used. This merely illustrates that either method may be employed without sacrificing much accuracy.

An investor could also investigate the effect of assuming that the effective yield volatility is equal to the historical yield volatility.[5] Exhibit 15–2 shows that the OASs on the FNMA 9.30s calculated using historical price/yield volatility (77 and 80 basis points) do not differ significantly from the OASs found when the effective yield volatility is set equal to the historical yield volatility level (82 and 85 basis points). This is due to the fact that the option was not exercisable until 1995, so the small differences between volatility levels do not strongly affect the value of the option.

As another example, Exhibit 15–3 shows the OASs on the Southern California Edison (SCE) 10s of 01/15/20. The OASs calculated using the actual historical price (or yield) volatilities (116 and 137 basis points) differ from those found using the effective yield volatilities as a proxy for the historical yield volatilities (137 and 142 basis points). This is due to the fact that SCE 10s were currently callable and the bonds were priced at a premium. In this case, the embedded call option had a higher probability of being exercised, which resulted in greater negative convexity and price compression. From Exhibit 15–3, there appears to be a threshold volatility level such that the small differences in the price volatility (from 8.9 to 10.3 percent) are magnified into greater differences in effective yield volatility (from 11.5 to 17.0 percent). For the SCE 10s, the use of the historical price volatilities reveals an OAS pattern that would not have been discerned if only short-rate of Treasury volatilities were used.

IMPLIED VOLATILITY

The previous analyses started with an assumed level of volatility and used that level to compute option value and then the security's OAS. In contrast, implied-volatility analysis begins with the security's assumed sector spreads over Treasuries and then computes the option value, and hence the volatility implied by the market price. For a specific sector yield curve that

---

[5] The previous footnote discusses why these two quantities are not necessarily always equal.

E X H I B I T   15–3

Comparison of Computed OASs for Southern California Edison 10s of 1/15/20 Using Varying Volatility Measures

Volatility Type*	(Equivalent) Short-Rate Volatility (%)	(Equivalent) Price Volatility (%)	(Effective) Yield Volatility (%)	OAS (BPs)
Short-rate volatility	**10.0**	7.1	7.9	146
Short-rate volatility	**15.0**	8.9	11.5	137
30-day Treasury volatility†	19.8	9.6	**14.4**	126
60-day Treasury volatility‡	16.1	9.1	**12.4**	135
30-day price volatility	23.0	**10.3**	17.0	116
60-day price volatility	15.0	**8.9**	11.5	137
30-day yield volatility	14.8	8.3	**11.0**	137
60-day yield volatility	12.5	7.7	**9.4**	142

* Boldface figures represent assumed volatility levels that would be entered into an option valuation model. Remaining volatility figures are either the equivalent or effective volatilities resulting from the particular input level. The effective yield volatility is the volatility of the equivalent, duration-matched bullet bond.

† Based on closing prices and yields for SCE 10.0s and 10-year Treasury notes from 12/4/90 to 1/23/90.

‡ Based on closing prices and yields for SCE 10.0s and 10-year Treasury notes from 10/31/90 to 1/23/90.

defines the yields of noncallable bullets for different maturities (see Chapter 12), the value of the underlying bullet bond can be found readily. Thus, the object is to find the interest rate volatility for a given sector yield curve that equates the theoretical price of a bond with embedded options to its market price. This furnishes the implied volatility.

For a callable bond, if the implied volatility is higher than a benchmark volatility, the embedded option may be overvalued and the callable bond may be cheap. However, if the implied volatility is lower than a benchmark volatility, the option may be undervalued and the bond may be expensive.

Exhibit 15–4 shows that the implied yield volatility of the FNMA 9.30s was 21 percent. Compared to the historical Treasury yield volatility of 14 percent and the historical yield volatility of 6.7 percent for this FNMA issue, the FNMAs were cheap since the market was valuing the option as if the expected level of volatility was significantly higher than recent levels. Just as the above variations indicate that the FNMA 9.30s were cheap on an OAS basis, this analysis similarly shows that the securities were also cheap on an implied-volatility basis. Exhibit 15–4 also shows that the SCE 10s were similarly cheap on an implied-volatility basis.

SUMMARY

Given all the volatilities discussed in this chapter, several conclusions may be drawn. First, calculations over a range of volatilities are required since volatility changes with time and there is no one constant level of volatility. Second, depending on the specific option valuation model, the common use of 10 and 15 percent short-rate volatilities may not translate

E X H I B I T   15–4

Implied-Volatility Analysis

A. FNMA 9.30s of 2/10/00

	1-Year	2-Year	3-Year	4-Year	5-Year	7-Year	10-Year	30-Year
Treasury yield (%)	6.58	7.09	7.31	7.51	7.66	7.91	8.03	8.21
Spread (BPs)*	10	15	18	23	30	30	34	50
FNMA sector yield curve (%)	6.68	7.24	7.49	7.74	7.96	8.21	8.37	8.71
Implied yield volatility	21.0%							

B. SCE 10s of 1/15/20

	1-Year	2-Year	3-Year	4-Year	5-Year	7-Year	10-Year	30-Year
Treasury yield (%)	6.58	7.09	7.31	7.51	7.66	7.91	8.03	8.21
Spread (BPs)†	45	50	55	60	60	70	80	90
AA-rated sector yield curve (%)	7.03	7.59	7.86	8.11	8.26	8.61	8.83	9.11
Implied yield volatility	18.5%							

* Spreads for generic, noncallable FNMA issues are Prudential-Bache Capital Funding quotes as of the close on January 24, 1991.

† Spreads for generic, AA-rated, noncallable utility issues are Prudential-Bache Capital Funding quotes as of the close on January 24, 1991.

into similar yield volatility levels. Third, the effective yield volatility is a mechanism that allows short-rate volatilities to be translated into long-term yield volatilities when using one-factor interest rate models. Finally, the sector volatility should be more influential in the valuation of the option than the overall level of Treasury volatility.

16

Ⓖ **MEASURING, INTERPRETING, AND APPLYING VOLATILITY WITHIN THE FIXED-INCOME MARKET**

Keith Anderson
Managing Director
BlackRock Financial Management

Scott Amero
Managing Director
BlackRock Financial Management

Volatility is an important tool for both interpreting market history and evaluating investment strategies. Understanding volatility is a prerequisite for investing in fixed-income securities. In particular, volatility directly affects the pricing of options and the valuation of securities that have optionlike characteristics.

This chapter explains the connection between volatility and the value of fixed-income securities. We define volatility, discuss the differences between historical and implied volatility and between price and yield volatility, show how to calculate historical volatility, and explain how volatility affects market returns.

HISTORICAL VERSUS IMPLIED VOLATILITY

Volatility is the tendency of a quantity to change. Intuitively, some quantities are more volatile than other quantities. The return on an equity investment in an offshore oil exploration company, for example, is likely to be more volatile than the return on an investment in Treasury bills. Furthermore, the same quantity can be much more volatile in one time period than in another. Consider, for example, two months when 30-year bond yields averaged 9 percent, ranging from 8.90 to 9.10 percent in the first month and from 8 to 10 percent in the second month. Clearly, yields on the long bond were much more volatile in the second month, but how much more?

Volatility and option prices are directly linked. An option to buy or sell a security that is unlikely to change in price is worth much less than a similar option on a security that has wide price swings. The volatility of a financial instrument can be quantified by analyzing historical data or by analyzing current option prices. Volatility computed over a specific historical time frame is called *historical volatility*. The number of possible time frames is unlimited, but 10-day, 30-day, and 50-day time periods are used most often for fixed-income securities.

Volatility based on current prices and an option pricing model is called *implied volatility*. If a market exists for options on a particular security, the price of an option and all but one of the parameters in an option pricing model—the volatility of the underlying security—are known. Given the strike price, the price of the underlying security, time to expiration, short-term interest rates, and the type of option (put or call), the volatility *implied* by the price of a particular option can be calculated from an option pricing model through an iterative process. This implied volatility is often viewed as a reflection of the market's expectation of future volatility for the term of that option.

A question such as "What is the volatility of the Treasury 8⅞s of 8/15/17?" is therefore ambiguous. Because options on the 8⅞s are actively traded, both historical and implied volatility can be computed. Furthermore, historical volatility can be computed for different time frames, and implied volatility can be computed for different options contracts. The 30-day historical yield volatility and the implied volatility of 3-month at-the-money put options on the Treasury 8⅞s of 8/15/17 can vary dramatically.

CALCULATING HISTORICAL VOLATILITY

Historical volatility is generally expressed as the annualized standard deviation of the percentage daily changes of a series of prices, yields, or returns. Historical volatility can be based on 5 days of data or 5,000 days of data. Exhibit 16–1 illustrates the most commonly used calculation of historical volatility. The calculation of historical volatility is relatively straightforward and can be implemented in spreadsheet programs.

Although in most cases this method of calculation provides reasonable results when measuring historical variability, there may be some inconsistencies. Since volatility is measured as the variation of percentage changes, a security that increases in price by the same percentage each day will have a historical volatility of zero. This effectively underestimates the true variability of prices in a strictly trending market. For this reason, some formulas assume a constant value for the mean, such as zero. In addition, different assumptions about the number of days in a year (do weekends count, and if so, how much?) used to annualize historical volatility can lead to inconsistent results.

Other methods of calculating historical volatility alleviate some of the inconsistencies of the standard model. The most important modifications incorporate more information about intraday volatility. Some mod-

E X H I B I T   16–1

Calculation of Historical Volatility

Day	Security Price	% Price Change
0	100.00	
1	101.00	1.000%
2	100.50	0.4950
3	102.00	1.4925
4	101.00	–0.9804
5	99.50	–1.4851
6	100.25	0.7538
7	99.00	–1.2469
8	99.75	0.7576
9	99.25	–0.5013
10	98.00	–1.2594
	Average % daily price change:	–0.1964%
	Standard deviation (unbiased):	1.09%
	Number of trading days in a year:	254
	Annualization factor ($\sqrt{\text{days}}$):	15.94
	Annualized volatility (standard deviation × factor):	17.45%

els, for example, use other information such as the high, low, and open rather than simply the close and previous close to calculate historical volatility.[1] The additional information about the trading activity during the day generally provides more accurate measures of historical volatility.

Since historical volatility is a moving average, it is important to remember that it will be affected not only by the most recent price or yield change but also by the price of a yield change that no longer falls within the period analyzed. A dramatic change in 10-day price volatility, for example, could occur if a large change in price occurred today or 11 days ago. Exhibit 16–2 illustrates this phenomenon, showing the 5-day, 10-day, and 15-day historical yield volatilities of December Eurodollar futures from 10/15/87 to 11/10/87. All of the volatilities spiked up on 10/20/87 as a result of the stock market crash on October 19. The volatilities also show a pattern of decline. The 5-day volatility declined dramatically from 83.4 to 54.0 percent 5 business days later on 10/27/87; the 10-day volatility declined from 71.6 to 40.7 percent 10 business days later on 11/3/87; and the 15-day volatility declined from 59.6 to 35.1 percent 15 business days later on 11/10/87. Some methods of calculating historical volatility avoid this inconsistency by exponentially weighting the data so that a single day or observation never falls out all at once.

PRICE VERSUS YIELD VOLATILITY

As mentioned earlier, volatility can be measured for prices or yields. For securities such as commodities, equities, and Treasury bond and note futures that do not have yields, price volatility is the appropriate choice. Yield volatility, however, is recommended for most fixed-income securities. First, price volatility is somewhat inconsistent because the duration of a fixed-income security changes as time passes and as yield levels change. Some of the price changes therefore are attributable to the changing characteristics of the security. Second, yield volatility facilitates better comparisons across different maturities. Longer maturities have much higher price volatilities due to their long durations. Historically, the short end of the Treasury yield curve has been considerably more volatile than the longer end.

---

[1] One model that incorporates intraday data to calculate historical volatility uses the average daily percentage range [(high − low)/close] over the time period. If prices (or yields) move randomly, the average daily percentage range implies an annualized standard deviation, or volatility, of approximately

$$\text{Average daily range} \times \tfrac{15}{22} \times \sqrt{254}$$

E X H I B I T   16–2

December Eurodollar Futures: 5-Day, 10-Day, and 15-Day Historical
Volatilities (10/15/87 to 11/10/87)

Date	December Eurodollar Futures Yield	5-Day Closing Yield Volatility	10-Day Closing Yield Volatility	15-Day Closing Yield Volatility
10/15/87	9.46%	25.2%	20.5%	17.9%
10/16/87	9.56	25.2	18.3	17.8
10/19/87	9.36	33.1	24.4	21.5
10/20/87	8.20	99.0	70.7	57.5
10/21/87	7.95	88.4	71.2	58.7
10/22/87	7.60	79.8	70.2	60.7
10/23/87	7.77	85.0	71.7	61.9
10/26/87	7.46	83.4	72.0	62.9
10/27/87	7.64	54.0*	75.3	63.9
10/28/87	7.66	52.2	71.4	63.5
10/29/87	7.53	43.3	69.3	62.0
10/30/87	7.58	39.1	68.8	61.7
11/02/87	7.71	25.1	71.6	62.6
11/03/87	7.58	24.0	40.7*	62.7
11/04/87	7.50	24.4	38.5	59.8
11/05/87	7.31	27.7	24.5	58.8
11/06/87	7.37	28.2	32.1	58.6
11/09/87	7.44	24.6	26.1	59.6
11/10/87	7.46	23.5	22.4	35.1*

* Indicates when the yield change from 10/19 to 10/20 fell out of the historical
volatility calculation.

It is particularly important to look at implied yield volatilities rather
than implied price volatilities when evaluating over-the-counter options.
Implied yield volatilities enable investors to compare the relative values
of options on securities with different maturities more easily. For example, if a 3-month at-the-money put option on the 5-year is priced at 5 percent price volatility and a 3-month at-the-money put on the 10-year is
priced at 11 percent price volatility, a relative value comparison is difficult to make. Given the additional information that the options' prices

imply 14 and 18 percent yield volatilities, respectively, the put on the 5-year appears much cheaper on a duration-weighted basis.

Yield volatility can vary dramatically across the yield curve. Yields of shorter-maturity Treasuries are often much more volatile than those of longer-maturity issues. In periods of aggressive easing or tightening by the Fed, short-term rates have been more than twice as volatile as long-term rates. Technical factors can also cause certain sectors of the yield curve to be more volatile. Uncertainty over the Treasury's long bond authority, for example, could cause increased gyrations in 30-year Treasury yields.

Price and yield volatility are obviously related. Because of the inherent inconsistencies associated with price volatility, which measures the price variance of a security that changes in maturity and duration, there is no exact formula that links the two. Yield volatility, however, can be estimated from price volatility, and vice versa, using the following formula:

$$\text{Yield volatility} = \frac{\text{Price volatility} \times \text{Price}}{\text{Value of an 01} \times \text{Yield} \times 10,000}$$

The dollar value of an 01 is the average price change given a 1-basis-point decline in yield and a 1-basis-point increase in yield.

Implied yield volatilities of options on the Treasury bond and note futures contracts can also be estimated from the above formula. In this case, the price, yield, and value of an 01 of the bond or note that is cheapest to deliver into the futures contract are used to convert the implied price volatility of the options on futures to a yield volatility. A caveat regarding this methodology of calculating the implied volatility of futures is that it fails to take potential changes in the cheapest-to-deliver security into consideration.

DEVELOPING A VOLATILITY FORECAST

A volatility forecast is essential in evaluating options and securities that have embedded options. As previously discussed, the implied volatility of an option is often viewed as the market's expectation of future volatility. Investors who have expectations of future volatility that differ from the volatility implied by options pricing can increase portfolio expected returns by buying or selling options. Investors with higher volatility expectations than the implied volatility would consider options cheap, while investors with lower volatility expectations would consider options rich.

When developing a volatility forecast, investors generally begin by examining recent historical volatility. Historically, implied volatility of at-the-money put and call options on bond futures and 30-day historical or actual volatility of bond futures are very closely correlated. In fact, the average level of implied volatility of at-the-money options on bond futures rarely diverges from 30-day historical volatility for a sustained period. For example, when market expectations, as measured by implied volatility, are for higher volatility than recent experience suggests, these expectations are either met (actual volatility increases) or adjusted (implied volatility declines). Factors such as the scheduled release of important market information and supply and demand pressures can cause implied and historical volatilities to diverge.

THE IMPORTANCE OF SCHEDULED MARKET INFORMATION

In evaluating an option, particularly a short-term option, the appropriate volatility to use in pricing that option may depend on the scheduled release of market information during the time period. For example, a one-week option granted over the Thanksgiving holiday week may not be as valuable as a similar option granted during a week when many important economic figures are schedule to be released.

PATTERNS OF IMPLIED VOLATILITY

The volatility at which longer-term options are priced is generally less sensitive to recent levels of market volatility than that of shorter-term options. If near-term volatility is very low, a longer-term option typically will be offered at a higher volatility than that of a short-dated option. For example, if 1-month at-the-money call options on the long bond are offered at 8 percent implied yield volatility and long-term average historical yield volatility for 30-year Treasuries is approximately 14 percent, a 3-month option may be offered at 11 to 12 percent volatility. Although this relationship is not necessarily linear, generally the longer the term of an option, the less the pricing of that option will be influenced by recent levels of market volatility.

Out-of-the-money puts generally trade at higher levels of implied volatility than out-of-the-money calls. Retail investors typically use derivative products such as options to hedge against rising interest rates and therefore tend to be better buyers of put options and better sellers of call options. Two of the most common option strategies used by investors are purchasing out-of-the-money puts as a form of insurance and selling out-of-the-money calls as a yield enhancement strategy.

This supply and demand imbalance is typically reflected in higher levels of implied volatilities for out-of-the-money puts than for calls that are similarly out of the money.

IMPLICATIONS OF A VOLATILITY FORECAST

Volatility is an attempt to quantify the variability of yields or prices over time. A volatility forecast, therefore, is an implicit projection of the distribution of yields or prices over time. For example, a yield volatility forecast of 10 percent in an 8 percent interest rate environment implies that the distribution of possible yield levels in one year has a standard deviation of 80 basis points (10% × 8%). Furthermore, this suggests that there is roughly a 67 percent probability that rates in one year will fall within one standard deviation of the mean (8 percent) or between a level of 7.2 and 8.8 percent. There is roughly a 95 percent probability that rates will fall within two standard deviations of the mean or between a level of 6.4 percent and 9.6 percent.[2]

Given this relationship, probabilities can be derived for specific interest rate scenarios. Exhibit 16–3 shows the probability distributions derived from various yield volatility assumptions for a one-year time horizon. A lognormal distribution with a mean of 8 percent is used to assign similar probabilities to equal percentage changes in rates rather than equal absolute changes. This distribution also has the desirable effect of making it impossible to assign any probability to negative yields in the future. A higher volatility assumption implies a higher variation of yield levels or a greater probability of large interest rate moves. According to the exhibit, a portfolio manager must have a volatility forecast of at least 15 percent to assign a significant probability (more than 5 percent) to rates changing more than 150 basis points in either direction in one year.

VOLATILITY AND EXPECTED RETURN

The expected returns of positively or negatively convex securities are linked directly to the level of projected volatility. In a high-volatility environment where large interest rate moves are assigned high probabilities,

---

[2] Actually, the center or mean of the distribution will occur at the one-year forward interest rate, which may be slightly different from 8 percent depending on the shape of the yield curve. Second, a lognormal probability distribution of yields is generally used in practice. If rates are lognormally distributed, the 67 percent confidence interval will range from 7.24 to 8.84 percent.

E X H I B I T   16–3

Scenario Probabilities—One-Year Horizon

Yield Change	0%	5%	10%	15%	20%
−400 bp and below	0%	0.00%	0.00%	0.00%	0.10%
−350	0	0.00	0.00	0.03	0.47
−300	0	0.00	0.00	0.27	1.56
−250	0	0.00	0.05	1.32	3.71
−200	0	0.00	0.71	4.08	6.72
−150	0	0.04	4.15	8.66	9.83
−100	0	2.55	12.53	13.56	12.13
−50	0	24.50	21.98	16.58	13.03
0	100	46.83	24.57	16.56	12.48
+50	0	22.63	18.85	13.97	10.89
+100	0	3.28	10.54	10.24	8.80
+150	0	0.17	4.51	6.67	6.66
+200	0	0.00	1.54	3.94	4.77
+250	0	0.00	0.43	2.14	3.26
+300	0	0.00	0.10	1.08	2.15
+350	0	0.00	0.02	0.51	1.37
+400 and above	0	0.00	0.00	0.40	2.07

positively convex securities, which outperform less convex securities when interest rates change substantially, will have higher expected returns. One way to link volatility and convexity to expected return is to look at the weighted average expected returns (WAVERs) of securities with different convexity characteristics given various volatility assumptions. The difference between the WAVER given a volatility projection and the WAVER in a 0 percent volatility environment represents the expected total return pick-up or give-up due to convexity.

Exhibit 16–4 shows the projected returns of three hypothetical securities in various interest rate scenarios. The three securities have similar durations but different convexity characteristics. WAVERs for each security are also provided for 0, 5, 10, 15, and 20 percent yield volatility assumptions. The WAVERs are created by assigning probabilities, implied by the volatility assumptions, to each interest rate scenario. Given a 15 percent volatility assumption, the three securities have the same WAVERs. Security A has a

E X H I B I T 16–4

Weighted Average Expected Returns of Securities with Varying Convexity and Yield

Interest Rate Scenario	[A] Positive Convexity, Low Yield	[B] No Convexity, Moderate Yield	[C] Negative Convexity, High Yield
–200 bp	31.3%	28.0%	24.7%
–150	24.3	23.0	21.7
–100	17.8	18.0	18.2
–50	11.8	13.0	14.2
0	6.3	8.0	9.7
+50	1.8	3.0	4.2
+100	–2.2	–2.0	–1.8
+150	–5.7	–7.0	–8.3
+200	–8.7	–12.0	–15.3
Yield Volatility		**WAVERs**	
0%	6.30%	8.00%	9.70%
5	6.63	8.00	9.37
10	7.26	8.00	8.74
15	8.00	8.00	8.00
20	8.58	8.00	7.42

6.3 percent expected return given 0 percent volatility and an 8.0 percent expected return given 15 percent volatility. The additional 1.7 percent is the expected total return pick-up due to convexity. Security C, on the other hand, has an expected total return give-up of 1.7 percent (9.7% – 8.0%) given a 15 percent volatility assumption. The expected return of security B, which has no convexity, is not dependent on the level of volatility because the security's return pattern is linear with respect to yield changes.

A direct relationship exists between expected return and volatility and convexity for fixed-maturity securities. The formula that relates the expected return pick-up to convexity and yield volatility is

$$\text{Expected return pick-up} \approx (C \times t \times Y^2 \times V_y^2)$$

where

C = Convexity
T = Investment horizon in years
Y = Yield
V_y = Yield volatility

This formula is derived from the relationship between price changes and yield changes.[3]

The formula can also be applied to variable-maturity securities such as mortgages. For these securities, however, the expected return pick-up is less precise because some of the parameters of the formula, such as convexity, are dependent on the specific prepayment model used to derive the cash flows of the mortgage security.

---

[3] The formula commonly used to predict price changes from yield changes is

$$\frac{\Delta P}{P} = -D_m \Delta Y + \tfrac{1}{2} C (\Delta Y)^2 + \text{Residual}$$

where D_m is modified duration and C is convexity.

APPLICATIONS

17

HEDGING WITH OPTIONS AND OPTION PRODUCTS

Jane Sachar Brauer, PhD
Vice President
Merrill Lynch

Laurie S. Goodman, PhD
Managing Director
PaineWebber

The interest rate variability of the past 15 years has fostered the development of new financial products that give market participants greater flexibility in their risk/return profiles. Among the most important of these innovations are two option products: debt options and caps. These products have allowed investors and issuers alike to design risk/return profiles that fit their preferences more closely than the alternatives in the absence of options. In this chapter, we look at the hedging uses of debt options and caps. The first section considers the hedging use of options in asset management. It examines when money managers might want to use debt options to hedge their portfolios, given their interest rate expectations and the costs of these instruments. We consider both over-the-counter option markets and the exchange-traded markets. The next section discusses the use of debt options and caps in liability management in light of the fact that issuers have emerged as very active users of the options markets. The third section turns to the use of options in asset/liability management. Financial institutions often find themselves in a position where they have implicitly written options as a result of comparative advantage and institutional restrictions. The only way to hedge the risk arising from a short options position is to buy options. As we will demonstrate, caps are the option product of choice.

USING OPTIONS IN ASSET MANAGEMENT

Asset managers concerned about the risk of rising rates have a variety of debt tools that may help to reduce or restructure that risk. To that end, interest rate, or debt, options can be especially powerful. The key to asset hedging is to understand the risk/return profile of the portfolio being hedged, the risk profiles of the available hedging tools, and how these factors can be combined to produce the desired profile.

Symmetric versus Asymmetric Risk

Options offer a risk profile that differs substantially from that of futures. They therefore become an alternative structuring tool in the control of risk. A short futures position has a symmetric return; when rates rise by 10 basis points, the gain on the security will be of roughly the same magnitude as the loss when rates fall by 10 basis points. When a short futures position is established with a long cash position, the money market return is locked in until the future sale date. If prices go up, the loss on the short sale offsets the gain on the asset. If prices go down, the gain on the short sale offsets the loss on the asset.

In contrast, options have an asymmetric risk/reward profile that can be used to protect against price declines but allows the investor to profit if the market rallies. (The basics of options are discussed in Chapter 1.) A put option becomes more valuable as the price of the underlying security falls below the strike price. However, it expires worthless at any price above the strike price. A call option becomes more valuable the higher the price of the underlying security, but expires worthless at any price below the strike price. The maximum loss on either option is the option premium. Thus, options can be used to create an asymmetric return from a symmetric portfolio, a symmetric return from an asymmetric portfolio, or a modified asymmetric return from an asymmetric portfolio.

The decision to use a short hedge or a long put to hedge a bond portfolio depends on your views on the direction and magnitude of interest rate changes in the future, your comfort level regarding unfavorable outcomes, and your investment goals. If you strongly believe that rates will rise substantially, you should choose a short hedge to lock in its return. However, if you want to protect yourself from a possible rise in rates but you also believe that rates could fall, buying a put option, which limits the loss while allowing for upside potential, may be more appropriate. A long put added to a portfolio has the same risk characteristics of a long call option: upside potential with limited downside risk. If rates rise, this option strategy will cost more than a short hedge. It will perform far better than an unhedged bond, as it will provide a floor on the return. In the event that rates fall, this strategy will have a greater return than a short hedge.

A Simple Example

Let us consider an example in which you, the investor, are hedging a call-free bond portfolio with Treasury bond puts. For this example, assume your portfolio consists of one bond, an 8⅞ long-term Treasury bond selling at 98–12. As rates rise, the market value of the portfolio declines, and as rates fall, the market value of the portfolio rises. This asset has symmetric risk: The same type of gain (loss) occurs in opposite directions when rates fall (rise).

Next, suppose you expect rates to rise in the near future and want to protect against this risk. You strongly believe that rates will not fall, and you are willing to forgo gains if rates do fall in exchange for protection if rates rise. In other words, you are looking for a symmetric "risk-free" or neutral return on your portfolio. In this case, you would choose a symmetric hedge, a short cash or futures position, to offset your long cash position. Options would not suit your risk needs. The portfolio hedged with options is shown in Exhibit 17–1. Note that the position hedged with futures provides a return comparable to that of a "risk-free" money market instrument under all interest rate scenarios.

Suppose instead that you now expect rates to fall over the next month but want protection if rates rise. For that protection, or insurance, against an adverse change in interest rates, you are prepared to pay a premium. If you are right, your gain is the market move less the premium. If you are wrong, you lose only your premium.

The purchase of a four-week, at-the-money Treasury put on the 8⅞ at a price of 1.56 points, when combined with the bond you own, would give you your desired profile by allowing you to benefit from a decline in interest rates. In this transaction, you would purchase a put option entitling you to sell the bond at 98–12 (strike price) at any time before the expiration date of the option. The strike could be defined in terms of yield instead of price. For example, the option could have been specified to sell the 8⅞ at a 9 percent yield.

If the price falls below the put's strike price, you will realize a loss on the portfolio, but you will also realize an offsetting profit on the puts in the following way. Suppose the 8⅞ falls to a price of 95–12. The portfolio then falls by 3 points. But the option has value in either of two ways. If you purchase the Treasury securities in the open market at 95–12 and "put" them,

EXHIBIT   17–1

1-Month Profit/Loss on an 8⅞ Long-Term Treasury Bond
Unhedged and Hedged with Futures & Options

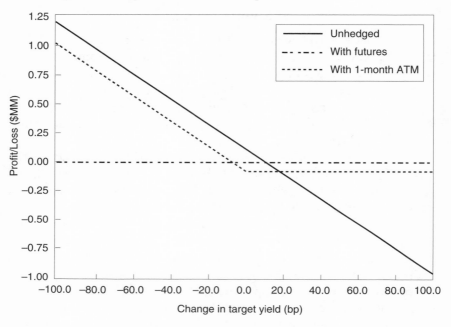

or sell them to the writer of the option at the price represented by the strike price—that is 98–12—the put, as exercised, is worth 3 points.

Alternatively, you could sell the put itself back to the writer; the value of the put is the same 3 points of so-called "intrinsic value," the difference between the open market price and the strike price. Thus, if the market price falls below the strike price, the gain of 3 points from the put will offset your 3-point loss on the portfolio, less the cost of the option, for a capital loss of 1.56 points instead of 3 points on the unhedged bond.

If the price falls by an amount equal to the cost of the option, the hedged position will have a capital loss of 1.56, as will the unhedged bond. On the other hand, if prices do not fall below the strike price, the option will expire worthless, reducing the minimum return at all prices above the strike price, as shown in Exhibit 17–1. You will own an asset that will not have fallen much in value beyond the cost of the put and may have appreciated greatly. In this case, if prices had risen 3 points, the hedged position would have a capital gain of 1.44 points versus 3 points for the unhedged position. If prices rise substantially, of course, the hedged position will consistently produce a return somewhat smaller than the unhedged position. This is the cost of the unused insurance. Note that to compute the holding period return, you must include the coupon income.

Options at Different Strike Prices

Put options are similar to insurance. You, the investor, pay a premium for protection against rising interest rates. The size of this premium depends on the strike price, which is determined by the desired "deductible." Of course, the less the protection, the lower the price.

The strength of a market opinion can determine which strike price to choose: whether to protect a cash position against any and all adverse movements or to protect only against a larger movement (at a lower premium cost).

For example, suppose you are the manager of a fixed-income portfolio. You want to earn a certain minimum rate of return over the next month, but you expect rates to rise. You could buy an at-the-money put option, in which the market price is the strike price; an out-of-the-money option, in which the market price is higher than the strike price; or an in-the-money option, in which the market price is lower than the strike price. Exhibit 17–2 shows the return profile of the long 8⅞ bond hedged with puts in and out of the money by 2 points, as well as an at-the-money put.

An in-the-money option, if exercised today, has value. In our example, this value (the intrinsic value) is 2 points. The price of the option, which comprises both intrinsic value and time value, must be greater than that. In this case, the price is 2.85. If rates fall (prices rise), the bond with an in-the-money put option will underperform the unhedged bond by $2.85. It will underperform the bond hedged with the at-the-money option (cost 1.56) by 1.29 (2.85 – 1.56). If interest rates rise a great deal (prices fall), the bond with the in-the-money option will outperform the unhedged bond by an amount dependent on the price and will outperform the bond with the at-the-money option by 0.71 (1.56 – 0.85).

In Exhibit 17–2, it appears as if the bond with the in-the-money option has a zero return if rates rise. This is because the gain on the option plus the bond is $2. The cost of the option is $2.85. The 0.85 loss on the option is roughly equal to the monthly coupon income on the 8⅞ bond. Note that if prices fall more than 0.85, the bond hedged with the in-the-money option will outperform the unhedged bond.

An out-of-the money option is the least likely to be exercised and is therefore the least expensive option hedging alternative. A one-month

E X H I B I T   17–2

1-Month Profit/Loss on an 8 ⅞ Long-Term Treasury Bond
Unhedged and Hedged with Options

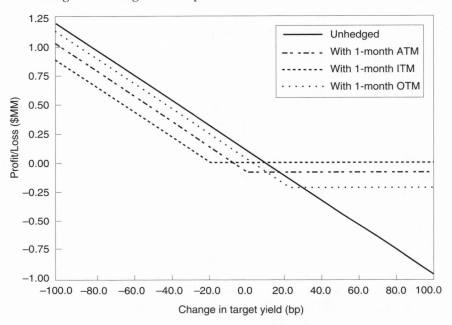

option 2 points out of the money sells for $0.72. Thus, if rates fall (prices rise), the bond hedged with an out-of-the-money option will underperform the unhedged bond by $0.72. On the other hand, if prices do fall, the first few points will be a direct loss to your return, as will be the premium. Thus, prices must fall more than $2.72 to outperform the unhedged bond (the out-of-the-money amount plus the premium). An at-the-money put, struck at today's price, fits somewhere between the in- and out-of-the-money options.

Exchange-Traded versus Over-the-Counter Options

Exchange-traded options exist on physicals, or actual bonds, including options on U.S. Treasury bonds, notes, and bills. Generally these markets are not liquid enough for the execution of transactions of any size. Options on financial futures are much more liquid. Options on bond futures are the most liquid long-term contract, and options on Eurodollar futures are the most active short-term contract. Options on the nearby futures contracts are the most liquid, although trades can generally be done on the three futures contracts closest to maturity. In addition to the exchange-traded options, securities dealers make over-the-counter markets in a variety of underlying credit instruments, and each option is customized according to the requirements of the investor.

Whether you use OTC options versus exchange-traded options, or options on futures versus options on bonds, depends on your need to tailor the hedge to a specific date, security, strike price, or the liquidity of the market. Exchange-traded options, if appropriate, can be less costly than OTC options, since they eliminate the dealer's bid-ask spread. Sometimes, however, exchange-traded options will not meet your needs. Expiration dates are spaced three months apart, strike prices are spaced 2 points apart and, the longest expiration date is only nine months out. Moreover, the universe of bonds on which they are based is small. The advantage, however, is that exchange-traded options are more liquid; if you no longer need the option, you can resell it at any time. By contrast, OTC options often can be resold only to the original seller, with fairly large transaction costs.

Over-the-counter options play an important role in providing longer-term protection. All exchange-traded and most OTC options expire in one year or less. If these short expiration dates do not meet your needs as a portfolio manager, you may choose to buy puts and roll them over as time passes. However, there is a risk in rolling options; since price is a direct function of volatility, if market volatility rises, the price of the roll will rise. On the other hand, if volatility is high and you believe the market will become more stable, a rolling put strategy may be less costly than purchasing a long OTC option.

Hedging Floating-Rate Assets

Thus far, we have discussed using options to hedge a note or bond portfolio. You can also use options to hedge a portfolio consisting of floating-rate assets to create a floor on your return. Suppose you would like to hedge against a decline in rates. You can achieve an effective floor on you return by purchasing a series of call options on a floating-rate security, such as Eurodollar or 3-month U.S. Treasury bill futures, and so on. When rates fall (prices rise), you exercise the call option, purchasing the securities at the lower strike price and reselling them at the market price. This hedge will offset the difference between your specified floor and the actual rate on the floating-rate note. Let us demonstrate this hedge with a simple example.

Suppose you buy a 4-month call on 3-month Eurodollar futures with a strike price of 93 for 8 basis points annually, or $200 per $1 million. Today's 3-month LIBOR is 7.25 percent. You expect rates to rise, but if they do not, you will earn no less than a 7 percent annual rate minus the cost of the call, or 6.92 percent. This is the floor you have effectively purchased. If rates rise above 7 percent, you do not exercise the option; you receive the floating rate less the option premium. If rates fall below 7 percent, you exercise the call option. Your net return is the 7 percent floor less the 8-basis-point premium. Thus, if rates fall below 6.92 percent, the hedged return outperforms the unhedged return.

Basis Risk: Hedging a Diversified Portfolio

Every hedge involves a *basis risk*. Basis risk arises when an unexpected change in the price of the hedge is not reflected in a change in the price of the bonds in your portfolio. This basis risk can arise from any number of sources: changes in credit risk or risk perceptions of the bonds in your portfolio; changes in the shape of the yield curve, which is differentially reflected in the hedge and in your portfolio; or changes in supply or demand that may affect your portfolio differently than the hedge. There is minimal basis risk in owning a bond and buying an option on that underlying bond. However, in most hedging situations, your portfolio will consist of bonds that are quite different from the ones in which option markets are made. This requires that you estimate how your bonds will move relative to the bonds underlying the option. In a situation where a portfolio of financial sector (corporate) bonds is hedged with an option on Treasury futures, any subsequent flight to quality will cause the bonds in the portfolio to underperform those of the hedge. The widening of the basis results in losses on the financial sector bonds that are not fully offset by gains from the short futures position.

The financial sector bonds may be shorter or longer in maturity than the cheapest bond off which the futures contract is pricing, creating yield curve risk. When using exchange-traded options to hedge a 3-year instrument, for example, you must choose between the basis risk of an option on a 3-month futures and an option on a 10-year futures or, alternatively, purchase a more expensive OTC option. Moreover, the maturity of the cash bond off which the Treasury future is priced might change, causing the original hedge ratio to be incorrect.

Costs

In contrast to futures, options protection is expensive because it is one-sided: If rates go up, you gain; if rates go down, you do not lose. The explicit cost of obtaining this payoff structure is the option premium.[1]

Because the costs are not small, you must decide what risk you are willing to bear. You can reduce the price of the option if you choose an out-of-the-money option and/or shorten the expiration date. For example, if you expect a change in Federal Reserve policy within the next three weeks, a two-month option represents an unnecessary cost.

Option prices are also a function of volatility. The more volatile the market, the higher the hedging cost for a market maker and the higher the price to the buyer. Of course, in volatile markets you will have a higher level of concern about asset protection than in stable markets. Consequently, you will be more willing to pay more for this protection.

Calculating a Hedge Ratio

Hedging the 8⅞ with an option on the same bond and a specific expiration date in mind is simple. One option is used to hedge one bond.

The next simplest hedge is one in which you, the portfolio manager, want to hedge one bond, say, the 8⅞, with an option on another bond, say a long-term 14 percent Treasury bond. You use a hedge ratio that is the same as that used to establish a short position in the 14 percent coupon cash bond. Analytically, it is the ratio of the price changes for equal yield changes. If the 14s move 0.75 points for a 10-basis-point change in rates but the 8⅞s move 1.00 points, you will use a hedge ratio of 1.00/0.75, or 1.33 options on the 14s to hedge every 1.0 of 8⅞s. Thus, if you have $20 million of the 8⅞s to hedge and want an options position in the 14s, you will buy put options on $26.6 million of the 14s.

The general formula used to calculate the amount of the hedge to be purchased is given by

$$DHR = \frac{\Delta P_{MP}}{\Delta P_{H}} \tag{1}$$

where

$$DHR = \text{The hedge ratio, or the amount of the duration}$$
$$\text{hedge to be purchased}$$

---

[1] The buyer of an option is not required to post margin. Therefore, the cost is precisely the premium.

ΔP_{MP} = The change in the price of your portfolio for a
         10-basis-point fall in rates

ΔP_{H} = The change in price of the hedging instrument
         for a 10-basis-point fall in rates

If you cannot, or decide not to, buy options on the bonds in your portfolio, bond futures options rather than OTC options will be your more likely alternative. The principle for computing the hedge ratio is exactly the same when futures are used as the hedging instrument as when cash is used. The hedge ratio is simply the relative price sensitivities.

The hedge ratio when using futures is based on the cheapest-to-deliver (CTD) bond. The CTD bond is the most likely bond to be delivered against the bond futures contract. It is the bond with the highest return on a long cash–short futures transaction. A correction must be made for the conversion factor. This factor "adjusts" the bonds so they are all comparable with a hypothetical 8 percent, 20-year bond. The futures price moves with the price of the cheapest-to-deliver bond divided by the factor. Thus, when hedging with an option on futures, the hedge ratio is given by

$$\text{DHR} = \frac{\Delta P_{MP}}{\Delta P_{CTD}/\text{Factor}} \qquad (2)$$

where

ΔP_{CTD} = The change in price of the CTD bond for a 10-basis-point
         fall in rates

To see how this might be used, assume your portfolio has a market value of \$50 million and a modified duration of 6.5 years. It will rise in value by \$325,000 for a 10-basis-point fall in rates. Suppose the cheapest-to-deliver bond is a 7.25 percent issue with a modified duration of 10.46 years and its current price is 81.656 (in decimals). The change in the price of 100,000 par amount of the cheapest-to-deliver bond is 854.12 (10.46 × 81.656) for a 10-basis point fall in rates. The factor is 0.9167. Thus, the rise in the price of the futures contract for a 10-basis-point fall in rates is (854.12/0.9167), or \$931.73. The hedge ratio is 325,000/931.73, or 349 contracts.

This hedge assumes that the yield on the hedging instrument will move by the same amount as the yield on the asset. If you believe that rates will not move equally, you can adjust the hedge by the relative volatility of yields based on the "beta," or slope, of a regression equation as given by

$$\Delta Y_{MP} = \alpha + \beta \Delta Y_{H} \qquad (3)$$

where

ΔY_{MP} = The change in the yield of the bond(s) in your portfolio

ΔY_{H} = The change in the yield of the hedging instrument

Note that this is sometimes estimated using yields instead of yield changes.

The optimal regression hedge ratio (RHR) is then given by

$$RHR = DHR \times (\beta) \qquad (4)$$

Thus, if the beta (β) was 0.8, the yield movements on your bond would be less than the yield movements on the CTD bond. The regression hedge ratio in the above example would involve purchasing 279 contracts.

Another way to calculate a regression hedge ratio is to apply regression analysis to historical price changes. The "beta," or slope of the line, would indicate the relative price sensitivity of the instruments and therefore the number of options to buy.

If data are available for regression analysis, this approach may be preferred to duration hedging in cases where yields are not expected to move equally and the nature of the relative yield movement is not known with certainty without performing a historical analysis. Two such examples are using Treasury bond futures to hedge a tax-exempt portfolio and using Treasury bond futures to hedge a mortgage-backed security.

Simulating Options with Futures

There are situations in which you, as an investor, cannot find an exchange-traded put option to meet your needs. To create the desired payoff structure of the hedging instrument, you have three alternatives: (1) You can purchase an OTC put option; (2) you can simulate a put option by adjusting the size of the short cash or futures hedge frequently according to a specific portfolio strategy; or (3) you can continuously replace some of your long bonds with money market instruments, and vice versa, using a dynamic asset allocation model so that your portfolio return looks like that of an option.

Futures, because of their greater liquidity and lower transaction costs, are the easier and less expensive way to simulate an option. Moreover, the creation of a synthetic option enables you to create an optionlike return at the exercise (strike) price and expiration date of your choosing. If tailoring

the exercise price and expiration date on exchange-traded options is important to you, this strategy must be viewed as a less expensive alternative to
OTC option purchases. A synthetic strategy does, however, require that you
adjust positions frequently as the market changes.

To understand synthetic options, you have to understand the concept
of the *delta* of an option. The delta of an option is the hedge ratio of the
option to the underlying instrument, in other words, the change in the
price of the option relative to the change in the price of the underlying
instrument.

The return profile of the option at expiration was discussed in earlier chapters. To review, when the market price is at the option strike price,
the option is at the money, if the price rises, the put becomes worthless;
and if the price falls, the put becomes valuable. The solid line in Exhibit
17–3 shows the return of the put at expiration. The dotted line shows the
price of the option one month before expiration. The slope of the dotted
line is the delta hedge ratio. The higher the price of the underlying security, the less likely the put is to be exercised and therefore the fewer

EXHIBIT   17–3

Put Option Value 30 Days to Expiration and at Expiration

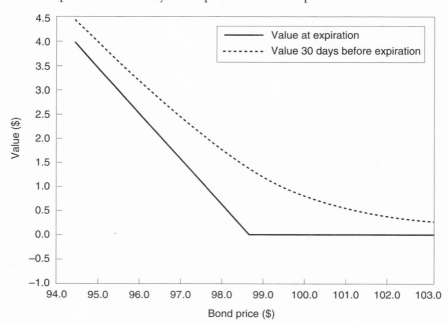

futures are needed as a hedge. The lower the price, the more likely the put is to be exercised and the more futures contracts are needed as a hedge. When the bond is priced at the money, the hedge ratio is 0.5. This means that one put option priced at the money will move half as much as the futures contract. If the market rallies, the position is overhedged; it if drops, the position is underhedged. Because the hedge ratio changes as the price changes, you frequently have to readjust. In- and out-of-the-money deltas do not need to be adjusted as frequently as at-the-money deltas, because they do not change as much as at-the-money options when the price of the underlying bond changes. You can calculate the delta by using an option pricing model.

The creation of a synthetic option using futures contracts requires that you multiply the number of futures contracts required to hedge the bond by the delta of the option.

Earlier in this chapter, we explained how you would compute the number of options on bond futures to hedge a portfolio. Equation 5 shows you how to compute the number of futures to be sold (purchased) to create a long position in a synthetic put (call) option:

$$\Delta P_{MP} \times \text{Delta} = \Delta P_{CTD} / \text{Factor} \times \text{DHR} \tag{5}$$

where

$$\text{delta} = \text{the delta on the synthetic option.}$$

Solving for the amount to be purchased, we obtain

$$\text{DHR} = \frac{\Delta P_{MP} \times \text{Delta}}{\Delta P_{CTD}/\text{Factor}} \tag{6}$$

To illustrate how this may be used, we use the same example as before. Your bond portfolio has a market value of $50 million and a modified duration of 6.5 years. It will rise by $325,000 for a 10-basis-point fall in rates. The cheapest-to-deliver bond is a 7.25 percent issue with a modified duration of 10.46 years. Its current price is 81.656 (in decimals); its factor is 0.9167. The change in the price of $100,000 par of the cheapest-to-deliver bond is 854.12 for a 10-basis-point fall in rates. Thus, the price sensitivity of the futures contract is 931.73. We want to create a synthetic put option with a strike price of 86 expiring on July 15. There are no exchange-traded July options contracts. The two nearest options on bond futures are the June contract, expiring in late May, and the September contract, expiring in late August. The delta on this option would be 0.36. Thus, the appropriate hedge ratio to use for a synthetic option would be the sale of 126 [(325.000/931.73) × 0.36)] bond futures. Note that as the delta rises (that is, as interest rates rise), you would sell more bond futures. For example, if the hedge ratio were 0.48, you would sell more bond futures, at a lower price. As the delta falls, you would buy back bond futures, at a higher price.

The cost of creating a synthetic option is the loss that results from selling futures contracts as the price falls and buying them back as the price rises. You may choose to create a synthetic option to achieve the desired expiration date for a particular strike price. You may also choose to create a synthetic option if you believe the market will be less volatile than the premium for an OTC or exchange-traded option implies. In this case, the cost of delta hedging will be less than the cost of purchasing an option from an option writer.

Hedging Assets with Embedded Options

You can also use synthetic options to hedge assets with embedded options. Examples of assets with embedded options include a floater with a cap or floor, a callable bond, and a mortgage pass-through. To obtain a symmetric risk profile from a security with an embedded option, you may want to consider hedging the embedded option with an option to obtain a risk profile similar to that of a simple floater or a call-free bond. Often the characteristics of the embedded options are such that a synthetic option must be created to hedge the embedded option. If you are seeking a neutral position, you may also need to hedge the call-free underlying bond with a short cash or futures position.

Let us first consider hedging callable bonds. We separate the callable bond into two parts: the call-free bond and the call option. Theoretically, you could buy a call similar to the embedded call of the bond and short call-free bond or futures. Many embedded calls, however, cannot be exercised for 5 to 10 years. Because the long option market is not very liquid, you may choose to hedge with a short futures position that combines the option hedge and the call-free hedge. This requires that you adjust the hedge ratio; that is, you establish a short futures hedge and construct a synthetic long call option position to offset the embedded call. The synthetic call involves a long position in bond futures. On net, the futures position will be short.

It is important to realize that you can view a 10-year bond callable in 5 years as a 5-year bond coupled with an issuer put in 5 years on a 5-year bond; that is, the issuer may choose to extend the bond or terminate it in 5 years depending on the 5-year market rate at the time. In this case, you would need to hedge a 5-year bond and a put in 5 years on this bond. To hedge the 5-year bond plus the put, you would need the same short futures position as above.

To hedge a capped floater, you might buy a cap to offset the cap on the floater. (Caps are discussed more fully in the next section.) As an alternative, you could buy a Eurodollar put on the floater. If rates rise (prices fall), you buy the securities and "put" them to the seller of the option. The difference between the put price and the market value, which equals the intrinsic value, will compensate for the loss on the cap yield. This is the difference between the market floating rate and the cap yield.

If the floater has a floor, you have implicitly purchased a long call; that is, you have the right to lend at a rate that is higher than the market rate in a low-rate environment. If you do not believe that rates will fall, you may increase your return by removing the floor. You could offset the floor by writing call options at the strike yield represented by the floor.

LIABILITY MANAGEMENT

Options have become quite important in liability management. Generally, they take two forms (1) hedging an anticipated fixed-rate debt issuance or (2) capping a current floating-rate debt issue.

Hedging a Future Debt Issuance

One of the most common problems facing issuers occurs when they consider the current interest rate level favorable but are reluctant to lock it in either because they believe there is a chance that rates could go lower or because they are not sure of their funding needs in the near future.

Options offer the answer in either case. If you, the borrower, believe rates could go lower, an option provides the ideal hedging vehicle. It enables you to lock in a maximum borrowing rate and take advantage of lower rates if rates fall. The cost of this protection is the option premium. If you are not sure of your funding needs, options can guarantee a maximum all-in funding cost. If the funding is needed, the protection is helpful. If the funding is not needed and there is a gain on the option, the option can be exercised or liquidated. The maximum loss is the option premium.

Like investors, issuers can use either exchange-traded or over-the-counter options. OTC options can be customized to lock in borrowing costs. There is no basis risk; that is, you can lock in both the base rate and your credit spread for the desired period. The disadvantage to over-the-counter options is that they are expensive to unwind before expiration. Thus, if you are unsure of exactly when funding may be needed, an exchange-traded option will be preferable. Since most issuers have some degree of funding uncertainty, exchange-traded options are used far more commonly than OTC options. If your credit spread fluctuations are small, you may well prefer to use an exchange-traded option, since it is important to hedge only the base rate. It is unnecessary to pay more for a customized product.

We now discuss how to set up a hedge on a prospective new issue. To hedge a given amount of a new issuance, you purchase the exact amount of an over-the-counter option. By contrast, with an exchange-traded option, you must establish and readjust a hedge ratio. The calculations for establishing a hedge ratio are identical to that for investors. Assume you want an option with a strike price of 86 that expires on, say, August 20 of the same year which we assume is the exact expiration date of the September option on the bond futures contract. The duration hedge ratio would be calculated as follows:

$$\text{DHR} = \frac{\Delta P_{\text{BI}}}{\Delta P_{\text{CTD}}/\text{Factor}} \qquad (7)$$

where

ΔP_{BI} = The change in your bond issuance for a 10-basis-point fall in rates

Assume you want to float a \$50-million, 20-year bond issue. The coupon on the bond is to be 10 percent. If rates move down 10 basis points, the issuance cost of the bonds will rise by \$431,930. We showed in the previous section that the change in \$100,000 face value of the cheapest-to-deliver bond—the 7.25 percent issue—is 854.12 and the factor is 0.9167. Thus, the rise in the price of the futures contract from a 10-basis-point fall in rates is 854.12/0.9176, or 931.73. From equation 7 you should purchase 464 September put options with a strike price of 0.86.

If the desired option expiration date does not match the expiration date of the options on bond futures, you can create a synthetic option with the desired expiration date. Combinations of June and September options to replicate a July expiration date will be highly unsatisfactory. The June contract will expire before the option is to mature; the September contract will expire after the option is needed. Moreover, the exchange-traded option will be worth more than its intrinsic value in July; it will also have some time value remaining. Thus, to tailor the expiration date, a synthetic option must be constructed. If the desired strike price does not match the strike price on existing exchange-traded options, you can either create a synthetic option with the desired strike price or use a combination of the nearest two strike prices. Thus, if you wanted a strike of 87 on September options on bond futures, you could create a risk/return profile that is similar—but not identical—by using September put options with strike prices of 86 and 88.

To create a synthetic option, you can use futures contracts and adjust the hedge ratio on a frequent basis as we discussed in the previous section. The correct initial hedge ratio is the duration hedge ratio times the delta on the synthetic option. Thus, if you, as an issuer, want to create a synthetic option expiring in July with a strike price of 86, the delta of the synthetic option will be 0.36. Thus, the correct initial hedge ratio for the synthetic option will be 464 × 0.36, or 167. This means you should short 167 September futures contracts to create the appropriate synthetic position.

In sum, you can use either over-the-counter, exchange-traded, or synthetic options to hedge a debt issuance. Over-the-counter options provide more protection for a greater cost; they are expensive to resell prior to maturity. Exchange-traded options are, however, easy to sell at any time. If the characteristics of the option desired by the issuer do not match those of the option traded on the exchange, a synthetic option can be created using futures. This position must be rebalanced frequently. It is, of course, easy to liquidate a futures position.

Capping a Debt Issuance

Caps are interest rate agreements that place an upper bound on your borrowing costs. If you buy a LIBOR-based cap at 11 percent, the counterparty agrees that if LIBOR rises above 11 percent, he or she will pay you the difference between the prevailing rate and 11 percent. Thus, if you purchased a cap that settled semiannually on $100 million and LIBOR rose to 13 percent, you would receive $0.02 \times \frac{1}{2} \times \$100,000,000$, or $1 million. Your total borrowing costs would be

Interest cost	$0.13 \times \frac{1}{2} \times \$100,000,000$	=	$6,500,000
Receipt from cap	$0.02 \times \frac{1}{2} \times \$100,000,000$	=	–$1,000,000
			$5,500,000

Note that net cost corresponds to an interest rate of 11 percent ($0.11 \times \frac{1}{2} \times \$100,000,000$). Because of the type of protection provided, capping is most applicable for floating-rate issuers.

Caps are available based on a wide range of money market indices, including Treasury bills, commercial paper, LIBOR, the prime rate, and the rate on certificates of deposit. LIBOR-based caps are, by far, the most common. Generally, you will have to pay more for other indices. You select the floating-rate index you prefer, as well as the maturity of the cap (up to 10 years), the ceiling rate, the start date, and the payment frequency (three or six months). Most caps are written for maturities of three to seven years. Caps are usually paid for with an up-front fee. Up-front costs are higher as the cap term gets longer or as the strike yield is reduced.

Caps are option products. Consider a three-year cap that pays every six months. The cap may be regarded as a series of five options: a 6-month option, a 12-month option, an 18-month option, a 2-year option, and a 2½-year option. This is because cap payments are determined by the LIBOR rate at the beginning of the period and paid at the end. The rate for the first six months is determined immediately and hence has no option component. The payment for the period from 6 to 12 months is determined by LIBOR at month six. These caps would then be priced as a series of five independent options. The cap market under two years does not exist, but you can create a synthetic cap using Eurodollar futures out to this point. That is, you can create each option synthetically with the appropriate futures position.

Exhibit 17–4 compares three alternatives to an issuer of 5-year debt: plain vanilla floating-rate debt, floating-rate debt plus a cap, and floating-rate debt plus a swap. Floating-rate debt plus a swap transforms the floating-rate debt into fixed-rate debt. In a low–interest rate environment, you will probably prefer to borrow at a floating rate without a swap or cap. In a high-interest rate environment, both the swap and the cap provide an upper limit on your borrowing costs. However, the maximum rate on the cap is higher than the swap rate, as the swap fixes a rate, while with a cap you can take advantage of the situation when rates go down.

Most caps are marketable instruments;[2] if somewhere into the life of the issue you no longer want the cap, it can be resold. For example, suppose you purchase a five-year cap when you initially issue your floating-rate debt. After two years, you become convinced that rates will stay low for the remainder of the cap term. It would be in your interest to resell the cap.

A variation on the cap is the floating-rate collar. The collar market was created for issuers who prefer capped floating-rate liabilities but con-

---

[2] Occasionally caps are embedded in a floating-rate issue; that is, the issue itself has a cap rate. These are not separately marketable.

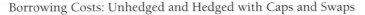

E X H I B I T   17–4

Borrowing Costs: Unhedged and Hedged with Caps and Swaps

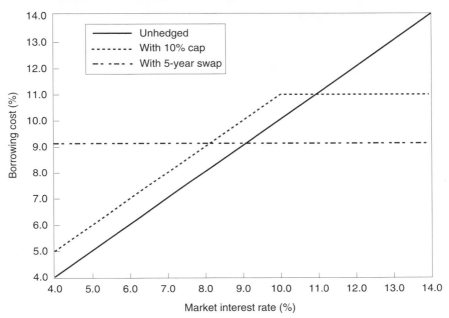

sider caps too expensive. With a collar, you purchase a cap and sell a floor at the same time. The selling of the floor offsets some of the cost of the caps. For example, with LIBOR at 7.50 percent, if you purchased a 10 percent cap and sold a 7 percent floor for five years, the net cost of the collared position would be an up-front fee of $2.93 rather than $3.69 on the cap alone.

Exhibit 17–5 shows the risk/return profile of a collared position vis-à-vis a capped position and an unhedged position. As you can see, when rates are low, both the unhedged positions and the capped position are preferable to the collar. As rates rise, the collar looks quite attractive; it is more favorable than either capped debt or hedged debt.

Another cap product is the forward cap. You may want to use the forward cap if you expect to issue debt in the future and believe that rates will go up by more than the expectations implied by the existing yield curve. If you decide not to issue the debt, you can sell back the cap. This type of transaction requires that a counterparty write one cap (the longer cap) and buy another cap (the shorter cap). As a result, the transaction costs on this type of hedge are greater than on a normal cap.

EXHIBIT 17–5

Borrowing Costs: Unhedged and Hedged with Caps and Floors

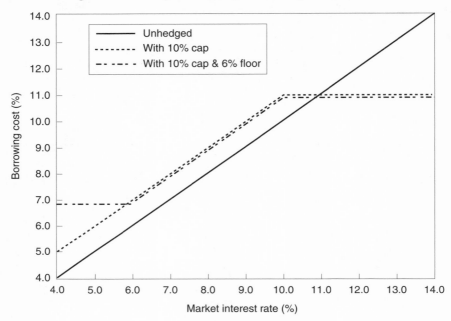

ASSET/LIABILITY MANAGEMENT

Option products are just beginning to play an important role in asset/liability management. We expect this role to increase over the next few years as institutions begin to consider risk management decisions in a macro sense, that is, from the point of view of the entire balance sheet.

Asset/liability management applies primarily to financial institutions that hold financial instruments on both sides of their balance sheets. Adjustments can be made on either side of the balance sheet or by using risk management products such as swaps, caps, futures, and options. There is a very large role for option products because many of the liabilities contain embedded options. The role of option products in asset/liability management perhaps can be best illustrated by focusing on a particular type of financial institution. In this section, we focus on life insurance companies. Life insurance companies have a comparative advantage in issuing liabilities that have a savings component as well as an insurance component. This is because insurance policies are tax-advantaged forms of saving; that is, the implicit interest income is not taxable. Because of this built-in advantage, many individuals wish to invest a substantial amount of savings in insurance policies.

Think about some of the basic types of insurance products for individuals:

Insurance Only	Insurance and Savings	Savings Only
Term insurance	Whole life	Single-premium deferred annuity
	Universal life	
	Single-premium whole life	
	Variable universal life	

Interest-sensitive embedded options are contained in whole life policies, universal life policies, single-premium whole life policies, and single-premium deferred annuities. The two most important of these options are essentially embedded put options the issuer has written. If rates rise, insurance companies, as the writers, will be adversely affected because more and more policyholders will exercise these options.

In whole life policies, the single most important option is the option to take out a policy loan at a fixed rate of interest. While this feature has not been offered for the last several years, it is an important option because of the volume of whole life policies outstanding. Currently, insurance policies offer the policyholder the ability to borrow at a floating rate of interest, generally the dividend crediting rate plus a spread. The ability to borrow at a floating rate of interest is a convenience, but it is not a valuable option to policyholders. On the other hand, the ability to borrow at fixed rates afforded by old policies is valuable to policyholders. As market interest rates rise above the fixed borrowing rate on the policy, policyholders have an incentive to borrow against the policy instead of incurring alternative forms of debt. Policyholders also have an incentive to borrow at the fixed rate and invest the proceeds of their loans in higher-yielding securities.

The second option, which is common to universal life, single-premium whole life, and single-premium deferred annuities, is the lapse option. Whole life policyholders also have this option, but it is usually preferable to borrow at fixed rates than to let the policy lapse. Policyholders, at their option, may let the policy lapse and accept its cash surrender value. They will exercise this option if they are not satisfied with the interest rate at which their earnings are being credited. This rate is determined by the insurance company. Insurance companies usually purchase medium-term bonds. As rates go up, the entire portfolio cannot be credited at the new rate because it is actually yielding a blend of the old and new rates. The company will usually make a partial adjustment to the new rate. Policyholders who are unhappy with the rate will let their policies lapse and receive the cash surrender value. Looked at differently, the cash surrender value is based on book value and hence is higher than the market value of the securities backing it in a rising interest rate environment.[3]

Insurance companies receive an asymmetric payoff because of these options. The only way to offset an option that has been written is to buy a similar option. These embedded options extend over a number of years. Thus, caps are better suited to hedge these embedded options than short-term options would be.

To use caps effectively, insurance companies must estimate their option payoffs at different levels of interest rates. As rates increased from 8 to 9 percent, for example, fewer caps would be needed than if interest rates rose from 8 to 10 percent. This is because with a 2-percentage-point rise in rates, more policyholders would let their policies lapse than with a 1-percentage-point move. The best solution for insurance companies is to use caps at different strike prices. For example, a company may want to buy some 9 percent caps, some 10 percent caps, some 11 percent caps, and some 12 percent caps. This strategy is called *layering caps.*[4]

Other financial institutions also have assets or liabilities with embedded options. Depository institutions, for example, hold mortgage assets in their portfolios. These instruments, of course, prepay as rates fall. Commercial banks make fixed-rate loans. These loans can be prepaid. As rates decline, corporate clients will prepay expensive borrowing and take out new loans at market interest rates. If an institution writes interest rate options that are embedded in other financial products, the only way to offset these options is to purchase or create similar options.

---

[3] In universal life policies, there is a symmetric option as rates fall. In these policies, holders have a great deal of flexibility as to their annual premiums. As rates fall, the crediting rate generally does not fall as much and policyholders tend to overdeposit. The insurance company has written both a put option and a call option in these policies.

[4] An excellent introduction to the use of caps by insurance companies can be found in Chapter 20 in Frank J. Fabozzi, ed., *Fixed Income Portfolio Strategies* (Chicago: Probus Publishing, 1989).

SUMMARY

In this chapter, we investigated the hedging uses of options. This chapter is meant to be an introduction rather than an inclusive list of all hedging applications. These instruments have broad appeal to money managers, bond issuers, and asset/liability managers. The key point for readers is that options are extremely flexible instruments with many hedging applications.

To use options effectively, money managers must explicitly state their interest rate expectations and desired risk/return profile. This, coupled with the portfolio profile of current holdings, will indicate whether options would be an appropriate hedging vehicle. Similarly, issuers and asset/liability managers must articulate their desired risk/return trade-off to determine whether or not to hedge with options.

SCENARIO ANALYSIS AND THE USE OF OPTIONS IN TOTAL RETURN PORTFOLIO MANAGEMENT

Keith Anderson
Managing Director
BlackRock Financial Management

Scott Amero
Managing Director
BlackRock Financial Management

Total return fixed-income portfolio management is typically approached as a trade-off between risk and return. Duration is the most commonly used measure of interest rate risk, and yield is the most commonly used measure of return. The fixed-income portfolio management process is generally a two-step approach. First, the manager determines the appropriate level of interest rate exposure to incur; second, the manager selects the specific securities that will comprise the portfolio. In this manner, a manager creates a fixed-income portfolio with a duration level that is consistent with both the performance objectives and the interest rate forecast.

Managers typically use the duration of a particular performance benchmark as a starting point in determining the appropriate duration of their portfolios. The appropriate benchmark is the index or liability stream against which performance will be measured. This duration level may then be modified to reflect the manager's individual interest rate forecast.

Managers who are bullish generally will construct a portfolio with a higher duration than that of the performance benchmark. The degree to which managers are willing to deviate from the benchmark will depend not only on their confidence in their interest rate forecasts, but also on their ability to withstand variability between the performance of their portfolios and the benchmark portfolio. For example, if the performance benchmark is an index with a duration of 5 years, a manager who is bullish may be hesitant to "bet the ranch" and construct a portfolio with a duration of 10 years, particularly if the repercussions of being wrong for three months may be the loss of the account or his or her job. Unfortunately, positioning a portfolio with a relatively high duration to dramatically outperform a benchmark on the upside will also result in a dramatically poor relative performance on the downside. Portfolio managers, however, are not limited to securities or portfolios that have patterns of returns that are symmetric with respect to interest rate changes.

Duration is an incomplete measure of the interest rate risk of an individual security or a portfolio of securities. Duration is helpful in understanding how the price of a security will react to a small change in interest rates, but it can be a very misleading gauge of how a security or a portfolio will react to large changes in interest rates. Duration is particularly misleading when variable maturity securities such as callable bonds and mortgage securities are included in a portfolio.

In this chapter, we will discuss why single-point risk and return measures such as duration and yield do not completely describe the risk and return of fixed-income securities. We will introduce scenario analysis as a portfolio management tool that can be used to better quantify the risk and return of an individual security or a portfolio of securities.

We will also introduce the use of options in total return portfolio management and discuss how they can be used to create portfolio return profiles that are attractive to those of their performance benchmarks.

SCENARIO ANALYSIS

Scenario analysis is an analytical tool used to determine the pattern of total returns for a single security or portfolio of securities over a range of interest rate scenarios for a given time horizon. Scenario analysis is important because duration and yield do not fully describe the risk and return of fixed-income securities. The change in price and return of a fixed-income security is not a linear function with respect to interest rates as duration might suggest. A thorough scenario analysis will capture these nonlinear effects, such as convexity, which can dramatically affect the potential returns of fixed-income securities. Scenario analysis, combined with weighted-average expected return (WAVER), will also highlight the expected performance of fixed-income securities with varying convexity characteristics in different volatility environments.

Convexity

Fixed-income portfolio managers should consider convexity, in addition to duration and yield, as a parameter on which to structure a portfolio. The combination of duration and convexity provides better insight than duration alone into the price and return behavior of a security or portfolio of securities in varying interest rate environments. In a theoretical context, *convexity* can be defined as the second moment of price changes with respect to changes in yield. Modified duration is the first-order term of this relationship.

On a more pragmatic level, convexity can be thought of as the portion of bond price movements that is not predicted by duration. Modified duration analysis makes the implicit assumption that bond prices change linearly with respect to yield. Exhibit 18–1 shows that the actual price of a fixed-maturity security does not change linearly with yield. For a pos-

E X H I B I T   18–1

Actual versus Duration-Predicted Price Change

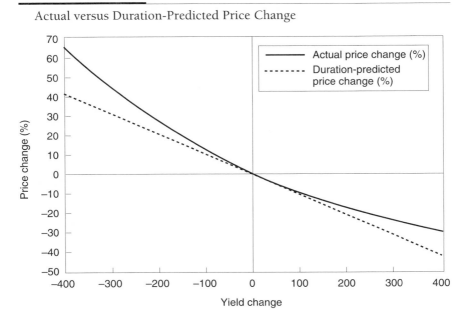

itively convex security such as this one, convexity represents the positive difference between the actual price of the security given a change in
yield and the price of the security predicted by duration alone. In other
words, prices of positively convex securities always outperform the
prices predicted by duration alone. For a negatively convex security,
convexity represents an underperformance in actual price compared to
the price predicted by duration. All else being equal, the returns of portfolios with positive convexity are expected to exceed those of portfolios
with negative convexity.

Exhibit 18–2 shows the results of a scenario analysis on three
hypothetical securities, A, B, and C, all of which yield 8 percent and
have a modified duration of 10 years. Security A has positive convexity,
security B displays no convexity, and security C has negative convexity.
If interest rates are unchanged over the time period considered, convexity will have no impact on returns. If interest rates change substantially
in either direction, the positively convex security (A) will outperform
both the security with no convexity (B) and the security with negative
convexity (C).

In this case, A is clearly preferable to both B and C, and B is clearly preferable to C. Positive convexity is valuable to a portfolio manager

E X H I B I T   18–2

Scenario Analysis: 1-Year Total Returns of Securities
with Varying Convexity

Interest Rate Scenario	(A) Positive Convexity	(B) No Convexity	(C) Negative Convexity
−200 bp	33.0%	28.0%	23.0%
−150	26.0	23.0	20.0
−100	19.5	18.0	16.5
−50	13.5	13.0	12.5
0	8.0	8.0	8.0
+50	3.5	3.0	2.5
+100	−0.5	−2.0	−3.5
+150	−4.0	−7.0	−10.0
+200	−7.0	−12.0	−17.0

Assumed reinvestment rate: 8.0%.

and negative convexity is detrimental provided there are no differences in yield. In general, however, positively convex securities offer lower yields than negatively convex securities, making the portfolio manager's decision more difficult.

Consider three similar securities, A*, B*, and C*, but assume security A* yields only 6.3 percent, security B* yields 8.0 percent, and security C* yields 9.7 percent. Exhibit 18–3 shows the one-year total returns of A*, B*, and C*. In this case, security C* has the most attractive yield and the least attractive convexity characteristics, and determining which security offers the best relative value is more difficult.

Security A* outperforms B* and C* in stable interest rate environments because of its low yield but outperforms them when interest rates change substantially in either direction because of its positive convexity. Security C*, on the other hand, outperforms A* and B* in stable environments because of its high yield but significantly underperforms them in volatile environments. The lower yield of security A* represents a payment for positive convexity, while the higher yield of C* represents compensation for negative convexity. The relative attractiveness of the three securi-

E X H I B I T 18–3

Scenario Analysis: 1-Year Total Returns of Securities with Varying Convexity and Yield

Interest Rate Scenario	(A*) Positive Convexity, Low Yield	(B*) No Convexity, Moderate Yield	(C*) Negative Convexity, High Yield
−200 bp	31.3%	28.0%	24.7%
−150	24.3	23.0	21.7
−100	17.8	18.0	18.2
−50	11.8	13.0	14.2
0	6.3	8.0	9.7
+50	1.8	3.0	4.2
+100	−2.2	−2.0	−1.8
+150	−5.7	−7.0	−8.3
+200	−8.7	−12.0	−15.3

Reinvestment is assumed to occur at the yield of each security.

ties depends on the investor's assessment of the likelihood of large changes in interest rates. If the portfolio manager expects a great deal of interest rate volatility, security A^*, the lowest-yielding security, may offer the best relative value.

Volatility

Volatility is a statistical measure of the variance of yields, prices, or returns around a center or average point. Historical volatility is the annualized standard deviation of the percentage daily yield, price, or return changes of a particular security measured over a specified number of trading days. Historical volatility is not a unique number and can have substantially different values when measured over different time periods.

Volatility is an attempt to quantify the variability of yields, prices, or returns over time. A yield volatility level of 10 percent in an 8 percent interest rate environment implies that the distribution of possible yield levels in one year has a standard deviation of 80 basis points ($0.10 \times 8\%$). This means that there is roughly a 67 percent probability that rates in one year will fall within one standard deviation of the mean (8 percent), or between a level of 7.2 and 8.8 percent. Further, there is roughly a 95 percent probability that rates will fall within two standard deviations of the mean, or between a level of 6.4 and 9.6 percent.[1]

Exhibit 18–4 shows the relationship between volatility and the 67 percent confidence interval as a function of time. A higher volatility assumption implies a higher variation of yield levels, or a greater probability of large interest rate moves. In an environment where large interest rate moves are assigned greater probabilities, positive convex securities, which outperform less convex securities when interest rate levels change substantially, are more valuable. Therefore, investors should be willing to sacrifice more yield to obtain positive convexity in higher-volatility environments.

Exhibit 18–5 shows the probability distributions derived from various yield volatility assumptions for a one-year time horizon. A mean yield of 8 percent and a lognormal distribution of future interest rates are assumed in the exhibit. A lognormal distribution is used to assign similar probabilities to equal percentage changes in rates rather than equal

---

[1] Actually, the center or mean of the distribution will occur at the one-year forward interest rate, which may differ slightly from 8% depending on the shape of the yield curve. Second, a lognormal probability distribution of yields is generally used in practice. If rates are lognormally distributed, the 67% confidence interval will range from 7.24% to 8.84% ($8e^{-0.10}$ and $8e^{0.10}$).

Range of Yields within One Standard Deviation of Mean
(67% Probability Confidence Interval)

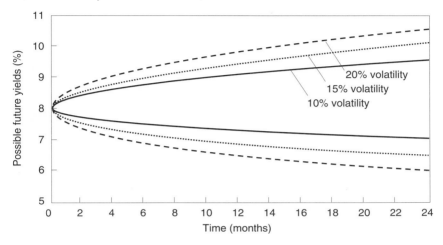

absolute changes. This distribution also has the desirable effect of making it impossible to assign any probability to negative yields in the future. According to the exhibit, a portfolio manager must have a volatility forecast of at least 15 percent to assign a significant probability (more than 5 percent) to rates changing more than 150 basis points in either direction in one year.

Weighted-Average Expected Return

Investors can better quantify the effect of convexity by looking at weighted-average expected returns (WAVERs). WAVER provides investors with an expected return that is based on assigning probabilities to a range of interest rate scenarios. The weightings are based on the probabilities of each interest rate move occurring given a selected volatility assumption. WAVER, however, is also a single point measure and may not fully reflect the return characteristics of the security being analyzed.

Exhibit 18–6 restates the one-year total returns of the three hypothetical securities, A^*, B^*, and C^*, whose yield differences offset their convexity differences. Weighted-average expected returns for each security are also provided for 10, 15, and 20 percent volatility assumptions. The

E X H I B I T   18–5

Scenario Probabilities: 1-Year Horizon

Yield Change	Annualized Yield Volatility				
	0%	5%	10%	15%	20%
−400 bp and below	0%	0%	0%	0%	0.10%
−350	0	0	0	0.03	0.47
−300	0	0	0	0.27	1.56
−250	0	0	0.05	1.32	3.71
−200	0	0	0.71	4.08	6.72
−150	0	0.04	4.15	8.66	9.83
−100	0	2.55	12.53	13.56	12.13
−50	0	24.50	21.98	16.58	13.03
0	100	46.83	24.57	16.56	12.48
+50	0	22.63	18.85	13.97	10.89
+100	0	3.28	10.54	10.24	8.80
+150	0	0.17	4.51	6.67	6.66
+200	0	0	1.54	3.94	4.77
+250	0	0	0.43	2.14	3.26
+300	0	0	0.10	1.08	2.15
+350	0	0	0.02	0.51	1.37
+400 and above	0	0	0	0.40	2.07

WAVERs are created by assigning probabilities, implied by the volatility assumptions, to each interest rate scenario. An investor expecting 15 percent yield volatility would be virtually indifferent among A*, B*, and C*. Therefore, 15 percent yield volatility is the break-even volatility among the three securities. Investors who expect higher than 15 percent volatility should purchase the more convex security A*, while those with lower volatility expectations should buy C*.

The yields of two securities with similar durations but different convexity characteristics suggest a break-even or "implied" volatility. This implied volatility is the volatility assumption at which the two securities will have the same WAVER. Investors who anticipate a higher level of volatility than the implied volatility effectively place greater

E X H I B I T   18–6

1-Year Total Returns of Securities with Varying Convexity and Yield

Interest Rate Scenario	(A*) Positive Convexity Low Yield	(B*) No Convexity Moderate Yield	(C*) Negative Convexity High Yield
−200 bp	31.3%	28.0%	24.7%
−150	24.3	23.0	21.7
−100	17.8	18.0	18.2
−50	11.8	13.0	14.2
0	6.3	8.0	9.7
+50	1.8	3.0	4.2
+100	−2.2	−2.0	−1.8
+150	−5.7	−7.0	−8.3
+200	−8.7	−12.0	−15.3
Yield Volatility	**WAVERs**		
10%	7.26%	8.00%	8.74%
15	8.00	8.00	8.00
20	8.58	8.00	7.42

probabilities on large interest rate moves than market pricing suggests. These investors therefore would find the security with more positive convexity relatively cheap.

Although all bonds that have fixed cash flows have positive convexity, the degree of positive convexity varies even among bonds of the same duration. Higher-coupon bonds have more positive convexity than lower-coupon bonds of the same duration. Exhibit 18–7 shows the modified duration of three Treasury bonds with similar maturities given various yield levels. The three bonds have the same duration at the 8 percent yield level. Furthermore, they all have positive convexity because their durations extend as yields decline, providing additional price appreciation. However, the higher-coupon issue, the 12s, has the highest degree of positive convexity, providing the most duration extension in a rally.

Modified Duration of Varying Convexity for Three Fixed-Maturity
Treasury Issues

	Coupon Rate		
Yield	0%	7%	12%
5%	5.00 years	5.11 years	5.18 years
6	4.98	5.05	5.10
7	4.96	4.99	5.01
8	4.93	4.93	4.93
9	4.91	4.87	4.85
10	4.88	4.81	4.77
11	4.86	4.76	4.69

Exhibit 18–8 graphically presents the return difference between the
30-year Treasury bond at the time of this analysis (8¾s of 5/15/17) and a
similar-duration zero-coupon bond (STRIPS). The 8¾s have a lower yield
but higher positive convexity. The 8¾s outperform the zero-coupon issue
when interest rates move more than 70 basis points in either direction.
Therefore, investors who expect a large move in rates, or a high level of
volatility, should prefer the more convex 8¾s. The effect of these convexity
differences, however, is relatively small and can be overwhelmed by yield
spread changes between the two issues. Convexity differences between variable-maturity and fixed-maturity securities of the same duration, however,
can have a more dramatic impact on returns.

Variable-Maturity Securities

Many fixed-income securities have uncertain maturity dates due to call or prepayment provisions. These securities have embedded options which affect the
prepayment of principal and account for their asymmetric return patterns or
convexity. GNMA securities, for example, have an implicit short call option
position. The homeowner has the option to prepay the mortgage loan at any
time. If interest rates decline, homeowners may find it economical to refinance
their mortgages and will, in effect, "call" the loan from the investor. This prepayment option reduces the upside potential of the mortgage security.

Although GNMA securities are U.S. government guaranteed, they
often provide significantly higher yields than Treasury securities to com-

E X H I B I T   18–8

30-Year Treasury* versus Similar-Duration STRIPS
(1-Year Horizon)

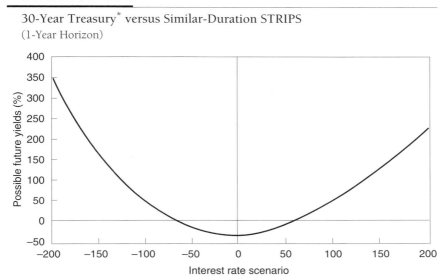

* 30-year Treasury bond at the time of this analysis was the 8 3/4s of 5/15/17.

pensate investors for the embedded short call options. Due to these embedded options, GNMAs have dramatically different return patterns than similar-duration Treasuries. Exhibit 18–9 shows one-year holding period returns of the current-coupon GNMA at the time of this writing and the Treasury seven-year over a range of interest rate scenarios. The current-coupon GNMA is expected to outperform the Treasury seven-year in stable and increasing interest rate environments, but underperforms dramatically as interest rates decline because of the embedded short call options.

When determining the relative attractiveness of GNMAs versus Treasuries, the portfolio manager must answer two separate questions. First, which pattern of returns best matches the investment objectives and market outlook? Second, are the embedded options fairly priced? Most prior analysis has focused on the second question, providing "option-adjusted spreads" to show whether or not the embedded options in GNMAs are fairly priced. The more important question, however, is whether or not the portfolio manager wants to be short call options and, consequently, short convexity. Portfolios heavily weighted in GNMAs will generally underperform in a market rally because of the embedded short call options.

E X H I B I T   18–9

1-Year Total Returns
(Current Coupon GNMA versus 7-Year Treasury)

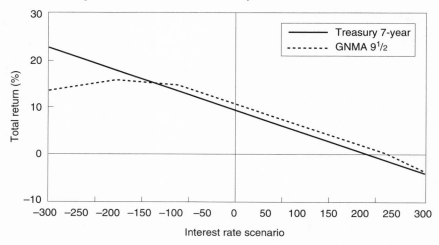

The availability of options and securities with embedded options provides the portfolio manager with the tools to mold portfolio returns. The portfolio manager can use these tools to create a return pattern that has the greatest likelihood of meeting his or her objectives. Given a desired return pattern, the manager must determine the cheapest way to obtain it. At that point, the question of whether or not the embedded options are "fairly priced" becomes more relevant.

OPTIONS

The asymmetry of the return patterns of highly positively and highly negatively convex securities is reminiscent of the asymmetric return patterns of options. The buyer of an option pays a fee to obtain an asymmetric return pattern in which losses are limited to the initial fee but profits are virtually unlimited. The seller of an option receives a fee to accept a return pattern in which the maximum profit is the initial fee but losses are virtually unlimited. Portfolios that are net long options have positive convexity, while portfolios that are net short options, implicit or explicit, generally have negative convexity.

Due to their asymmetric return patterns, options are excellent building blocks for reshaping portfolio return patterns. Options can be bought or sold to add and subtract potential returns in different interest rate scenarios.

For example, an investor who expects bond prices to be relatively stable could obtain incremental return in a stable environment by selling options. The sale of options reduces the returns of the portfolio in large interest rate moves, but provides additional returns if prices are stable.

The cost of purchasing options, or the cost of positive convexity, is highly dependent on market volatility. Volatility is a key input into the options pricing formula. Exhibit 18–10 shows the prices of six-month over-the-counter options on the Treasury 8¾s of 5/15/17 (the 30-year bond at the time of this analysis) given various volatility assumptions. In a 10 percent yield volatility environment, the cost of a six-month at-the-money call is $22^{23}\!/_{32}$, but in a 15 percent volatility environment, the price is 4 points.

The investor's decision about whether or not to purchase convexity in the form of options should be based not only on the absolute cost or volatility but also on the relative cost or volatility. If an investor can purchase the at-the-money call in Exhibit 18–10 at 4 points, an implied yield volatility of 15 percent, but believes that actual volatility will be 20 percent over the next six months, the cost of the option is relatively cheap.

Options allow portfolio managers to create the portfolio return patterns that best match their market outlook and investment objectives. Managers not only can adjust their duration based on their view of the direction of rates but also can adjust the convexity of their portfolios by buying and selling options. In this way, portfolio managers can create virtually any desired pattern of returns.

E X H I B I T   18–10

Premiums of 6-Month Options on Treasury 8¾s of 5/15/17[*]
in Varying Volatility Environments (Points and 32s)

Yield Volatility	2-Point Out-of-the-Money Call	At-the-Money Call	2-Point In-the-Money Call
8%	1–10	2–06	3–13
10	1–26	2–23	3–28
12	2–11	3–08	4–11
15	3–04	4–00	5–03
17	3–21	4–18	5–18
20	4–14	5–11	6–10
25	5–24	6–21	7–18

[*] 30-year Treasury bond at the time of this analysis.

OPTION STRATEGIES TO STRUCTURE
PORTFOLIO RETURN PATTERNS

In this section, we describe several option strategies that allow a portfolio manager to structure the pattern of expected total returns of a particular security. The first four are basic strategies that involve the buying or selling of either calls or puts in combination with a 30-year Treasury bond.

Second, we will examine strategies that entail the purchase or sale of both puts and calls in combination with a 30-year Treasury bond. These strategies dramatically alter the pattern of total returns and are an effective means of taking a position on the future level of interest rate volatility, independently of the direction of future interest rates.

Finally, we will provide an example of a strategy that combines multiple option contracts to create a pattern of returns that would be best suited for a manager with a specific forecast of both the direction and the magnitude of future interest rate changes. In this section, we will introduce the use of out-of-the-money options. Out-of-the-money options give the holder of the option the right to buy (calls) or sell (puts) the underlying security above (calls) or below (puts) the price of the underlying security. Options of various strike prices provide the manager with additional flexibility to mold patterns of returns to the desired shape.

Buying Calls

An investor who purchases call options pays an initial fee, or premium, for the right to purchase a specific security as a specified price for a given period of time. The investor's loss on the call options is limited to the initial premium, but the gain can be substantiated if the price of the underlying bond increases dramatically. Purchasing call options therefore creates an asymmetric return pattern with favorable returns in a declining interest rate environment. Exhibit 18–11A displays the payoff profile of a long call options on a 30-year Treasury bond.

Exhibits 18–11B and 18–11C show graphically and tabularly the return patterns of a 30-year Treasury bond combined with various amounts of long call options. The long call option position increases the upside potential of the portfolio but reduces the returns in stable and increasing yield environments. The long position in call options also adds positive convexity to the Treasury position and therefore provides higher expected returns in high-volatility environments and lower expected returns in low-volatility environments. For example, if a portfolio manager were to buy one call option for every two Treasury bonds (50 per-

E X H I B I T   18–11A

Payoff Profile: Long Call Option
(Buy: 6-Month 102–27 Call on Treasury 8³/₄s of 5/15/17[*] @ 4–00)

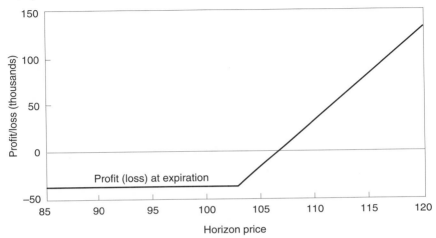

[*] 30-year Treasury bond at the time of this analysis.

cent), the weighted-average expected returns in 10, 15, and 20 percent yield volatility environments would be 2.84, 3.89, and 5.11 percent, respectively. A manager can increase the convexity of the portfolio by buying a greater percentage of call options in combination with Treasury bonds. The cost of this convexity is simply the premium paid for the call options, which is reflected in the lower returns in stable and rising interest rate environments.

Selling Calls

An investor who sells call options receives an initial fee or premium but is obligated to deliver a specific security at a specified price for a given period of time. The investor's gain on the short call option is limited to the initial premium, but the potential loss is virtually limitless. Selling call options therefore creates an asymmetric return pattern with favorable returns in a stable or rising interest rate environment. Exhibit 18–12A displays the payoff profile of a short call option on a 30-year Treasury bond.

Exhibits 18–12B and 18–12C show graphically and tabularly the return patterns of a 30-year Treasury bond combined with various amounts of short call options. The combination of Treasury bonds and short call options is commonly referred to as a *buy-write* or *covered call* strategy.

6-Month Total Returns of Treasury 8³/₄s of 5/15/17* with
Various Long Call Options Positions
(Options Position Expressed as a Percentage of Face Value)

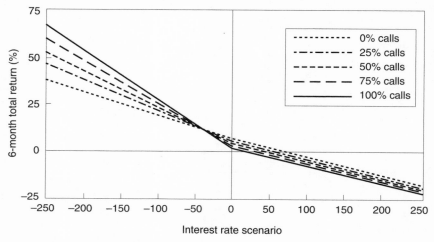

* 30-year Treasury bond at the time of this analysis.

A one-to-one combination (100 percent) is said to be *fully written*, while less than one call option per bond is referred to as *ratio writing*. The short call option positions reduce the upside of the portfolio but provide additional return in stable and rising interest rate environments. The short position in call options also reduces the convexity of the portfolio and therefore provides higher expected returns in low-volatility environments and lower expected returns in high-volatility environments. For example, if a portfolio manager were to sell one call option for every two Treasury bonds (50 percent), the weighted-average expected returns in 10, 15, and 20 percent yield volatility environments would be 4.13, 3.89, and 3.83 percent, respectively.

A manager can reduce the convexity of the portfolio further by selling a greater percentage of call options in combination with Treasury bonds. The compensation for selling this convexity is the additional return generated in stable and rising interest rate environments. At the extreme, a manager who writes calls against 100 percent of his or her Treasury bonds has effectively capped the upside return potential of the portfolio.

Buying Puts

An investor who buys put options pays an initial fee or premium for the right to sell a specific security at a specified price for a given period of

E X H I B I T   18–11C

6-Month Total Returns of Treasury 8¾s of 5/15/17* with Various Long Call
Options Positions (Options Position Expressed
as a Percentage of Face Value)

Interest Rate Scenario	0%	25%	50%	75%	100%
−250 bp	38.26%	45.70%	53.03%	60.26%	67.38%
−200	30.06	35.53	40.91	46.22	51.45
−150	22.64	26.31	29.94	33.51	37.03
−100	15.90	17.95	19.98	21.97	23.94
−50	9.77	10.35	10.92	11.48	12.03
0	4.19	3.42	2.66	1.92	1.19
+50	−0.91	−1.85	−2.78	−3.69	−4.59
+100	−5.57	−6.48	−7.37	−8.25	−9.12
+150	−9.85	−10.72	−11.59	−12.43	−13.27
+200	−13.78	−14.62	−15.46	−16.28	−17.09
+250	−17.39	−18.21	−19.02	−19.81	−20.60
Yield Volatility			**WAVERs**		
10%	3.47%	3.15%	2.84%	2.53%	2.23%
15	3.89	3.89	3.89	3.89	3.89
20	4.48	4.80	5.11	5.41	5.71

* 30-year Treasury bond at the time of this analysis.

time. The investor's loss on the put option is limited to the initial premium, but the gain can be substantial if the price of the underlying bond decreases dramatically. Purchasing put options therefore creates an asymmetric return pattern with favorable returns in an increasing interest rate environment. Exhibit 18–13A display the payoff profile of a long put option on a 30-year Treasury bond.

Exhibits 18–13B and 18–13C show graphically and tabularly the return patterns of a 30-year Treasury bond combined with various amounts of long put options. The long put option position reduces the downside of the portfolio, but also reduces the returns in stable and decreasing yield environments. The long position in put options also adds positive convexity to the Treasury position and therefore provides higher expected returns in high-volatility environments and lower expected returns in low-volatility environments. For example, if a portfolio manager were to buy one put

E X H I B I T   18–12A

Payoff Profile: Short Call Option
(Sell: 6-Month 102–27 Call on Treasury 8³/₄s of 5/15/17* @ 4–00)

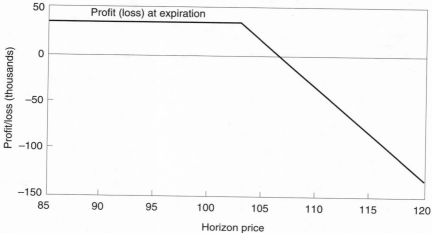

* 30-year Treasury bond at the time of this analysis.

E X H I B I T   18–12B

6-Month Total Returns of Treasury 8³/₄s of 5/15/17* with
Various Short Call Option Positions
(Option Position Expressed as a Percentage of Face Value)

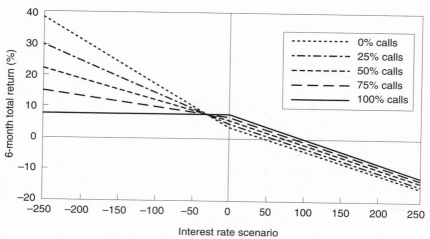

* 30-year Treasury bond at the time of this analysis.

E X H I B I T   18–12C

6-Month Total Returns of Treasury 8¾s of 5/15/17* with Various Short
Call Option Positions (Option Position Expressed
as a Percentage of Face Value)

Interest Rate Scenario	0%	25%	50%	75%	100%
−250 bp	38.26%	30.71%	23.04%	15.26%	7.36%
−200	30.06	24.51	18.88	13.16	7.36
−150	22.64	18.90	15.11	11.27	7.36
−100	15.90	13.81	11.69	9.55	7.36
−50	9.77	9.18	8.59	7.98	7.37
0	4.19	4.96	5.75	6.56	7.37
+50	−0.91	0.04	1.01	1.99	2.99
+100	−5.57	−4.66	−3.72	−2.77	−1.81
+150	−9.85	−8.96	−8.06	−7.15	−6.22
+200	−13.78	−12.92	−12.05	−11.16	−10.27
+250	−17.39	−16.56	−15.72	−14.86	−13.99
Yield Volatility			**WAVERs**		
10%	3.47%	3.79%	4.13%	4.46%	4.81%
15	3.89	3.89	3.89	3.89	3.89
20	4.48	4.16	3.83	3.49	3.15

* 30-year Treasury bond at the time of this analysis.

option for every two Treasury bonds (50 percent), the weighted-average expected returns in 10, 15, and 20 percent yield volatility environments would be 2.83, 3.89, and 5.11 percent respectively.

A manager can increase the convexity of a portfolio by buying a greater percentage of put options in combination with Treasury bonds. The cost of this convexity is simply the premium paid for the put options, which is reflected in the lower returns in stable and declining interest rate environments.

Selling Puts

An investor who sells put options receives an initial fee or premium, but is obligated to buy a specific security as a specified price for a given period

Payoff Profile: Long Put Option
(Buy: 6-Month 102–27 Put on Treasury 8³/₄s of 5/15/17* @ 4–00)

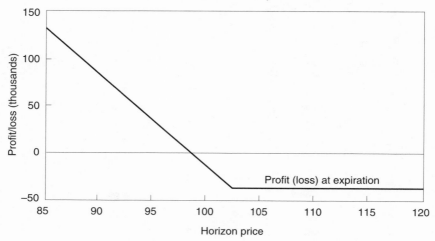

* 30-year Treasury bond at the time of this analysis.

6-Month Total Returns of Treasury 8³/₄s of 5/15/17* with
Various Long Put Option Positions
(Option Position Expressed as a Percentage of Face Value)

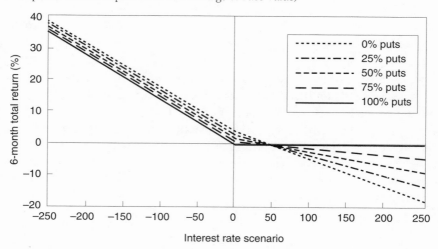

* 30-year Treasury bond at the time of this analysis.

E X H I B I T   18–13C

6-Month Total Returns of Treasury 8¾s of 5/15/17[*] with Various Long Put Option Positions (Option Position Expressed as a Percentage of Face Value)

Interest Rate Scenario	0%	25%	50%	75%	100%
−250 bp	38.26%	36.95%	35.67%	34.41%	33.18%
−200	30.06	28.83	27.63	26.44	25.28
−150	22.64	21.48	20.34	19.22	18.13
−100	15.90	14.80	13.73	12.67	11.64
−50	9.77	8.73	7.72	6.72	5.74
0	4.19	3.20	2.24	1.29	0.36
+50	−0.91	−0.79	−0.68	−0.57	−0.46
+100	−5.57	−4.26	−2.97	−1.70	−0.46
+150	−9.85	−7.43	−5.06	−2.74	−0.45
+200	−13.78	−10.35	−6.99	−3.69	−0.45
+250	−17.39	−13.04	−8.76	−4.57	−0.45

Yield Volatility	WAVERs				
10%	3.47%	3.15%	2.83%	2.52%	2.21%
15	3.89	3.89	3.89	3.89	3.89
20	4.48	4.80	5.11	5.42	5.72

[*] 30-year Treasury bond at the time of this analysis.

of time. The investor's gain on the short put option is limited to the initial premium, but the potential loss is virtually limitless. Selling put options therefore creates an asymmetric return pattern with favorable returns in a stable or declining interest rate environment. Exhibit 18–14A displays the payoff profile of a short put option on a 30-year Treasury bond.

Exhibits 18–14B and 18–14C show graphically and tabularly the return patterns of a 30-year Treasury bond combined with various amounts of short put options. The short put option positions increase the downside of the portfolio, but provide additional returns in stable and declining interest rate environments. The short position in put options also reduces the convexity of the portfolio and therefore provides higher expected returns in low-volatility environments and lower expected returns in high-volatility

E X H I B I T   18–14A

Payoff Profile: Short Put Option
(Sell: 6-Month 102–27 Put on Treasury 8³/₄s of 5/15/17* @ 4–00)

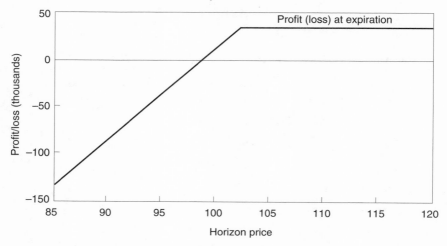

* 30-year Treasury bond at the time of this analysis.

E X H I B I T   18–14B

6-Month Total Returns of Treasury 8³/₄s of 5/15/17* with Various
Short Put Option Positions
(Option Position Expressed as a Percentage of Face Value)

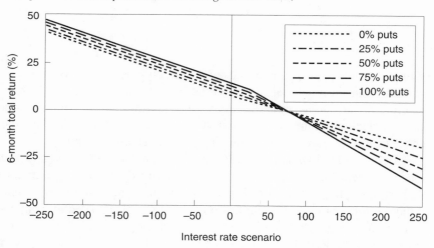

* 30-year Treasury bond at the time of this analysis.

E X H I B I T   18–14C

6-Month Total Returns of Treasury 8¾s of 5/15/17[*] with Various Short Put
Option Positions (Option Position Expressed as a Percentage of
Face Value)

Interest Rate Scenario	0%	25%	50%	75%	100%
−250 bp	38.26%	39.59%	40.95%	42.33%	43.74%
−200	30.06	31.31	32.59	33.89	35.22
−150	22.64	23.82	25.02	26.25	27.50
−100	15.90	17.01	18.15	19.31	20.49
−50	9.77	10.83	11.90	13.00	14.12
0	4.19	5.19	6.21	7.26	8.32
+50	−0.91	−1.03	−1.15	−1.27	−1.40
+100	−5.57	−6.92	−8.28	−9.68	−11.10
+150	−9.85	−12.31	−14.82	−17.38	−19.99
+200	−13.78	−17.27	−20.83	−24.46	−28.16
+250	−17.39	−21.83	−26.36	−30.97	−35.68
Yield Volatility			**WAVERs**		
10%	3.47%	3.80%	4.14%	4.48%	4.83%
15	3.89	3.89	3.89	3.89	3.89
20	4.48	4.15	3.82	3.49	3.14

[*] 30-year Treasury bond at the time of this analysis.

environments. For example, if a portfolio manager were to sell one put
option for every two Treasury bonds (50 percent), the weighted-average
expected returns in 10, 15, and 20 percent yield volatility environments
would be 4.14, 3.89, and 3.82 percent, respectively.

A manager can reduce the convexity of the portfolio further by selling a greater percentage of put options in combination with Treasury
bonds. The compensation for selling this convexity is the additional
return in stable and declining interest rate environments.

Buying Both Calls and Puts

Buying a straddle involves the purchase of both at-the-money calls and
at-the-money puts. The investor's loss on the straddle is limited to the ini-

tial premium paid for both the put and the call, but the gain can be substantial if prices change dramatically in either direction. Purchasing a straddle therefore creates an asymmetric return pattern that has favorable returns in very volatile environments. Exhibit 18–15A displays the payoff profile of a long straddle on a 30-year Treasury bond.

Exhibits 18–15B and 18–15C show graphically and tabularly the return patterns of a 30-year Treasury bond combined with various long straddle positions. The long option position adds positive convexity to the Treasury bond and therefore provides higher expected returns in high-volatility environments and lower expected returns in low-volatility environments. The long straddle position decreases total returns in stable environments but increases the returns in scenarios where interest rates change dramatically.

Selling Both Calls and Puts

Selling a straddle involves the sale of both at-the-money calls and at-the-money puts. The investor's gain on the short straddle position is limited to the initial premium received for both the put and the call, but the loss can be substantial if prices change dramatically in either direction. Selling

E X H I B I T   18–15A

Payoff Profile: Long Call Straddle
(Buy: 6-Month 102–27 Call on Treasury 8³/₄s of 5/15/17* @ 4–00)
(Buy: 6-Month 102–27 Put on Treasury 8³/₄s of 5/15/17* @ 4–00)

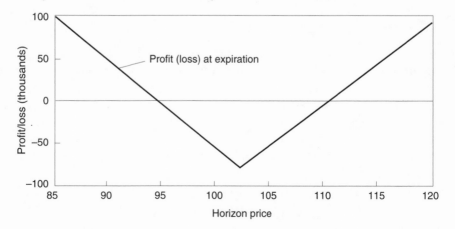

* 30-year Treasury bond at the time of this analysis.

6-Month Total Returns of Treasury $8^3/4$s of 5/15/17[*] with Various
Long Straddle Positions
(Option Position Expressed as a Percentage of Face Value)

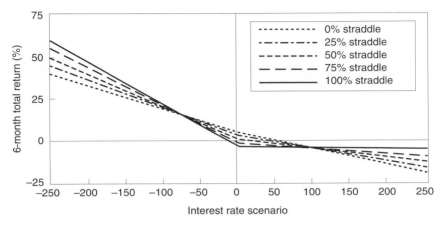

* 30-year Treasury bond at the time of this analysis.

a straddle therefore creates an asymmetric return pattern that has favorable returns in stable environments. Exhibit 18–16A displays the payoff profile of a short straddle on a 30-year Treasury bond.

Exhibits 18–16B and 18–16C show graphically and tabularly the return patterns of a 30-year Treasury bond combined with various short straddle positions. The short option position reduces the convexity of the Treasury position and therefore provides higher expected returns in low-volatility environments and lower expected returns in high-volatility environments. The short straddle position increases total returns in stable environments but decreases the returns in scenarios where interest rates change dramatically.

Multiple Option Strategy

Option strategies are not limited to the six strategies just discussed. The availability of different strike prices makes the number of possible option strategies virtually infinite. For example, one multiple option strategy involves the sale of a straddle and the purchase of a strangle. In other words, the investor sells at-the-money calls and at-the-money puts and purchases out-of-the money calls and out-of-the-money puts. An out-of-

E X H I B I T   18–15C

6-Month Total Returns of Treasury 8¾s of 5/15/17[*] with Various
Long Straddle Positions (Option Position Expressed as a Percentage
of Face Value)

Interest Rate Scenario	0%	25%	50%	75%	100%
−250 bp	38.26%	44.33%	50.21%	55.89%	61.40%
−200	30.06	34.26	38.31	42.24	46.04
−150	22.64	25.13	27.54	29.87	32.13
−100	15.90	16.85	17.76	18.65	19.51
−50	9.77	9.31	8.87	8.44	8.03
0	4.19	2.45	0.77	−0.85	−2.43
+50	−0.91	−1.73	−2.52	−3.28	−4.02
+100	−5.57	−5.17	−4.77	−4.39	−4.02
+150	−9.85	−8.32	−6.84	−5.40	−4.01
+200	−13.78	−11.21	−8.73	−6.33	−4.01
+250	−17.39	−13.88	−10.48	−7.19	−4.01
Yield Volatility			**WAVERs**		
10%	3.47%	2.83%	2.22%	1.63%	1.06%
15	3.89	3.89	3.89	3.89	3.89
20	4.48	5.11	5.72	6.30	6.86

[*] 30-year Treasury bond at the time of this analysis.

the-money call has a strike price higher than the current market price and
will be valuable only if prices rise above the strike before expiration. An
out-of-the-money put has a strike price below the current market price
and will be valuable only if prices fall below the strike price before expiration. Exhibit 18–17A displays the payoff profile of the combination of
a short straddle and a long strangle on a 30-year Treasury.

Exhibits 18–17B and 18–17C show graphically and tabularly the
return patterns of the 30-year Treasury with and without the option strategy described above. The short straddle produces more income than the
cost of the strangle, boosting returns in stable interest rate environments.
The option strategy performs poorly in moderate market moves (50 to
100 basis points), but is protected against large moves by the strangle.

E X H I B I T   18–16A

Payoff Profile: Short Straddle
(Sell: 6-Month 102–27 Call on Treasury 8³/₄s of 5/15/17* @ 4–00)
(Sell: 6-Month 102–27 Put on Treasury 8³/₄s of 5/15/17* @ 4–00)

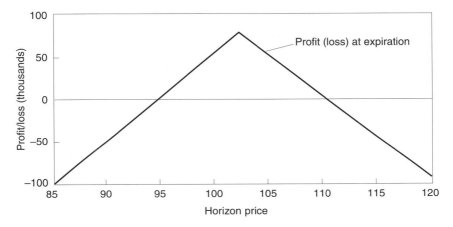

* 30-year Treasury bond at the time of this analysis.

E X H I B I T   18–16B

6-Month Total Returns of Treasury 8³/₄s of 5/15/17* with Various
Short Straddle Positions
(Option Position Expressed as a Percentage of Face Value)

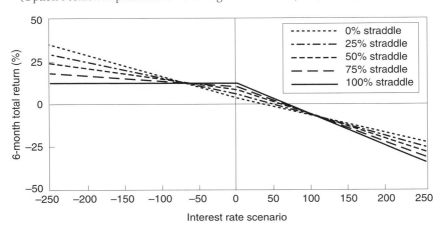

* 30-year Treasury bond at the time of this analysis.

E X H I B I T   18–16C

6-Month Total Returns of Treasury 8¾s of 5/15/17[*] with Various
Short Straddle Positions (Option Position Expressed as a Percentage
of Face Value)

Interest Rate Scenario	0%	25%	50%	75%	100%
−250 bp	38.26%	31.97%	25.47%	18.73%	11.75%
−200	30.06	25.72	21.23	16.57	11.75
−150	22.64	20.06	17.39	14.62	11.76
−100	15.90	14.92	13.90	12.85	11.76
−50	9.77	10.24	10.73	11.24	11.76
0	4.19	5.98	7.84	9.77	11.76
+50	−0.91	−0.07	−0.81	−1.71	−2.65
+100	−5.57	−6.00	−6.44	−6.89	−7.36
+150	−9.85	−11.43	−13.07	−14.77	−16.53
+200	−13.78	−16.43	−19.17	−12.02	−24.96
+250	−17.39	−21.03	−24.79	−28.68	−32.72
Yield Volatility			**WAVERs**		
10%	3.47%	4.13%	4.82%	5.53%	6.28%
15	3.89	3.89	3.89	3.89	3.89
20	4.48	3.83	3.15	2.44	1.70

* 30-year Treasury bond at the time of this analysis.

The strategy therefore allows the investor to take advantage of declining
volatility without the potential for virtually unlimited losses that the short
straddle alone has.

SUMMARY

A total return portfolio manager must look beyond duration and yield as
risk and return measures of fixed-income securities. Convexity, volatility,
and, most important, the specific pattern of returns with respect to interest rate movements are paramount in gauging the potential risk and return
of fixed-income investments.

E X H I B I T   18–17A

Payoff Profile: Short Straddle and Long Strangle
(Sell: 6-Month 102–27 Call on Treasury $8^3/4$s of 5/15/17* @ 4–00)
(Sell: 6-Month 102–27 Put on Treasury $8^3/4$s of 5/15/17* @ 4–00)
(Buy: 6-Month 108–27 Call on Treasury $8^3/4$s of 5/15/17* @ 4–00)
(Buy: 6-Month 96–27 Put on Treasury $8^3/4$s of 5/15/17* @ 4–00)

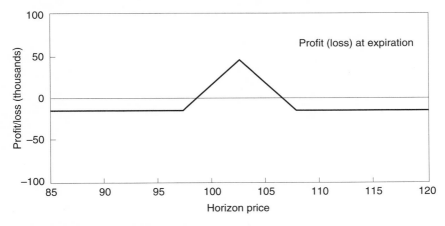

* 30-year Treasury bond at the time of this analysis.

E X H I B I T   18–17B

6-Month Total Returns of Treasury $8^3/4$s of 5/15/17* with Long Straddle and Short Strangle

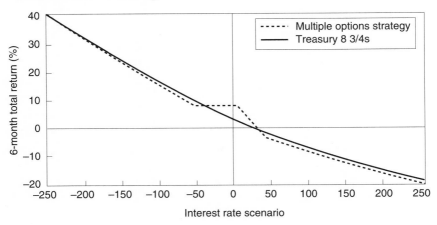

* 30-year Treasury bond at the time of this analysis.

E X H I B I T   18–17C

6-Month Total Returns of Treasury 8¾s of 5/15/17* with Long Straddle
and Short Strangle

Interest Rate Scenarios	Treasury 8 3/4s 5/15/17	Treasury 8 3/4s with Long Straddle and Short Strangle
−250 bp	38.26%	38.56%
−200	30.06	29.99
−150	22.64	22.23
−100	15.90	15.19
−50	9.77	8.78
0	4.19	8.04
+50	−0.91	−0.85
+100	−5.57	−7.26
+150	−9.85	−11.73
+200	−13.78	−15.84
+250	−17.39	−19.62

* 30-year Treasury bond at the time of this analysis.

All fixed-income securities exhibit some degree of convexity, positive or negative, which can greatly affect their potential risk and return. Fixed-maturity securities, for example, exhibit some degree of positive convexity, which is a valuable attribute that enhances the expected return of a security not fully captured by duration and yield. For fixed-maturity securities of the same duration, higher-coupon issues exhibit a greater degree of convexity than lower-coupon issues. The effect of convexity is magnified in variable-maturity securities such as callable corporates and mortgage securities. These securities contain embedded options, which can dramatically affect their expected returns. Conventional measures of risk and return, such as duration and yield, are of minimal value when analyzing variable-maturity securities and can be very misleading as portfolio management tools.

A prudent portfolio manager must look beyond single-point measures of risk and return and perform scenario analysis to expose the behavior of these securities in changing interest rate environments. Models that attempt to quantify the value of the embedded options within these securities can be helpful, but a manager should first determine whether or not the pattern of returns of a particular security is consistent with both his or her objectives and forecast of interest rates and future levels of volatility. Only then is the question of relative value of the embedded options valid.

Finally, total return portfolio managers should consider using options to create portfolio return patterns that reflect their views of both the direction and the volatility of future interest rates. Managers who utilize explicit options to structure return patterns are not confined by the availability of fixed-income securities that have embedded options. Thorough scenario analysis of various fixed-income securities and derivatives provides a better understanding of their behavior in volatile interest rate environments. Armed with the knowledge of the return patterns of individual securities, the portfolio manager can construct a portfolio that, compared to the benchmark, has an attractive return pattern.

19

⑥ COVERED CALL WRITING STRATEGIES

Frank J. Jones, PhD
Chief Investment Officer
Guardian Life

Beth A. Krumholz

Options are extremely flexible hedging and investment vehicles. A wide variety of strategies that are not only bearish and bullish but neutral can also be constructed via options. Further, these strategies can be constructed with either limited or unlimited profit and loss potentials.

This chapter describes a particular type of neutral strategy, a covered call writing strategy. For over two decades, managers of equity portfolios have generated additional income on their portfolios and provided some protection against price declines by writing calls on stock options against their stock portfolios. This strategy is particularly effective during times of relatively stable stock prices.

CALL WRITING

This chapter focuses on writing calls on the options on Treasury bond futures contracts against actual Treasury bonds and other closely related bonds, such as corporate bonds and mortgage-related bonds. Since the options themselves, however, are based on the Treasury bond futures contract, such covered call writing on actual bonds is an indirect strategy; options on Treasury bond futures are written against actual bonds. This complexity, the relationship between the Treasury bond futures contract underlying the option and the bond in the portfolio, is considered in the next section.

This section considers the covered call writing strategy in general as it applies against any underlying instrument, whether it be stocks, bonds, or futures contracts. The next section specifically considers writing calls on the Treasury bond futures options against actual Treasury bonds.

Specifically, this section summarizes various types of call writing; that is, selling calls against the instrument underlying the Treasury bond futures option itself: the Treasury bond futures contract.

Naked Call Writing

Naked call writing consists of writing or selling calls without having a related offsetting position in the underlying market. Exhibit 19–1 shows the profit/loss profile from only selling a March 70 call at a premium of 3 versus the price of the futures contract at the expiration of the option. It is important to note that this graph and the other profit/loss graphs in this chapter apply only at the *expiration of the option*, when no time value remains in the call premium. Assume that the price of the futures contract was 70 at the time the option was sold; that is, the call was at the money.

E X H I B I T   19–1

Naked Call Writing
(Short One Call)

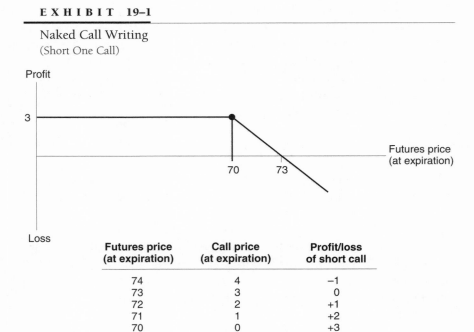

Futures price (at expiration)	Call price (at expiration)	Profit/loss of short call
74	4	−1
73	3	0
72	2	+1
71	1	+2
70	0	+3
69	0	+3
68	0	+3
67	0	+3

The naked call write in this example provides for a *limited profit* (of 3), if the futures price remains the same or declines (since the option expires worthless and the seller collects the initial time value of the option) and for an *unlimited loss* if the futures price increases (since the option seller will have to "buy" a futures contract at the higher market price and deliver it at the strike price of 70).

Writing a Treasury bond futures call without owning the underlying futures contract is called *naked call writing*. It provides for a limited profit (if the futures price remains constant or decreases) and an unlimited loss (if the futures price increases). Thus, this is either a neutral or bear strategy.

Covered Call Writing

Writing or selling a call while owning the amount of the instrument under-lying the call is called *covered call writing*. In the context of the Treasury bond futures option, a covered call write involves being short one call and long one futures contract.

The profit/loss profile for only the underlying long Treasury bond futures contract, priced initially at 70, is shown in Exhibit 19–2. It has unlimited upside potential (if the futures price increases) and unlimited downside potential (if the futures price decreases).

A standard covered write involves a combination of selling one call (a neutral/bear strategy) and buying one futures contract (denoted by 1/1—a bull strategy). Its profit/loss profile is a combination of Exhibits 19–1 and 19–2 and is shown in Exhibit 19–3, along with the profit/loss profile for the underlying long futures contract. As indicated in Exhibit 19–3, a covered write has a limited profit, the premium, if the futures price increases (since the option will be exercised and the call writer will "deliver" the futures contract he or she holds as cover) and an unlimited loss if the futures price decreases (since the call will expire worthless and there will be a loss equal in value to the difference between the strike price and the final level of the futures contract).[1] Thus, the covered write is obviously a neutral/bull strategy.

Ratio Call Writing

Covered call writing involves selling one call and buying one futures con-tract. A closely related strategy is called *ratio call writing*, in which more than one call is sold against an underlying long futures contract.

---

[1] Note that the profit/loss profile for a covered call (1/1) is the same as that for a short put.

E X H I B I T   19-2

Long Futures

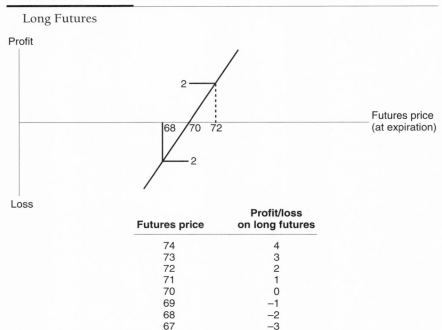

Futures price	Profit/loss on long futures
74	4
73	3
72	2
71	1
70	0
69	−1
68	−2
67	−3

The rationale for this strategy is based on the likely change in the call price relative to the change in the price of the underlying futures contract. This relationship is measured by the call's *delta*, which is defined as the ratio of the change in the call premium to the change in the underlying futures price. The delta for a call is less than or equal to 1.

At-the-money calls frequently have deltas approximately equal to 0.5 to obtain a completely *neutral* position between long futures and short calls—that is, a position for which a slight change in the futures price does not affect the profit/loss of the combined long futures/short call position—a number of calls equal to the reciprocal of the delta would have to be sold against the futures contract.

The profit/loss possibilities for long futures, short call, and short call/long futures (1/1) strategies are summarized in Exhibit 19–4.

A very common strategy, the *ratio write*, consists of selling two calls against one long futures contract. This covered write would be neutral if the call's delta were 0.5. Consider the results of a ratio write: The profit/loss profile would be a combination of Exhibit 19–3, a covered write, and Exhibit 19–1, an additional short call, and is shown in Exhibit 19–5. Since two calls are sold instead of one, the premium collected is

E X H I B I T   19–3

Covered Call Writing
Short One Call against Long One Futures Contract

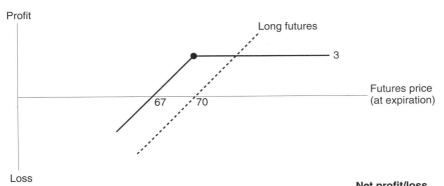

Futures price (at expiration)	Call price (at expiration)	Profit/loss on long futures	Profit/loss on short call	Net profit/loss on short call/ long futures
74	4	4	−1	3
73	3	3	0	3
72	2	2	1	3
71	1	1	2	3
70	0	0	3	3
69	0	−1	3	2
68	0	−2	3	1
67	0	−3	3	0
66	0	−4	3	−1

twice as great (6 rather than 3) as for a covered write. In either case, the amount of premium collected is equal to the maximum profit, which occurs when the underlying price at expiration equals the strike price.

Since the standard covered write (1/1) has unlimited loss potential if futures prices decrease and a naked short call has unlimited loss potential if the futures price increases, this ratio write, which is a combination of these two, has unlimited loss potential for either increasing or decreasing prices, but twice the profit potential (which is limited) as a covered call for stable prices. As shown in Exhibit 19–5, in this example, losses occur outside the futures price range from 64 to 76. Thus, this ratio write strategy is a neutral strategy; that is, it profits with stable prices, with unlimited loss potential for either price increases or decreases.[2] Thus, while a short call is a bear strategy and a covered write is a bull strategy, a ratio write is a neutral strategy.

---

[2] Note that the profit/loss profile for a ratio write is the same as that for a sell straddle, which is a combination in which both puts and calls are sold.

EXHIBIT 19-4

Summary of Strategies

	Futures Price Increases	Futures Price Constant	Futures Price Decreases	Type of Strategy
Long futures	Profit— unlimited	No profit/ loss	Loss— unlimited	Bull
Short call (naked call write)	Loss— unlimited	Profit	Profit— limited	Neutral/ bear
Short one call/ long one futures (covered call write)	Profit— limited	Profit	Loss— unlimited	Neutral/ bull
Short two calls/ long one futures (ratio [2/1] call write)	Loss— unlimited	Profit	Loss— unlimited	Neutral

Writing two calls against one futures contract is a basic theme in ratio call writing. An important variation on this theme is considered next.

Delta Neutral Call Writing

One-for-one and two-for-one covered writing strategies have been considered. As indicated earlier, if the reciprocal of the delta of the call is used as the number of calls sold, a neutral or completely offset covered call write will result, at least initially. This is called a *delta neutral*, or just a *neutral covered write*. In this case *small* changes in the futures price will cause completely offsetting profits and losses in the futures position and the call positions, and there will be no net profit or loss on the net position.

For example, if the delta of an at-the-money June 70 call on a futures contract is 0.67 (1/0.67 = 1.5), 15 calls will be sold against 10 futures contracts for a delta neutral covered write. If the futures price then increased from 70 to 71, the profit on the long futures position would be $1,000 times 10 contracts for a total profit of $10,000.[3] The short calls would then decline in value by 0.67 (since the futures increased by 1.0 and the call's delta is 0.67). So the total loss on the short calls would be 15 × 0.67 × $1,000 for a total loss of $10,000. Therefore, the net profit/loss would be zero; this is a neutral position.[4]

---

[3] Each 1.0 price change in the Treasury bond futures contract is worth $1,000.

[4] In practice, the delta would not remain constant with 1.0 moves from 70 to 69 or 71 in the underlying futures price, but his example assumes that the delta remains constant over this range to keep the arithmetic simple.

E X H I B I T   19–5

Ratio Call Writing
(Short Two Calls against Long One Futures)

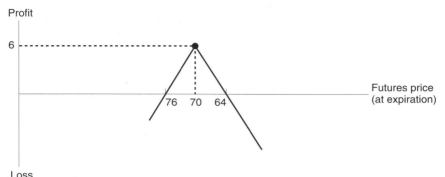

Futures price (at expiration)	Call price (at expiration)	Profit/loss on long futures	Profit/loss of short 2 calls	Net profit/loss of short 2 call/ long futures
77	7	7	−8	−1
76	6	6	−6	0
75	5	5	−4	1
74	4	4	−2	2
73	3	3	0	3
72	2	2	2	4
71	1	1	4	5
70	0	0	6	6
69	0	−1	6	5
68	0	−2	6	4
67	0	−3	6	3
66	0	−4	6	2
65	0	−5	6	1
64	0	−6	6	0
63	0	−7	6	−1

However, for large increases or decreases in the futures price, this position would not remain neutral. Why? Because for significant futures price increases or decreases, the call's delta increases or decreases, respectively. Specifically, if the futures price increases, the call becomes more in the money and its delta increases (toward 1.0 for the deep-in-the-money calls). If the futures price decreases, the call becomes more out of the money and its delta decreases (toward zero for deep-out-of-the-money calls). Thus, the initial weight of 15, based on the initial delta of 0.67, would be too low or too high, after the futures price increased or decreased, respectively, by a significant amount.

Consider the example summarized in Exhibit 19–6. The delta of a call at the initial futures price of 70 is 0.67. For small (by assumption) increases or decreases in the futures price, say, to 71 or 69, there is no

E X H I B I T   19–6

Futures Price Change, Delta, and Profit/Loss Position

	Futures Price	Delta	Hedge Ratio	Profit/ Loss on Future	Net Loss on Call	Profit/ Loss
Initial	70	0.67	15	—	—	—
Small	69	0.67	15	−10	+10	0
change	71	0.67	15	+10	−10	0
Large	60	0.60	16.67	−100	+90*	−10
change	80	0.80	12.50	+100	−120†	−20

* (.6 × 15 × 10)

† (.8 × 15 × 10)

incremental profit or loss on the overall position; profits or losses on the long futures are offset by equal losses or profits on the short calls.

However, if larger changes in the futures price occur, the call's delta will change, increasing as the futures price increases, and vice versa. If the hedge ratio of 15, based on the original delta, 0.67, is used, it will then be inappropriate for significant futures price changes in either direction. Also, in either case, as shown in Exhibit 19–6, there will be an incremental loss in the long 10 futures/short 15 call position.

Thus, the maximum profit occurs at the initial futures price, and small futures price changes do not affect the profit. But significant futures price changes in either direction cause incremental losses in the position.

Thus, to keep the position neutral against price changes, the number of calls will have to be continually changed as the futures price increases or decreases and the delta increases or decreases. That is, to maintain neutrality as the futures price increases, some calls will have to be liquidated, and if the futures price decreases, additional calls will have to be sold. The frequency of the adjustment of the positions must, of course, recognize transaction costs. The management of delta neutral call writes is considered in a later section.

In view of this discussion, it can be observed that a routine 2/1 covered write might be slightly bullish, slightly bearish, or neutral depending on the initial value of the delta of the call written.

Variable Ratio Write (Trapezoidal Hedge)

Typically, in covered, ratio, or neutral call writes, at-the-money calls are sold because at-the-money calls have the greatest time value. This is an obvious choice when the futures price is close to a call strike price. However, when the futures price is between call strike prices, instead of writing calls on either the nearest in-the-money or nearest out-of-the-money calls, there are advantages to writing calls on a combination of each, thereby straddling the futures price will call strike prices.

Consider the following example of a covered call write. Assume that the June Treasury bond futures contract price is 71, the June 70 call is priced at 4, and the June 72 call is priced at 3.5 (or $3^{32}\!/_{64}$, since call premiums are expressed in 64ths), written 3–32. Consider two cases:

1. A portfolio manager sells two June 70 calls against one June futures contract.

2. A portfolio manager sells two June 72 calls against one June futures contract.

Exhibits 19–7 and 19–8 provide the calculation of profit/loss profiles for these two covered writes. Note the equations for calculating the maximum profit and the downside and upside break-even points in the notes to the exhibits. The profit/loss profiles are shown in Exhibit 19–9, and the critical parameters of these profiles are summarized in Exhibit 19–10.

Given the initial futures price of 71, when writing the two in-the-money calls (70 strike price), the maximum profit is 7 (at the strike price of 70) and the range of profitability is from 63 to 77, from 8 below to 6 above the initial futures price. Thus, this strategy is slightly bearish, since its profit range extends farther on the downside than on the upside.

On the other hand, when writing two of the out-of-the money calls (72 strike price), the maximum profit is 8 (at the strike price) and the range of profitability is from 64 to 80, from 7 below to 9 above the initial futures price. This strategy is thus slightly bullish, since its profit range extends farther on the upside.

Implementing slighting bearish or bullish strategies is appropriate if this is consistent with the investor's outlook. Also, an investor who wanted to be somewhat more bearish or bullish (although basically neutral) could write two 68 or 74 calls, respectively.

But, as shown in Exhibits 19–11 and 19–9, to implement a perfectly neutral strategy (neutral in the sense that the profit range is symmetric around the initial price), the investor would write one 70 call and one 72 call against one futures position. This is called a *variable ratio write*. As indicated in Exhibit 19–11, there are three differences in this variable ration write from either pure June 70 call or June 72 call covered writing strategies:

E X H I B I T   19–7

2/1 Write with June 70 Call

Futures Price at Expiration	Profit: Call Price at Expiration	Long 1 Futures (@ 71)	Profit: Short 2 Calls (70 @ 4)	Net Profit: Long 1 Futures/ Short 2 Calls
78	8	7	2 × (–4) = –8	–1
77 (up)	7	6	2 × (–3) = –6	0
76	6	5	2 × (–2) = –4	1
75	5	4	2 × (–1) = –2	2
74	4	3	2 × 0 = 0	3
73	3	2	2 × 1 = 2	4
72	2	1	2 × 2 = 4	5
71	1	0	2 × 3 = 6	6
70 (max)	0	–1	2 × 4 = 8	7
69	0	–2	2 × 4 = 8	6
68	0	–3	8	5
67	0	–4	8	4
66	0	–5	8	3
65	0	–6	8	2
64	0	–7	8	1
63 (down)	-8	0	8	0
62	0	–9	8	–1

Notes:

$$\text{Maximum profit} = \text{Strike price} - \text{Futures price} + 2 \times \text{Call price}$$
$$= 70 - 71 + 2(4)$$
$$= -1 + 8 = 7 \text{ (maximum profit occurs at the strike price)}$$
$$\text{Downside break-even point} = \text{Strike price} - \text{Maximum profit}$$
$$= 70 - 7 = 63$$
$$\text{Upside break-even point} = \text{Strike price} + \text{Maximum profit}$$
$$= 70 + 7 = 77$$

1. The maximum profit in the variable ratio write is less than that for either of the single strike price writes (6.5 versus 7 at a price of 70 for the 70 call and 8 at a price of 72 for the 72 call);

2. The maximum profit occurs over a range of expiration futures prices (from 70 to 72, the range between the two strike prices) rather than at a single price (70 for the 70 call and 72 for the 72 call).

E X H I B I T   19–8

2/1 Write with June 72 Call

Futures Price at Expiration	Call at Expiration	Profit: Long 1 Futures (271)	Profit: Short 2 Calls (72 @ 3.5)	Net Profit: Long 1 Futures Short 2 Calls
81	9	10	$2 \times (-5.5) = -11$	-1
80 (up)	8	9	$2 \times (-4.5) = -9$	0
79	7	8	$2 \times (-3.5) = -7, 1$	1
78	6	7	$2 \times (-2.5) = -5$	2
77	5	6	$2 \times (-1.5) = -3$	3
76	4	5	$2 \times (-0.5) = -1$	4
75	3	4	$2 \times 5 = 1$	5
74	2	3	$2 \times 1.5 = 3$	6
73	1	2	$2 \times 2.5 = 5$	7
72 (max)	0	1	$2 \times 3.5 = 7$	8
71	0	0	7	7
70	0	-1	7	6
69	0	-2	7	5
68	0	-3	7	4
67	0	-4	7	3
66	0	-5	7	2
65	0	-6	7	1
64 (down)	0	-7	7	0
63	0	-8	7	-1
62	0	-9	7	-2

Notes:

$$\text{Maximum profit} = \text{Strike price} - \text{Futures price} + 2 \times \text{Call price}$$
$$= 72 - 71 + 2(3.5)$$
$$= +1 + 7 = 8 \text{(maximum profit occurs at the strike price)}$$
$$\text{Downside break-even point} = \text{Strike price} - \text{Maximum profit}$$
$$= 72 - 8 = 64$$
$$\text{Upside break-even point} = \text{Strike price} + \text{Maximum profit}$$
$$= 72 + 8 = 80$$

3. The range of profitability is symmetrical around the original futures price (from 63.5 to 78.5, 7.5 below and above the original futures price of 71), making this ratio covered write a perfectly neutral strategy in this sense.

Profit/Loss Profiles for 2/1 Covered Writes
(Initial Futures Price = 71)

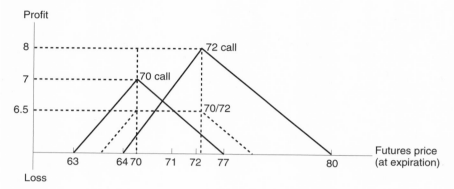

Overview

Call writing against a long position in the underlying instrument can be done in a variety of ways to give a variety of profit/loss profiles. The selection of the number of calls sold, and the choice of the call strike prices used are important decisions in implementing the strategy consistent with the investor's investment needs and view of the market. Continually managing these positions is also important.

WRITING TREASURY BOND FUTURES CALLS AGAINST TREASURY BONDS

Basics

The discussion in the previous section considered writing Treasury bond futures calls against the actual security underlying the option, the Treasury bond futures contract. But portfolio managers are more likely to write such calls against actual Treasury bonds, bonds that may or may not be deliverable on the Treasury bond futures contract, or other, closely related bonds, such as corporate or mortgage-related bonds.

This section considers writing options on the Treasury bond futures options contract against actual Treasury bonds. Writing calls against other types of bonds is very similar. In this application, three instruments are involved, directly or indirectly: Treasury bonds, Treasury bond futures contracts, and Treasury bond futures options, as summarized in Exhibit 19–12.

E X H I B I T   19–10

Critical Parameters

	(70 Call @ 4) Case (1)	(72 Call @ 3.5) Case (2)
Maximum profit	7	8
Price of maximum profit	70	72
Downside break-even price	63(–8)	64(–7)
Upside break-even price	77(+6)	80(+9)

To effectively implement such call writing strategies requires an understanding of the specifications of the Treasury bond futures options contract and Treasury bond futures contracts. A general summary of the contract specifications follows.

	Treasury Bond Futures Contract	Option on Treasury Bond Futures Contract
Denomination	$100,000	$100,000 (one Treasury bond futures contract)
Deliverable grade	Treasury bonds with maturity (or call, if callable) greater than 15 years	Treasury bond futures contract
Months traded	March, June, September, December,	Same as Treasury bond futures trading months (strike prices are in 2-point increments, e.g., 64, 66, etc.)
Trading unit	$\frac{1}{32}$ of 1% of par ($31.25)	$\frac{1}{64}$ of 1% of par ($15.63); ($\frac{2}{64}$ is valued at $31.25)
Last day of trading	Eighth to last business day of delivery month (1:00 P.M. EST)	First Friday (1:00 P.M. EST) preceding by at least five business days the first notice day for the corresponding Treasury bond futures contract (first notice day is last business day of preceding month)

Options on the Treasury bond futures contract are based on one Treasury bond futures contract. Upon exercise and assignment, the long call is assigned a long futures position at the call's strike price and the

E X H I B I T   19–11

2/1 Write with One June 70 and One June 72 Call

Futures Price at Expiration	70 Call Price at Expiration	72 Call Price at Expiration	Profit/ Loss: Long 1 Futures	Profit/ Loss: Short 1 70 Call	Profit/ Loss: Short 1 72 Call	Net Profit/ Loss
79	9	7	8	−5	−3.5	−0.5
78 (up)	8	6	7	−4	−2.5	+0.5
77	7	5	6	−3	−1.5	+1.5
76	6	4	5	−2	−0.5	+2.5
75	5	3	4	−1	+0.5	+3.5
74	4	2	3	0	+1.5	+4.5
73	3	1	2	1	+2.5	+5.5
72 (max)	2	0	1	2	+3.5	+6.5
71 (max)	1	0	0	3	+3.5	+6.5
70 (max)	0	0	−1	4	+3.5	+6.5
69	0	0	−2	4	+3.5	+5.5
68	0	0	−3	4	+3.5	+4.5
67	0	0	−4	4	+3.5	+3.5
66	0	0	−5	4	+3.5	+2.5
65	0	0	−6	4	+3.5	+1.5
64	0	0	−7	4	+3.5	+0.5
63 (down)	0	0	−8	4	+3.5	−0.5

short call is assigned a short futures position at the strike price. For puts, the long is assigned a short futures position at the strike price and the short is assigned a long futures position at the strike price.

To effectively write Treasury bond futures calls on actual Treasury bonds requires an adjustment based on the relation between the Treasury bond held and the Treasury bond futures contract. Consider the relationship between deliverable Treasury bonds and the Treasury bond futures contract. The Treasury bond futures contract is based on an 8 percent par coupon, 20-year Treasury bond. To adjust the invoice price for the delivery of other coupons (all coupons are deliverable) and other eligible matu-

EXHIBIT 19–12

Options on T-Bond Futures

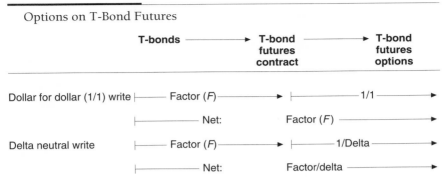

rities, the invoice price for the delivery of Treasury bonds is set equal to the futures settlement price times a conversion factor (F) provided by the Chicago Board of Trade.[5]

Thus, as is the common practice in futures hedging, to hedge $100,000 of Treasury bonds, F futures contracts are sold rather than one futures contract. This hedge ratio equates the gains or losses on the Treasury bond with the losses or gains on the futures positions.[6] The appropriate hedge ratio will be denoted by H.

Since the relation between the Treasury bond and the Treasury bond futures contract is determined by this hedge ratio, and the option is based on the futures contract, the number of calls sold on underlying Treasury bonds must also be adjusted by the futures hedge ratio. Thus, if to hedge $100,000 of a specific Treasury bond with Treasury bond futures contracts requires H futures contracts, H calls should be sold to do a 1/1 covered write on these Treasury bonds. To do a delta neutral covered write on this Treasury bond, a number equal to H/Delta calls would be sold. These relationships are summarized in Exhibit 19–12.

---

[5] This conversion factor equals the price at which the deliverable bond, with the deliverable bond's coupon and maturity, yields 8% times 0.01.

[6] This adjustment applies precisely only to the cheapest deliverable bond on the futures contract. Several Treasury bonds are deliverable on the futures contract, but one is the cheapest to deliver by the short and is usually delivered. For noncheapest deliverable Treasury bonds, the conversion factor must be multiplied by the quotient of the dollar value of the price change due to a 1-basis- point yield change in the bond being hedged divided by the dollar value of the price change due to a 1-basis-point yield change in the cheapest deliverable bond to determine the hedge ratio.

Effect of Futures Convergence

Since Treasury bond futures options are based on Treasury bond futures contracts, the option premiums respond directly to changes in Treasury bond futures prices. Obviously, Treasury bond futures prices depend on Treasury bond prices (specifically, the price of the cheapest deliverable Treasury bond). Thus, Treasury bond futures option premiums depend indirectly on Treasury bond prices. However, the relationship between Treasury bond futures prices and Treasury bond prices—the difference is called the *basis*—must be considered in writing calls on Treasury bonds.

Treasury bond futures prices relate to Treasury bond prices as follows:

1. When the Treasury yield curve is upward sloping (long-term rates are higher than short-term rates), futures prices are less than cash prices and futures prices decrease the longer the maturity of the futures contract.

2. When the Treasury yield curve is downward sloping, futures prices are greater than cash prices and increase with maturity.

These results are shown in Exhibit 19–13.

At the maturity of a futures contract, the futures price equals the cash price (the cash price of the cheapest deliverable adjusted for the conversion factor, as specified in the futures invoice price). This process is called *convergence*. Thus, as convergence occurs, Treasury bond futures prices increase relative to Treasury bond prices with an upward-sloping yield curve, and vice versa. Futures price increases cause losses to short futures positions and gains to long futures positions.

E X H I B I T   19–13

Futures/Cash Price Relationships

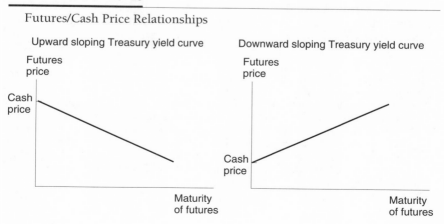

Short calls, if exercised, are assigned short futures contracts. Thus, with an upward-sloping yield curve, convergence leads to an increase in the call premium and a loss to sellers of calls. Another way to express this phenomenon is that with an upward-sloping yield curve, if cash prices remain constant, futures prices increase and thus call premiums increase, causing a loss to writers of calls.

This is an important result for call writers. The convergence that occurs between Treasury bonds and Treasury bond futures (with an upward-sloping yield curve) causes premium increases and, as a result, losses to covered call writers. Such losses tend to offset the profits that accrue to the call writers (sellers) due to the decrease in time value.

With an upward-sloping yield curve, convergence also causes losses in the two common forms of hedging or insuring fixed-income securities, selling futures and buying puts. Thus, with an upward- sloping yield curve, convergence works against the three common forms of hedging, insuring or generating income from a fixed-income portfolio.

Of course, with a negatively sloped yield curve, futures prices decrease relative to cash prices due to convergence, causing premium decreases and profits to call writers. With a negatively sloped yield curve, convergence similarly benefits those who sell futures or buy puts.

Another intrinsically related relationship should be recognized in assessing the impact of convergence on the effectiveness of covered writing strategies with either positive or negative yield curves. Consider a positive yield curve for which convergence works against a call writer. The positive yield curve means that the long-term interest rate exceeds the short-term interest rate. Specifically, in terms of the Treasury bond held, this means that the coupon return on the bond exceeds the financing cost on the bond (explicit or opportunity cost), which is based on short-term rate. Thus, the longer the bond is held, the greater the dollar value of the excess return of the coupon return over the financing cost. Further, this increasing return countervails the negative effect of convergence on the short call; in fact, these two effects have the same antecedent. The positive yield curve causes both the convergence, which causes the loss to the short call, and the generation of an excess of coupon return over financing cost, and these two results tend to offset each other.[7]

---

[7] Of course, the futures contract convergence depends on the relationship between the coupon return and the financing cost of the cheapest deliverable bond, while the actual dollar gain from carrying the Treasury bond depends on the relationship between the coupon return and the financing cost of the bond actually held, and these two will not necessarily be exactly the same.

In a 1/1 covered writing strategy (on the cheapest deliverable Treasury bond), if the futures contract were accurately priced (on the basis of carry), these two factors would exactly offset each other, and the profit on a covered write would be due only to the compression of time value of the call premium. However, for a covered writing strategy in which more than one call is sold, there will be a greater negative effect from convergence than a positive effect from carrying the bond. There will thus be an offset to the premium compression of short calls.

This discussion applies in the opposite direction with a negative yield curve. But in general, a negative yield curve causes convergence, which benefits a call writer, but leads to a loss from carrying the bond, since the carry cost will be greater than the coupon return. The effect of cash/futures convergence on covered writing strategies should be recognized.

One other theoretical consideration should be recognized. While most theories have limitations, the theory for pricing options on stocks and other underlying instruments is generally thought to be accurate. However, a widely accepted theory for determining the price relationship between an underlying and an option and the future on the underlying has not yet been developed. Thus, there may be more uncertainty in the delta used for delta neutral writing of calls on Treasury bond futures contracts on underlying Treasury bonds than for delta neutral call writing on stocks or other underlying instruments directly. This adds a risk to the covered call writing strategies.

MANAGING THE COVERED WRITE

Since most covered writing strategies have unlimited risk on either the upside or the downside, it is important to monitor and manage such positions. There are two important ways to manage a covered write: managing the strike price and managing the hedge ratio.

Managing the Strike Price: Rolling Down and Rolling Up

A common method of managing covered writes is rolling the strike price of the calls written down or up. This involves decreasing the strike price of the calls written if the underlying price decreases or increasing the strike price of the calls written if the underlying price increases. Rolling is achieved by buying back the calls previously written and selling new calls at lower or higher strike prices.

Consider, for example, the covered write consisting of selling two June 72 calls at 3.5 and buying a Treasury bond futures contract at 71 discussed earlier in this chapter. To be consistent with this example, consider again managing the covered write on a Treasury bond futures contract rather than on a Treasury bond. The 3.5 premium in this example is entirely time value, since the call is out of the money. As indicated in Exhibit 19–8, at expiration (when there is no time value in the call premium), the maximum profit is 8 at a futures price of 72. The downside and upside break-even points are 64 and 80, respectively. Of course, prior to expiration, the call would have some time value left, and the maximum profit would be less than 8 and the down- and upside breakeven points closer together.

Roll-Down

Consider the appropriate response to a decrease in the futures price from 71 to 67, as summarized in Exhibit 19–14. With a break-even range of 64/80, this covered call write is, after the price decrease, close to the downside loss area below 67 and thus is at this time a bull strategy. The covered writer may want to reestablish a neutral position and would accomplish this by rolling down to a lower strike price. This is accomplished by buying back (and liquidating) the two 72 calls at an assumed price of 1. Two 68 calls would then be sold at an assumed price of 2.5 to roll down to a 2/1 covered write with 68 calls, thereby reestablishing a neutral position.

As shown in Exhibit 19–14, at the liquidation of the 72 strike price 2/1 covered write, the investor has a profit of 1, which is the net of a loss of 4 on the long futures (from 71 to 67), and a profit of 5 on the two 72 calls (sold at 3.5 and bought back at 1). The decrease in the 72 call premium is due to a decrease in time value, which resulted from the passage of time, and to the call moving from at the money to out of the money.

The investor then sells two 68 calls at 2.5 to reestablish the neutral position. This new covered write has, at expiration, a maximum profit of 6 (at the price of 68) and break-even points of 62/74, thus being neutral given the current price of 67. While the covered write with the 68 call, with the futures price of 67, provides a break-even range of 62/74, which is slightly bullish, a slightly bearish situation would have resulted from rolling to the 66 strike price instead. A trapezoidal hedge (66/68) could, of course, give a neutral break-even range.

It is important to note that even though the break-even range of the original 72 strike price covered write was 64/80, these break-even points applied to expiration, when the 72 call premium had no time value

E X H I B I T   19–14

Roll-Down of Covered Write

A. Initial futures price = 71	B. Subsequent futures price = 67
72 Calls @ 3.5 (intrinsic value = 0; time value = 3.5)	72 calls @ 1.0 (intrinsic value = 0; time value = 1.0)
	68 calls @ 2.5 (intrinsic value = 0; time value = 2.5)
	Roll-down:
Sell two 72 calls @ 3.5	Buy two 72 calls @ 1 Sell two 68 calls @ 2.5 Profit/loss on initial covered write:
Maximum profit = 8 (at 72) Break-even points: 64/80	– Loss on futures = 71 – 67 = 4 – Profit on calls 2 × (3.5 – 1) = 5
	Net gain (loss) = –4 + 5 = 1 (profit)
	New covered write:
	Long 1 futures Short two 68 calls @ 2.5 Maximum profit: 6 (at 68) (68 – 67 + 2 × 2.5)
	Break-even points: 62 (68 – 6)/ 74(68 + 6)

remaining. In this example, the futures price had decreased to 67 prior to expiration and the 72 call premium still had 1.0 time value in it. Thus, at this time prior to expiration, if the futures price had declined to 67, the original covered write would have been not at a break-even, as it would have been at expiration, but at a loss of 2.0 as follows:

$$\text{Loss on futures: } 64 - 71 = -7$$
$$\text{Gain on 72 calls: } 2 \times (3.5 - 1) = 5$$
$$\text{Net loss: } 2$$

Thus, prior to expiration, when the time value of the call premium has not completely collapsed, the break-even points are closer to the original futures price than they are at expiration. In this example, at the time prior to expiration considered, the lower break-even point would be 66 rather than 64.

E X H I B I T   19–15

Roll-Up of Covered Write

A. Initial futures price = 71	B. Subsequent futures price = 75
72 calls @ 3.5 (intrinsic value = 0; time value = 3.5)	72 calls @ 4 (intrinsic value = 3; time value = 1.0)
	76 calls @ 2.5 (intrinsic value = 0; time value = 2.5)
	Roll-up:
Sell two 72 calls @ 3.5	Buy two 72 calls @ 4 Sell two 76 calls @ 2.5
Maximum profit = 8 (at 72) Break-even points: 64/80	Profit/loss on initial covered write: – Profit on futures = 75 – 71 = 4 – Loss on calls 2 × (4 – 3.5) = 1 Net gain (Loss) = 4 – 1 = 3 (gain)
	New covered write:
	Long 1 futures Short two 76 calls @ 2.5 Maximum profit: 6 (at 76) (70 – 75 + 2 × 2.5) Break-even points: 70 (76 – 6)/82 (76 + 6)

Roll-Up

Now consider the management in response to an increase in the futures price from 71 to 75. This roll-up of the initial covered write is summarized in Exhibit 19–15. When the futures price increases from 71 to 75, the premium of the 72 calls correspondingly increases to 4, and there is a net profit on the initial position of 3 as follows:

$$\text{Gain on futures position: } 75 - 71 = 4$$
$$\text{Loss on 72 calls: } 2 \times (4 - 3.5) = 1$$
$$\text{Net gain: } 3$$

But at a futures price of 75, the 72 covered write strategy is no longer neutral, since its break-even points are 64/80.

To reestablish a neutral position, the writer may liquidate the two 72 calls at 4.0 and sell two 76 calls at 2.5. This new position has break-even points of 70 and 82 and is again approximately neutral. To be exact, it is slightly bullish. Rolling to a strike price instead of the 76 strike price would have provided a slightly bearish covered write position. Again, a trapezoidal hedge (74/76) would provide a neutral break-even range.

The profit from the initial covered write resulted in the decline in time value from 3.5 to 2.5 in the 72 call, which resulted from both the passage of time and the call moving from at the money to in the money. If the futures price had moved from 71 to 75 in a very short period of time, the premium would not have decreased as much due to the passage of time, and the profit of the initial covered write would have been less. In addition, as discussed for the roll-down, even though the break-even points for the initial covered write were 64/80, these break-even points applied to expiration, and thus, since the time at which the futures price was at 75 in this example was assumed to be prior to expiration, the break-even range at this time would be narrower.

To have the potential to roll a covered call down or up before a loss is incurred, it is desirable to have both the next higher and lower strike prices within the profit or break-even range. This is one reason for using a trapezoidal covered write: It broadens the profit range. But since the break-even points refer to expiration, even if the expiration break-even points include the next higher and lower strike prices, a quick and significant price increase or decrease may provide a price outside the profit range at that time.

The basic philosophy of a covered write is to profit from the reduction in the time premium of a short call, as it decreases over time, while the price of the underlying remains approximately the same. By rolling the strike price of the call down or up as the price of the underlying changes, there are two advantages. First, as indicated earlier, it allows the covered writer to reestablish a neutral position. Second, and more important, it allows the covered writer to buy back a call that has moved from at the money to either in or out of the money and sell a call that is at the money. This is beneficial for the writer, because at-the-money calls have the maximum time value; that is, they have greater time value than in-the-money or out-of-the-money calls. Thus, the covered writer is buying a call whose time value has declined for this reason and selling an at-the-money call with greater time value.

Of course, one way to respond to a quick and significant upward or downward move in the underlying price is to liquidate the covered write. This should be done if the basic view has changed and it is now expected that the underlying price will subsequently be volatile. However, if the basic view is that the underlying price will be stable at the new price, rolling up or down to reestablish a new neutral position may be appropriate.

Another aspect of neutrality, discussed earlier, concerns the hedge ratio, that is, the number of calls written against the underlying. This too can be managed as the price of the underlying changes.

Managing the Hedge Ratio

As discussed earlier, the neutrality of a hedge is affected by the number of calls sold. An initially neutral covered write is achieved by selling a number of calls equal to the reciprocal of the delta of the call. A 1/1 write is neutral/bullish as discussed previously, and selling a large number of calls against one underlying will be neutral to bearish. However, as discussed earlier, as the underlying price increases or decreases, the delta increases or decreases, respectively, and the initially delta neutral covered write is no longer neutral.

Thus, to maintain neutrality, the delta neutral covered writer should adjust the number of calls written as the underlying price changes. As summarized in Exhibit 19–16, as the underlying price increases, the delta increases. Thus, the number of calls held short should be decreased rela-

E X H I B I T   19–16

Delta Neutral Call Writing

In the limit, becomes a 1/1 write
(covered write)

                Underlying Price Increase
                • Delta increases
                • Hedge ratio decreases
                  (Emphasizes futures/bonds relative to short calls)
                        Liquidate (buy back) calls
                        Buy more futures/bonds

      Initial Price—Delta Neutral

                Underlying Price Decrease
                • Delta decreases
                • Hedge ratio increases
                  (Emphasizes short calls relative to futures/bonds)
                        Sell more calls
                        Sell futures/bonds

In the limit, becomes a naked write
(large number of calls relative to futures/bonds held)

tive to the amount of the underlying security held. To achieve this, calls can be bought (liquidating short calls) or more of the underlying asset purchased. In the limit, for a delta equal to 1 for deep-in-the-money calls, the writer will have a 1/1 or covered write.

On the other hand, as the underlying price decreases, the delta decreases and the number of calls that should be held short against the underlying should be increased. This can be accomplished by selling more calls or selling some of the underlying. In the limit, as the price decreases toward zero for a deep-out-of-the-money call, the delta approaches zero, the hedge ratio approaches infinity, and the covered write becomes a naked write (with a very large number of calls sold against the amount of the underlying).

The hedge ratio can be changed frequently, by buying or selling calls or the underlying, to adjust to changes in the underlying price. Frequent changes, however, lead to large commissions and may be time consuming. This trade-off must be considered.

While managing a covered write by rolling the strike price up or down and by adjusting the delta hedge ratio have been discussed separately, they are usually done together. In fact, a writer who had an initial delta neutral position and then decided to roll up or down due to underlying price changes, would use the delta of the new call sold to determine the number of calls at the new strike price to be sold (the hedge ratio). The writer would thus combine a roll and a hedge ratio adjustment.

While delta adjustment should always be made for a roll for a delta neutral strategy, delta adjustments can be made even without rolling to new strike prices, that is, at the same strike price(s). Whether or not making a hedge ratio adjustment without a strike price roll should be done depends to some extent on the width of the strike price intervals. The smaller the strike price intervals, the less the need for delta adjustment prior to the need for a strike price roll.

Protecting Profits

Protecting profits entails a covered writing strategy that has already accrued profits due to the passage of time and the stability of prices and the reassessment of the strategy to protect those profits.

Consider the covered writing strategy in Exhibit 19–7. Originally, two June 70 calls were sold for 4 when the underlying was priced at 70. The original break-even range was 63/77, and the maximum profit was 8 at the strike price of 70. Assume that as time passes, the underlying price decreases from 71 to 70 and the June 70 call premium declines to 2. Thus, at this time there is a profit of 4 on the position. The writer may wish to protect this profit while still attempting to gain the remaining 4 of the initial maximum profit of 8. This can be done by considering the present position as an initial position and initiating a new, incremental ratio writing strategy.

At this new initial position, the (incremental) maximum profit will be 4 ($70 - 70 + 2 \times 2 = 4$) and the break-even points will now be 66 ($70 - 4$)/74($70 + 4$). By considering the new position as an initial position and then considering only the incremental returns, having already incorporated the profits of 4, the incremental maximum profit will be 4 and the incremental break-even points will be 66/74. The covered write could then be closed out at either of these prices to lock in the previous profit of 4.

This example was for a 2/1 ratio write. If the call write had been a delta neutral write, the number of calls written could have been adjusted for the new delta of the call at this time also. If there had been a small change in the underlying price, but a profit was nevertheless realized, it may be desirable to roll down or up to a different strike price while using the narrower break-even points, which would lock in the accumulated profit. In addition, it may be desirable to roll back to a more deferred contract with the narrower break-even points. However, since premium collapse accelerates near expiration, it may not be desirable to roll back too soon.

Thus, by using such an adjustment, a manager can consider accumulated profits as if realized while continuing to attempt to realize incremental profits. The manager can continue to bring the break-even points closer together and finally roll into the next expiration series.

Overview of Strategy Management

Call writing is a strategy with many potential types of outcomes, depending on the particular application. Naked call writing is a bearish strategy; it has limited downside profit potential but unlimited upside risk. A (1/1) covered call write combines a short call (bearish) with an equal dollar value of the underlying (bullish) and is net a bullish strategy; it has limited upside potential but unlimited downside risk.

In a (2/1) ratio write, calls are sold with a greater dollar value than the value of the underlying held, in effect adding bearish naked calls to a bullish covered call. Ratio writes thus become neutral strategies. Ratio writes have unlimited upside risk (if exercised, the investor does not own enough underlying to deliver on the short calls) and unlimited downside risk (unlimited loss potential due to the decline in the value of the under-lying security). By selling additional calls, the profit of the call writing strategy if the price remains the same increases.

This observation related to the fundamental concept of call writing: profiting from the erosion of the time value of the call premium if the under-lying price remains the same (and the intrinsic value of the call premium remains the same). The more calls sold, the greater the profit from the ero-sion of time value. Further, this concept dictates that at-the-money calls be written because they have the greatest time value. In addition, at-the-money calls are most neutral in the sense of a symmetric break-even range. But by selling more naked calls, the profit/loss profile of the strategy changes.

An important aspect of a call writing program is its bullish/bearish sentiment, which relates to the range of probability with respect to the current price. This is illustrated in Exhibit 19–17.

Two factors determine the bullish/bearish inclination, the number of calls sold and the strike price(s) in the write. Consider the number of calls sold first. Obviously, in a ratio write, naked calls which are bearish, are added to a covered call; so the more calls sold, the more bearish the strat-egy. Thus, a 3/1 ratio write is more bearish than a 2/1 ratio write. Also, a ratio write based on the call's delta is neutral, at least at the initial price.

E X H I B I T   19–17

Bearish/Bullish Call Writes

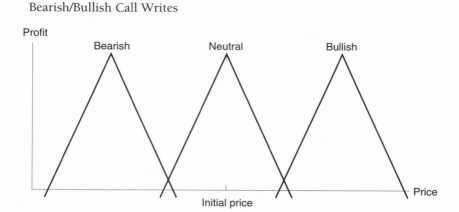

With respect to the choice of the strike price (or prices), the higher the strike price(s) of the call (that is, the more out of the money) the more bullish the strategy. Higher strike prices provide more profit potential on the upside, because they are less likely to be exercised for upward price moves, and, if so, only at the higher strike price. However, relative to at-the-money calls, writing out-of-the-money calls provides less premium, because the time values are less.

On the other hand, writing in-the-money calls makes the strategy more bearish but also provides less income due to time value than at-the-money calls. Thus, the choice of strike prices is an important decision in call writing strategies.

This section provides the basis for managing or altering covered writing strategies as the underlying price increases or decreases. Consider a call writer who initially establishes a delta neutral covered write with the at-the-money strike price call and plans to profit as the time value of the premium erodes. If the market moves up or down, there may be two outcomes:

1. The writer will not achieve the maximum profit, although he or she may still be in the profit range.

2. The writer will no longer have a neutral position but a bearish position (if the market moves up) or a bullish position (if the market moves down).

If the call writer wishes to reinstitute a neutral position (and ensure that there is no loss if the market continues in the same direction), two factors that affect bullish/bearish sentiment will have to change: the number of calls written (based on the delta) and the strike price of the call. Obviously, if the cash price moves up or down soon after the covered write is established, there will be little erosion of time value and thus little, if any, profit in the strategy.

As indicated above, the basic concept of covered call writing is to profit from the erosion of time value of the calls written with stable underlying prices. In this context, the profit/loss profiles throughout this chapter apply to the time of option expiration, when the time value had become zero. These profiles thus provide the maximum profit, since the time value erosion was at its maximum.

Obviously, for a short holding period, the maximum profit would be much smaller since the time value would not erode completely. Also obviously, if the underlying price moved up or down considerably soon after the covered write was established, there may be little profit; in fact, since the break-even points would be close to the initial price, there may even be a loss.

CONCEPTUAL OBSERVATIONS

"There's no such thing as a free lunch." In portfolio management, this aphorism is usually translated into the following statement about risk and return: "In order to increase the average or expected return of a portfolio, the variance of the return (risk) must be increased." When portfolio returns are described by a normal distribution, portfolios can be altered only along mean-variance lines. However, the options markets provide a way to expand the set of investment alternatives by increasing the range of return characteristics the investor can control. "Indeed, the range of returns that can be created through the use of the option markets makes the two-dimensional trade-offs of conventional mean-variance portfolio theory obsolete."[8]

The return distribution for portfolios is generally thought to be symmetric around the mean. But as options are added to a portfolio, the distribution can be changed into a number of different forms. The upper and lower tails of the distribution can be truncated, leaving the investor with little risk of a loss or little potential for a large gain, or a large portion of the probability distribution can be centered in a particular range, giving a high probability of receiving that range of returns. Writing call options on a portfolio provides a specific application of these concepts.

Several important observations can be made from studies of covered call writing strategies. The usual attraction of a covered call writing program is that it increases the probability of a moderate return; that is, the mode of the return distribution, as measured by the highest point of the probability distribution, is higher. But due to elimination of the potential for high gains, the mean return for a portfolio covered with short calls is lower. Thus, a portfolio with short calls has a higher mode, or most likely return, but a lower mean return due to the elimination of the potential for very high returns, that is, the truncation of the upper tail of the return distribution. But if the environment is thought to be one with a small probability of a prolonged price increase, covered call writing may be optimal.

Increasing the strike price (writing more out-of-the-money calls) increases the potential for larger returns, thereby reducing the degree of truncation of the upper tail. In addition, for more out-of-the-money calls, the level (return) of the mode is higher, but the probability of this most likely return is lower.

---

[8] Richard Bookstaber and Roger Clarke, "Options Can Alter Portfolio Return Distributions," *Journal of Portfolio Management*, Spring 1981, p. 63.

By comparison, the return distribution of a portfolio perfectly hedged with short futures contract will have a 100 percent probability of a specific return—a certain return. Theoretically, this certain return would be the risk-free rate. Both upper and lower tails will be truncated; but in practice, due to basis risk, there will be some variation in the return distribution. Further, the level and distribution of this return depend on the level of the futures price relative to the cash price at the time the hedge is put on.

Thus, the addition of options, in this case covered calls, to a portfolio can significantly alter the risk/return choice pattern usually considered to be confined to normally distributed portfolio returns. But this broader range of choices makes even more important the specification of the portfolio manager's investment goals regarding risk and return.

SUMMARY

Equity managers have been using covered call writing strategies as a means of enhancing the yield on their portfolios and providing a degree of downside protection since the advent of exchange-traded calls on stocks in 1973. With the introduction of options on the liquid Treasury bond futures contract during 1982, fixed-income portfolio managers can now accomplish the same objectives.

However, as explained in this chapter, while covered call writing is basically a neutral strategy, its degree of neutrality or bullishness/bearishness can be affected by the number of calls written against the underlying bonds and the strike price(s) of the calls written.

The first section of this chapter discussed some of the fundamental concepts of covered call writing that apply to stock options as well as Treasury bond futures options. The second section discussed the special considerations in using the Treasury bond futures options to write calls on specific Treasury bonds and related general covered call writing concepts to writing Treasury bond futures calls on specific Treasury bonds.

The third section discussed the management of covered call writing strategies, which is very important since all covered writes have unlimited loss potential in at least one market direction and some in both market directions.

Before engaging in a covered call writing program, however, the purpose of such a program should be clear. First, covered call writing should not be done to hedge a bond or a bond portfolio. Short futures and long puts are hedges in that they limit the maximum loss of a bond or a bond portfolio, although in different ways. Writing calls against a bond or a bond portfolio does not limit the loss; in a declining market the loss in a covered call portfolio is unlimited.

Rather, covered call writing is a yield enhancement strategy for an expected neutral environment. In rapidly rising markets, covered call writing strategies are not optimal because the maximum appreciation that can be experienced is determined by the strike price of the calls written (plus the initial time value of the premium). In declining markets, the underlying asset held depreciates in price and, while the loss in the value of the asset held is mitigated by the initial value of the call premium, there is nevertheless an unlimited loss on the bond or portfolio.

In stable markets, however, the covered call writer experiences neither the actual loss on the portfolio, due to a declining market, nor the opportunity loss due to not participating to the limit of a rising market; rather, the writer benefits from the premium received from selling the calls. If the underlying price remains stable and there is no increase in the volatility of the call, the passage of time will lead to a reduction in the time value of the call premium and a profit in the calls sold. This is the basis for profiting from covered call writing: to realize the profit from the decrease in the time value component of the premium due to the passage of time.

The risks of covered call writing strategies are

1. An increase in the market price, leading to a loss on the call (and an exercise of the call).
2. A decrease in the market price, leading to a loss on the underlying asset.
3. A significant move in the market price in either direction soon after the covered write is initiated, leading to a loss.
4. An increase in the implied volatility in the call, leading to an increase in the call premium and a loss on the calls sold.
5. The use of a delta in delta neutral covered writing that is too high or too low.

As indicated, however, covered call writing can be used as a means of yield enhancement in a stable environment and of reducing the variability of the return on the portfolio, not as a hedge. How, fixed income managers can use the same mechanism to achieve the yield enhancement/risk reduction results that equity managers have used extensively for at least a decade.

APPENDIX   19–A

Rate of Return on a Covered Write on a Treasury Bond

This appendix provides the method for calculating the rate of return on a covered write with the Treasury bond futures option contract on an actual Treasury bond. The formulas are as follows:

$$TI = PC_1 + AIP - NO \times OP_1$$
$$RCU = (PC_2 - PC_1) - NO \times IV$$

where

$$IV = \max ((FP - K), 0)$$

so

$$RCU = (PC_2 - PC_1) - NO \times \max ((FP - K), 0)$$

$$RR = \frac{RCU + AIE}{TI} \times \frac{360}{ND}$$

TI = Total investment
PC_1 = Initial cash price
PC_2 = Final cash price
OP_1 = Initial call price
OP_2 = Final call price
FP_2 = Futures price at expiration of call
NO = Number of calls written
K = Strike price of call
F = Conversion factor of bond
AIP = Accrued interest paid (at purchase of bond)
AIE = Accrued interest earned (over holding period)
ND = Number of days in holding period
RR = Rate of return (over holding period)
RCU = Return on call/underlying
IV = Intrinsic value of call at expiration

1. Out of the money (expires worthless) $OP_2 = 0$:

$$FP_2 < K$$
$$FP_2 - K < 0$$
$$\max((FP_2 - K), 0) = 0$$
$$RCU = PC_2 - PC_1$$

$$RR = \frac{RCU + AIE}{TI} \times \frac{360}{ND}$$

$$= \frac{PC_2 - PC_1 + AIE}{PC_1 + AIP - NO \times OP_1} \times \frac{360}{ND}$$

2. In the money (will be exercised):

$$FP_2 > K$$
$$FP_2 - K > 0$$
$$\max((FP - K), 0) = FP_2 - K$$
$$OP_2 = FP_2 - K, \text{ the intrinsic value, at expiration}$$
$$RCU = PC_2 - PC_1 - NO \times (FP_2 - K)$$

$$RR = \frac{RCU + AIE}{TI} \times \frac{360}{ND}$$

$$= \frac{PC_2 - PC_1 - NO \times (FP_2 - K) + AIE}{PC_1 + AIP - NO \times OP_1} \times \frac{360}{ND}$$

3. General

$$RCU = PC_2 - PC_1 - NO \times OP_2$$

$$\text{where } OP_2 = \begin{cases} FP_2 - K \text{ if in the money at expiration,} \\ 0 \text{ if out of the money at expiration} \end{cases}$$

$$RR = \frac{PC_2 - PC_1 + AIE - NO \times OP_2}{PC_1 + AIP - NO \times OP_1}$$

$$= \frac{(PC_2 - NO \times OP_2) - PC_1 + AIE}{PC_1 + AIP - NO \times OP_1}$$

(a) For out-of-the-money options, $OP_2 = 0$ and

$$RR = \frac{PC_2 - PC_1 + AIE}{PC_1 + AIP - NO \times OP_1}$$

For the cheapest deliverable, $FP_2 = (1/F) \times PC_2 < K$ at expiration. Thus, $PC_2 < (F \times K)$ at expiration for the call option to be out of the money.

(b) For the in-the-money option, $OP_2 = FP_2 - K$ and

$$RR = \frac{PC_2 - NO \times (FP_2 - K) - PC_1 + AIE}{PC_1 + AIP - NO \times OP_1}$$

$$= \frac{PC_2 - NO \times FP_2 + NO \times K - PC_1 + AIE}{PC_1 + AIP - NO \times OP_1}$$

For a dollar-for-dollar covered write, $NO = F$ and, since the factored basis (B) is $B = PC_2 - F \times FP_2$,

$$RR = \frac{B + NO \times K - PC_1 + AIE}{PC_1 + AIP - NO \times OP_1}$$

Observations

1. For out-of-the-money call options at expiration ($FP_2 < K$), the covered writer keeps the entire premium, OP_1; that is, the writer does not lose due to premium OP_2, since $OP_2 = 0$. There may be a capital gain of $PC_2 - PC_1$ but PC_2 can go up no more than to a level that makes the option at the money, that is $PC_2 = F \times K$. There may also be an unlimited capital loss.

2. In-the-money call options may be exercised at any time prior to expiration or at expiration. In this case $OP_2 > 0$, so this amount is subtracted from the return of the out-of-the-money result, and thus the overall return may be negative if it ends up suffi-ciently in the money. At expiration, OP_2 equals the intrinsic value ($FP_2 - K$).

The *AIE* refers to the actual period until exercise. At exercise, the covered writer (short call) is assigned *NO* short futures positions. The writer will then be short futures/long cash bond. The assumption is then that the writer liquidates the *NO* short futures positions (at $NO \times FP_2$) and the cash bond (at PC_2). It is for this reason that the factored basis appears in the *RR* equation.

(6) # CAPPING THE INTEREST RATE RISK IN INSURANCE PRODUCTS

David F. Babbel, PhD
Associate Professor
Wharton School
University of Pennsylvania

Peter Bouyoucos
Vice President
Morgan Stanley

Robert Stricker
Vice President
Citicorp

KEEPING RISK UNDER A CAP

During the past several years, interest rate caps have been increasingly sought by insurers. An interest rate cap is an agreement that provides protection against rising rates by making a payment to the holder when rates exceed a specified level. In this chapter, we consider a cap valuation and how cap strategies apply to other insurance products, such as SPDAs (single-premium deferred annuities), universal life, and single-premium life.[1]

All authors were employed by Goldman, Sachs & Co. at the time the paper was written. An earlier version of this paper was published by Goldman, Sachs & Co., under the same title, in March 1988.

[1] In an earlier paper on caps for insurers, we described how interest rate caps could be used to hedge the lapse and policy loan risk on whole life policies. See David F. Babbel, "Capping the Risks of Life Insurance Policy Loans and Lapses," *Insurance Perspectives*, November 1986, Goldman, Sachs & Co.

All these products contain an investment element, and the insurer has written a put option allowing policyholders to cash out of their policies based on book value rather than market value. An expected future cost has been incurred once the option is written, regardless of whether the insurer charges for it or chooses to hedge the risk associated with it.

In addition to these options on the liability side of the balance sheet, insurers write options on the asset side in the form of callable corporate bonds and mortgage securities. This combination of options typically places insurers in a short straddle position, as we described in an earlier paper on asset/liability management.[2] Economically, they are worse off if rates move too far in either direction. Because these options are often written out of the money, and because book value accounting tends to mask the underlying economics, insurers were comfortable with a short straddle in the past, when markets were less volatile. However, as volatility has increased, policyholders have become more sophisticated, and competition has become keener, insurers more than ever before now need to consider hedging their economic surplus against sudden, dramatic shifts in interest rates. This is especially pertinent to insurers doing business in New York because, as a result of Regulation 126, insurers are required to demonstrate the adequacy of their reserves under different interest rate scenarios.

The dramatic growth in recent years of interest rate–sensitive products makes it especially important for insurers to adopt an effective asset/liability management strategy. To offer competitive yields, the insurer typically feels a need to extend out along the yield curve. The policyholder is generally given the option, however, to cash out early at predetermined surrender values. While early cashouts are not expected to be a problem for moderate increases in interest rates, a sudden spike in interest rates, especially in conjunction with an inverted yield curve, could create a serious surplus strain from these products.

A simulation of results for a typical SPDA product serves to illustrate the impact of interest rate volatility. Exhibit 20–1 shows accumulated surplus over 5, 10, 15, and 20 years, based on 40 random interest rate scenarios[3] and using the 7 scenarios suggested by New York Regulation

---

[2] David F. Babbel, and Robert Stricker, "Asset/Liability Management for Insurers," *Insurance Perspectives*, May 1987, Goldman, Sachs & Co.

[3] The 40 random scenarios were generated by a two-factor equilibrium model of the term structure of interest rates originally proposed by Michael Brennan and Eduardo Schwartz in "A Continuous Approach to the Pricing of Bonds," *Journal of Banking and Finance*, 1979, pp. 133–55. They are considered more consistent with economic principles than the rather arbitrary New York Seven Scenarios. However, a more precise simulation would include several thousand scenarios. The scenarios and SPDA analyses were provided by Tillinghast, and are used with its kind permission. Goldman, Sachs performed the cap analysis using identical scenarios.

126 for comparison. While the upside is comparable using both sets of assumptions, the 40-scenario simulation clearly illustrates the downside risk that stems from granting options in a volatile interest rate environment. Important to note is the ability of caps to hedge this downside risk. The cap payoff can be managed so as to offset the negative surplus impact of high interest rate scenarios.

As Exhibit 20–1 indicates, interest rate caps appear to offer one solution to help hedge products with policyholder options against a large increase in interest rates. Consequently, we anticipate that purchases of these instruments by insurers will increase.

Among the many potential applications of interest rate caps, insurers can use them to

1. Hedge against book value cashouts and adverse selection on interest rate–sensitive products because of rising interest rates.

2. Hedge against the risk of rising policy loan usage on traditional, fixed-loan-rate whole life policies.

3. Offset a portion of the "negative convexity" risk of certain assets, such as high-coupon collateral PO's (principal-only strips) that may suffer from a slowdown in prepayments when rates are high.

E X H I B I T   20–1

Comparison of Accumulated SPDA Surplus and Cap Payoff

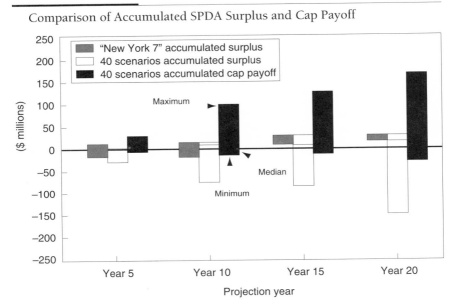

4. Protect a portfolio against an upward shift in interest rates, while allowing it to capture the upside of long bond returns if interest rates decline, that is, protect against the potentially negative consequences of going too long on assets relative to liabilities.

5. Tailor specific investment-related products that provide high current fixed rates of interest plus a guarantee of higher interest if rates move upward.

6. Allow for competitive crediting strategies on life products in rising interest rate environments for an insurer basing amounts credited on portfolio yield where the competition bases amounts credited on new money rates.

7. Hedge against any inflationary impact on property-casualty claims cost if short-term interest rates are related to inflation rates.

In the balance of this chapter, we will describe how caps work: what their specifications are, how they are valued, and how they can be used to hedge a bond portfolio and an interest rate–sensitive insurance liability.

DESCRIPTION OF INTEREST RATE CAPS

How Do Caps Protect?

An interest rate cap is a type of interest rate insurance contract. The buyer of the insurance pays a *premium* for protection against rising interest rates. The cap provides this protection in two different ways.

First, the buyer of an interest rate cap will receive payments from the seller, to the extent that the underlying interest rate index rises above a prespecified trigger level. The difference between this trigger level and the initial market level of rates can be thought of as the *deductible*. The greater the difference, the larger the deductible. This implies less protection and hence lower cost. For example, if interest rates are currently 8 percent and a 10 percent cap is purchased, rates would need to rise 2 percentage points before any payments would be received from the cap. If a 12 percent cap were purchased, rates would have to increase by 4 percentage points before any payments were received. Naturally, the 10 percent cap costs more than the 12 percent cap because the buyer is receiving more protection. As with any insurance contract, the trade-off among premium, amount of protection, and deductible is a function of your risk profile. The more risk averse you are, the greater the protection that you should purchase and the lower the deductible should be.

Payment protection is available with a specified frequency, such as quarterly, that corresponds to the buyer's particular liabilities. Cap payments, for example, can be used to credit higher dividends to policyholders when rates rise, thereby making existing policies more attractive and reducing lapses and withdrawals.

The second form of protection, market value protection, arises from the fact that caps are marketable instruments. An interest rate cap will increase in value with the level of interest rates. This is particularly useful in situations where liabilities can be "put" back to the insurer in high interest rate environments. The gain from the sale of the cap can offset a portion of the loss on currently held assets, which may need to be liquidated to fund the unplanned payout on the liability. The gain will also help reduce the need to use new cash flows to retire old liabilities.

Both of these features, payment protection and market value protection, are very important to life insurance companies.

Cap Contract Specifications

Interest rate caps, like other over-the-counter instruments, can be custom tailored to the particular needs of different buyers. By combining the various specifications, you can design virtually any level and pattern of protection (see Exhibit 20–2). The attributes you may specify include the following.

Underlying Index   Underlying indexes may include LIBOR, commercial paper, U.S. Treasury bills, and the prime rate. LIBOR and commercial paper caps are the most prevalent. The index will typically have a term of 1, 3, or 6 months.

E X H I B I T   20–2

Interest Rate Cap Contracts: Summary of Features

1. Contract type	Over-the-counter
2. Underlying index	LIBOR, CP, T-bills, prime (1-, 3-, 6-month rates)
3. Index reset	Daily to annually over term
4. Term of contract	3 months to 12 years
5. Strike level	Desired index level
6. Payment: Upfront	Percentage of notional amount
Amortized	Level payment over entire term

Frequency of Reset of Index The frequency of reset and the term of the index need not be identical, although generally they are. For instance, you could create a cap for a liability that floats off 3-month LIBOR and is repriced monthly. The determination of cap payments is made only on the actual reset dates. Reset periods range from daily to annually. When the reset dates are more frequent than the payment dates, the payment will be calculated based on the average of the underlying index on the reset dates.

Timing of Cap Payment Cap payments are typically made in arrears. For example, a standard 3-month LIBOR cap would have resets beginning on the effective date and ending 3 months prior to the maturity date. Payments on the cap would occur on each succeeding reset date (i.e., starting 3 months after the effective date and ending on the maturity date).

Term of Cap Agreement Interest rate caps typically have terms from 3 months to 12 years. The choice of term for the cap is based on the term of the underlying asset or liability being hedged, on the relative price of caps for various terms, and on the desired level of sensitivity to interest rates. Caps with longer terms will cost more and have greater dollar sensitivity to changes in interest rates than caps with shorter terms, all else being equal.

Strike Level The strike (trigger) level is the level of the underlying index above which the buyer receives payments. This will typically be a constant level for the life of the cap agreement, although this is not necessary. The higher the strike level, the higher the deductible. Since a higher strike level means the buyer must shoulder more of the risk of rising rates, this also implies a lower premium.

Notional Amount This is the underlying amount of principal on which cap payments are based. To fully cap the interest payments on a floating-rate liability, the buyer would purchase caps with a notional amount equal to the total liability principal. Alternatively, the buyer may want to provide partial market value protection, assuming that only a portion of the liability will need to be repurchased when interest rates rise. (This is often the situation when offsetting a put option that has been granted to policyholders.) In this case, the notional amount (as well as other features, such as the strike level or time to expiration) may vary over time. This may be constructed as a single cap or, more likely, as a series of individual caps layered on top of one another.

Method of Payment The buyer will typically pay the seller an up-front sum equal to a percentage of the notional amount. For example, if the underlying amount is $100 million and the associated premium is 2.5 percent, the buyer will pay the seller $2.5 million.

Alternatively, the payment may be amortized over the term of the cap agreement. This method of payment exposes the writer to credit risk and is reflected in the price. If the contract is sold before expiration, the original buyer will need to reimburse the original seller for the present value of remaining payments.

Credit Risk Since interest rate caps are over-the-counter agreements, the buyer must be careful to assess default risk in choosing an appropriate counterparty. Counterparties spanning a range of creditworthiness are usually available.

Cap Payoff Characteristics

If, on the reset dates, the level of the underlying index is above the strike level of the cap, the seller must make a payment to the buyer. The payment will be calculated using the following formula:

$$\left(\begin{array}{c}\text{Index} \\ \text{level}\end{array} - \begin{array}{c}\text{Strike} \\ \text{level}\end{array}\right) \times \left(\begin{array}{c}\text{Actual days} \\ \text{in period}\end{array} / 360\right) \times \left(\begin{array}{c}\text{Notional} \\ \text{amount}\end{array}\right)$$

Thus, if 3-month LIBOR is at 11 percent on the reset date, the strike level is 10 percent, the number of days in the reset period is 91, and the notional amount is $100 million, the seller will pay the buyer

$$(11\% - 10\%) \times (91/360) \times (\$100,000,000) = \$252,778$$

If three-month LIBOR is at 10 percent or below on the reset date, no payment is due.

Exhibit 20–3 shows average monthly levels for 3-month LIBOR from January 1978 through December 1987. The two horizontal lines represent 8 percent and 10 percent strike levels for hypothetical 10-year caps purchased in January 1978. Exhibit 20–4 shows the actual payouts for $100 million notional amount of such caps. As you can see, substantial payouts at the assumed cap levels would have occurred during 1979–82. Although the 8 percent cap pays out more frequently and in greater amounts than the 10 percent cap (as would be expected), the 8 percent cap's up-front premium would have been larger because of the lower deductible.

EXHIBIT   20–3

3-Month LIBOR from 1978 through 1987: 8% and 10% Interest
Rate Cap Levels

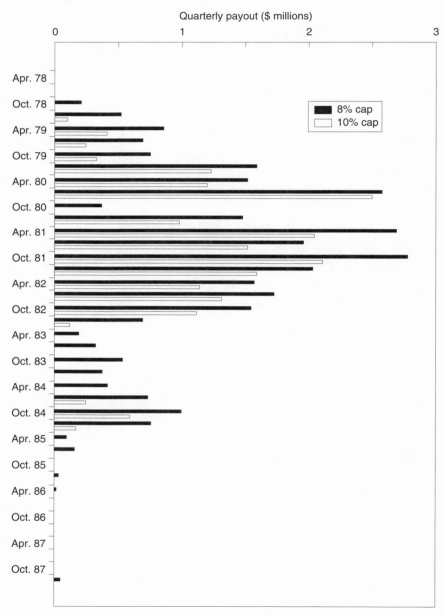

E X H I B I T   20–4

Hypothetical Cap Payouts from 1978 to 1988: 8% and 10% Interest Rate Caps (on 3-Month LIBOR), $100 Million Notional Amount

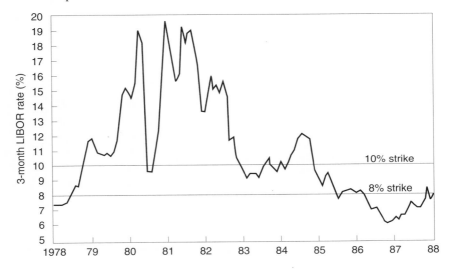

CONSIDERATIONS IN VALUING CAPS

An Interest Rate Cap as a Strip of Caps

How do the various contract specifications affect the value of interest rate caps? One way to think about this is to regard a cap of a certain term, such as 5 years, as a series of one-period caps. We depict this in Exhibit 20–5. A 5-year cap on an index that resets semiannually can be valued as nine separate caps, each covering different periods in the future. (Remember that there is no cap on the first period, since the interest rate is known when the cap is bought.) Because each potential cap payment occurs at different times, each with its own forward rate, a cap derives its value across the yield curve. This implies that the level and shape of the yield curve will be important determinants of cap values.

A second important point from Exhibit 20–5 is that the value of a cap should decline as it approaches maturity (assuming no changes in interest rates and volatility). Not only does the time value of each cap decline, but over time there are fewer and fewer 1-period caps remaining. This also means that, all else equal, longer-term caps are worth more than shorter-term caps.

E X H I B I T   20–5

Cap Value Equals Sum of 1-Period Caps: 8% Flat Spot Curve,
10% Strike Level

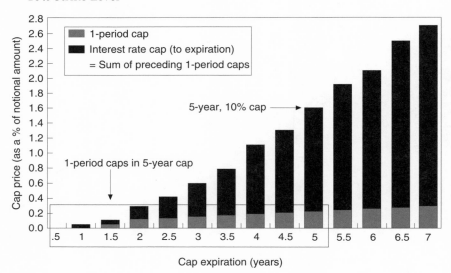

Cap expiration (years)

Impact of Expected Short Rate Volatility

Exhibit 20–6 portrays theoretical prices for caps of various terms and interest rate volatilities. Each line represents prices for various terms at each
level of volatility. The main conclusions are that (1) all else equal, greater
expected volatility is correlated with higher cap values, and (2) as a cap
ages, changes in volatility (as well as changes in interest rates) may have a
greater impact on value than aging alone. For example, a 5-year cap currently valued at 0.8 percent assuming 16 percent volatility (point A in
Exhibit 20–6) should theoretically be worth 0.65 percent in six months
(point B), but could be worth 1.0 percent (point C) if volatility increases to
20 percent.

Exhibit 20–7 shows historical volatility levels. It depicts a 40-day
rolling average volatility of 3-month LIBOR. Although a graph of
implied volatilities (i.e., implied in actual market prices) would be more
appropriate in assessing historical cap pricing, this chart is still useful.
In general, volatilities between 15 and 30 percent are not unusual for 3-
month LIBOR (although short periods with much higher volatilities
have occurred.)

EXHIBIT 20–6

Price versus Expiration Volatility: 8% Flat Spot Curve, 10% Strike Level

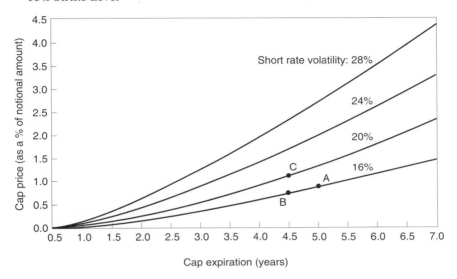

Cap expiration (years)

Impact of the Yield Curve

The general level of interest rates and the shape of the yield curve are important determinants of the value of caps. The unlimited number of combinations makes the precise impact quite difficult to summarize. However, if we focus on the "at-the-money" cap, an increase in the general level of interest rates should increase the value of the cap. The cap, in a sense, becomes more "in the money." The effect is directionally the same as lowering the strike level.

Steepening of the yield curve, while holding short-term rates at current levels for this same "at-the-money" cap, should also increase its value, all else equal. This is because a steeper yield curve contains higher implied forward short rates. The effect is to increase the degree to which future 1-period caps are near to or in the money.

Relationship to Interest Rate Swaps and Floors

Interest rate swaps are arrangements whereby parties "swap" interest payments. There is no exchange of principal. The most common type of swap is one in which the two parties exchange fixed for floating payments. For

EXHIBIT 20-7

History of 3-Month LIBOR Volatility: 40-Day Rolling Average

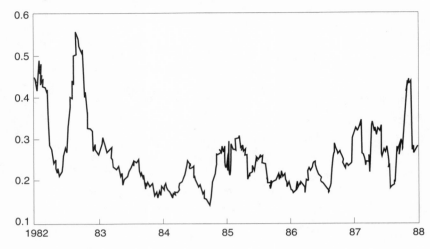

example, if the rate to swap 5-year fixed for 3-month LIBOR is 10 percent, the fixed payer will make fixed payments equal to 10 percent annually and receive 3-month LIBOR. (This is considered a "fair swap" if the 10 percent fixed rate, over 5 years, corresponds to a combination of forward 3-month LIBOR rates implied in the cap yield curve over the same period.)

Interest rate floors are like caps in that they are also interest rate insurance contracts. Unlike caps, however, floors provide protection against falling interest rates. Hence a floor on 3-month LIBOR with a 10 percent strike level entitles the owner to payments from the seller if 3-month LIBOR falls below 10 percent on reset dates. Such payments would be based on the notional amount and the difference between 3-month LIBOR and the 10 percent strike level.

You can create an interest rate floor by entering into a swap (pay floating, receive fixed) and purchasing a cap. The swap will entitle the floating payer to receive 10 percent fixed payments in exchange for floating 3-month LIBOR. The cap will make payments to the holder whenever 3-month LIBOR is above 10 percent. Combining the two positions, for rates above 10 percent, the net payout is always zero because the cap payment received plus the fixed receipt will exactly equal the floating payment due of 3-month LIBOR. For rates below 10 percent, the cap does not make payments and the net cash received equals the difference between the 10 percent fixed rate received and the floating index paid. This payout pattern, across all levels of interest rates, is the same as that of an interest rate floor.

The general relationships[4] among swaps, caps, and floors are

Cap = Floor + Swap (receive floating, pay fixed)

Floor = Cap + Swap (pay floating, receive fixed)

Thus, floors can either be purchased outright or created synthetically with a swap and a cap. Another implication is that the valuation of caps and floors is related to interest rate swap market levels.

Price Sensitivity of Caps

Interest rate caps are highly convex instruments with very large negative durations that are rapidly changing.[5] Because caps increase in value with interest rates in increasing amounts, this negative duration and positive convexity serve to cushion the decline in value as rates fall and to accelerate the increase in value as rate rise. This behavior is shown in Exhibits 20–8 and 20–9. These charts depict, for flat yield curves, the theoretical pricing of caps of different terms and strike levels. (Because the value of a cap also depends on a complex combination of volatility levels and the shape of the yield curve over the entire term, these simplified "price/yield" graphs can be misleading.)

Exhibit 20–8 shows the impact of term on price sensitivity. It shows caps of 3, 5, and 7 years with 10 percent strike levels across interest rates. Exhibit 20–8A shows cap prices as a function of interest rates for various maturities, while Exhibit 20–8B shows changes in cap prices for 100-basis-point moves in interest rates. We can discern some general relationships. First, for all levels of interest rates, longer caps are worth more than those with shorter terms, all else equal. Second, for all caps, the actual price change accelerates as interest rates rise (although the curve straightens out beyond the strike level) and decelerates as rates fall. This effect is more pronounced the longer the term of the cap.

Exhibit 20–9 isolates the impact of strike level on price sensitivity. It shows 8, 10, and 12 percent strike levels for 5-year caps across interest rates. In general, the lower the strike level, the greater the price and its

---

[4] These relationships hold most precisely for like term and strike levels and a flat yield curve.

[5] For a discussion of duration and convexity, see Frank J. Fabozzi, *Fixed Income Mathematics* (Chicago: Probus Publishing, 1988), Chapters 10 and 11.

Price Sensitivity by Term of Cap: Price versus Interest Rates

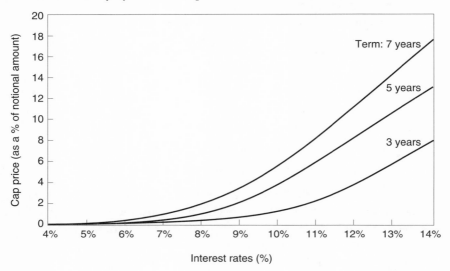

change across interest rates. In addition, as rates rise and the caps become more in the money, the change in price becomes close to linear.

These exhibits, although simplified by yield curve shape and volatility assumptions, are useful for understanding the price behavior of different caps. In particular, an asset/liability manager may determine that he or she will require about $10 million to offset a capital loss if rates rise to 11 percent. Based on assumptions about price sensitivity, the manager determines the amounts of 8, 10, 12 percent and layered combinations of 5-year caps that are necessary to reach the target. This is shown in Exhibit 20–10. If the hedge were initiated with interest rates at 8 percent, the cost of the hedge would vary inversely with the strike level. This makes sense, because the cap with a low strike level is more "in the money" and the probability of cap payouts is greater than for higher strike levels.

Another interesting point in this analysis is that for interest rate levels above 11 percent, the 12 percent caps become more valuable than the other hedge alternatives. This greater convexity of the 12 percent caps, compared with that of the 8 percent and 10 percent caps, is due to the greater amount of 12 percent caps needed for the hedge as a result of their lower dollar sensitivity.

Finally, the sophisticated asset/liability manager understands that the hedge will under- or overperform to the extent that the shape of the

Price Change versus Interest Rate Change

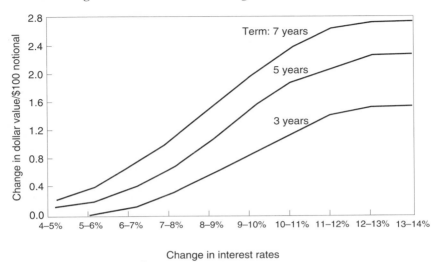

Change in interest rates

yield curve or the volatility changes during the hedging horizon. Thus, a cap position needs to be managed just as an immunized bond portfolio needs to be managed over time because of duration drift.

ADDING CAPS TO A BOND PORTFOLIO

Interest rate caps can have an impact on both the cash flow and market value of a portfolio over time. Exhibit 20–11A shows market values, over a range of interest rates, of an asset (7-year noncallable 9 percent bond) and of a combination of the bond with a 7-year, 10 percent strike level, interest rate cap. At 9 percent, the bond has a value of $100 and the asset/cap combination has a value of $100. The asset/cap consists of approximately $96 principal of the bond and $4 market value of the cap.

As rates fall below 9 percent, the 7-year bond steadily increases in value. The asset/cap also gains, although its value remains below that of the bond. This is because the cap value declines as rates fall, and the portfolio looks more and more like the bond with $96 principal. This "economic cost" is the upside potential forgone in exchange for protection against rising interest rates.

As rates rise, the chart becomes more interesting. Because the cap performs well in a rising rate environment, the asset/cap portfolio outper-

Price Sensitivity by Strike Level: Price versus Interest Rates

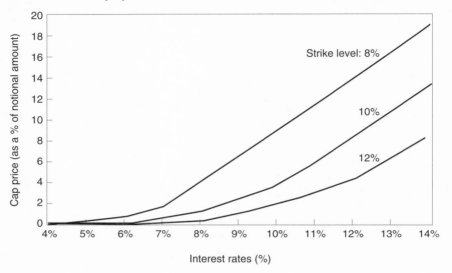

forms the bond.[6] Because the asset/cap portfolio is shorter in duration and more convex than the bond, it performs much better when rates rise.

In Exhibit 20–11B, we revisit the situation 4 years into its life. The asset is now a three-year bond, and the cap has 3 years remaining to expiration. Compared with the initial situation, the price/yield curves for the bond and asset/cap portfolios are much flatter.

Compared with Exhibit 20–11A, the asset/cap portfolio appears to perform below the bond for a much wider range of interest rates. This, of course, ignores any payments that may already have been received from the cap and assumes no change in expected short rate volatility, general yield levels, or shape of the yield curve. To the extent that these elements increase the value of the cap, the comparison would look much more favorable.

EXAMPLE: INTEREST-SENSITIVE LIFE INSURANCE

To illustrate the operational features of a cap hedge, we have selected an application geared toward single-premium whole life insurance. The

---

[6] An interest rate range of 4% to 14% is consistent with a much higher level of volatility. If the cap were purchased in a 9% interest rate environment and at a volatility of 20%, and if interest rates suddenly moved plus or minus 500 basis points, the asset/cap combination would be worth considerably more than is indicated in Exhibit 20–11A.

E X H I B I T   20–9B

Price Change versus Interest Rate Change

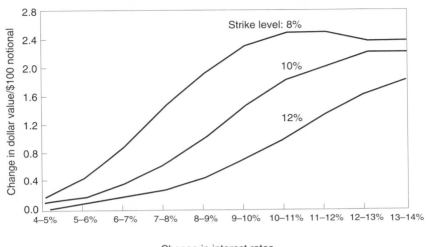

techniques discussed, however, can be modified and applied to other interest-sensitive and traditional life products to protect against surrenders from rising interest rates. We want to emphasize that hedging an interest rate-sensitive life insurance product is not an exact science. Not only must the option characteristics of the liabilities be approximated based on limited data, but the estimates of future cap payoffs are also subject to variation because underlying assumptions about volatility and shape of the yield curve change.

Consider a mutual insurer with a closed book of single-premium whole life business. Such an insurer may have a clientele that consists of a time-varying portion of policyholders who are sensitive (to different degrees) to interest rate spreads on competing products and another portion who are, for practical purposes, insensitive to interest spreads. When interest rates spike, some among the interest rate–sensitive portion of policyholders are likely to surrender their policies at the available cashout value and redeploy the funds obtained elsewhere. This action could potentially produce a drain on surplus if assets are liquidated at a capital loss to accommodate the cash demands of surrendering policyholders.

To avoid this potential surplus drain, the insurer can do one of two things. First, it can base amounts credited to policyholders (in the form of dividends and increments to cash values) on new money rates (instead of

E X H I B I T   20–10

Alternate Ways to Hedge Expected Market Risk at 11%: 8% Caps,
10% Caps, 12% Caps or Layered Combination

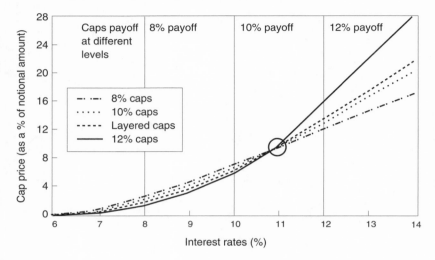

portfolio yield) to minimize surrenders during periods of rising rates. But
this has unfortunate consequences. To keep a segment of policyholders
from lapsing, the insurer must provide higher credited earnings to every-
body when market yields rise, not just to the group that is prone to lapse.
Moreover, unless the insurer has invested very short term, with the historically lower yields that such a strategy entails, it may be subjected to a
large divergence between the new money rate and the portfolio yield; that
is, the portfolio yield may be less than the new money rate on which dividends are based. This can have adverse economic consequences for the
insurer. But if it does forgo the higher yields from investing long term, its
policies may be unattractive during periods of steady or declining rates.

A second approach the insurer can take is to provide for sudden
lapses when rates spike by having investments that provide capital gains
when cash is needed most. One instrument available for accomplishing
this objective is an interest rate cap. The key insight to keep in mind when
using caps in such an application is that when a lapse occurs, a liability
goes off the books. Thus, a group of assets can also be liquidated. Unlike
the policy loan hedge, described elsewhere,[7] where periodic cap pay-

---

[7]   Babbel, "Capping the Risks of Life Insurance Policy Loans and Lapses."

7-Year Cap Hedge: Impact on Portfolio over Time
(Market Value at T(0)—over Changing Rates)

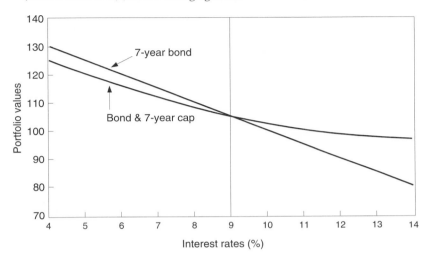

ments were relied on to offset entirely the lost interest on reserves placed in policy loans, a hedge against surrenders involves the liquidation of caps at their market value when cash demands require it. The caps are no longer required to hedge against surrenders, as a policyholder can surrender only once. In setting up an appropriate cap strategy, several steps may be followed. There are obviously varying degrees of fineness in the construction of an offsetting cap hedge, but the following steps are fundamental to any hedge strategy.

1. *Set up a time profile of policy reserves on existing business, assuming normal surrenders and mortality.* A hypothetical time profile of the total amount of policy reserves outstanding appears in Exhibit 20–12. Such a profile can be generated by company actuaries.

2. *Estimate the amounts of reserves over time that would be subject to abnormal lapse experience resulting from interest sensitivity—"hot money."* This is usually done by estimating the percentages of reserves likely to be subject to abnormally high lapses over time because of spikes in interest rates and multiplying these percentages by the amounts of policy reserves scheduled to be outstanding at each point in time. The resulting

E X H I B I T   20–11B

Market Value after 4 Years—over Changing Rates

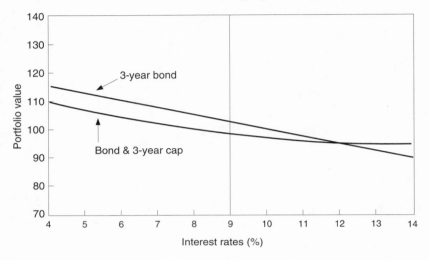

products form a time profile of "hot money" that will be on the books in the *absence of* an interest rate spike. Once spreads between yields implied by dividends/cash value increments and those available elsewhere become of sufficient magnitude, policyholders representing the "hot money" will begin to surrender their policies until ultimately only the lethargic portion remains. Exhibit 20–12 also portrays an example of a schedule of potential hot money.

3. *Determine the potential surplus drain associated with interest rate spikes of varying levels.* There are several ways to go about this step. A first, broad-brush approach is to compute the duration of assets supporting current and scheduled reserves at each point in time and then multiply the duration numbers by interest rate spreads that could give rise to excess surrenders. These products would then be multiplied by the amounts of hot money from the schedule of step 2 to give the total potential surplus drain at each point in time. Exhibit 20–13 provides an example, which shows loss exposure beyond what would be incurred from the first 100-basis-point rise in interest rates. (We assume the insurer is willing to absorb losses associated with a 100-basis-point upward move.)

Interest Spread Sensitivity Money Profile

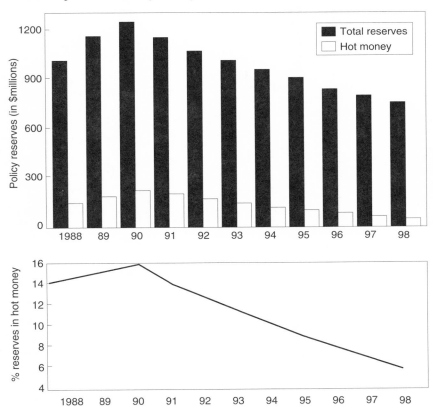

The broad-brush approach is likely to exaggerate the levels of potential surplus drain, as it ignores the convexity of assets.

A more refined approach is to compute the actual implied (as distinguished from duration-implied) capital losses on the portion of the asset portfolio that would need to be liquidated in the event of sudden cash demands from surrendering policyholders. These calculations would be made for various interest levels at various future times, take into account the evolution of portfolio value over time as assets came closer to maturity, and incorporate reinvestment assumptions. In the stylized example that follows, we took the more refined approach.

    4. *Construct a payoff matrix of caps having maturities that span the period over which protection is desired.* This step involves

E X H I B I T   20–13

Duration-Implied Exposure to Capital Loss* Due to Lapse

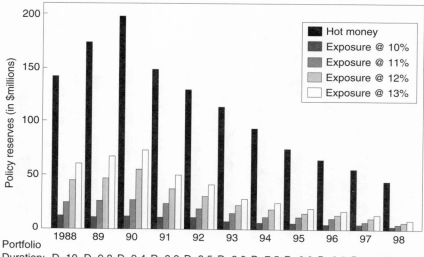

* Assumes insurer absorbs capital loss associated with first 100-basis-point move.

use of a cap pricing model, as the payoffs associated with a cap portfolio at any point in time include liquidation value as well as periodic payments. The payoff matrix would include the theoretical market values of caps at different interest rate levels with varying remaining maturities and different trigger levels. It would focus on how these values change under rising interest rates, and may include some periodic payment amounts as well. Exhibit 20–8 and 20–9 provide the type of information from which such a cap payoff matrix can be derived. Obviously, a good cap pricing model is required if the payoff matrix is to be viable. It is useful to include a few caps with trigger levels far out of the money, along with caps having triggers near those that engender surrenders, to hedge for any nonlinearities in the demand for cash.

5. *Select the cap combination that provides for payoff amounts from step 4 consistent with the potential surplus drain from step 3.* Several techniques can be used to accomplish this step, ranging from careful eyeballing and experimentation to sophisticat-

E X H I B I T   20–14

Cap Strategy: Purchases and Sales

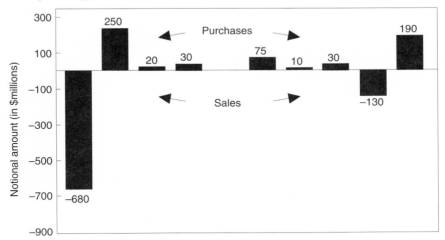

ed dynamic programming. To determine the cap strategy illustrated in Exhibit 20–14, we used an approach in between these
two extremes in complexity, based on a simple spreadsheet
backwards solution procedure. The procedure starts with buying
sufficient caps to protect against abnormal surrenders during the
final (10th year) period of the horizon.[8] These 10-year caps will
be more than adequate to hedge the potential hot money existing in year 9, so some 9-year caps are sold until the net amount
of remaining protection available in the 9th year is at the level
desired. The portfolio manager then looks at how much net protection is already on the books for the 8th year from the purchase of 10-year caps and the sale of 9-year caps, and either
buys or sells 8-year caps based on the difference between
desired and already existing cap protection. The manager follows this approach until reaching the current date.

---

[8] If the 10-year caps were bought with a trigger rate 100 basis points above the current rate, a notional
amount of principal close to the product of the projected duration and the potential hot money
would be sought. In the example, portfolio duration in the 10th year is projected to be 5.0
years, and potential hot money is $40 million; thus, a notional principal near $200 million
would be sought for 10-year caps. If the caps were bought with triggers further out of the
money, a higher notional principal would be needed.

E X H I B I T   20–15A

Exposure at 10% Interest Rates

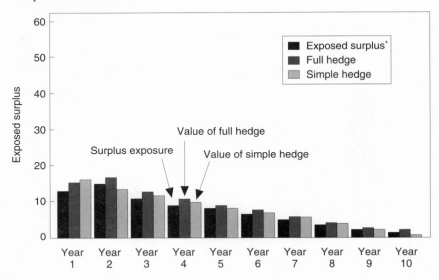

* First 100-basis-point move not included

The illustration involves buying and selling caps of maturities ranging from 1 to 10 years, all at trigger levels of 9 percent. We refer to this
strategy as a full hedge because it utilizes the full range of cap maturities
available and, apart from the first 100-basis-point rise in interest rates, it
aims at minimal surplus exposure. Exhibits 20–15A through 20–15D
show how well this full hedge strategy offsets the potential surplus drain
associated with expected policy surrenders resulting from future interest
rate increases. Exhibit 20–15A illustrates a 200-basis-point increase;
Exhibit 20–15B, a 300-basis-point increase; Exhibit 20–15C, a 400-basis-
point increase; and Exhibit 20–15D, a 500-basis-point increase. The full
hedge cap portfolio hedges well against surrenders, regardless of whether
they occur sooner or later and regardless of whether they occur at interest spreads of 200 to 500 basis points or beyond. If only a portion of the
hot money leaves the company at a certain spread, only a pro rata share
of the cap portfolio is sold off to cover that portion, and the remainder is
kept to cover subsequent lapses. The total estimated net cost of the illustrated cap strategy, assuming that the insurer is willing to absorb capital
losses associated with the first 100-basis-point rise in interest rates, is
under $4.5 million for this hypothetical example. Viewing the up-front

E X H I B I T   20–15B

Exposure at 11% Interest Rates

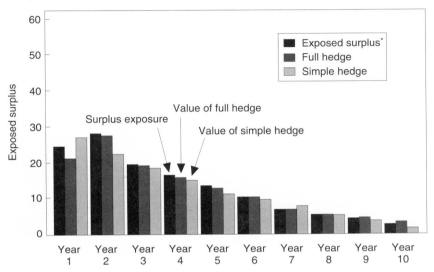

* First 100-basis-point move not included

cap payment as a cost, however, is ignoring the expected return on that investment.[9] It is more proper to view the payment as an investor with a positive expected return and a payoff that behaves in a manner that offset potential losses on other assets.

The amount of protection for any one year from the full hedge approach (as shown in Exhibits 20–15A through 20–15D) does not always exactly match the surplus exposure at every level of interest rates. More precision is available than that associated with the illustrated cap strategy by substituting some 9 percent caps with caps further out of the money. However, in practice, it is more likely that a portfolio manager will require less precision, which results in a simpler program with fewer caps. Furthermore, many insurers may be reluctant to sell off caps in those years where they have excess protection. At any point in time, certain maturity and trigger level ranges of caps are more highly traded than

---

[9] In the SPDA example of Exhibit 20–1, although the median return on the caps under the 40 random scenarios was negative, the expected return (average) was greater than zero. That is because of the asymmetric nature of returns on caps, which offer a large upside and limited downside potential.

E X H I B I T   20–15C

Exposure at 12% Interest Rates

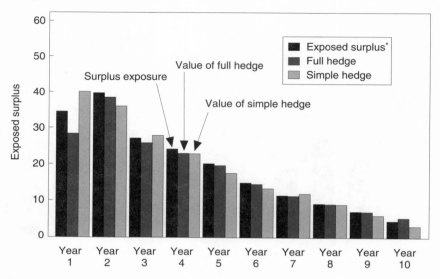

* First 100-basis-point move not included

others, for example, 2-, 3-, 5-, and 7-year caps that are 2 or 3 percent out of the money.

To construct a simpler hedge using these more liquid caps, we used a backwards solution approach based on trial and error using a Lotus spreadsheet to calculate net exposure for each year for various combinations of caps. One such simplified hedge involves purchasing 10-year, 9 percent caps with a notional amount of $110 million; 7-year, 12 percent caps with a notional amount of $70 million; and 5-year, 12 percent caps having a notional amount of about $500 million. While this simplified approach would not provide as uniform a pattern of protection as the full hedge strategy, it would still provide a very good hedge, does not require selling caps, would allow the insurer to operate in the more liquid segments of the market, and would have a cost somewhat lower than the full strategy (approximately $500,000 less in this particular case). As shown in Exhibits 20–15A through 20–15D, the "simple hedge" strategy (which utilizes only 3 different cap maturities, two of which have triggers far out of the money) underprotects against lapse exposure in certain years and overprotects in others, especially the first year. The amount of over- or underprotection depends on the level of interest rates. Of course, all of these are shown with respect to

E X H I B I T   20–15D

Exposure at 13% Interest Rates

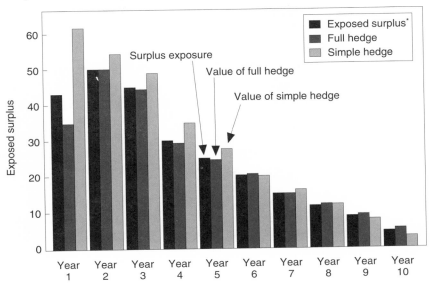

* First 100-basis-point move not included

certain stated assumptions regarding volatility and shape of the yield curve, which might not exactly hold in practice.

SUMMARY

The growth of interest-sensitive life insurance products in conjunction with increased interest rate volatility has created greater asset/liability management challenges for insurance companies. The risk of book value cashouts resulting from a dramatic increase in interest rates can no longer be ignored. Interest rate caps provide a form of catastrophe insurance against this risk, albeit requiring an up-front investment. Because of competitive pricing pressures, there is often little room left in the margins to allow for hedging. This does not necessarily mean that the hedges are too expensive. Rather, insurers may not be adequately charging for this risk in their products. Nonetheless, once an insurer has granted an option to policyholders, it has incurred an expected future cost. The question is whether the insurer wishes to hedge some of this potential future cost.

Interest rate caps are a relatively new instrument, and historical pricing data are limited. Fortunately, however, they can be viewed as a series of options. As such, they can be fairly valued using modern option pricing techniques, given yield curve shape and interest rate volatility assumptions. It is these theoretical values that should be used to judge whether current market values are fair.

Limited data are also available on the cashout risk of interest-sensitive life insurance products. While it is clear that this risk exists, quantifying it is more difficult. Therefore, developing an appropriate hedge strategy is more an art than a science. In this chapter, we suggested a methodology whereby you estimate potential cashouts and the resulting surplus drain each year. Starting in the last year, you then estimate how many caps you need to hedge that risk, and then work backward. Unfortunately, you will typically end up underhedged in some years and perhaps overhedged in others. This lack of precision should not pose practical problems in most situations, however. Insurers are in the business of accepting risk, and therefore would generally not want to eliminate all risk. Rather, they want to eliminate the risk of catastrophe in the form of excess cashouts that could seriously impair their viability as a firm. Thus, the objective is not to construct a perfect hedge but to obtain a layer of excess coverage at an affordable cost.

PUTABLE SWAPS: TOOLS FOR MANAGING CALLABLE ASSETS

Robert M. Stavis
Managing Director
Salomon Brothers Inc

Victor J. Haghani
Partner
Long-Term Capital Management

The putable interest rate swap combines swaps and options, two of the fastest-growing areas of financial innovation in the past decade. Unlike a traditional swap, the putable swap carries the right to cancel the swap agreement. Hence it is sometimes referred to as a *cancelable* or *terminable* swap. Interest rate swaps are flexible agreements that are easily tailored to specific asset or liability management needs. Putable swaps are an exciting new way to customize a swap agreement, which makes them particularly useful in managing callable assets.

Previously, investors often entered into interest rate swaps in conjunction with fixed-rate bond positions. The "asset-based swaps" created synthetic floating-rate assets at attractive spreads to LIBOR (London Interbank Offered Rate). However, the universe of noncallable fixed-rate bonds has been limited; as a result, many of the bonds used in the asset-based swaps had embedded call options. As the market rallied, the assets behind the swaps were called away, and investors were left with long interest rate swap positions with high fixed coupons. In the lower interest rate environment, similar-quality, high-yielding replacement assets were not available, and the swaps were expensive to reverse, creating losses on the traders. Putable swaps provide a means to mitigate these losses resulting from early redemption.

The introduction of an optionlike agreement on an interest rate swap opens up a new dimension in the world of swap applications. Put and call options on swaps can be applied in myriad ways. This chapter focuses on the putable swap, which is a combination of an interest rate swap and a put option on that swap. The approach we use follows:

1. We examine the components of corporate bond risk and return.
2. We review the transformation of noncallable fixed-rate assets into synthetic floating-rate assets through the purchase of interest rate swaps.
3. We discuss the problems posed by the call provisions embedded in corporate debt.
4. We introduce the putable interest rate swap as a means of managing the risk of callable assets.
5. We discuss how the terms of a putable swap affect its cost.

RISK AND RETURN FROM NONCALLABLE CORPORATE BONDS

Investors traditionally have looked to the long-term corporate bond market for higher yields. The yield on a long-term, noncallable corporate bond can be considered the sum of two components: a benchmark interest rate based on the bond's maturity and a "credit spread." The usual benchmark is the U.S. Treasury yield curve. The spread reflects a combination of factors, including the risk of credit downgradings, the risk of default, and a premium for liquidity.

The interest rate risk associated with holding fixed-rate assets is traditionally measured through the use of duration,[1] which provides a gauge of how much the bond's value will decrease if interest rates increase.

---

[1] Robert W. Kopprasch, "Understanding, Duration and Volatility," Chapter 5 in Frank J. Fabozzi and Irving M. Pollack, eds., *The Handbook of Fixed Income Securities* (Homewood, IL: Dow Jones-Irwin, 1987).

ASSET-BASED INTEREST RATE SWAPS WITH NONCALLABLE BONDS

Many investors desire to separate the credit risk component from the interest rate risk associated with long-duration, fixed-rate corporate bonds. One way to achieve this is to purchase, or "go long", an interest rate swap.[2] These asset-based swap transactions allow investors to create high-yielding, synthetic floating-rate assets. The hedged position has a duration similar to that of a money market security.

The mechanics of this trade are straightforward: The investor buys a noncallable, high-yielding corporate bond and enters into a long swap position. The swap position, if structured with an at-the-market coupon, generates no cash flow up front. This combination provides the investor with a synthetic floating-rate asset. The yield to maturity the investor receives is a function of the floating-rate index (usually three-month LIBOR) plus the difference between the fixed coupon on the bond and the fixed level of the swap.[3] Exhibit 21–1 illustrates the period cash flows generated by a simple asset-based swap.

The asset in this example is a 10-year noncallable, 10 percent coupon bond at par. The investor also goes long an interest rate swap, on which he or she pays a fixed rate and receives a floating rate. For the purpose of this example, assume that an at-the-market swap can be entered into at 8 percent semiannually (Treasuries plus the swap spread) versus three-month LIBOR quarterly. The investor's yield is a function of the quarterly LIBOR payments and the excess 2 percent (10% – 8%) of the semiannual coupon. Exhibit 21–2 shows the net flows to the investor. Exhibit 21–3 shows the net flow on an adjusted quarterly basis: The investor earns quarterly LIBOR plus 195 basis points. The swap does not involve an up-front payment; in effect, it is a variation of the at-the-market swap.

---

[2] Purchasing or "being long" an interest rate swap means that the investor is obligated to pay a fixed coupon periodically and will receive a coupon based on a floating-rate index. This position has the same interest rate sensitivity as being short a fixed-rate bond and long a floating-rate note. For a thorough discussion of the swap market, see Robert Kopprasch, John Macfarlane, Daniel R. Ross, and Janet Showers, "The Interest Rate Swap Market: Yield Mathematics, Terminology and Conventions," Chapter 58 in *The Handbook of Fixed Income Securities*.

[3] If the synthetic floating-rate position is liquidated before the maturity of the underlying asset, the return the investor realizes will be a function of the price at which he or she can sell the asset and reverse the swap position. In theory, this holding period return should be the same as that which would be earned through the purchase and resale of an actual floating-rate note. In practice, however, there are more components to the return of the synthetic position, including changes in the relationship between swap market spreads and the credit spread of the particular bond that was purchased.

E X H I B I T   21–1

Periodic Flows from an Asset-Based Swap*

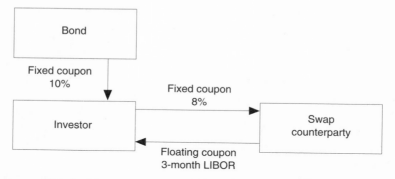

* Investor pays $100 for bond. No up-front swap fees. Fixed flows are semiannual. Floating flows are Actual/360.

The fixed coupon on the swap is raised by 200 basis points to match the fixed coupon on the underlying asset. To avoid any up-front payment while maintaining the 8 percent all-in cost of the swap, the floating side of the swap must also be increased by 200 semiannual-equivalent basis points (resulting in the 195 quarterly actual/360 basis points). In other words, the swap still has an *effective coupon* of 8 percent semiannually. When analyzed in this way, an asset-based swap transaction can be easily compared with other floating-rate securities. Although this trade seems quite attractive, it is difficult to implement because of the relative scarcity of noncallable corporate bonds.

It is important to point out that the synthetic floating-rate security created in an asset-based swap will have a spread to LIBOR that will reflect the credit of the underlying fixed-rate bond. There can be attractive opportunities to create high-yielding, synthetic floating-rate notes by starting with lower credit bonds. Alternatively, higher credit bonds can be used to create synthetic floaters with commensurately lower spreads to LIBOR.

THE PROBLEMS OF CALLABLE ASSETS

Callable corporate bonds pose another risk to investors. In addition to the interest rate and credit risks inherent in noncallable securities, early redemption is also a risk.[4] To compensate investors, callable bonds offer higher yields than comparable noncallable issues.

---

[4] The term *callable* should be interpreted broadly as including all types of early redemption, including cash calls, refundings, and sinking fund options. This call risk is related to interest rates. See *The Effective Duration of Callable Bonds,* Salomon Brothers Inc, March 1987.

E X H I B I T   21–2

Net Flows from an Asset-Based Swap

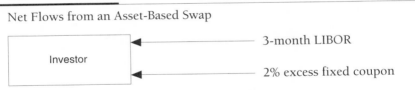

Investors have become more sensitive to the effect of call risk since the bond market rally of late 1986, in which callable assets significantly underperformed the market. One reaction to this has been the development of bond pricing models that consider the effect of embedded options on bond price sensitivity and yield. The models do this by valuing the callable corporate as a combination of a noncallable bond and a call option. The investor who is long the callable corporate is effectively long a noncallable corporate (with the same coupon and maturity as the callable bond) and short a call option on that bond.

By analyzing the call option component of the bond, these models can provide investors with a more accurate understanding of callable bond behavior. In addition, they provide investors with a measure of "option-adjusted spread," which can be used as an indicator of relative value. Bonds that are cheap on an option-adjusted spread basis should be good candidates for asset-based swaps provided that their risk of being called can be managed.

These models identify specific callable corporate issues that have attractive spreads after subtracting the fair value of the call premium. However, extracting the credit spread without being subject to market risk is a more difficult proposition when the target bond is callable than when it is noncallable. To gain a better understanding of this problem, we examine how the traditional asset-based swap transaction described earlier goes wrong when the underlying fixed-rate bond is callable.

Consider the position in a 10-year, 10 percent bond callable at par in 7 years combined with a 10-year swap (see Exhibit 21–4). Ignoring the call risk, the position would seem to create a synthetic 10-year floater at LIBOR plus 195 basis points. If the bond is called after seven years because of a decline in interest rates,[5] the investor will be repaid the principal and will be left with a long position in a three-year swap. If the investor purchased

---

[5] A decline in interest rates is not even necessary for the bond to be called. In a constant positive yield curve environment, the bond might be called to take advantage of a three-year rate that is below the original coupon rate of the bond, because the bond is "rolling down the yield curve."

E X H I B I T 21–3

Adjusted Net Flows from an Asset-Based Swap

a replacement three-year bond, he or she would end up with a much lower spread to LIBOR (possibly negative), because the replacement assets would have a lower yield than the original fixed-rate asset. Alternatively, if the investor attempted to offset the swap position, he or she would be required to pay a fee to sell the swap, because the swap carries the obligation to pay an above-market effective fixed coupon.

Our synthetic floating-rate position carries a significant interest rate risk that is not normally associated with floating-rate assets. In fact, we tried to eliminate interest rate risk in the creation of the synthetic floater. The solution is clear: Investors who want to earn higher corporate yields by taking on credit risk without subjecting themselves to call risk must buy options to offset the calls they have implicitly sold when they buy callable assets.

In theory, call options on specific corporate issues should be obtainable. The cost would be prohibitive, however, because of the difficulties the option writer would have in hedging his or her exposure. Debt options based on Treasuries traded on various exchanges exist, but they have expiration dates well within one year. Furthermore, the traditional over-the-counter (OTC) debt options market is generally limited to shorter-dated (also less than one year) options on Treasury and mortgage securities.[6]

Longer-term OTC Treasury options, if available, would not necessarily be a good solution to the problem. A Treasury-based call option would not benefit from a tightening of general corporate credit spreads as a call option on a corporate bond would. To illustrate this point, imagine a situation in which the general level of interest rates is basically unchanged, but credit spreads for corporate issues narrow, causing some corporate issues to be called. A call option on Treasuries attempting to offset the impact of those calls would not generate a payoff, because the underlying bond would not have experienced a commensurate increase in price.

---

[6] Interest rate caps and floors, while available with long-dated expirations, are based on money market rates, and therefore are not the best offsets to the risk in callable corporates.

E X H I B I T   21–4

A Traditional Asset-Based Swap with a Callable Bond

Terms of the Bond	
Maturity	10 years
Coupon	10% semiannual
Call provision	Callable in seven years
Call price	100 (single call price)
Bond price	100
Terms of the Swap	
Maturity	10 years
Fixed coupon	10% semiannual
Floating coupon	LIBOR plus 195
All-In cost	8.00%

The option on the swap embedded in a putable swap provides a solution to the practical problems previously discussed. It can have long-dated expiration and exercise provisions matching those found on the calls embedded in corporate bonds. In addition, the LIBOR swap market is a good hedging vehicle for corporate bonds, because swap spreads are driven in part by spreads in the corporate market.

USING A PUTABLE SWAP TO MANAGE A CALLABLE ASSET

A Simple Example

The putable interest rate swap is the best solution yet to the problem of hedging the risks of a callable corporate bond. It is the most appropriate tool for creating synthetic floating-rate positions devoid of call risk. As an example, consider the same callable security that we analyzed previously. To convert this bond into a synthetic floater, the investor would enter into a putable swap (see Exhibit 21–5).

Exhibit 21–6 shows the periodic cash flows associated with the transaction. We examine two possible scenarios. First, if the bond is not called, the investor receives LIBOR plus 165 basis points until the maturity date. In the event that the bond is called, the investor will receive

E X H I B I T   21–5

A Simple Asset-Based Putable Swap with a Callable Bond

Terms of the Bond	
Maturity	10 years
Coupon	10% semiannual
Call provision	Callable in seven years
Call price	100
Bond price	100
Terms of the Putable Swap	
Maturity	10 years
Fixed coupon	10% semiannual
Floating coupon	LIBOR plus 165
Put provision	Putable in 7 years
Option type	European
All-In cost of nonputable swap	8.00%
Cost of put option	31 semiannual basis points

LIBOR plus 165 basis points to the call date. On the call date, the investor receives the principal from the issuer and puts (cancels) the swap.[7] The putable swap does not guarantee the LIBOR plus 165 basis points for the original maturity of the bond. However, it does protect the investor from the risk described earlier when the bond was called and the investor was left with a swap position at a loss.[8]

The Cost of the Putable Swap Transaction

In this case, the cost of the put option is built into the putable swap coupon. The calculation of the up-front cost of the put can be accomplished by determining the value of the swap purchased, as if the swap had no put option. Because we know that an at-the-market, 10-year swap (see Exhibit

---

[7] Even if the bond is not called, the investor could put the swap back. The exercise of the putable swap is not contingent on the bond being called.

[8] This uncertain maturity of the synthetic floater superficially seems similar to the uncertain maturity of an actual floater, which typically is callable in the last five years of its life. However, the events that tend to cause early redemption in each case are different. In the case of the synthetic floater, early redemption will most likely be caused by a downward shift in interest rates. Alternatively, the actual floater will most likely be called if the issuer's credit spread narrows.

E X H I B I T   21–6

The Periodic Flows of the Simple Example

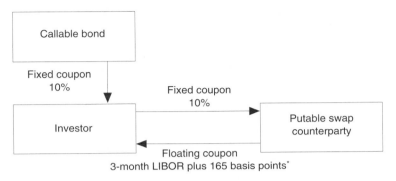

* Coupon is adjusted for put cost. Investor pays $100 for package.

21–4) has a coupon of 8 percent versus LIBOR flat, we can determine the up-front cost of a nonputable swap with a coupon of 10 percent and variable-rate flows of LIBOR plus 165 basis points. This swap would require a payment of 2.1 points up front to the buyer of the swap. Because the investor purchasing the swap is receiving no points up front, we can infer that the option must be costing 2.1 points. This cost is equivalent to the present value of the 31-basis-point increment in the all-in cost of the putable swap versus the all-in cost of the generic swap (8.31 − 8.00).

A More Realistic Example

Most asset-based putable swap transaction are mechanically more complex than the transaction described previously, yet are conceptually similar. A more realistic example will enable the reader to better understand the putable swap transaction and demonstrate the flexibility in tailoring the putable swap to a particular asset. Exhibit 21–7 summarizes our example. The major differences in this transaction are the payment of points up front, the presence of a call schedule with multiple call dates and prices, exercise payments, and non-European exercise. Exhibits 21–8, 21–9 and 21–10 show the cash flows from this transaction at initiation, periodically, and on a call date, respectively.

The transaction involves an up-front payment of 2.5 points to the swap buyer. When this is combined with the 102.50 cost of the bond, the base cost for the entire transaction is brought down to par (see Exhibit 21–8). This payment represents the net of the up-front swap payment the

E X H I B I T   21–7

A More Realistic Asset-Based Putable Swap with a Callable Bond

Terms of the Bond	
Maturity	3/15/97
Coupon	10% semiannual
Call provisions (date and price)	3/15/94 to 3/14/95 @ 103
	3/15/95 to 3/14/96 @ 102
	3/15/96 to 3/14/97 @ 101
	3/15/97 @ 100
Terms of the Putable Swap	
Maturity	3/15/97
Up-front payment	2.50 paid to investor (swap buyer pays fixed)
Fixed coupon	10% semiannual
Floating coupon	LIBOR plus 136
Put provisions (date and price)	3/15/94 to 3/14/95 for 3 points
	3/15/95 to 3/14/96 for 2 points
	3/15/96 to 3/14/97 for 1 point
Option type	Deferred American
All-in cost of nonputable swap	8.00
Cost of put option	24 basis points

investor *would receive* for agreeing to pay what is effectively an above-market fixed coupon and the up-front points the investor must pay for the put option on the swap.

Exhibit 21–9 demonstrates the simplicity of the resulting cash flows. As long as the bond is not called, the investor earns LIBOR plus 136 basis points. The swap is structured so that the fixed coupon on the bond and the fixed coupon on the swap perfectly offset each other.

The putable interest rate swap was structured with a schedule of put dates to match the call schedule of the target issue. The putable swap has a "deferred American" exercise. This means that it cannot be exercised initially, but after some point it can be exercised at any time over its remaining life. This is analogous to the call feature of the corporate bond, which also has a deferred American exercise. Because the bond is callable

E X H I B I T   21–8

Realistic Example: Initial Flows

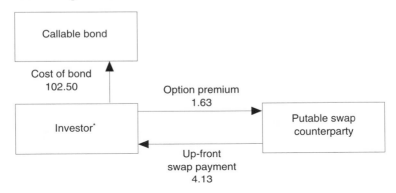

* Net upfront payment to investor = 4.13 − 1.63 = 2.50
  Net cost to investor = 102.5 + 1.63 − 4.13 = 100.00

at a premium to par, the swap is structured with an exercise payment designed to match the amount by which the call price is above par. If the bond is called, the investor receives the call premium buy pays an equal amount to offset the long swap position. Call prices over par can be considered adjustments to the strike price of the option the investor has implicitly sold to the issuer. Correspondingly, the exercise payments paid to cancel the swap can also be considered adjustments to the strike of the put option on the swap.

In Exhibit 21–10, which describes the cash flows in the event of a call, we assume that the bond is called as per the schedule on March 15, 1994. The investor is paid 103 points by the issuer, but passes 3 points along for the right to cancel the swap. This effectively gives the investor back the initial investment of 100. In the event of a call, the investor has paid 100 points initially, receives LIBOR plus 136 over the life of the bond, and ends up with 100 points.

In summary, this synthetic floating-rate note pays LIBOR plus 136 basis points as long as the bond remains outstanding.[9]

---

[9] In fact, the 136-basis-point amount is based on the assumption that the investor exercises the right to put the swap if and only if the underlying bond is called. However, the investor can sometimes achieve a better return. For instance, the investor may be able to exercise the put option, even if the bond is not called, and buy another swap at more favorable terms. It may also be possible that when the issuer calls the bond, the investor would do better by selling the swap in the market than by exercising the put to cancel the swap.

Realistic Example: Periodic Flows

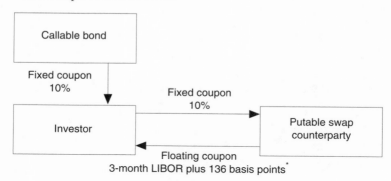

*Coupon is adjusted for put cost.

DETERMINANTS OF VALUE OF A PUT ON
AN INTEREST RATE SWAP

Swap market terminology is often confusing. Adding options to swaps
certainly does not alleviate this confusion. However, to be consistent with
swap market terminology, the term *put on a swap* is used to describe the
right to sell a swap (receive a fixed rate). Because a short position in an
interest rate swap effectively represents being long the bond market, a put
option on an interest rate swap is effectively a call on the market. The
pricing of puts on swaps therefore is related to the determinants of value
of a call option on the bond market.

Effective Fixed-Coupon Level

The higher the effective fixed coupon (fixed coupon minus spread to variable index) on the swap, the greater the value of being able to put the
swap back to the floating-rate payer. Exhibit 21–11 shows the effect of
changing the effective fixed-coupon level on the up-front points earned
(or paid) by the swap purchaser in a traditional and a putable swap. It also
shows the cost of a put option on a swap over a range of effective fixed
coupons. The net up-front points (positive or negative) generated by the
putable swap are simply the points generated by the traditional swap
minus the cost of the put option.

E X H I B I T   21–10

Realistic Example: Cash Flows at Call Date

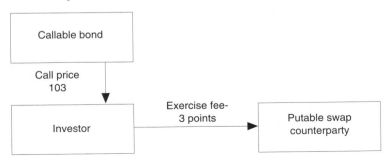

All else held constant, the higher the coupon, the more valuable is the option to, at some future date, sell (or cancel, in the case of the linked putable swap transaction) the swap for a fixed exercise fee. While the value of the put option rises as the effective fixed coupon is increased, the points generated up front by a higher effective coupon on the underlying swap grow even faster. Therefore, although an increase in the fixed coupon raises the cost of the put option, the net effect on the package is a decrease in the up-front fee paid by the purchaser of the putable swap.

Swap Maturity

Generally, the longer the time to final maturity of the swap at the exercise date of the option, the more valuable the option on that swap will be. This is a result of the increased price sensitivity (duration) of the swap with the greater maturity.

Exercise Payments

The greater the exercise payment that must be paid to exercise the option, the lower the value of the swap option. A larger positive exercise payment is equivalent to a more out-of-the-money option. If appropriate for a particular application, a more in-the-money option could also be created by having a payment paid to the holder of the option at exercise.

E X H I B I T   21-11

The Effect of Different Fixed Coupons

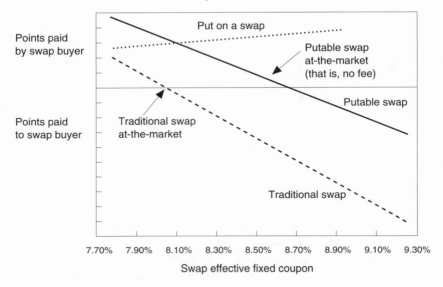

Time Until Exercise

European Swap Options

As the time to expiration of a European swap option is extended (holding the maturity of the swap constant), a variety of factors influences its value. On the one hand, longer options allow more time for the swap market to move in favor of the option holder. On the other hand, because the underlying swap is aging over the life of the option, it is important to consider what the maturity of the swap will be at the exercise date of the option. Initially, increasing the time to expiration raises the value of the swap put option. Eventually, however, the lessening remaining maturity and hence the decreasing duration of the swap dominate, lowering the value of the put option. In the limit, when the expiration date of the option equals the maturity date of the swap, the option will have no value. Exhibit 21–12 demonstrates this for 5-, 7- and 10-year swap puts.

American Swap Options

Two statements can be made about the valuation of American options. First, American options will always have values greater than or equal to

E X H I B I T   21–12

European Swap Option: Time until Expiration Effect

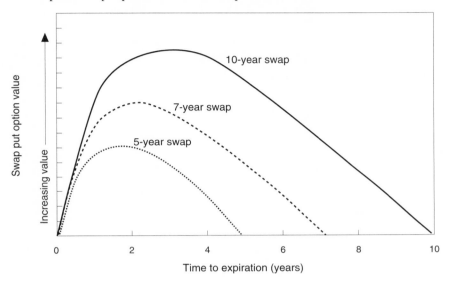

those of their European counterparts. Second, as time to expiration increases (again holding final maturity constant), the value of the American put on a swap will never decrease. Exhibit 21–13 demonstrates this effect, comparing the value of a European put with that of an American put on a 10-year swap.

SUMMARY

There are several direct extensions of the development of putable swaps. The first natural extension of the trades outlined in this chapter is for asset managers to use a portfolio of putable swaps to manage entire portfolios of callable assets. The flexibility of the putable swap transaction will allow portfolio managers to mold the risk/return patterns of their portfolios to better meet their objectives.

The second application of the putable swap is to manage the "call" risk in mortgage-backed securities. The flexibility of the interest rate swap has already made it an important part of "risk-controlled arbitrage" (the mortgage market version of the asset-based swap). Putable swaps will allow for better management of the calls embedded in the underlying mortgage securities. A risk-controlled arbitrage combining some tradi-

E X H I B I T   21–13

American Swap Option: Time until Expiration Effect

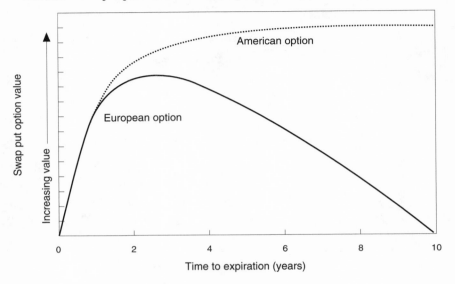

tional and some putable swaps will provide more protection from the dangers of the mortgage assets prepaying too quickly and the investor being left with onerous swap positions.

Putable swaps demonstrate the continuing development of derivative securities that relate to different sectors of the financial marketplace. Development in the market will lead to the disaggregation of putable swaps into the long swap position plus the put on that swap. This will lead to new applications of puts on swaps alone, as well as the development of an active market in calls on swaps. Applications on the asset side could include using puts on swaps to lengthen the duration of a callable bond portfolio by offsetting the embedded call options. Calls on swaps (which would be equivalent to puts on the bond market) could be purchased to provide a floor on a long-term corporate bond portfolio. Investors could also write options on the swap market in an effort to generate higher current yields. In addition, liability managers will be able to use options on swaps to manage callable debt.

These new developments in the swap market enable asset/liability managers to have more control over the performance of their portfolios.

It is another link that allows for risk transfer among various market participants. Managers who utilize their new options in the construction of swap positions will be able to better meet their investment and borrowing objectives.

22

USING OPTIONS TO ENHANCE THE TOTAL RETURN OF A MORTGAGE PORTFOLIO

Laurie Goodman, PhD
Managing Director
Mortgage Strategy Group
PaineWebber

Linda Lowell
First Vice President
Mortgage Strategy Group
PaineWebber

Jeff Ho
Vice President
Mortgage Strategy Group
PaineWebber

All mortgage investors are aware that mortgages are a combination of two elements: a long position in a noncallable bond and a short position in a call option. While options embedded in mortgages are far more complicated than plain vanilla interest rate options, interest rate options can be valuable and flexible tools in the day-to-day management of a mortgage portfolio. Options can be used to manage the negative convexity associated with current-coupon pass-throughs. They can also be valuable tools for monetizing the positive convexity in mortgage derivatives. In this chapter, we examine several trade concepts that utilize options. All of our examples will use over-the-counter (OTC) options, but the same analysis applies to exchange-traded options.

We gratefully acknowledge the assistance of Diane May, John Coleman, Sara Pinneo, and Diana Rich in the preparation of this chapter.

First, we give an overview of the markets in which OTC options on Treasuries and mortgages are traded. Then we discuss the most common use of options in a mortgage portfolio: covered call writing. An important variant of this approach is writing call options on portfolios of derivatives that are very positively convex to monetize the convexity. Next, we discuss buying call options to add both duration and convexity to current-coupon pass-throughs so that current coupons can be judged against discount pass-throughs or 10-year notes. Finally, we discuss ways to take advantage of situations in which the investor expresses a view on the directionality of mortgage–Treasury spreads. While the trades discussed in this chapter are by no means all-inclusive, they provide a good introduction to many uses of options in mortgage portfolio management.

OTC TREASURY AND MORTGAGE OPTION MARKETS

Portfolio strategies employing mortgage options typically are executed in the over-the-counter markets made by many of the large securities firms active in the mortgage-backed securities market. Strategies employing Treasury options may be executed in both exchange-traded and OTC markets. Exchange-traded options are discussed in Chapter 2.

Over-the-counter-markets in Treasury and mortgage options have matured over the last 8 to 10 years. Most broker/dealer firms maintain an options trading activity that is fueled by customer demand carried over from U.S. Treasury and mortgage pass-through trading. While OTC Treasury options will never become as liquid as Chicago Board of Trade (CBT) options on Treasury note and bond futures, they have become sufficiently standardized to provide dealers with markets liquid enough to shrink bid-asked spreads in this product down to those of the U.S. Treasury obligations themselves.

Along with the narrowing bid-asked spreads that accompany any mature market, trade conventions have also been standardized. Most dealers make markets on any U.S. Treasury coupon security longer than 1½ years. The most liquid issues are always the current 2-year, 5-year, and 10-year notes and the current 30-year bond. These issues are traded on the screens; that is, interdealer brokers encourage liquidity on these issues by providing a forum for trading options on each issue. These contracts commonly expire one week, two weeks, one month, two months, and three months from any given trade date. Although customers can buy or sell options that expire on any day, these five expiration dates make up a majority of the business done. Treasury options may be American style or

European style; the former is the more common, as CBT futures options are also American style. Treasury options expire at 4:00 P.M. Eastern time in most cases.

In Treasury options, 75 percent of trading with investors is in writing covered calls. Call options sold on positions held for the purpose of bringing in extra yield on the position are by far the most common customer trade. Not surprisingly, those dealers who see the most customer flow usually turn out to be net sellers to other dealers in the interdealer broker market.

There are several reasons customers choose to use the OTC market to hedge their portfolios. Most important is the fact that they are able to transact in options on the specific securities in which they have positions. This eliminates the so-called basis risk (the risk that the price changes on bonds held by an investor will not be matched by the price change on the option's underlying security) inherent in using CBT futures options. Furthermore, the customer may specify precisely which day the option will expire and at exactly which strike price. This tailoring advantage brings many customers to the OTC market with their hedge and speculative trades.

In mortgage options, the conventions and end users differ. First, expiration dates of options commonly correspond with the monthly settlement dates of the mortgage collateral set by the Public Securities Association (PSA). Mortgage options usually expire one week prior to PSA settlement, and two weeks prior is the second most popular convention. Most dealers make markets on good delivery paper only (paper in which the exact pools to be delivered are to be arranged (TBA) later). That is, dealers do not transact in options on specified pools of collateral. The most common varieties of TBA on which mortgage markets are made are 30-year conventional FNMAs, 30-year FHLMC Gold, 30-year GNMA Type I, 15 year FNMA Dwarf paper, and Gold 15-year paper. A few dealers also make markets on GNMA 15-year paper, ARMs, and balloons. Mortgage options are always European style. This is because the underlying security is a forward transaction, and there is no dollar advantage in carry to owning the forward mortgage ahead of time. Mortgage options also expire at 4:00 P.M. Eastern time.

The main impetus for a mortgage options market comes from mortgage bankers hedging their security pipelines. Originators are unsure of what percentage of their loan commitments will actually close; borrowers' decisions are highly rate dependent. If rates rise, a higher-than-expected portion of the pipeline will close, as borrowers have locked in a rate better than that currently available. Similarly, if rates fall, a lower-than-expected portion of the pipeline will close. Mortgage bankers often hedge their pipelines with a combination of forward sales of securities and options. Mortgage originators who are bearish sell a large portion of their loan commitments as mortgage pass-throughs for forward delivery and buy out-of-the-money calls. If the market trades off as expected, the mortgages have already been sold at favorable prices. If the market rallies and fewer mortgages close, the out-of-the-money calls provide protection. Alternatively, originators who are bullish may sell forward a smaller amount than they expect to actually close and buy puts to cover themselves if the market trades off. In the event the market does trade off, the puts provide protection on the additional loans closed.

From 1991 through most of 1994, the most common end users of mortgage options were mortgage bankers who bought puts to hedge pipelines laden with much more rate-sensitive refinancings. The effect on the market of this demand was to make out-of-the-money puts on mortgages very expensive, since there were many natural buyers and no natural sellers. Since OTC mortgage and Treasury options are often used to hedge each other (mortgage option desks in particular were short mortgage options and long Treasury options), options' volatility generally rose during that time period. Another effect was that mortgage volatility richened to Treasury volatility. In the environment at this writing (winter 1995), with mortgage originations down roughly 70 percent from their peak in 1993, mortgage volatility has come back into line.

These option products can be extremely valuable to mortgage investors, but historically they have been underutilized. In the following sections, we outline four trades that use options to augment the performance of a mortgage portfolio. These trades are representative, not exhaustive. Options are very flexible instruments; when an investor has a view to express, options always offer a way to do it.

COVERED CALL WRITING

One of the most commonly used strategies for mortgage portfolio managers is covered call writing. In a covered call, an investor "writes" or sells a mortgage option on a security that he or she owns, taking the premium into income. If the market rallies, the investor's security is called away at the strike price. Thus, if the market remains constant or sells off, the premium income helps cushion the loss on the security. Exhibit 22–1 shows the return profile of the covered call position, as well as the profile of the long position in the underlying and the short position in the call. We use closing prices as of Thursday, February 9, 1995, for this analysis. The March price of the FNMA 8.5s was 99:13. We look at writing a one-

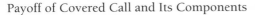

E X H I B I T   22–1

Payoff of Covered Call and Its Components

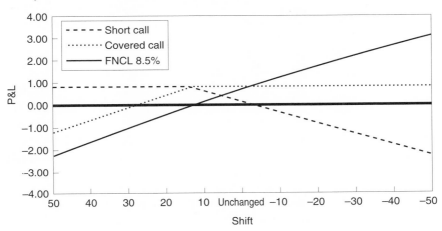

month at-the-money forward call option (March expiration, strike 99:13) at a premium of 0:14+.

Let us compare this strategy to (1) holding the securities and not writing the call and (2) selling the securities. If the market stays at current levels, the most profitable alternative is to do the covered call writing strategy. If the market trades off, covered call writing is clearly more profitable than holding the security outright, since the investor pockets the premium. It is important to realize that a rally offers little protection; the investor is trading away the upside. If the market were unchanged, the price of the security would be 99:21. That is, forward prices would have converged to current prices; the security would have moved up in price by 8 ticks, corresponding to the roll. Thus, if the market stays unchanged, the investor is better off by only 6+ ticks having written a covered call versus just owning the security outright. The investor is hurt in this instance when the market rallies more than 4 basis points. Essentially, the investor is trading his or her upside in the security for the premium income.

Should an investor who is negative on the market sell covered calls or simply sell the security? The answer depends on how negative the investor is and how sure of his or her judgment. If the market trades off more than 14 basis points, the investor is better off having sold the security. If the market trades off less than this amount, stays unchanged, or rallies, the investor is better off with the covered call position, since he or she has earned the premium income. Thus, as long as FNMA 8.5s stay around current levels, the covered call strategy makes sense. If the market trades off substantially, the investor is better off having sold the security. Note that the time frame on this trade is very short: March options expire one week before the TBA delivery date (i.e., on March 6, 1995, as TBA delivery is March 13, 1995).

It is important to realize that these option positions can be tailored to the portfolio manager. It is not necessary to write an at-the-money forward option; a different strike price can be used. A higher strike price (more out-of-the-money) will generate less premium income but will create a larger cushion if the market rallies. Similarly, there is nothing magic about a one-month option. The period can be shorter or longer. For shorter periods, the option premium is proportionately larger; for longer periods, it is proportionately smaller. As of the close on February 9, 1995, the PaineWebber options desk was quoting three-month options (May settle, at-the-money forward, strike 98:31) at 0:28, not quite double the one-month premium for an option three times as long. In general, for at-the-money options, an investor must quadruple the time to expiration to double the premium.

WRITING OPTIONS TO MONETIZE POSITIVE CONVEXITY

Another use for options is to monetize the positive convexity now inherent in many mortgage positions. This technique is rarely used by portfolio managers, but we believe it makes a great deal of sense. During the 1991–93 rally, it was practically impossible to find positive convexity in the mortgage market; securities came in only two flavors, negatively convex and more negatively convex. This painful situation existed because there were no outstanding pass-throughs priced substantially under par. At any given point in time, the lowest coupon traded was the current coupon, which generally had a price above 98. In fact, the rally was so sharp that in some periods there were no coupons under par. Exhibit 22–2 shows the price configuration in the mortgage market as of December 31, 1993, for 30-year mortgages with coupons of 6.5 percent and above and 15-year products with coupons of 6 percent and above. As can be seen, this product was all over par. Consequently, the only positively convex securities in the market were the higher-coupon IOs.

In contrast, as Exhibit 22–2 also shows, by winter 1995 over half of the mortgage market had a dollar price of 95 or below. Thirty-year GNMAs with

EXHIBIT   22–2

Distribution of Prices

| Price Range | Breakdown of 30-Year | | | |
| | 12/31/93 | | 2/9/95 | |
	Balance ($mm)	% of 30-Year	Balance ($mm)	% of 30-Year
<90	$ 0	0	$133,201	15
90–95	0	0	336,641	39
95–100	0	0	224,911	26
100–105	355,731	45	124,657	14
>105	441,835	55	43,802	5
Total	$797,566	100	$863,212	100
Coupon*	8.05		7.78	
Price*	105:04		95:26	

| Price Range | Breakdown of All† | | | |
| | 12/31/93 | | 2/9/95 | |
	Balance ($mm)	% of Total	Balance ($mm)	% of Total
<90	$ 0	0	$133,201	11
90–95	0	0	482,915	41
95–100	0	0	380,874	32
100–105	633,910	57	145,842	12
>105	473,299	43	43,802	4
Total	$1,107,209	100	$1,186,634	100
Coupon*	7.76		7.53	
Price*	104:19		96:20	

* Weighted average.
† Includes 15-years.

coupons of 7.5 percent and lower and 30-year conventionals with coupons of 7 percent and lower actually had positive convexity on the basis of the PaineWebber OAS model. Furthermore, selected CMO tranches backed by the lower-coupon collateral possessed considerable positive convexity. For example, POs and structured POs backed by discount collateral had very little extension risk from their current levels. Contraction risk on these bonds is a nice feature: The price moves toward par quickly as the bond shortens.

This asymmetry is picked up in the convexity measures. Similarly, inverse floaters often have a great deal of positive convexity, particularly the long-average-life tranches priced at a discount. Investors win if the market rallies because the average life of the security contracts and the coupon increases. If the market trades off, the security should not extend much, since prepayment rates have little room to slow from current levels. Moreover, the coupon can never go below zero, giving most LIBOR floaters relatively little downside from the forward rates implicit in the current yield curve. For example, the convexity of FNR 93–184 M, a super PO backed by 7s, was 5.60; the convexity of LIBOR-based inverse floaters ranged between 5 and 12. In contrast, the convexity of a 27-year zero was 3.4.

The problem stopping many investors in this environment from adding convexity to their portfolios is that there is a cost to the convexity, and that cost is usually a lower base-case yield. Many investors are reluctant to buy instruments with a great deal of positive convexity because they yield less than comparable instruments with less positive convexity. This should not be a deterrent. Holding positively convex instruments allows the portfolio manager to write call options against the position. In essence, the value of these embedded options can be monetized by writing options against the position.

Exhibit 22–3 shows how this technique can be applied to a super PO position. This instrument has a relatively low base-case total rate of return, 6.92 percent; however, it does relatively much better if interest rates fall than it suffers if interest rates rise. That is, if interest rates fell 200 basis points, the security would return 76.15 percent, versus –31.06 percent if interest rates rose 200 basis points. We can monetize these options by writing an at-the-money one-year call option on a 10-year note. That is, we write an option such that if the yield on the 7.50 percent Treasury note of 2/15/05 is lower than current yields (7.58 percent, the close as of Thursday, February 9, 1995), the call will be exercised. The compensation for writing this option is the premium of 2 points up front. This can significantly raise the total rate of return on the portfolio in the base case and in the cases where interest rates rise. Adding $1 million face of options for each $1 million face of the super PO improves the base-case rate of return by just over 700 basis points. (This is because the dollar price of the security is just above 30:00.) If rates rally substantially, the options entail a cost, but the cost is much lower than the upside on the super PO. Thus, the investor is lowering the upside in a major market rally to cushion the downside. If rates fall 200 basis points, the total rate of return is only 48.92 percent, versus 76.15 percent without the options. If rates rise, the premi-

EXHIBIT 22-3

Writing Options against a Positively Convex Mortgage Security

(A Long Position in FNR 93-184 M Plus a Short Position in an OTC Call Option on the 10-Year Note)

PORTFOLIO

	Face	Price	Accrued Interest	Proceeds	Duration	Convexity	OAS
FNR 93-184 M	1,000,000	30:16	0	305,000	26.8	5.6	-66
Call *	-1,000,000	2:00	0.0000	-20,000			
				285,000			

Interest Rate Scenario

	-300	-200	-100	-50	unchanged	50	100	200	300
ROR									
FNR 93-184 M	160.36	76.15	36.24	20.49	6.92	-4.71	-14.65	-31.06	-44.94
Portfolio	128.98	48.92	24.17	17.67	13.95	2.02	-8.25	-25.23	-39.59
TERMINAL VALUE									
FNR 93-184 M	990,172	581,486	425,546	370,709	326,455	290,792	261,962	217,620	183,332
Call	-219,063	-140,000	-67,500	-33,125	-313	0	0	0	0
Portfolio	771,109	441,486	358,046	337,584	326,143	290,792	261,962	217,620	183,332
7.5% 2/15/05 at Horizon Date									
Yield	4.58	5.58	6.58	7.08	7.58	8.08	8.58	9.58	10.58
Price	121:11	113:14	106:06	102:24	99:15	96:11	93:10	87:20	82:12

*This is a 1-year option on a 10-year Treasury (7.5%, 2/15/05) struck at the money; that is, the strike yield is 7.58%, the same as the yield as of the close of Thursday, February 9, 1995.

um obviously cushions the downside on the security. A 200-basis-point rise in rates would cause the value of the portfolio (super PO + short call option on the 10-year note) to drop by 25.23 percent, versus 31.06 percent in the absence of the option on the 10-year note. In short, options can be used to monetize the embedded options in very convex mortgage securities. We believe that writing options against very convex portfolios should be more widespread than it is among investors.

USING OPTIONS TO AUGMENT UP- AND DOWN-IN-COUPON MORTGAGE TRADES

In this market environment, current-coupon mortgages have gotten very cheap relative to their siblings backed by discount collateral. Between the end of December 1994 and February 1995, the market witnessed a creeping bullishness, reflecting the fact that formerly strong economic numbers were now coming in more mixed. This resulted in an 18-basis-point drop in the yield of the 10-year note. However, the movement in the price spreads between mortgage securities is far larger than the size of this rally would suggest. Essentially, many mortgage portfolio managers were in a position where the duration bet and the relative value decision were not separable. For many portfolio managers, the most efficient way to express a bullish sentiment in such a situation is to move down in coupon. That is, if there were no institutional constraints and if current coupons were cheap relative to discounts, it would make more sense to stay in current-coupon mortgages and buy 10-year Treasury notes to extend duration. Many mortgage portfolio managers cannot do this; their holdings are confined to mortgages. For them, the most efficient way to express a duration bet is to move down in coupon. Suppose an investor has made a duration bet at the expense of a relative-value decision. If the investor faces these types of institutional constraints, he or she has made the right trade-off: If the market moves substantially in either direction, the duration bet will be far more important than the relative-value decision.

To see how current-coupon mortgages are cheap relative to discounts, we can look at a historical price spread analysis, which we refer to as the "perfect price spread." Exhibit 22–4 shows how discount mortgages traded relative to their current-coupon counterparts over the February 1994 to February 1995 period. (The columns on the far right show the value of the perfect price spread over the February 1994 to February 1995 period; values over the November 1994 to February 1995 [12-week] period and August 1994 to February 1995 [26-week] period

EXHIBIT 22–4

Perfect Price Spread Analysis

	02/09/95 Perfect Coupon	02/09/95 Price Spread	12-Week Period				26-Week Period				52-Week Period			
			Average	Max	Min	%R*	Average	Max	Min	%R*	Average	Max	Min	%R*
GNMA 30-Year Perfect Price Spread (8.52% perfect current coupon)														
+100 bp	9.52	4.63	4.82	5.91	4.49	10	5.04	6.06	4.40	14	4.78	6.06	3.95	32
+50 bp	9.02	2.26	2.48	2.86	2.22	6	2.60	3.09	2.22	5	2.52	3.09	2.17	9
−50 bp	8.02	−2.51	−2.63	−2.51	−2.79	100	−2.74	−2.51	−3.03	100	−2.76	−2.51	−3.03	100
−100 bp	7.52	−5.32	−5.43	−5.28	−5.65	90	−5.67	−5.28	−6.05	95	−5.76	−5.28	−6.13	96
−150 bp	7.02	−8.39	−8.44	−8.21	−8.72	63	−8.83	−8.21	−9.37	84	−8.99	−8.21	−9.55	86
FNMA 30-Year Perfect Price Spread (8.55% perfect current coupon)														
+100 bp	9.55	4.55	4.64	5.42	4.33	21	4.71	5.49	4.15	30	4.44	5.49	3.59	51
+50 bp	9.05	2.20	2.35	2.89	2.05	18	2.43	2.93	2.05	17	2.32	2.93	1.92	28
−50 bp	8.05	−2.17	−2.37	−2.11	−2.72	91	−2.47	−2.11	−2.83	93	−2.49	−2.11	−2.95	94
−100 bp	7.55	−4.55	−4.79	−4.46	−5.24	89	−5.01	−4.46	−5.52	92	−5.14	−4.46	−5.85	94
−150 bp	7.05	−7.16	−7.36	−7.09	−7.83	91	−7.71	−7.09	−8.28	95	−7.90	−7.09	−8.77	96

* %R = percentile within the range, assuming a uniform distribution between the minimum and maximum.

are shown left to right. The perfect current-coupon FNMA, the security that will sell at par for corporate settlement, is the 8.55 percent. This is interpolated from the price of the FNMA 8.5s and 9s. It follows that the perfect −100-basis-point coupon would be the 7.55 percent. We interpolate between the 7.5s and the 8s to construct the price on this hypothetical security. It would sell at a discount of 4.55 from par. This is shown in the third column on the left. Tracking this perfect price spread series over the past year (the last four columns on the right), we can see that the perfect −100 coupon has been priced, on average, at a discount of 5.14. The minimum displayed by this series has been a discount of 5.85, and the maximum has been a discount of 4.46. The current discount of 4.55 is very near the maximum value over the prior year. Assuming a uniform distribution between the minimum and the maximum, the current discount is in the 94th percentile within the range. This analysis does not allow for the effect of a yield curve flattening, and thus it can be argued that discounts should be richer to currents than they have been. However, even when we look at this trend over the past 12 weeks, when the yield curve was both steeper and flatter than it is now, we are still in the 89th percentile. That is, over the past 12 weeks, this discount averaged 4.79; at 4.55, it is still nearly 8 ticks cheap.

Investors who want to take advantage of this mispricing but keep their duration equal to that on a lower-coupon mortgage can use options. In particular, they can purchase a fraction of a call option on the 10-year note. Consider moving up in coupon from FNMA 7.5s to FNMA 8.5s and purchasing a fraction of a call on a 10-year note. We purchase the fraction of the 10-year note call generated by the excess carry on the 8.5 percent mortgage; that is, FNMA 8.5s roll at roughly 8 ticks per month, while FNMA 7.5s roll at 6 ticks per month. Thus, over a three-month period, we will have 6 ticks with which to buy Treasury call options. The cost of a 3-month at-the-money forward call option on the 10-year Treasury is 1:10+; thus, 6 ticks can purchase 0.141 of an option.

Exhibit 22–5 shows the results for this analysis: buying $1 million face of FNMA 8.50, buying 0.141 of $1 million face of an option, and selling $1 million face of a FNMA 7.5. The prices for the FNMA 7.5s and 8.5s for each interest rate scenario are model driven; that is, we estimate how the security has behaved under these same interest rate scenarios in the past. As can be seen, this trade performs very well. Because the 8.5s are relatively cheap, with the addition of options it outperforms in all scenarios by +/−50 basis points. It would take a rally of 90 basis points for the 8.5-plus-options combination to underperform the 7.5s; that is, at this point, the 8.5s have

E X H I B I T   22–5

Current-Coupon Pass-Through Plus Call versus Discount Pass-Through*

	Drop/Month	Forward Price
FNCL 8.5%	8	98:31
FNCL 7.5%	6	94:14
10-year Treasury		98:29
10-year Treasury option ATM fee		1:104
Face amount of option[†]		141,176
Face amount of each pass-through		1,000,000

							P&L			
Shift	10-Year Treasury Yield	FNCL 8.50%	FNCL 7.50%	10-Year Treasury Price	Long Treasury Call	FNCL 8.50%	Call+ 8.50%	FNCL 7.50%	Difference
125	8.83	91:02	86:03	91:12	−1,875	−79,085	−80,960	−83,308	2,348
120	8.78	91:15	86:16	91:22	−1,875	−74,879	−76,754	−79,258	2,504
110	8.68	92:10	87:10	92:10	−1,875	−66,653	−68,528	−71,282	2,754
100	8.58	93:03	88:03	92:29	−1,875	−58,674	−60,549	−63,470	2,921
90	8.48	93:28	88:27	93:17	−1,875	−50,943	−52,818	−55,822	3,004
80	8.38	94:20	89:19	94:06	−1,875	−43,459	−45,334	−48,338	3,004
70	8.28	95:11	90:11	94:26	−1,875	−36,223	−38,098	−41,018	2,920
60	8.18	96:01	91:02	95:15	−1,875	−29,234	−31,109	−33,862	2,753
50	8.08	96:23	91:24	96:03	−1,875	−22,493	−24,368	−26,871	2,503
40	7.98	97:12	92:14	96:24	−1,875	−15,999	−17,874	−20,043	2,169
30	7.88	97:32	93:03	97:13	−1,875	−9,753	−11,628	−13,380	1,752
20	7.78	98:19	93:24	98:03	−1,875	−3,755	−5,630	−6,881	1,251
10	7.68	99:05	94:12	98:24	−1,875	1,996	121	−546	667
Unchanged	7.58	99:23	95:00	99:14	−1,116	7,500	6,384	5,625	759
−10	7.48	100:08	95:19	100:04	−152	12,756	12,604	11,632	973
−20	7.38	100:24	96:06	100:26	821	17,765	18,586	17,474	1,111
−30	7.28	101:07	96:24	101:16	1,802	22,526	24,328	23,153	1,175
−40	7.18	101:22	97:10	102:06	2,792	27,039	29,831	28,667	1,164
−50	7.08	102:03	97:27	102:29	3,791	31,305	35,096	34,017	1,079
−60	6.98	102:16	98:11	103:20	4,798	35,324	40,122	39,203	919
−70	6.88	102:28	98:28	104:11	5,815	39,095	44,910	44,225	684
−80	6.78	103:07	99:11	105:02	6,840	42,618	49,459	49,083	376
−90	6.68	103:18	99:26	105:26	7,875	45,894	53,769	53,777	−7
−100	6.58	103:28	100:09	106:17	8,919	48,923	57,841	58,306	−465
−110	6.48	104:04	100:23	107:09	9,972	51,703	61,676	62,672	−996
−120	6.38	104:13	101:04	108:01	11,035	54,237	65,272	66,873	−1,601
−125	6.33	104:16	101:11	108:13	11,570	55,411	66,980	68,912	−1,932

* 3-month horizon.
[†] Amount of calls determined by additional positive carry of 8.5% over 7.5%.

little room to appreciate, while the 7.5s continue to appreciate. The 0.141 of a 10-year note option is insufficient to offset this effect.

Another conceptual possibility for adding options to this position is to buy a fraction of a 10-year note. This strategy has two problems. First, if the market declines, the investor will at some point be net long and very susceptible to price declines; that is, the price action of the 7.5 and 8.5 will be very similar, and the fraction of a 10-year note will make the position too long. Second, if volatility jumps, the value of current-coupon mortgages will decline relative to discounts. The investor is essentially short convexity. If, as we suggested earlier, an investor buys a call option, the option will increase in value if volatility increases, protecting the position. In other words, the option has a great deal of positive convexity, hedging the negative convexity in the current-coupon pass-through.

USING OPTIONS TO BET ON THE DIRECTIONALITY OF MORTGAGE/TREASURY SPREADS

Mortgage option trades can be an excellent way to take advantage of a conviction that mortgage spreads are related to market direction. Many investors believe mortgage spreads are directional: Mortgages will widen and Treasuries will outperform if the market trades up, and mortgages will tighten if the market trades off. If investors simply lighten up on mortgage exposure versus Treasuries, they are implicitly betting that spreads will widen. If spreads narrow in a bear market, the investors lose. Using options, investors can construct trades with positive payoffs geared toward the scenarios in which yields fall and spreads widen and incur no losses in the bearish scenarios by buying call options on the 10-year Treasury and selling call options on current-coupon mortgages. Investors can also construct scenarios in which mortgages tighten as the market trades off and there are no losses in the bullish scenarios by buying Treasury puts and selling mortgage puts. If investors buy mortgages and sell Treasuries, they are implicitly betting that spreads will tighten regardless of market direction. A guide to mortgage options combinations is shown in Exhibit 22–6. Investors can, of course, use combinations of these strategies, such as buying a Treasury straddle and selling a mortgage straddle to bet that spreads are strictly directional.

Let us look at an example of how a combination of mortgage and Treasury options can be used to bet on the directionality of the mortgage/Treasury spread. Given the configuration of the mortgage market as of February 9, 1995, the trade we believe makes sense is to bet that if the

EXHIBIT 22–6

Mortgage/Treasury Option Combinations

	Treasury Market Rallies	Treasury Market Trades Off
Mortgages tighten	Sell Treasury calls Buy mortgage calls	Buy Treasury puts Sell mortgage puts
Mortgages widen	Buy Treasury calls Sell mortgage calls	Sell Treasury puts Buy mortgage puts

market trades off, current-coupon conventional mortgages will tighten. We like this trade for three reasons. First, current-coupon conventional mortgages look slightly cheap at current levels. Second, mathematically the spread on a given coupon should tighten as the market trades off, as the value of the call option the investor has implicitly written declines in value, allowing the spread to the Treasury curve to tighten. Finally, as the market has rallied investors have been bullish, and, as we discussed in the previous trade, moved down in coupon. If bearish sentiment prevails once more, investors will return to the currents and premiums.

To put on this bet, we must buy Treasury puts and sell mortgage puts. Intuitively, we want to buy puts on the security that will decline more as the market moves down (the Treasury). Exhibit 22–7 shows the payout from this strategy. To achieve a fee-neutral combination, we buy 0.65 Treasury put options for each mortgage put option we sell. As shown in Exhibit 22–7, the fee for an at-the-money forward, three-month option on FNMA 8.5s is 0:276 and the fee for the Treasury put option of the same maturity is 1:10+. If rates are unchanged, both options expire worthless, and the base case has a zero profit. Intuitively, both mortgages and Treasuries go up in price as the forward prices converge to the current prices, and both puts expire worthless. If the market sells off and the spread tightens, the trade does very well.

All of the spread-tightening scenarios show a profit in Exhibit 22–7. Essentially, as spreads tighten, the mortgages decline in value by less than the Treasuries, producing a profit on the trade since we have purchased the Treasury puts. If the market sells off and spreads widen, the trade loses. If the market rallies, all options expire worthless and no profit and loss impact occurs.

E X H I B I T   22–7

FNCL 8.5%, 10-Year Treasury Option Spread Payoff

Treasury option fee/strike			1:10+		98:28+
Mortgage option fee/strike			0:276		98:31
Buy Treasury/sell mortgage option ratio			0.6529		
Treasury option face		$	652,941		
Mortgage option face		$–1,000,000			
Option expiration			May 1995		

		Spread Scenario			
Change	5	Base Case	–5	–10	–15
Level	113	108	103	98	93
Bp Shift					
40	–4,859	–2,356	160	2,688	5,227
20	–3,424	–872	1,692	4,269	5,038
Base Case	0	0	0	0	0
–20	0	0	0	0	0
–40	0	0	0	0	0

SUMMARY

This chapter illustrated four mortgage positions for which the utilization of option positions would be beneficial. Mortgage investors would do well to look to the options market on a regular basis to see if options can be used to take advantage of mortgage mispricings that could otherwise not be captured. In our examples, we showed how options can be used to generate premium income, monetize positive convexity, take advantage of mispriced pass-throughs, and bet on the directionality of mortgage/Treasury spreads. This is but a subsample of trades in which investors might find options appealing as a mortgage portfolio management tool. Mortgage investors should feel as comfortable around options as they do around mortgages; both are debt instruments with option-like payoffs.

I N D E X

A

Akkus, Deniz, 287n
Alternative options, 60–63
American options, 4, 78, 185n, 274–277
  Black-Scholes model and, 181–182
  calls, on the bond's spread, valuation and, 304–308
  puts, credit risk derivative valuation and, 299–304
  swap options, 478–479
Amero, Scott, 331, 369
Anarella, Debbie, 465n
Anderson, Keith, 331, 369
Anson, Mark J.P., 225
Arbitrage-free binomial pricing model; see Binomial pricing model
Arbitrage pricing, 171–174
Asset management; see Hedging
Asymmetric vs. symmetric risk, 346–347
Atlantic options, 4
Audley, David, 283, 287n, 294n, 296n, 319, 323n

B

Babbel, David F., 366n, 437, 437n, 438n, 454n
Back-end fee, 159
Backward induction, 253
Barone-Adesi, Giovanni, 263, 263n, 272, 275–276, 277
Barone-Adesi-Whaley model, 263, 272, 275–276, 278
Barr, William A., 127
Barrier options, 50–56
Barter, Brit, 225n
Basis risk, hedging and, 352
Bear spreads, 29
Bear Stearns & Co., 127n
Benchmarks, volatility, 322–323
Bermuda options, 4
Best-of-two options, 60–62
Bhattacharya, Anand K., 143

Binomial pricing model
  arbitrage-free, 188–192, 251–252
    violation of, 185–186
  with embedded options, 201–223
    interest rate tree, 204–219, 251–252
      example, 220–223
    node values, 208–210
    putable bonds, 222
    volatility and standard deviation in, 208
  using yield to maturity, 182–186, 194–196, 200
Binomial term structure, 228–231
Black, Fischer, 24n, 178, 201, 201n, 226, 226n, 230n, 237, 237n, 238, 239, 241, 245–246, 246n, 253n, 263, 263n, 272, 273, 273n, 274, 274n, 279n, 297, 297n, 298, 313n
Black and Cox model of coupon corporate bond pricing, 298–299
Black-Derman-Toy model, 201
Black price-based model, 273–274, 277
Blackrock Financial Management, 331, 369
Black-Scholes pricing model, 177–182, 200, 320
  embedded options and, 247
  interest rates and, 278
  short terms to expiration and, 194–196
  volatility and, 179–180
Bliss, Ehud, 254n
Bloomberg, 267n
Bond over stock (BOS) options, 62–63
Bond portfolios, interest rate caps in, 451–463
Bonds
  callable; see Callable bonds
  cheapest-to-deliver (CTD), 39, 354
  indicatives of, 249–250
  noncallable, risk and return from, 466
  putable, valuation of, 222
  valuation of, binomial model for, 201–223
Bookstaber, Richard, 173n, 186n, 190n, 428n
Botta, Trish, 465n
Bouyoucos, Peter, 366n, 437
Brauer, Jane Sachar, 345

Breidbart, S., 177n
Breit, John, 143n
Brennan, M.J., 275, 275n, 438n
Brown, Scott, 312n
Bullish strategies, SYCURVE options and, 83–85
Buy-writes, 31–32

C

Callable bonds; *see also* Calls
    option pricing and, 196–197
    putable swaps for managing; *see* Interest
        rates, swaps for managing
    valuation model for, 245–259
        arbitrage-free interest rate trees, 251–252
        interest rate models
            inputs for, 248–250
            selection of, 246–248
        interest rate volatility calibration, 253–256
        intuitive approach, 288–292
        present value factors and, 250–251
        richness/cheapness analysis, 253–256
Calls, 4–5; *see also* Callable bonds
    American options, 304–308
    on the bond's spread, 304–308
    buying, 382–383, 391–392
    on calls, 137–140
    conceptual observations, 427–429
    covered, 31, 401–435
    delta neutral, 406–408, 423–424
    down-and-in, 50–52
    down-and-out, 53–55
    European options, 242
    hedge ratio management, 423–424
    intrinsic value and, 11
    long, 6–8
    management of, 418–423
    mortgage portfolios and, 486–488
    MOTTO options, 90–93
    naked, 402–403
    pricing of, 12–13
    profits, protection of, 424–425
    protection period for, 249
    put/call parity, 5–7, 218–219
    on puts, 137–140
    ratio, 403–406
    rolling down, 418–421
    rolling up, 418–419, 421–423
    selling, 383–384, 392–393
    SPREAD-LOCK options, 111–112
    spread options, 102–103

Calls, continued
    strategy management, 425–427
    strike price management, 418–423
    T-bond futures, 412–418
        convergence and, 416–418
    trapezoidal hedges, 408–412
    variable ratio, 408–412
Cancelable swaps (putable swaps); *see* Interest
    rates, swaps for managing
Caplets, 66–67
Capping a debt issuance, 361–364
Caps and floors; *see* Insurance products;
    Interest rates
Carlson, Erik, 287n
Carr, Peter, 275n
Carry, 17–18
Chase Manhattan Bank, N.A., 311
Cheapest-to-deliver (CTD), 39, 354
Chicago Board of Trade (CBT), 39–41, 261–281
Chin, Richard, 283, 287n, 294n, 296n, 319,
    323n
Clancy, R. P., 182n
Clarke, Roger, 428n
Classic pure option strategies, 26–29
Coleman, John, 483n
Collars, interest-rate, 153–154
Commissions, 130
Compound options, 67–71, 137–140, 158–162
    conventional options vs., 159–161
    uses of, 162
Conservative strategies, SYCURVE options
    and, 85–86
Contingent premium options, 66–67
Contracts, 37–48
    Eurodollar futures, 42–46
    nondollar interest rate futures, 46
    OTC interest rate options, 46–47
    specification and delivery procedure, 264–267
    T-bond futures, 39–40
    T-note futures, 40–42
Convergence, and calls against T-bond futures,
    416–418
Convexity, 20–22, 371–374
    positive, 488–491
    strategies, 25
Cornell, B., 309, 309n
Corridors, interest-rate, 154–156
Costs
    of hedging, 353
    of putable interest rate swaps, 472–473

Coupon levels, and putable interest rate swap valuation, 476–477
Coupon payments, Black-Scholes model and, 180–181
Coupon rates, of bonds, 249
Courtadon, George, 279n
Covered calls; *see* Calls
Covered writes, on T-bonds, 432–435
Cox, John C., 179n, 181, 181n, 225n, 229n, 241, 241n, 245n, 275, 275n, 279n, 297, 297n, 298, 306, 306n
Cox-Ingersoll-Ross model, 245
Credit exposure, 131
Credit risk
    derivatives, valuation of; *see* Valuation
    interest rate caps and, 443
Credit spreads, 248–249
CROSS options, 75–76, 103–108
    equivalent portfolio, 107–108
Curtin, William J., 33n

D

Das, S., 298, 298n
Davey, Laura, 465n
Debt, issuance of
    capping, 361–364
    hedging, 359–361
Deductibles, insurance, 440
Deferred premium options, 63–71
Deferred strike options, 71–73
Delta hedging, 19–20
Delta neutral calls, 406–408, 423–424
DeMoivre-LaPlace theorem, 242
Derivatives, 7
    credit risk, valuation of; *see* Valuation
    spread options; *see* Spread options
Derman, Emanuel, 201, 201n, 226n, 245–246, 246n, 253n, 279n, 313n
Detkar, Daniel, 314n
Differential equation approach, for option pricing, 192–193
Directionality strategies, 24–25
Discount factor, SYCURVE options, 114
Discounting procedure, option pricing and, 175
Dothan, Uri L., 279n
Down-and-in calls, 50–52
Down-and-out calls, 53–55
Drastal, John, 33n
DUOP structure, 93, 98
    spread options, 76

Duration, 369–370
Dyer, Lawrence J., 167, 169n, 182n

E

Effective maturity, 321–322
Effective yield volatility, 321–322
Either-or options, 60–62
Embedded options, 245, 245n
    binomial pricing model and; *see* Binomial pricing model
    in caps, floors and collars, 225–243
    sector yield curve and, 285
    valuation of, 319–329
Empirical volatility, 33–34
Epstein, Sheldon, 198n
Equivalent portfolio
    ISO options, 101–102
    SYCURVE options, 80–81, 87–88
Eurodollar futures, 42–46
European options, 4, 78, 178, 185n
    calls, 242
    puts, 238
    swap options, 478
Exchanges, futures, 37–38
Exchange-traded options
    mortgage-backed securities, 129–131
    OTC options vs., 350–351
Exercise, of options, time until, 478–479
Exercise payments, 477
Exotic options, 49–73
Expected return, and volatility, 338–341
Expiration date, 4, 128, 130
    short terms to, 194–196
    SYCURVE options, 114

F

Fabozzi, Frank J., 3, 3n, 127n, 143n, 167n, 169n, 192n, 198n, 201, 201n, 203n, 220n, 221n, 222n, 230n, 294n, 314n, 366n, 437n, 449n, 466n
Fabozzi, T. Dessa, 3n, 143, 167n, 294n
Faguet, Dmitri, 275n
Fallout risk, mortgage-backed securities, 134–136
Fee income strategies, 25
The First Boston Company, 331
Fixed-date resettable strike option, 59–60
Flat convexity, 21–22, 23
Flat gamma, 21–22, 23
Flesaker, B.L., 297, 297n

Flesaker, Hughston, Schreiber and Sprung
    approach (FHSS), 297
Flexible Treasury Options, 40, 47
Floating-rate assets, hedging, 351–352
Floorlets, 66–67
Floors
    caps and; *see* Interest rates, caps and floors on
    contingent, 66–67
FNMA (Federal National Mortgage
    Association), 322–328
Forward contracts, vs. options, 7–9
Forward yield spread, SYCURVE options,
    114–115
Fuji Securities Inc., 127
Future debt issuance, hedging, 359–361
Futures contracts
    exchanges for, 37–38
    options vs., 7–9
    simulating options, 355–358

G

Gamma hedging, 20–22
Gartland, William J., 3
Gastineau, Gary L., 49
General Electric Capital, 295
GNMA (Government National Mortgage
    Association), 91–97, 378–380
Goldman, Sachs & Co., 75, 75n, 76n, 77, 77n,
    91n, 201, 437, 437n, 438n
Goodman, Laurie S., 345, 483
Grannan, Lawrence E., 37
Green, K., 309, 309n
Guardian Life Insurance Co., 401

H

Haghani, Victor J., 465
Harrison, J., 186n
Hayre, Lakhbir, 312n
Heath, David, 279n
Hedge ratio
    calculation of, 353–355
    management of, covered calls and, 423–424
Hedging, 345–367
    asset management and, 346–359
        asset/liability management, 364–366; *see
            also* Insurance products
        basis risk and, 352
        costs of hedge, 353
        embedded options, 358–359
        example, 347–349

Hedging, continued
    asset management and, continued
        exchange traded vs. OTC options,
            350–351
        floating-rate assets, 351–352
        hedge ratio calculation, 353–355
        options at different strike prices, 349–350
        option simulation with futures, 355–358
        symmetric vs. asymmetric risk, 346–347
    liability management and, 359–364
        asset/liability management, 364–366;
            see also Insurance products
        capping a debt issuance, 361–364
        future debt issuance hedges, 359–361
    mortgage servicing rights, 311–318
    of pipeline risk, mortgage-backed securities,
        133–136
    pricing of options and, 18–23
    spread options and; *see* Spread options
    trapezoidal, 408–412
Historical volatility
    calculating, 332–334
    implied vs., 331–332
    of price, 324–325
    of yield, 325–326
Ho, Jeff, 483
Ho, Thomas S.Y., 245, 245n, 279n, 280n
Hogan, M., 177n
Ho-Lee model, 245–246, 279–281, 280n
Hughston, L., 297, 297n
Hull, John, 238n, 245–246, 246n, 253n, 279n,
    280n
Hunter, Susan Mara, 91n

I

IMM (International Monetary Market), 42–46
Implied volatility, 34–35
    historical volatility vs., 331–332
Index, underlying, 144, 441
    reset frequency, 442
Ingersoll, Jonathan E., Jr., 225n, 245n, 279n
In options, 50–52
Installment options, 65
Insurance products, 364–366
    and interest rate caps, 437–464
        advantages of, 439–440
        in bond portfolios, 451–463
        cap agreement, term of, 442
        cap payment timing, 442
        contract specification, 441–443

Insurance products, continued
  and interest rate caps, continued
    credit risk and, 443
    described, 440–441
    fundamental steps, 455–459
    index, underlying, 441
    reset frequency, 442
    interest-sensitive life insurance, 452–463
    notational amount, 442
    payment method, 443
    payoff characteristics, 443–445
    strike level, 442
    valuation of, 445–451
Interest rates
  caps and floors on, 143–158; *see also*
      Insurance products
    cap/floor parity, 156–158
    caps
      advantages, 147–148
      described, 145–151
      embedded options valuation, 226–233,
          237–239
      participating caps, 148–151
    collars, 153–154
      embedded options valuation, 228–231,
          233–237
    contingent, 66–67
    corridors, 154–156
    embedded options in, 225–243
    features of, 144
    floors
      described, 151–153
      embedded options valuation, 228–231,
          233–237
    pricing of, 144–145
    termination of, 158
  collars on, 153–154
    embedded options valuation, 228–231
  corridors and, 154–156
  modeling
    binomial method, 201–223
    inputs for, callable bond valuation,
        248–250
    and intuitive approach to valuation,
        292–293
    selection of, callable bond valuation,
        246–248
    short-rate volatility and, 320–321
    for T-bond futures, 278–281
  negative, Black-Scholes model and, 180

Interest rates, continued
  risk and, insurance products; *see* Insurance
      products
  spikes in, 456–457
  swaps for managing
    and floors, interest rate cap valuation,
        447–449
    putable, 465–481
    and bonds, noncallable
      asset based swaps and, 467–468
      risk and return from, 466
    callable assets
      examples of, 471–476
      problems with, 468–471
    costs of, 472–473
    valuation of, 476–479
  term structure of, 228–231
  volatility of, calibration and callable bond
      valuation, 253–256
Interest-sensitivity
  life insurance and, 452–463
  policy reserves and, 455–456
Intrinsic value, 10–11
ISO-DUOP options, 98, 102–103
ISO options, 75–76, 97–103
  equivalent portfolio, 101–102
  puts and calls, application of, 102–103

J

Jacob, David P., 167, 167n, 169n, 173n, 182n,
    186n, 190n, 191n, 192n, 196n, 197n
Jamshidian, Farshid, 225n, 246n
Jarrow, Robert, 279n
Jones, Frank J., 401

K

Kalotay, Andrew J., 201, 201n, 230n
Karasinski, Piotr, 230n, 245–246, 246n, 253n,
    279n
Kopprasch, Robert W., 466n, 467n
Kreps, D., 186n
Krumholz, Beth A., 401

L

Langsam, Joseph, 173n, 186n, 190n
Latainer, Gary, 197n
Lauterbach, Kenneth, 312
Lawrence, Andrew, 33n
Lee, San-Bin, 245, 245n, 279n, 280n
Letica, Nicholas C., 3, 33n

Leverage speculation strategies, 25
Levy, Hiam, 317n
Liability management; *see* Hedging
Liquidity, option, 130
Lognormal random walk, 206
"Long bond," 39
Long calls, 6–8
Long convexity, 21, 23
Long puts, 6–9
Long securities, 6–7
Long-terms to expiration, option pricing and, 196–198
Long volatility, 21, 23
Lookback options, 58–60
Lord, Graham, 191n
Lowell, Linda, 483

M

McDermott, Scott, 75
Macfarlane, John, 467n
Market data, 248–249
   volatility and, 337
Maturity dates
   of bonds, 249
   of swaps, 477
May, Diane, 483n
Mean reversion, 295
Merrill Lynch & Co., 245n, 255n, 345
Merton, R.C., 273, 273n, 297, 297n, 303
Monte Carlo simulation, 192
Morby securities (MBS) market, 32
Morgan Stanley, 167n, 177n, 195n, 196n
Mortgage-backed securities, 90–97, 127–141
   exchange-traded options, 129–131
   hedging pipeline risk, 133–136
   option pricing and, 197
   OTC options on, 128–131
   pipeline risk, hedging, 133–136
   portfolio returns and, 140–141, 483–498
      convexity, positive, monetizing, 488–491
      covered call writing, 486–488
      mortgage option markets, 484–486
      and mortgage/Treasury spreads, directionality of, 496–498
      OTC Treasury market, 484–486
      up-and-down-in-coupon trades, 491–496
   prepayments, pricing and, 131–133
   servicing rights, 311–318
   short-term options on forwards, 196
   split fee options, 137–140, 159

Mortgage-backed securities, continued
   Treasury options, 129–131
Mortgage over Treasury options; *see* MOTTO options
Morton, Andrew, 279n
MOTTO options, 75–76, 90–97
   puts and calls, structuring of, 90–93
   underlying securities, choosing, 93–94
Murphy, Michelle, 465n

N

Naked calls, 402–403
Negative interest rates, Black-Scholes model and, 180
Nondollar interest rate futures, 46
No regrets options, 56–63
Noris, Peter D., 198n
Noskiewicz, Robert, 311
Note-over-bond trade (NOB), 41
Notional amount, interest rate caps and floors, 144, 442
Nutt, Steven L., 37

O

Option-adjusted spread (OAS), 192, 283, 285–287, 287n, 313–314
Options
   alternative, 60–63
   American, 4, 78, 185n, 274–277
      Black-Scholes model and, 181–182
   barrier, 50–56
   best-of-two, 60–62
   bond over stock (BOS), 62–63
   buy-writes, 31–32
   calls; *see* Calls
   classic strategies, 26–29
   compound, 67–71, 158–162
      conventional options vs., 159–161
      uses of, 162
   contingent premium, 66–67
   contracts; *see* Contracts
   convexity strategies, 25
   deferred premium, 63–71
   deferred strike, 71–73
   defined, 4–9
   directionality strategies, 24–25
   either-or, 60–62
   European, 4, 78, 178, 185n
   exotic (nonstandard), 49–73
   fee income strategies, 25

Options, continued
  vs. forward contracts, 7–9
  vs. futures, 7–9
  "in," 50–52
  installment, 65
  leverage speculation strategies, 25
  liquidity of, 130
  lookback, 58–60
  on mortgage-backed securities; *see* Mortgage-
    backed securities
  mortgage over Treasury; *see* MOTTO options
  no regrets, 56–63
  "out," 53–55
  outperformance, 60–63
  over-the-counter (OTC); *see* Over-the-counter
    (OTC) options
  overview, 3–35
  portfolio insurance, 30–31
  and portfolio return patterns, 382–396
    calls
      buying, 382–383, 391–392
      selling, 383–384, 392–393
    multiple option strategy, 393–396
    puts
      buying, 384–387, 391–392
      selling, 387–393
  practical strategies, 29–32
  price of; *see* Pricing, of options
  protective put buying, 30–31
  puts; *see* Puts
  reset, 58–60
  roll-down, 55–56
  roll-up, 55–57
  and scenario analysis, 380–381
  simulation of, with futures, 355–358
  slope-of-the-yield-curve; *see* SYCURVE
    options
  spread; *see* Spread options
  spread trades, 28–29
  stock over bond (SOB), 62–63
  straddles, 26
  strangles, 27–28
  strategies, 24–32
  synthetic, 355–358
  up and on, 159
  valuation of; *see* Valuation
OTC options; *see* Over-the-counter (OTC)
  options
OTC Treasury market, for mortgages, 484–486
Out options, 53–55

Outperformance options, 60–63
Over-the-counter (OTC) options
  vs. exchange traded options, 350–351
  interest rate, 46–47
  mortgage-backed securities, 128–131

P

PaineWebber, 345, 483
Pair-offs, 4
Parity, interest rate caps and floors, 156–158
Partial lookback options, 59
Participating caps, 148–151
Participating swaps, 150
Payments
  exercise, and putable interest rate swap valua-
    tion, 477
  method of, interest rate caps, 443
Payne, Richard, 312
Payoffs, interest rate caps and, 443–445,
  457–459
Pierides, Yiannos A., 297, 300n
Pinkus, Scott, 91n
Pinneo, Sara, 483n
Pipeline risk, hedging, 133–136
Policy reserves
  interest sensitivity and, 455–456
  time profile of, 455
Pollack, Irving M., 466n
Portfolio analysis, total return and, 382–396
  calls
    buying, 382–383, 391–392
    selling, 383–384, 392–393
  multiple option strategy, 393–396
  puts
    buying, 384–387, 391–392
    selling, 387–393
Portfolio insurance, 30–31
Portfolio returns, mortgage-backed securities
  and, 140–141
Portfolio strategies, practical, 29–32
Premiums, insurance, 440
Prepayments, mortgage-backed securities and,
  131–133
Present value, callable bond valuation and,
  250–251
Price risk, mortgage-backed securities, 134
Price sensitivity, and interest rate cap valuation,
  449–451
Price volatility
  historical, 324–325

Price volatility, continued
  yield volatility vs., 334–336
Pricing
  of callable bonds; *see* Callable bonds
  of interest rate caps and floors, 144–145
  of options, 9–24; *see also* Valuation
    arbitrage-free binomial model, 188–192
    arbitrage pricing, 171–174
    basics, 169–177
    binomial model
      with embedded options, 201–223
        caps, floors and collars, 225–240
      using yield to maturity, 182–186,
        194–196, 200
        arbitrage-free pricing, violation of,
        185–186
    Black-Scholes model; *see* Black-Scholes
      pricing model
    and callable and putable bonds, 196–197
    delta hedging and, 19–20
    differential equation approach, 192–193
    discounting procedure, 175
    factors influencing, 13–18
    gamma hedging and, 20–22
    hedging and, 18–23
    intrinsic value, 10–11
    long-terms to expiration, 196–198
    models for, 23–24
      arbitrage-free binomial, 188–192,
        201–223
      binomial
        with embedded options, 201–223
        caps, floors and collars,
        225–240
        using yield to maturity, 182–186,
        194–196, 200
      Black-Scholes; *see* Black-Scholes
        pricing model
      choosing among, 193–194
      comparisons of, 177–193
      differential equation approach,
        192–193
      Monte Carlo simulation, 192
      next generation, 198
      test of, 199
      yield-curve models, 186–193, 200
    Monte Carlo simulation, 192
    mortgage-backed securities, 130, 197
      prepayments and, 131–133
    put prices vs. call prices, 12–13

Pricing, continued
  of options, continued
    short terms to expiration and, 194–196
    strike price and, 14
    SYCURVE options, 81–82
    theta hedging and, 23
    and time to expiration, 14–16
    time value, 10–11
    underlying securities and, 14, 17–18,
      176–177
    volatility and, 16–17, 174–175
    yield-curve models, 186–193, 200
Profits
  covered calls and, 424–425
  profit/loss graphs, 4
Protective put buying, 30–31
Prudential-Bache Capital Funding, 322, 323
Prudential Securities Inc., 283, 291, 294, 295,
  319
Public Securities Association (PSA), 92
Putable bonds
  option pricing and, 196–197
  valuing, 222
Putable interest rate swaps; *see* Interest rates,
  swaps for managing
Puts, 4, 5
  buying, 384–387, 391–392
  intrinsic value and, 11
  MOTTO options, 90–93
  pricing of, 12–13
  protective, 30–31
  put/call parity, 5–7, 218–219
  selling, 387–393
  SPREAD-LOCK options, 111–112
  writing, 31–32

Q

Quality options, 263

R

Ramamurthy, Shrikant, 283, 287n, 294n
Rate of return, covered writes on T-bonds,
  432–435
Ratio calls, 403–406
Refunding costs, 291–292
Rendelman, Richard, 225n
Request for quote (RFQ), 270
Reset frequency, underlying indexes and, 442
Reset options, 58–60

Returns
    from bonds, noncallable, 466
    for covered writes on T-bonds, 432–435
    enhancing; *see* Mortgage-backed securities,
        portfolio returns and; Portfolio analysis,
        total return and; Scenario analysis
    expected, volatility and, 338–341
    portfolio, mortgage-backed securities and,
        140–141
    WAVER (weighted average expected return),
        339–340, 375–378
Rich, Diana, 483n
Richard, Scott F., 91n
Richness/cheapness analysis, 253–256
Risk
    basis, 352
    from bonds, noncallable, 466
    credit; *see* Credit risk; Valuation
    interest rate; *see* Insurance products
    pipeline, 133–136
    price, 134
    symmetric vs. asymmetric, 346–347
Roll, Richard, 91
Roll-down calls, 55–56
    covered, 418–421
Roll-up calls, covered, 418–419, 421–423
Roll-up puts, 57
    and roll-down calls, 55–56
Ronn, Ehud I., 245, 245n, 254n, 261
Ross, Daniel R., 467n
Ross, Stephen, 179n, 181, 181n, 225n, 229n,
    241, 241n, 245, 275, 275n, 279n
Rubinstein, Mark, 179n, 181, 181n, 229n, 241,
    241n, 275, 275n, 306, 306n

                            S

Salomon Brothers Inc, 225, 465, 465n, 468n
Sarnat, Marshall, 317n
Scenario analysis, 369–381
    convexity and, 371–374
    options and, 380–381
    and variable-maturity securities, 378–380
    and volatility, 374–375
    WAVER and, 375–378
Scholes, Myron, 24n, 178, 273, 273n
Schreiber, L., 297, 297n
Schumacher, Michael, 314n
Schwartz, E.S., 275, 275n, 438n
Sector OAS estimation, 294–295
Sector price, 285–287, 289–290

Sector spreads, 290–291
Sector yield curve, valuation and, 284–285
Self-hedging, 135–136
Selvaggio, Robert D., 311
Settlement frequency, 144
Short convexity, 22, 23
Short-rate volatility, 322–323
    and interest rate cap valuation, 446–447
    interest rate models and, 320–321
Short terms to expiration, 194–196
Short volatility, 22, 23
Showers, Janet, 467n
Sitte, M., 196n
Slope-of-the-yield-curve options; *see*
        SYCURVE options
Southern Bell, 291–292
Split fee options, 137–140, 159
Spot yield spread, 82
    SPREAD-LOCK options, 75–76, 108–112
        puts and calls, application of, 111–112
Spread options, 75–125
    CROSS, 75–76, 103–108
        equivalent portfolio, 107–108
    DUOP structure, 76
    ISO, 75–76, 97–103
        equivalent portfolio, 101–102
        puts and calls, application of, 102–103
    ISO-DUOP, 98, 102–103
    MOTTO, 75–76, 90–97
        puts and calls, structuring of, 90–93
        underlying securities, choosing, 93–94
    SPREAD-LOCK, 75–76, 108–112
        puts and calls, application of, 111–112
    SYCURVE; *see* SYCURVE options
    SYCURVE-DUOP, 76, 88–90
Spread trades, 28–29
Sprung, L., 297, 297n
Stafford, Christine, 311
Standard deviation, in binomial pricing model,
        208
Stavis, Robert M., 465, 465n
Stock over bond (SOB) options, 62–63
Straddles, 26
Strangles, 27–28
Strategy management, 24–32
    covered calls, 425–427
    multiple option, 393–396
    SYCURVE options, 83–86
Stricker, Robert, 366n, 437, 438n
Strike level, 442

Strike premiums, 68
Strike prices, 4, 14, 128
  different, 349–350
  management of, 418–423
Strike rate, 144
Strikes, 130
Strike yield spread, 114
Strips, 66–67
Surplus drain, from interest rate spikes, 456–457
Swaps; *see* Interest rates
Switchback options, 60
SYCURVE-DUOP options, 76, 88–90
SYCURVE options, 75–90, 97–99
  application of, 82–86
  bullish strategy and, 83–85
  conservative strategy and, 85–86
  equivalent portfolio, 80–81, 87–88
  pricing, 81–82, 114–125
    formula for, 120–124
Symmetric vs. asymmetric risk, 346–347
Synthetic options, 355–358

T

Terminable swaps (putable swaps); *see* Interest
  rates, swaps for managing
Terminated options, 4
Theta hedging, 23
Thomasson, Richard, 98n
Tiger Management Corporation, 283
Tilley, James, 191n
Tillinhast, 438n
Time profile, of policy reserves, 455
Time to expiration, 14–16
Time until exercise, 478–479
Time value, 10–11
Timing options, 263–264
Toevs, Alden L., 192n, 197n
Toft, Klaus Bjerre, 261
Total returns, enhancing; *see* Mortgage-backed
  securities, portfolio returns and; Portfolio
  analysis, total return and; Scenario
  analysis
Toy, William, 201, 201n, 226n, 245–246, 246n,
  253n, 279n, 313n
Trapezoidal hedges, 408–412
Treasury securities
  bonds
    covered writes on, 432–435
    futures, 39–40, 261–281
      American options, 274–277

Treasury securities, continued
  bonds, continued
    futures, continued
      calls against, 412–418
      convergence and, 416–418
      contract specification and delivery,
        264–267
      delivery procedure, 264–267
      flexible, 267–270
      interest rate models for, 278–281
      specifications for, 268–269
      strategies for, 270–272
      valuation of, 272
  and mortgage/Treasury spreads, 496–498
  note futures, 40–42
  options on, mortgage-backed securities,
    129–131
  OTC market for, 484–486
  underlying, MOTTO options and, 93–94
  yield curve, 248
  yield volatility and, 324

U

Underlying index, 144, 441
  reset frequency, 442
Underlying securities, 128, 129, 176–177
  financing of, 17–18
  MOTTO options, 93–94
  price of, 14
Up-and-down-in-coupon trades, mortgage
  portfolios, 491–496
Up and on options, 159
Up-front premium, 144, 159

V

Valuation; *see also* Pricing
  of credit risk derivatives, 297–309
    American call on the bond's spread,
      304–308
    American put options, 299–304
    Black and Cox model of coupon corporate
      bond pricing, 298–299
  of embedded options, 220–223, 319–329
  of interest rate caps, 445–451
  intuitive approach to, 283–296
    callable bond example, 288–292
    computations vs. intuition/historical data,
      284
    estimation of option value, 287–288
    interest rate model effects, 292–293

Valuation, continued
  intuitive approach to, continued
      mean reversion and, 295
      refunding costs and, 291–292
      sector OAS estimation, 294–295
      sector yield curve and, 284–285
  of mortgage servicing rights, 311–318
  of putable interest rate swaps, 476–479
  of T-bond futures, 272
Variable-maturity securities, 378–380
Variable ratio calls, 408–412
Vasicek, Oldrich, 279n
Volatility, 21–23, 33–35, 331–341
  benchmarks, 322–323
  in binomial pricing model, 208
  Black-Scholes model and, 179–180
  defined, 174–175
  and embedded options, 319–329
  expected return and, 338–341
  forecasts of, 336–338
  historical, 331–334
  implied, 326–328
      historical vs., 331–332
      patterns of, 337–338
  interest rate, 253–256
  long, 21, 23
  market information and, 337
  price
      historical, 324–325
      yield vs., 334–336
  scenario analysis and, 374–375
  short, 22, 23

Volatility, continued
  T-bond futures and, 272, 272n
  of underlying securities, 16–17
  yield, 249
      historical, 325–326
      price vs., 334–336
      treasury instruments, 324
Volin, Susan, 294n

W

WAVER (weighted average expected return),
      339–340
  scenario analysis and, 375–378
Whaley, Robert E., 263, 263n, 272, 275–276, 277
White, Alan, 238n, 246, 246n, 253n, 279n, 280n
Wildcard options, 264
Williams, George O., 201, 201n, 230n
Wilson, Richard W., 222n
Window date, 159

Y

Yield curves
  and interest rate cap valuation, 447
  models of, for option pricing, 186–193, 200
Yield volatility, 249
  historical, 325–326
  price volatility vs., 334–336
  SYCURVE options, 116–120

Z

Zimmerman, Thomas, 312